STRESS, HEALTH AND PSYCHOLOGICAL PROBLEMS IN THE MAJOR PROFESSIONS

E. Lakin Phillips

The George Washington University

Founder and Executive Director
School for Contemporary Education
Springfield, Virginia

UNIVERSITY
PRESS OF
AMERICA

Copyright © 1982 by

University Press of America, Inc.

P.O. Box 19101, Washington, D.C. 20036

Printed in the United States of America

ISBN (Perfect): 0-8191-2774-4
ISBN   (Cloth): 0-8191-2773-6

Library of Congress Catalog Card Number: 82-17556

Table of Contents

INTRODUCTION

One of the remarkable events--or series of events in modern society is how much the professions are changing. This complex set of facts is documented in the daily press, in some of the research literature produced by the professions themselves, and in other fields of endeavor.

A second noteworthy fact is how little the professions are, themselves, registering and taking seriously these changes; how little the changes are conceptualized in clear and salient ways by leaders in the many professions. Few have realized the enormity of the processes going on that breed discomfort, malaise and confusion of goals among professional people.

Documenting the changes in the professions and their helath (and related) problems is not difficult. Although the reference section of this book numbers in the hundreds, over ten times this number of references (abstracts, articles, books, periodicals, etc.) have been consulted, showing the enormity of the problem of health matters in the professions.

Some books argue that the professions are often leeches on the populus (Illich et al, 1977; Illich, 1976; Ridgeway, 1968; Lynn, 1965; Carlson, 1975) but few of them treat the professions in relation to what the professions are doing to their own membership on the one hand and to (and against) society on the other hand. Most existing literature on the professions recognizes that they are arrogant, preemptive and insular; but seldome does the literature relate these attitudes of professions to the kinds of deterioration going on within the professions or how professions as organizations impact their membership in unhealthful ways. It is true that for ages keen observers have been unwilling to be "taken in" by the professions, but only recently has this skepticism and observational actuity lead as well to an understanding of the "internal" problems of the professions. Especially important is the health status (psychological and physical) of the members of various professions, how these health problems have (presumably) arisen, and how extensive they are.

Problems with the health of professions have arisen at several levels--documented in these pages--

and possibly for the same set of reasons spanning all levels. First is the level of selection of professional trainees. The clamor for advanced and specialized training grows apace; one has to have "courses" or "degrees" to certify that one knows anything. Educational practices related to selection and training of professionals is riddled with criticisms of unfairness, biased selection procedures based on particular kinds of quantitative tests, ethnic prejudice, economic favoritism, and other "selection" procedures; all the while extoling the virtues and benefits of professional careers. Coupled with this set of selection procedures is the entering bias of tyro professionals who are unrealistic about themselves and idealistic and naive about the professions they are entering.

A second set of factors determining the ultimate health problems of professions relates to the training itself, the indoctrination process. The idealism gives way in three or four years of training; the fledging professionals become more hardened to the realities of the professional system--as a system--and become increasingly more like their elder mentors who have largely given up idealism or interest in professional service. Replacing the interest in service are increasing interests in economic gain, prestige and power. The more successful in this indoctrination process the more materialistic the professional members become.

The second set of factors--the indoctrination process (it is more than technical training, these formative years: they are explicit attempts to make the fledging professional toe the mark of the profession itself and take on its ideological, economic and social values)--is one that leads to the third set of conditions, viz., that the professional members upon graduation and entry into their chosen professions are no longer oriented toward society and service to society; they are oriented toward their own advancement and economic gain; such as advancement becomes an end in itself. There is, of course, nothing wrong with economic or professional advancement; but when the idealistic ends (originally subscribed to) are almost totally subordinated to the materialistic ends, the profession and the professional members have taken on a different coloration, become sensitive to different goals in life, and follow different routes to professional realization and growth. This different route-- the materialistic quest, one might call it--tends to

vi

harden the young professional against service in favor of material gain. The more successful the profession--materially speaking--such as medicine, dentistry, executive positions in industry--the more this change seems to take place, and the more the health problems arise later among the participants. The more sole professions subscribe to the material gains route, the more these professions contrast with other professions that do not subscribe to the materia l gains route--here we note the roles of nursing, teaching and the clergy, particularly. These latter-named professions are just recently beginning to try for a place in the (economic) sun, and are coming into conflict with otherprofessions that are better established, more powerful and with greater professional expertise in dealing with adversity (e.g., nursing vs. medicine). The more powerful professions are also more "political," that is, they cultivate and value power, prestige and influence.

Fourthly, as one might expect, the materialistic route leads to material gains and quests. The notions of service and dedication as initial motivators for the fledging professional now lead to service as defined not by the professional's client, or by society, but by what the professional can offer that gains him/her the desired ends. Thus all theprofessions have evidenced a proliferation of services and skills not necessarily needed by society or by the professional's client. The new definition of service and professional expertise becomes dependent upon gadgetry and other appurtances the professional can use and manipulate, all the while increasing the charges for services without demonstrating adequate need or productive outcome for the client or for society. This has been the point made by Illich et al, 1977; by Bradshaw, 1978; by Knowles and his associates, 1977; by Chu and Trotter, 1974; by Jencks, 1979; and by many others. Needless to say, the indoctrination process given the fledging professional is by now beginning to pay off in terms of economic gains and in terms of power and prestige. The professional can now point to the enormous range of services and skills available, thereby making the client and the public generally more dependent upon the professional armamentarium available. People are taught to think that professional services are necessary, not about what they can do for themselves, saving the hardest problems or the most refractory ones for the professional. We run to the physician or the lawyer or the teacher long before we need to do so, thereby increasing our own dependency and simultaneously enhancing the professional's power and economic position.

A fifth outcome in the long road to the under-standing of the health of professions is the stress, tension and anxiety visited upon the professional who tries (and often does!) play God. No one can bear up long under all this strain: Trying to think for other trying to do for them what they can well and should do for themselves, and charge them dearly for the service The public pays the professional handsomely for that which it often does not need; but since the senario is a good one for the professional, it is kept active. But not without cost: The health of professions is suffering badly no matter where we look. And worst of all, the professional does not know in any large and steady sense how much the life s/he is leading contri-butes to his/her own health problems and how much the whole enterprise may be largely unnecessary. One charade leads to another. Today we have extant over two-hundred-fifty psychotherapies (Herink, 1980), so-called, not because they are needed, and certainly not because they are different or particularly useful, but because the charade must go on. Two-hundred-fifty psychotherapies to reduce the stress, tension and anxieties incurred by a previous set of charades; the show must go on.

One cannot help drawing an analogy between this display of professional expertise and the American industrial complexes: the military/industrial complex the medical/industrial complex, the educational/indus-trial complex, the agribusiness/industrial complex, and the publishing/industrial complex, and so on. All the industrial complexes produce gadgetry, allegedly "necessary" adjuncts to life, things and services to make one "whole," and attempt to promote the impressio and belief that only more material gain and growth can solve our personal problems, make life meaningful, or defeat our enemies. The professional world is by now so much a part of the industrial complex that it is almost impossible to untie them. And if we look closely at the men (there are **very few** women involved) who run these complexes we identify people who are as ill as the rest of us--the chief executive officers-- who sit on the industrial thrones vieing minute by minute with adversaries for power, prestige, and money to the tune of salaries in the hundreds of thousands of dollars per year, with increasingly more far-flung conglomerates to push around the world. Are these masters of the corporations "sicker" than others, as

some would say, because they run the machines that run
the rest of us? Looking closely at these corporations
and as professions as organizations, we see many similarities between them. Professions as organizations
are becoming more and more like corporations and are
becoming adjuncts to the various industrial complexes.

Since individuals sometimes run amok we might
expect these large industrial machines, the huge corporations, to run amok. They do, indeed. We are now
witness to the decline and possible destruction of the
giant American automobile industry because it has been
giving the public what it--the industry--wanted and not
what the public wanted or needed. As energy premiums
mount, the role of the automobile has to change; the
change may be so drastic as to destroy or greatly alter
the industry as we have known it for 75-80 years. Not
only that, with its unilateral power, the automobile
industry has become so impervious to social need that
its arrogance has led to its now defect-ridden status;
so much so that if the industry did not respond to
external change it might die of its own rot (Brown,
1980). More cars are returned for defects per year than
are now made each year, due to the occasional realization that the accumulation of defects has been going
on all these many years and ought to be remedied forth-
with; thus General Motors has to call back and repair
transmissions on over 4 million cars produced during
the 1975 - 1980 period (Brown, 1980). Perhaps DeLorean
was right about GM (Wright, 1979). Perhaps the daily
press is correct in pointing up repeatedly the monopo-
lizing and unilateral actions of the steel industry,
agribusiness, the petrochemical industry, and so on.
The various industrial complexes have service scarcely
in mind, and social responsibility is far from their
concern. How can an ideology like that of the various
industrial complexes and corporations act other than to
bring about ill health among us? Among the professionals
who run such industries? Among other professionals,
especially the health professionals, who take their
cues from the giant industrial complexes? Rowen (1980)
cites instances in which large corporations have fired,
abused, or reduced the salaries and bonuses of professional economists who have made unpopular or unwelcome
economic forecases that upset the plans and policies
of the giant corporations. Not only are the economic
blinders worn by the giant corporations a deterrent to
the industries and corporations themselves, people
suffer at individual levels with job loss, lowered
status, undue stress, humiliation, and chronic anxiety
and tension.

The sixth point, then, in the development of the problems relating to the health of professions is that society which values largely or only material gain, wealth and power, can only accumulate more stress, health and psychological problems. These effects will, in turn, affect the health of society and the health of professions and the professionals comprising them. This points up the often observed fact that the very strength which our society has had for many decades, viz., productivity, may be at the same time our greatest weakness. We are engaged in a highly redundant society-wide process of trying to reduce the stress we so vigorously promote in the name of progress. The hall-mark of progress has been continued growth and more acquisitions in the sense of large and larger conglo-merates, not public service, not the solution of pro-blems of the environment shared by all. People who do not go along with the master plans of giant industries and corporations find their way out of the melee (Terkel, 1974); or they stay in and develop a variety of health problems, become sloven workers, burn out or disinvest in their work.

This picture of large corporations, their effect on the economy and on society generally--not to mention professional who get caught in this web of influence--is corroborated by two recent publications (Carter, 1980; Vanik, 1980). Carter, writing in <u>Science</u> magazine, reviews briefly the <u>Global 2000 Report</u> which comprises a number of forecasts about how life will be in the year 2000. The report is far from an optimistic one. Predicted in this report are pressures from increasing world populations, especially the now-overcrowded areas in Asia and in some developing countries; fewer natural resources and energy sources to go around; the loss of important life-supporting capabilities in the environment (e.g., careless razing of forests, atmospheric concentration of carbon dioxide, less rangeland and cropland, etc.); increasing inflation to the extent of at least a 100 percent increase in the price of food; and greater vulnerability to both natural disaster and man-made disaster. These ominous predic-tions <u>could</u> lead us to develop hedges against our collective undertainties by stressing the solution of

x

our mutual[1] problems (health, the environment,
inflation, employment, housing, problems of the aged,
problems of infant mortality, education,and so on); or
they could lead the world, especially under the control
of giant corporations to become ever more avaracious as
bulwarks against their own losses of power, prestige
and money. What will happen to their professions if
the dire predictions contained in the Global 2000
Report come true? The professions will be expected to
become more competitive, to harbour more ill health,
to produce greater numbers of disabused, dropped-out,
dried-up members, and other malfunctioning persons.
Selection and training will be adversely affected and
the professions will change so much they will hardly
be recognizable. Mankind may not be able to adjust
to an contain the uprising stress, tension and anxiety
likely to come with a world as frought with problems
as those contained in the Global 2000 Report.

If one is skeptical about how much we can observe
signs of upcoming economic concentration and attendant
stress--as part of the picture derived from the Global
2000 Report--one has but to read the House of Representatives Congressional Record for June 27, 1980
(Vanik, 1980). Representative Vanik (Demoncrat-Ohio)
gave his eighth annual report on corporate tax studies.
He observes two trends over the past eight years:
certain companies and groups of companies are more adept
at extracting tax favors from the U. S. Government than
are other companies (i.e., avoiding taxes); and,
secondly, there has been a gradual and unwavering
decline in the amount of taxes paid by many corporations.
Some major American companies escaped paying any taxes
in 1978: Banks: J. P. Morgan & Co.; Industries: U.S.
Steel, General Dynamics, American Airlines, Occidental
Petroleum, and many others. This corporate power is
symptomatic not only of the ability to avoid paying
taxes, it further signals the power to run things as
they, themselves, see fit, for their own advantage and

---

[1] Everyone knows that inflation and recession are at
least annoying and sometimes crucial factors in the
conduct of our daily lives. Seir (1980), however, summarizes evidence that pressures from recession and
inflation are associated with a rise in the death rate.
As Seir's report states, "An expert calculates that over
a six-year period, a one-percentage-point rise in unemployment causes about 37,000 deaths". And that nearly
all major illnesses and causes of death are so affected.

to the detriment of others (e.g., the average citizen pays a higher <u>percentage</u> of income tax than do most large corporations). Vanik observes that ten years ago corporations paid 17 percent of the total revenues required to run the Federal Government; today, they contribute 14 percent, a significant drop in terms of costs associated with inflation and with increased governmental services; and the projection is that the corporate entities will pay about 11 percent of this total in the near future. Whether their contribution will go below that figure remains to be seen. The "eye" of the hurricane blasting us all is made up of the giant corporations that exercise unilateral power; and they, in turn, see the style of competition, economic struggle, and many of the quality-of-life problems that beset us all.

With the rampant materialism of these times--"materialism" used in the pejorative sense--it is no mystery that the professions are showing evidence of loss of integrity as professions, contributing materially to problems of health and well-being among members of professions, and showing an increasingly unfavorable stance toward society. The professions studied in this book are some of the ones showing the most problem-ridden status, but this book is not the whole story and cannot pretend to be. Some other professions evidencing stress but on which only scattered data exists include: Accountants, Architects, Airline Pilots, Airport Controllers, Foreign Service Officers, High Governmental Officials (members of Congress, Cabinet members, Presidents, and other high officials), Military Officers and Enlisted Personnel, Supreme Court Judges, University Presidents, Actors, Artists, and Musicians, and perhaps others. If present trends continue, all professions and perhaps all occupations will surface more and more signs of stress, along with mounting signs of stress in society generally. One purpose of this report is to raise the consideration of the health of professions to a higher state of awareness and to promote solutions to the problems so commonly observed.

One advantage in the present writing is that data on the health and related problems of various professions is most uneven. Data proliferate in regard to some of the health professions (Medicine, Nursing, Dentistry), but data are far more scarce for most other professions. Too, the types of studies relating to health matters are not uniform across professions. For example, data on suicide are far more adequate on the health professions than other professional groups, and the nature of killing illnesses, longevity, the occurrence of extreme psychological problems, family discord and divorce statistics are very scattered and often quite inconclusive over a range of professions. It is not possible, then, to rank the professions on each of several matters of health; the data are too incomplete. But this state of affairs can forcefully suggest to us where new studies might be placed and where more concerted attempts might be made to even out the picture of health matters among professions and their professional practitioners.

BIBLIOGRAPHY

Bradshaw, J. S., _Doctors on Trial_. N.Y.: Paddington Press, 1978.

Brown, M., GM accused of defects in '75-'80 autos, Washington _POST_, August 9, 1980, p. 1.

Carlson, R.J., _The End of Medicine_. N.Y.: Wiley, 1975.

Carter, L. J., Global 2000 Report: Vision of a gloomy world, _Science_, 1980, 209, 575-576.

Chu, F.D. and Trotter, S. _The Madness Establishment_. N.Y.: Grossman, 1974.

Herink, R., _The Psychotherapy Handbook_. N.Y.: New American Library, 1980.

Illich, I., _Medical Nemesis_. N.Y.: Pantheon Books, 1976.

Illich, I., Zola, I.K., McKnight, J., Caplan, J., and Shaiken, H. _Disabling Professions_. London: Marion Boyars, 1977.

Jencks, C. _Who Gets Ahead?_ N.Y.: Basic Books, 1979.

Knowles, J.H., (Ed.) _Doing Better and Feeling Worse: Health in the United States._ N.Y.: Norton, 1977.

Lynn, K.S. and the Editors of Daedalus, _The Professions in America_. Boston: Beacon Press, 1965.

Ridgeway, J. _The Closed Corporation: American University sities in Crisis_. N.Y.: Ballantine Books, 1968.

Rowen, H., Free speech on free trade at Ford: Killing the bad news bearers, Washington _POST_, August 10, 1980, p. 1.

Seir, G. F., Recessions cause death rate to rise, as pressures of coping take hold, _Wall Street Journal_ August 25, 1980, p. 17.

Terkel, S. _Working_. N.Y.: Avon Books, 1974.

Vanik, C.A. Annual corporate tax studies, _Congressional Record -- House_, June 27, H5828, 1980.

Wright, J. P. On A Clear Day You Can See General Motors. Grosse Point, Michigan, 1979.

CHAPTER I

THE PROFESSIONS--THEY ARE A' CHANGIN'

Work has always been a major part of a person's life. Children are asked at an early age, "What are you going to do (be) when you grow up?" as if to imply that one's whole being or doing hinged on one's work: What one was--one's worth--depended upon his or her work! Schools cause youngsters to reflect early on careers, jobs, personal assessment and self-examination with regard to the world of work. Prestige enters into this examination early and clearly: What one is expected to do is to be ambitious, set one's sights high, settle for nothing less than the best. Youth is expected to select a career or occupation that others will respect, nay even envy! The American Dream teaches aspiration, inspiration, getting ahead, and work--through education--the route to success.

As adults, work encompasses, us, even to the extent of excluding other considerations that may (or ought to) be equally important, such as family relationships, general educational/cultural development, broadened outlook on life associated with hobbies, volunteer work, or simply enjoyable use of leisure time. The absorption in work is expressed well in Adam Smith's remark: "...the understandings of the greater part of men are necessarily formed by their ordinary employment." William Faulkner, too, stated the overwhelming importance of work in the following: "You can't eat for eight hours a day nor drink for eight hours a day nor make love for eight hours a day-- all you can do for eight hours is work."

J. S. Dwight (1955), the poet, put a religious tinge on work:

> Work, and thou wilt bless the day
>   Ere the toil be done:
> They that work not, can not pray,
>   Can not feel the sun.
> God is living, working still,
>   All things work and move;
> Work, or lose the power to will,
>   Lose the power to love.

Carlyle said, "Blessed is he who has found his work; let him ask no other blessedness."

Work is ubiquitous. Much of our economy is geared
to, based on, evaluated by, and compared to other
societies on the basis of our ability to employ people
gainfully. Work is an _ought_; there shouldn't be any
unemployment in a well-run society (but there is!); we
strive to overcome unemployment caused by uncontrolled
economic factors) but we also strive to make people
want to work. We often say unemployment is spurious--
people could find work if they wanted to, we smugly
assert, knowing in the back of our minds that we, too,
could become unemployed for capricious reasons and
remain so as a result of factors beyond our control.
But work is nonetheless required, demanded, expected;
it is the modern categorical imperative in our social
and economic order.

Work is on everyone's mind most of the time. When
and where does one go towork? Does one like his/her
work? Where can one find a better job with more pay,
shorter hours, more personal recognition, greater chances
for advancement, with retirement and vacation and
health benefits to one's liking? Work serves _all_ of
life; it is the pivot for most of our existence.
Although we work only one-third of each living day,
that period of time ramifies into every other aspect of
our lives: Where we live (what we can afford in the
way of a house or neighborhood), how "high on the hog"
we live, how much we rely on ostentation as a sign of
successfully having arrived at a prestigious level,
resulting from hard work, where and when and how much
we vacation, what clubs and social groups we belong to,
and many more considerations. Although often onerous,
work is also prestigious, and we never let ourselves
or others forget the merits associated with our job,
our professional training or--even better--our professional standing.

Some people are obsessed with work; they find it
the only familiar territory for the use of their
energies, the main road to self-realization, the sine
qua non of daily living. Although these "workaholics"
are admonished and even condemned--they overwork in lieu
of better personal, family or affectional relationships,
it is said--they are also admired because if you want to
get a good lawyer, or physician, or accountant, or
psychologist, or nurse, you want someone who has taken
the time and effort to "work his way up to the top of
the ladder." We admire the best, even if they are workaholics and are presumably lacking in some other
department of life. It is the close family members of
the overworked that suffer the consequent indignities,

2

Work, long, hard toiling work has always been with mankind. As technology progressed, work became less laborious and arduous. The tractor replaced the walking plow; the automobile replaced earlier and slower transportation; the airplane now gets us across the continent in a few hours and saves the boredome and exhaustion of days of slow movement under uncomfortable conditions.

Because work has been necessary, restrictive and arduous, mankind had sought ways to improve upon work and working conditions. Children are encouraged to work harder than Dad and make moremoney, to find a profession that will bring the blessings of a fuller and less exhaustive life. Never mind if the professional too, is a workaholic; let him or her work with more finesse, earn more money, garner more prestige,and have the profession serve as an opening to the finer things in life. Children come to college to "better their elders" and find more rewarding work and professional satisfactions. Even if the father or mother of today's college student is already in a prestigious profession, the son or daughter must emulate the parent (or parents), not let the family down. They are to develop a more lucrative "practice" of some sort.

Finding a profession as an answer to hard and compelling work may not be a safe guide for the youth or young adult of today. Professions are as hard work in many ways as is manual labor./ The stress and strain of preparing for a profession, the perplexing and trying selection processes that determine who gets into professional school, the grueling hours of study and application over several years, guarantee that the winner of a professional degree has "been through the mill." No wonder many professionals try to find relief in exhausting physical exercise and highly competitive sports; no wonder many take to drugs, alcohol, affairs, and other means of assuaging the tensions stemming from overwork. When the plowman laid down his plow, he could rest; but can the architect rest at the end of the work day? Can the physician, dentist, clergyman, or psychologist go home to the family and not be plagued by phone calls and emergencies, or risk being uncaring and undevoted to his/her patients or parishioners?

If physical labor has changed toward less demands on the backs and brains of men, then professional work has increased in tension, anxiety and stress. While professions may offer benefits of a social and prestigious nature, they may not offer as many benefits of a

3

personal nature, devoid of stress and strain, as they
should; or as they once did. Professions cannot now be
counted on to produce what they once did in the way of
satisfaction due to the changes professions are undergoing.

Yes, work in the professions has changed in a
number of ways in recent years. Furthermore, people
also enter professions for different reasons from what
was true several decades ago. Although today's graduate
students (preparing for professions) are bright and
alert, they are often less devoted to scholarship and
the intellectual life than they were a few decades ago.
Today's physician has more technology at his/her disposal, yet the personal interest in the patient, the less
hurried care of the sick and wounded, and the role of
personal counselor are less well enacted by today's
physician than was true a generation or two ago.
Physicians today appear to look more to the "business
of being a doctor," than to the practice of medicine
in a personal and healing way. Lawyers look to the
influence they can exert from their chairs as "attorney
at law," and less to helping people untangle personal
(albeit legal) questions, prepare for life exigencies,
and solve disputes between adversaries. The adversary
nature of law and legal practice supervenes today,
and capital is made on this adversity. George Bernard
Shaw, the British playwright and sometimes acid wit, is
supposed to have said that professions are conspiracies
against the laity, which is to suggest that the unini-
tiated have a difficult time being treated fairly by
the professions and/or reaping the benefit that professional practice should afford the layman. Law,
medicine and many other professions appear to be more
out to preserve their own status than to serve the
public. Even President Carter remarked that law
practice sometimes involves the engagement of expensive
lawyers on each side of an issue, occasioning long
delays in the delivery of justice, and sometimes
resulting in the failure to protect the rights of the
citizen. Justice often overlooks the powerless and the
poor, those not knowledgeable in playing the "legal
games" one has to play in order to secure and advance
rights for fairness for all. The more altruistic motives
that characterized the tyro physician, lawyer or other
professional, hoary in the traditional past, has now
seemingly passed over to more commercial, business and
similar motives. While there are notable exceptions,
even members of the professions themselves sometimes
declare that professionalism, per se, has the upper han
in today's world.

Professions have changed also in that there has
been a proliferation of new professions since World
War II. Many new specialties have risen in the practice
of medicine: pediatric psychiatry, behavioral medicine,
surgical specialties on the hand and fingers among
orthopedic surgeons, brain surgery with subdivided
specialties concerning various parts and functions of
the brain, not to mention the whole range of pharmaco-
logical and psychopharmacological developments in
recent years. Law, too, has invented new specialties:
Land re-zoning law concurrent with the population
explosion has prompted the wider and more specialized
use of our terrain (sometimes to the benefit of the
bulldozer and asphalt pavements promoter, more than to
the maintenance of greenery); consumer law has arisen
to protect the rights of the citizen and the consumer
from the more opportunistic marketplace; law sensitive
to the poor and to minority groups has found a place
in the law school curriculum and in the public eye;
and law specializing in helping the handicapped secure
rights and opportunities has merited vigorous support
and has even led to fundamental changes in some cases.
Every profession has undergone cell subdivision many
times recently. Even philosophers complain that they
cannot easily talk with one another at their annual
meetings because philosophy that deals with linguistics
is so different from traditional philosophy, from
aesthetics, or semiotics or modern logic, so that
shared concepts are hard to identify and use. The
earlier apprenticeship training so characteristic of
architecture has gien way to professionalism that now
requires as much schooling as that of law, engineering
or teaching at the college level. Business, finance
and industry have spawned so many new professional sub-
fields that one can hardly keep track of changes. The
advent of computers with their programming requirements,
hardware specialists, software specialists and sales
contingents have generated new job fields by the dozens
and affected the training of persons numbering in the
millions. These changes will continue and expand.
Contrary to what many say, college training will not
subside in the 1980's but increase, because the advent
of more technical jobs and specialties will require
ever-higher degrees of training and expertise, adding
on months or years to training (N.Y. TIMES, 1979).
The higher the degree of specialization and requisite
education, the brighter the employment outlook. The
pyramid of professional occupations has not peaked, but
is jutting higher and higher.

        The changes are so rapid and compelling that they

have given rise to the terminology of "traditional" vs.
"nontraditional" occupations, with law, teaching,
medicine and the clergy being moretraditional occupations (yet spawning their own nontraditional fields),
and computer programming, management sciences, human
factors, behavioral medicine, engineering education and
administration, being newer and less traditional, yet
requiring as extensive background and advanced training
as the better known traditional fields. The more one
goes up the employment and educational ladder the more
optimistic is the outlook for vigorous employment and
continued growth, and the invention of still newer professions and specialties. The end, if there is one, is
not in sight; specialties and sub-specialties and sub-
sub-specialties abound and will thrive, even in the
face of momentary disruption through economic depres-
sions or recessions, as long as peoples' needs continue
to flourish and our technologies rise to meet these
needs.

Professions are also being challenged from a
different quarter today, that of questioning whether
one should even pick a profession. Skilled trades
workmen often make more money and obtain more benefits
than nurses who are trained far more intensively than
the skilled workmen (Washington POST, 1978), even
though nurses are assuming ever-increasing roles in
health care (Shabecoff, 1979). The transportation
services connected with school systems often pay
higher salaries to semi-skilled workers than are paid
to teachers and other educational specialists, with
unemployment and the vicissitudes of the economy under
better control by the tradesmen than by the professional
teachers. It is considered common for tradesmen to
strike, but prejudices against teachers, nurses,
physicians and other "public servants" striking for
higher wages, better working conditions or benefits
still draws a "no-no" from the public. Professions
are supposed to have a purity of purpose that non-professional work does not enjoy, yet this purity is often
fed back as a disadvantage to the professional nurse,
teacher or social worker. These conditions, among
others, often render the One Life-One Career Imperative
(Sarason, 1977, pp. 123-164) open to challenge. No
longer is it as imperative to make the one, mandatory,
"right" career choice and follow it throughout one's
life. No longer is it considered (looking back) as
fateful to have made the correct (or incorrect) choice,
or to attempt to "live with" a choice that may require
change and readjustment. Professionals are often heard
to remark, "I'm in the wrong profession--look at the

6

raises and benefits those people (tradesmen, iron/steel/ auto workers, etc.) have gotten--we (nurses, teachers) could <u>never</u> get that much consideration--I'm looking toward a change of work!"

The career choices of high school and college students is now less a matter of matching personal characteristics against job requirements in some near-perfect and synthetic fit that stays with one forever, than it is seeing large scale "job families" with which to align one's self, viewing vocational choice as a developmental and developing process, or opting for other choices up or down the prestige ladder (Super & Hall, 1978). Hobby areas can become job specialties if one so chooses--housewives become writers or painters or seamstresses. Dentists may engage in real estate specu-lation and make more money (if that is their objective) and often gain more personal satisfaction than they do from practicing their "chosen" profession.

Along with a lessening of the importance of one-career choices is the development of more open curri-cula in high school and college. Students have long said--but have not been remembered as saying--that "high school was a drag." They felt locked into narrow curricula that presumed to give them a leg up on a career choice, hence a career itself (Buxton, 1973; Coleman, 1973; Sarason, 1977). And the curriculum, narrow and pure, was a sure route--or as sure as one could find--to given career objectives. No wonder that many career choices, presumed to be based on a valid curriculum and to be a straightaway to later career success. have turned out to be unwise, unhappy or just plain miserable for many people (DeGrazia, 1964; Green, 1968; Nisbet, 1971; Terkel, 1974).

The presumptive free choice of a profession or career is being challenged more today. The choice is not "free." Boys are known to respond more than girls to parental influences and persuasiveness in vocational selection; girls may even consider that parental pres-sures are non-existent or not influential in their choices. Students from higher social and occupational levels have their choices made for them, compared to students from lower socio-economic levels, the children from "higher" levels aspire more, those from "lower" levels aspire less. While studies show that choice of major fields in college, or vocational choice in high school are often immature and incapable of being followed (the students lack the mature interest and abilities to follow their "choices"), there is much

educational pressure in high school and at the beginning level in college to get students to "declare a
major." Since many students shift their major field(s)
one or more times, it would appear rationally that it is
normal for new choices to be made and experimentation
with alternatives to be the mode (Titley and Vattano,
1976; Thoreson and Ewart, 1976). Many students have no
exposure to the world of work, save casual observations
or menial part-time work, hence have no early--or even
later experiences--on which to base career choice;
they "think professions" when they might well "think
skilled trades" or "think small business" (Card, 1978).
Training students in realistic professional or occupational choices consists in part in diverting them toward,
and training them in, more realistic expectations about
work, work roles in life, and the stresses and strains
associated with preparing for a career (Howell, Frese
and Sollie, 1977; Flanagan, 1977). Some studies have
shown that actual occupational and professional information are lacking for most students expected to make
career choices. As students gain more concrete information, their choices tend more toward realism at both
high school and college levels of education (Remenyi
and Fraser, 1977).

One often thinks of the choice of medicine to be
made early in life, owing to examples set by other
members of one's family, close association with physicians and the often-noted idealization of the practice
of medicine (Becker, 1961). With the development of
new specialties, including public health medicine,
medical research and medical-administrator, the
practice of medicine is not what it used to be. There
is today a notable "migration" of physicians from one
specialty to another. Moreoever, these changes in
migrations appear to be increasingly more common over
the past two decades, especially the last 5 years.
Such changes, if they continue, will influence medical
education, the planning for and distribution of physicians by specialty and other manpower considerations. In
recent years there has arisen a similar movement along
experimental and research psychologists going into
clinical psychology, which is a migration comparable
to specialty change among physicians. The to-be
clinical psychologist must return to school, develop
new skills, accumulate a body of experience in new
settings (clinics or hospitals), and learn to look at
psychological problems in somewhat different ways.
Economic factors, changing employment conditions, and
some "wearing out" or "drying up" of interest patterns
may account for these specialty changes among physician

8

and psychologists. It is possible that similar changes occur in accounting, dentistry, among airline pilots and other groups but they have not been well-documented to date. These changes in specialty portend changes in original training (how rigidly one has to hold to a given curriculum, whether one can train to be a generalist originally and then select specialty later without being wedded to them for life, whether any specialty is somewhat artificial at the curriculum level and becomes meaningful primarily with experience, and so on), and in the later career lines of many professionals. The one-life-one career notion is further challenged by these types of sub-specialty and specialty changes. The implications for vocational guidance and career information at the high school and college level are also real and will, in time, be felt (DeVoge, 1975; Howell, Frese, Sollie, 1977; Ekehammar, 1978; Bogie, 1976). Of interest is to learn whether specialty changes arebased on escaping from some boredom, a miscalculation of one's interests and skills, or whether the change is prompted by a move toward economic gain, less tension, more leisure, or because of geographic considerations. But changes there are, and they will likely continue:

A number of reasons, then, contribute to occupational and professional change:

1. Making original choice on the basis of insufficient information about one's interests, abilities, based mainly on school experiences, family pressures (Mortimer, 1976).

2. A failure to test out presumed interests in the actual world--even on a part-time or "intern" basis--of work, owing to lack of opportunity, improper guidance, and failing to understand the tenuous connection between armchair decisions about one's work and the actual world of work.

3. The complexity and relative unavailability of the salient experiences in the real world, especially where the professions are concerned (not as true for business-related and skilled trades fields).

4. Knowledge of the subtleties and the not-so-subtle aspects of some work fields (e.g., the importance of mathematics in becoming an engineer, even an economist!, the importance

of methodology/research design/statistics in
becoming a social scientist, especially a
psychologist, the importance of physiology
and anatomy in studying nursing, physical and
occupational therapy and so on), leading the
student to assume that what s/he "sees" a
professional do constitutes the entirety of the
profession (Sarason, 1977; Bogie, 1976).

5. The notion that one "discovers" a perfect
    match between one's capabilities and interests
    on the one hand and an occupation or profession
    on the other hand; a "get-the-right key"
    notion; rather than viewing choice as a deve-
    lopmental problem, a series of steps, sometimes
    circuitous, that are gradual, halting and
    probably without certainty or finality (Super
    and Hall, 1978).

Workers in the career and vocational guidance
field have long realized the shortcomings of the manner
of choosing a career evidenced by youth (Bogie, 1976;
Card, 1978; Ekehammar, 1978; Howell, Frese and Sollie,
1977; Flanagan, 1977), where some of the misfirings
result from the list of causes cited above. There
have been methods worked out to increase the "realism"
of vocational choice. One such exemplary program stems
from Flanagan's work and the work of Card in the same
Institute (Flanagan, 1977; Card, 1978). These
researchers have approached the problem of better
instructing the novice on career choices by paying more
attention to demographic, aptitude and sociopsycholo-
gical profiles of students, as well as providing the
student with a guide book on career planning, a career
handbook, a personalized report comparing the individual's characteristics with a number of career areas,
an examiner's manual, a counselor's handbook, and the
like. These more detailed approaches to career choices
may help reduce the error in first choices by high
school and college age students, and improve the basis
for choices that are positively made. One could say
that the changes noted in professions stem from a
variety of causes: changes in the profession as a
profession (i.e., medical practice and dentistry,
accounting and architecture are all different from
what they were 25 years ago owing to technological and
social changes); changes in the skills, aptitudes and
motivations of people who enter the profession now
compared to a generation ago; and changes in the person-
profession interaction due in part to the number of
"errors" made in selecting, pursuing and practicing a

10

profession or occupation. The vocational guidance and
career specialists attempt to inform the prospective
student of the first two types of changes and reduce the
likelihood of misfiring in the last type of contribution
to change (i.e., changes due to errors in aligning one's
self with a career line). Of course, all of these
factors and conditions intermingle to effect all manner
of changes but the most controllable factors are those
informational bases on which individuals make career
(especially professional) choices.

Not only are there problems with initial career
choices as we have seen above, there are an even larger
number of perplexing changes (new choices!) within the
career stream (Heddesheimer, 1976; Russell, 1976;
Social Action Research Center, 1973; Thomas, 1975;
Zytowski, 1976; Roberts, 1975) which contribute directly
to the oft-quoted "Professions--they are a' changin'"!
The commonest career changes--mid-career--have been
those brought on by a move from military service to
civilian life, the first and largest example stemming
from the World War II GI Bill of Rights for vocational
and educational assistance to servicemen and women
returning to civilian life. This process of change was
repeated on a smaller scale after the Korean and
Vietnam wars. While these changes provoked by an
almost total change of status from soldier or seaman
to civilian life, not typical of today's mid-career
changes, there are similarities. And thinking about
such changes was put into motion by career specialists
as they grappled with the problem of adapting skills
learned under military conditions to civilian life.
The military-civilian changes were based on codes and
descriptions of what a clerk (say) did in military life
that s/he could transfer directly, or indirectly, to
civilian occupations. At the levels of unskilled, semi-
skilled and skilled jobs, some military-to-civilian
status transfer was likely; on the professional level--
say, for example, in the work of the surgeon or the
bookkeeper--the transfer of skills was more direct and
less complicated.

Today we are facing a multitude of mid-career
changes that stem from factors related to the person
and to the nature of the profession itself, changes
that are far more subtle than were military-to-civilian
changes and even less well understood by the mid-career
changers themselves. Heddesheimer (1976) states that
there are two broad dimensions that intereact to provide
the occasion for mid-career changes: The person him/
her self who develops motivation for a career change,

which is owed to a large complex set of reasons; and
environmental changes that accumulate pressures toward
job or career change. Pressures toward individual motivational changes may embrace the search for more
satisfactions in one's work; a change in the person's
skills, in educational attainment, and in general
maturity or emotional development. The amount of
confidence one displays in his/her present self and
occupational/professional attainments vs. those anticipated through change come into play. Is the motivation for change one of escape from some deficits
(lack of satisfaction, boredom with work, etc.) or is
the motivation to change due to enlarging horizons and
further self-development?

As to changes provoked by the environment, these
may stem from changes in the location of work, in the
social composition of one's work group, in technological changes in the actual performance of the profession or job (e.g., acquiring computer-related skills
in accounting rather than doing accounting on a basis
common before computers came into wide usage), and
other, similar changes? The individual has to decide
for him/her self the origin of pressures to change in
mid-career and perhaps work out with a counselor or
therapist a set of criteria useful in making decisions
about mid-career changes and in carrying them out.

On the surface it seems illogical and wasteful for
people to change at mid-life into a new or different
occupation. Sometimes people who make such changes,
for whatever reasons, are called "dropouts," with the
implication that there must be something wrong with
their values, their mental health and attitudes, or
some other behind-the-scenes forces must account for
this irregular behavior. However, mid-career changes
are becoming more and more common, and occur as often
to people who are successful in their first careers as
they do to those less successful. In one interesting
study of mid-career changers (also referred to as"dropouts"), Roberts (1975) developed a conceptual framework for understanding such changes among people--
mostly men up to 55 years of age--based on several
factors: the initial and earlier frustrations the
career changers experienced, the occurrence of preci-
pitants that immediately occasioned the change; one's
access to alternative careers; how, when and where
the actual act of dropping out occurred, how it was
organized and executed; and the consequences the
change of career had on supportive groups and organizations and other individuals. Follow-up interviewing

12

of these career changers indicated that they were
happy with their change, were healthful in their
living, felt secure in the change, and were sometimes
supported by unusual means (working, for example on
skill levels below those for which they were originally
trained). The career changers indicated they were
content with their lots and resolved to remain "out"
of their original professions.

Should one think that impulsivity or rashness
enters into mid-career changes, whether changers are
considered as "dropouts" or whether they move up or
down the skill ladder. A study by Russell (1976)
found, in 836 cases that as many as 27 different
variables (relating to the individual and to the social/
work groups, and so on) are needed to account for
change. It is not surprising that out of these many
roles new identities may develop that would come to
dominate or redirect the person's major commitment in
life. Career changes, then, might be viewed as just
another set of changes impinging on the individual with
more or less compelling consequences. The most
demanding consequences would be that of going back to
school, part- or full-time, in order to retrain for
some new profession or specialty. Less commanding
changes during the adult years might spring from
hobbies being developed into occupations, or from one
joining up with one's spouse or friends to enter into
new business or professional ventures that mainly take
time, money and the enlargement of skills one already
possesses.

Since mid-career changes ultimately hinge on the
individual and his/her decision-making, there are
areas of self-examination that may make the mid-career
change a more constructive one (Hall, 1971, 1976).
Items to be contemplated and studied by one seeking
mid-career changes include: Recognition of one's
advancing age and the limitations associated therewith;
knowing one's energies, strength, bodily changes and
health condition; setting up and anticipating new
career goals and assessing their practicality; possibly
searching for new or different or revised life goals;
noting changes in family relationships and their
import; thinking about anticipated changes in actual
work relationships; considering whether one feels
"worn out" or "used up" thereby needing to "trade one's
self in on..." a different career; and matters relating
to job security, job mobility, and job stability
following upon making a mid-career change. Several or
all of these considerations may be taken up by the

mid-career changers; and they may be discussed with
profit with a vocational or career counselor.

But, as the advertisements say, "You're not alone."
Mid-career changes and their consequences need not
weigh heavily on the individual only. Organizations
and businesses are now contemplating entering more
actively into promoting mid-career changes among their
employees (Hall, 1976; Hall and Schneider, 1973). Help
from organizations--even among professional associations such as the clergy--may come in the form of
sending professionals back to school (full- or part-
time), may provide for lateral transfers within the
organization, sometimes offer special seminars and
continuing education to support preparation for new
specialties, often provide for degree programs at local
universities, suggest permit transfer to other units of
the organization in different geographic areas, and
the like. Several authors (Kaufman, 1974; Thompson and
Dalton, 1976) have suggested that it is not so much the
individual who becomes obsolescent--such as to require
a mid-career change or dropping out or early retire-
ment--but that organizations themselves may display
more obsolescence and need to "re-tool" their own
personnel outlook. Organizations (including professional societies) can help create new possibilities
for specialties and sub-specialties and otherwise
utilize more gainfully the as yet still vital resources
of the individual. Better organizational manpower and
career planning for individuals cannot only help the
individuals but can enhance the contributions to the
organization. The organization sometimes has more
degrees of freedom to refurbish individuals, make mid-
career changes viable, and offset their own obsolescence than can be done alone by each individual for
him/her self. This kind of teamwork between the individual up for mid-career change and the cooperative
posture and encouragement of the organization can
help prevent "dropouts" from the career mainstream
rather than risking making such dropouts necessary and
wasteful. However, it is still possible that individuals may yet prefer to "drop out" and seek new or
vastly different careers on their own and leave the
organization, their previous career pattern and their
profession wholly behind.

Although many measures may--and ought to be--
taken to start youth off better toward careers, and
flexibility might well be maintained inthe course of
careers so that changes are acceptable and heuristic,
there are still other changes and important matters

14

relating to professions as professions that need to be addressed. The issues around professions qua professions stems from changes within the <u>organization</u> of professions, the professional bodies themselves, the stresses and strains that become the hallmark of medicine, law, the clergy, teaching, and so on.

Over and above the practice of any profession in its day-to-day characteristics is the nature of the professional organization, per se. Much of the changing of professions stems not only from technological and knowledge changes but from the way the profession is organized. Professions shape and influence their practitioners, far more completely and subtlely than many think. These organizational changes in professions, then, have important impact on the individual; the individual becomes boxed in, squeezed between the alternatives of following the professional prescriptions on the one hand versus trying to find a personal life within the context of the profession. The question becomes: Can one be both--man (or woman) and professional? Can one enjoy the fruits of professional training and stimulation and still put up with, adjust to, and manage the stresses and strains brought on by the professional organization itself? Before going into the various professions and examining how they put typical stress on their practitioners, we will look in the next chapter at some characteristics of organizations (professions as organizations) in order to understand the role of stress. It is no longer the case that persons just go about their days practicing professions. The individuals become part of, become engulfed in, and surrounded by the profession as an entity, an entity that may often be at cross-purpose with the welfare of the individual professional as well as with the profession as a body of service to mankind. This professionalism, if it can be called that, turns up three characteristics: <u>stress</u> (stress created by the power of the profession, per se, to exact so much from the practitioner); <u>tension</u>, the felt pressure, the state of stress and strain between the practitioner and his/her professional stressors; and <u>anxiety</u>, stemming from a chronic state of conflict between the profession and the practitioner, arising from the stress created by the profession and the psychological and physical tensions visited on the individual practitioner. We will examine in the next chapter stress, tension and anxiety as the conceptually vital three-party explanation of the present state of the health of professions.

CHAPTER I

BIBLIOGRAPHY

Becker, H. S., Geer, G., Hughes, E.C., Strauss, A. L. *Boys in White*. Chicago: U. of Chicago Press, 1961.

Bogie, D.W. Occupational aspiration-expectation discrepancies among high school seniors, *Vocat. Guid. Quarterly*, 1976, 24, 250-5.

Buxton, C.E. *Adolescents in School*. New Haven, Conn.: Yale Univ. Press, 1973.

Card, J.J. Career commitment processes in the young adult years: an illustration from the ROTC/Army career path, *J. of Vocat. Beh.*, 1978, 12, 53-75.

Coleman, J.S. Youth: Transition to Adulthood. Report of the panel on youth of the President's Science Advisory Committee. Chicago: U. of Chicago Press, 1973.

DeGrazia, S. *Of Time, Work and Leisure*. Garden City, N.Y.: Doubleday Anchor, 1964.

DeVoge, S.D. Personality variables, academic major and vocational choice: a longitudinal study of Holland's theory, *Psychol. Reports*, 1975, 37, 1191-1195.

Dwight, J. S. *Barlett's Familiar Quotations*. Boston: Little, Brown & Co., 13th Ed., 1955.

Ekehammar, B.O. Toward a psychological cash-benefit model for educational and vocational choice, *Scandinavian J. of Psychology*, 1978, 19, 15-27.

Flanagan, J.C. Planning career goals based on data from Project Talent, *Vocat. Guid. Quarterly*, 1977, 25, 270-3.

Green, T. *Work, Leisure and the American Schools*. N.Y: Randon House, 1968.

Hall, D.T. A theoretical model of career sub-identity development in organizational settings, *Organ. Beh. & Human Perf.*, 1971, 6, 50-76.

Hall, D.T. _Careers in Organizations_. Santa Monica, Calif.: Goodyear, 1976.

Hall, D.T. & Schneider, B. _Organizational Climates & Careers_. New York: Academic Press, 1973.

Heddesheimer, J. Multiple motivators for mid-career changes, _Personnel & Guid. J._, 1976, 55, 109-111.

Howell, F. M., Frese, W., & Sollie, C.R. Ginzberg's theory of occupational choice: A reanalysis of increasing realism, _J. of Vocat. Beh._, 1977, 11, 332-346.

Kaufman, H. G. _Obsolescence and Professional Career Development_. N.Y.: AMACOM, 1974.

Mortimer, J.J. Social class, work and the family: Some implications of the father's occupation for familial relationships and son's career decisions, _J. of Marriage & the Family_, 1976, 38, 241-256.

New York _TIMES_ article: The job market is rosy, Sunday, January 7, 1979, p. 16 (Sect. 13).

Nisbet, R. _The Decredation of Academic Dogma_. N.Y.: Basic Books, 1971.

Osipow, S.H. _Theories of Career Development_. N.Y.: Appleton-Century Crafts, 1973.

Remenyl, A.G. & Fraser, B.J. Effects ofoccupational information on occupational perceptions, _J. of Vocat. Beh._, 1977, 10, 53-68.

Roberts, B.H. Middle-aged career dropouts: an exploration, _Gerontologist_, 1975, 15, 87.

Russell, R.L. Career change during mid-life; an investigation of the inter-relatedness of intra- and extra-organismic variables. Ph.D. Dissertation, Ann Arbor, Mich.: U. Of Mich. Films No. 76-10778,1976.

Sarason, S.B. _Work, Aging and Social Change._ N.Y.: the Free Press, 1977.

Shabecoff, P. Nurses assume bigger role in health care, Washington _POST_, March 25, 1979, p. 1.

Smith, E.A. _The Presbyterian Ministry in American_

<u>Culture: A Study in Changing Concepts</u>. Phila.: Westminster Press, 1962.

Social Action Res. Center, Berkeley, Calif., 1973.

Super, D.E. Vocational maturity theory, in Super, E.D. (Ed.) <u>Measuring Vocational Maturity for Counseling and Evaluation</u>. Washington, D.C.: National Vocational Guidance Assn., 1974.

Super, D.E. Vocational guidance: emergent decision-making in a changing society, <u>Bull. Intern. Assoc. Educ. Vocat. Guid.</u>, 1976, <u>29</u>, 16-23.

Super, D.E. & Bohn, M.J., Jr. <u>Occupational Psychology</u>. Monterey, Calif.: Brooks Cole, 1970.

Super, D.E. & Hall, D.T. Career Development: Exploration and Planning, in <u>Annual Rev. Psychol.</u>, Rosenzweig, M.R. & Porter, L.W. (Eds.), Palo Alto, Calif.: Annual Reviews, Inc., 1978.

Terkel, S. <u>Working</u>. N.Y.: Avon Books, 1974.

Thomas, L.E. Why study mid-life change? <u>Vocat. Guid.</u> Quarterly, 1975, <u>24</u>, 37-40.

Thompson, R.H. & Dalton, G.W. Are R & D Organizations obsolete? <u>Harvard Bus. Review</u>, 1976, <u>54</u>, 105-116.

Thoreson, C.E. & Dwart, C.K. Behavioral self-control and career development, <u>Counseling Psychologist</u>, 1976, <u>25</u>, 126-9.

Washington <u>POST</u> article: Under U. S. scale, janitors in L.A. earn more than nurses, Washington <u>POST</u>, December 3, 1978, p.1.

Zaccoria, J. <u>Theories of Occupational Choice & Vocational Choice & Vocational Development</u>. Boston: Houghton-Mifflin, 1970.

Zytowski, D.G. Predictive validity of the Kuder Occupational Interest Survey: A 12- to 19-year follow-up. <u>J. Counseling Psychol.</u>, 1976, <u>23</u>, 221-233.

CHAPTER II

STRESS, TENSION AND ANXIETY

Stress is a commonly used word to refer to all manner of unease and reactions to complexities in living. Stress ranges from mild setback, through chronic pressures, out to major catastrophies. In this chapter we will delineate some of the stress factors (often called "stressors") in the external world, in professional life, in one's style of living, and relate them to tensions and anxieties which are assimilated into the individual's make up and form his/her characteristic ways of reacting to the world.

Stress may be noted in one's life in that an employee may get a warning from the boss that if the employee's work does not improve, she/he will be fired. This is stress. Next, the employee may be required to produce a lengthy report on some aspect of his or her work; the assemblying of the data, the writing, the cooperation needed from others, and the whole organization of the matter may exert tensions on the individual in the form of worry, loss of sleep, self-doubts, ambivalence about asking others for help, and so on. At times, the employee may be free from tensions and enjoy life, but as she/he sits by the swimming pool on Sunday afternoon, thoughts about tomorrow, the report, getting into the writing, etc. may cause sweating palms, accelerated heart beat, loss of appetite, preoccupation with the issue, and more. These last signs are anticipatory; they are thoughts about what-might-be, what-ifs, and will-it-turn-out-alright; these are anxieties that interrupt one's otherwise normal behavior, that are anticipatory, intermittent, unpredictable, and difficult to control. Stress and tension may be controlled by environmental changes and arrangements (talking with the boss, enlisting help with the report, making headway on the report), but the doubts, worries, apprenhensions and so on are anxieties that may reoccur if and when the report is done and accepted; anxieties may play over the past and anticipate more of the same in the future. The anxieties may, in turn, persist, resulting in a general foreboding, in doubts about one's capabilities, and concern lest one be in the wrong profession or in the wrong company or job. These persistent anxiety states may, in time, give rise to other overt issues: Considering and deciding on mid-career change, dropping out, burning out, psychosomatic problems, ill health,

frequent sicknesses, family and marital problems,
excessive drinking, disruptions of one's life-style,
and the brooding presence of feelings of inadequacy.

The paradigm, then, for understanding and arranging
these multiplicity of factors affecting one's health
and psychological and professional well-being are:

STRESS (environmental, professional, arising
        in the organization)---

    TENSION (psychosomatic, individually felt,
             repetitive, debilitating)---

        ANXIETY (chronic or recurrent, covert/
                 overt, anticipatory)

leading to insults on one's integrity, confidence,
health, productivity, and social and professional life.

Stress is defined by Selya (1974) as having a
number of characteristics in addition to these already
cited--It is non-specific, it is a total bodily response
to a demand made on the body, and it is made in response
to something in the environment that requires adjustment. Stress may also be positive or negative, exciting
or depressing, pleasant or unpleasant; although most
stress is probably negative or unpleasant or aversive.

If stress occurred and did not touch one materially, then it would pass; there would be no tension
(except momentary) and no anxiety. If upon driving to
work a tree fallen across the road is encountered,
this is only momentarily stressful; sooner or later,
you'll pass through. Tensions may be matters of
inconvenience, momentary disruption; they, too, pass.
No recurrent thought covering the past and the future
occur as anxieties to plague the individual about his
driving to work. The whole matter is soon over. But
when the stress occurs in salient aspects of one's
life, tensions result, and anxieties build up. The
stress-tension-anxiety sequence is different and far
more compelling than the incident of the tree across
the road. We will be concerned with the saliency of
work, the saliency of one's profession in matters
relating to stress, tension and anxiety in this
chapter and throughout the rest of the book. It will
be the purpose of this book to show how these factors
are interrelated and to ferret out the general implications of professional stress on the tensions and
anxieties of individuals. Before addressing the

20

matter of how given professions have an unhealthful
impact on members, the general issues of stress, tension
and anxiety will be given consideration.

How do professions exact requirements (stress)
that lead to tension in the individual participants?
How are professions inherently stressful? There is an
abundance of evidence that professions are stressful in
a variety of ways. Some of them may be stated as
follows.

Sources of Stress

First, professions are lauded as the ultimate
objective of personal development, the prestige factor
mentioned in the previous chapter (Kanter, 1977).
Professions purport to offer "the most" in income,
status, opportunity for advancement, side benefits
(health insurance, retirement plans, good vacation
schedules), and association with persons of authority,
power and influence. As Kanter puts it, in quoting
both Adam Smith and Karl Marx, the job makes the
person. One can hardly think of any person among one's
acquaintances whose status is not integrally related
to his/her job or profession. What one then does with
the profession--attain eminence, make a lot of money,
wield power, etc.--are proofs of the value of the
profession and further icing on the cake. Eminence,
money, power would not have otherwise been available
in such abundance.

If professions are so lauded--as a second point--
then it is important to strive to attain professional
status, the number one goal in life. The youth looks
around to see what professions may be open to him or
her. As we have seen in Chapter I, the selection of a
profession is often a precarious and ill-thought-out
one, often leading to mismatching, stifling individual
development, and wasting otherwise useful talents that
might be better expended in alternative directions.
The rush to professional status is often hasty, waste
ful, circuitious, and open to easy frustration. The
early stages of selecting a profession are strewn with
many psychological carcasses; many are called but few
are chosen. The number of people applying to medical
school, law school, graduate school, and other professions may range from ten to one hundred times the
number actually accepted! Even once accepted, the
attrition rate in various professions may vary from ten
percent to seventy-five percent or higher.

A third source of stress among professions is that the profession itself may "create" demands, expectations, and acquiescence to authority that keep the individual participants in constant states of vigilance and obligation (Terkel, 1974; Presthus, 1962; Seidenberg, 1973; Levinson, 1964). Kanter says, "If jobs 'create' people, then the corporation is the quintessential contemporary people-producer" (Kanter, 1977, p. 3). The onus is not on corporations alone, however; organizations that act like or simulate corporate status--such as professional groups (Medicine, Law, etc.)--behave in much the same way and exact a toll of obedience, conformity and resultant shaping of individual participant behavior not unlike the more visibly structured corporation.

Schools of Thought

Two general schools of thought exist in relation to explanations of how professions create stress; how the individual relating to his/her job setting is thus stressed by the formal organization. One such school of thought is based on theories of motivation and incentive, where these two conditions link the individual with his or her job and job performance. People weigh factors that induce (motivate) them to participate in jobs, such as income, raises, opportunities for advancement, and the like. It is as if the individual and the organization were separate entities linked by strands of activity bearing such names as "salary," "incentive pay," "vacation plans," "work satisfaction" and the like. Bound together, these strands represent or typify one's motivation for work and the "pay-offs" resulting from the rewarded motivation are seen in terms of personal satisfaction and renewed incentives for more work. Conceived of in this way, the person-organization relationship is characterized as a jockeying for position over and over again, a virtual see-saw where, on occasion, it costs the company too much to give such-and-such raises, but the workers--even professionals--exert pressures of one sort or another (a subtle one is the lowering of morale!) to gain their ends. These jockeyings for position create inevitable tension and strife for the individual participants, not to mention stress in the organizational system as it attempts to deal with its own integrity and purported functioning.

A second school of thought linking the individual professional with his/her profession hingers on the group, the interpersonal relationships, formal and informal (Kanter, 1977, pp. 254-260; Crozier, 1964; Jay, 1971; Likert, 1961; Etzioni, 1969). Here the personal incentives linking the individual with the organization or profession are seen as subordinate to, the social structure, the simply "social" aspects aligning the individual with the group. In this "social" structure the face-to-face relationships, the kinds of leadership exerted by the organization, the tacit and explicit norms and cultural prescriptions loom large. These kinds of individual-organizational relationships may be illustrated in the earlier Hawthorne studies, in the work of the "social dynamists" such as Kurt Lewin, and other social psychologists. An increase in participation, in team-centeredness and in explicit role playing, all in more or less fluid social relationships and social groupings, are the nexus of relationships between individuals and the organization. Nevertheless, the more "social" type of individual-organization relationships may be full of tension, for social pressures, personal acceptance, and the like are often more "intrinsic" to the individual's needs than salary raises, bonuses and other benefits, especially if the latter are seen as "external" or "extrinsic." Pressures may be,and are, put on the individual by both intrinsic and extrinsic factors and relationships; it is not the case that one is benign and the other the opposite. The individual-organizational styles based on "social" factors do, however, emphasize participation and involvement and the assumption here is that stress on the individual is less if his/her rewards are intrinsic and based on participatory democracy and team-centered organizations at the management level.

A fourth source of stress from organizations and/or professions, making for tension at the individual level, stems from what Sarason (1977) called "great expectations." What people expect from their work--one's occupation or profession being far more than simply labor--is that respect be granted for their efforts, that personal satisfactions arise from the work, and that a larger self-fulfillment come in connection with the continued practice of the profession or work. These may all be subsumed under "work as experience," which is based on a fusion of both social and individual involvement in one's work. All this is part of the "American Dream," a promise that one could rise above the more routine and grudging matters of daily life by preparing for and engaging in a promising profession. A professional future promised much. This dream has been in evidence for many years but it was dealt a lethal blow by the great depression beginning

in the late 1920's and lasting at least until the end
of World War II. People then lost faith in themselves
and "the system," especially the economic system that
promised them much--hadn't education been the royal
road to self betterment, economic gain and personal
happiness?--but had failed to deliver on these promises.
Great personal tension in the form of suicides, family
disorganization, loss of personal ambition, and other
signs of social and personal disorganization followed
on the failure of the Great American Dream to deliver
on its promises. The Dream itself was the stressor.

The loss of faith in individual ambition and
initiative, and the corresponding loss of confidence in
the system offering the previously lauded promises of
personal gain, gave rise to much skepticism that may
have not yet been overcome. If we can have one
depression, why cannot we have another? Even if there
are only recessions, don't these produce qualitatively
similar disturbances in the expectations of persons,
and in the equilibrium between individual development
on the one hand and the stability of the system that
purports to offer constant opportunities for growth on
the other hand? Emanating from these broken promises,
these dashed expectations are such questions as: "How
can we depend upon education to fulfill our expectations?" "How can we change the system so it will be
capable of living up to its promises?" "How can one
know what to select inthe way of one's life work so
that s/he is not subject to the vicissitudes of economi
fluctuations, technological obsolescence, unusual
stress, competition from new professions, and the like?
In short, how can we reinstate our fond hopes and live
with the expectation they will be realized? All of
these questions, of course, pose as well the problem of
change and correction at the level of the individual--
"What can I do, as an individual to maintain my ambitions and fond hopes and not have to look to the larger
organization (or society) for change, stability or the
fulfillment of my dreams?" This emphasis may be wrong.
There may be little the individual can do to find his/
her way through themaze of on-going changes at the leve
of the profession, the organization, the larger entity,
if the individual wishes only to secure his/her own
blessings. In fact, the drift of events at the professional level may be just the opposite: One that rende:
living with the profession, the organization, more and
more complex, further removed from the dreams of the
past.

The organizations, the professions, the extant
bodies representing the major "callings" (law, medicine,
teaching, the clergy, and so on) are, themselves, undergoing so many changes--as Chapter I has cited and the
rest of this book will document--that the individual is
beset with the problem of hanging on for dear life,
rather than securing the fulfillment of the dreams of
the past. This may be a sad but true reality we all
have to face.

Stress From Organizations

The title of this chapter centers around
<u>organizational stress</u>, <u>individual tension</u>, and <u>anxiety</u>.
For years studies have been done of organizational
stress (Kahn, et al, 1964; DeGrazia, 1964; Miller,
1958). Job satisfaction affects and is influenced by
stress. Kahn and his associates found that job
satisfaction among professional and technical/mana-
gerial groups was not uniformly high, that such satisfactions among the "upper" occupational reaches were
often less than those on lower occupational levels,
and that the much taunted "ego satisfactions" from
professional work were often missing. We have largely
assumed in the past that only "grubby" work--unskilled,
dirty, unreliable work, sweat-producing and back-
breaking work--was unwelcome and would be traded off in
a minute for more refined work. The Kahn, et al study,
and others have shown that not only was hard labor
often unwelcome, but that the more cherished and
prestigious jobs also carried their untoward and stressful aspects, and that the problem of the amount of
dissatisfaction with professional work was being overlooked. Sarason (1977) makes the point throughout his
book that the amount of dissatisfaction among professional workers has been a neglected topic of study in
the vast range of studies of "worker satisfaction"
(and the various bases for these satisfactions among
laboring persons). Sarason syas: "It used to be that
highly educated, professional people viewed themselves, and were viewed by others, as an elite fortunate
in that they experienced work as fulfilling, challenging, and worthy, possessing few or none of the stifling
characteristics of labor. Job dissatisfaction was not
their problem, but that of the factory worker, clerk,
and others in simple, routine jobs" (Sarason, 1977,
p. 31). Sarason goes on to disabuse the reader of the
notion that even when highly educated people in the
professions, in managerial and highly technical roles
were dissatisfied, it was a negative comment on <u>their</u>
professionalism, competence, mental health or involve-

ment in their work. So strong was the stereotype that professional status meant high level satisfactions in work performance and involvement that even wide-ranging researchers who studied job satisfaction overlooked the dissatisfactions of the professional worker.

Passing the problem back more specifically to the organization (as the source of stress) is seen in the writings of Kanter (1977). Her comments connect the stress generated by the organization to the individual characteristics of workers and their states of tension. She avers that a functional analysis of social systems might explain and even subsume what is loosely called "individual psychology" (in the form of stress, anxiety, alienation of workers) and thereby put a large share of responsibility for change on the organization if individuals are to profit from less stress and happier work environments. It is as if Kanter and other students of organizations and professions (Merton, 1961; Argyris, 1969; Crozier, 1964; Thompson, 1967) said "the organization comes first" in explaining the tensions and anxieties, as well as many of the personality characteristics of workers, including professionals.

Another item about organizations and professional structures that may hinder individual adjustment, and cause stress in the organization (felt as tension and anxiety in the individual members) is that of <u>size</u>. The larger the professional group or organization, the more likely it will be poorly organized, fail to reach its goals, and lose conomic efficiency. This notion was well argued in Schumacher's book, <u>Small is Beautiful</u> (1973). Large organizations not only tend to depersonalize the roles of lower level workers, but cause many with high status to be powerless and dependent upon the nature of the structure of the organization itself. The larger size makes teamwork, face-to-face working relationships difficult or impossible, and renders individuals ineffectual unless they try to circumvent the formal structure by resorting to similarities in social conformity rather than basing their contacts on substantive issues that solve problems for the organization. The formal structure becomes an end in itself and protocol takes over where problem-solving ought to prevail. If problems cannot be solved, stress mounts in the organization, and the stress is rapidly conveyed to the individuals; chronic states of this type of ineffectual organizational functioning make for chronic anxiety states among the individual members, perhaps more so among the upper reaches of management and professional responsibilities,

26

whose members are caught between the need to be loyal to the organization on the one hand and to preserve some integrity for themselves and their subordinates on the other hand (Kanter, 1977, pp. 254-260).

Further substantiation of this general point comes from articles now appearing in the press. The New York TIMES carried an article by Dallas Newell (1979) under the title, "What makes companies work? Huddling?" with the points taken that organizations are often chaotic in their functioning, the ferment prevents work being done, frustrates individuals, and lowers efficiency. The answer to this ineffectual state of affairs is "huddling," meaning that informally a few persons get together, talk over the situation, aim for task-oriented analysis of the problem, and get some action started. The "huddlers" take on emergencies that arise unexpectedly (the overly gross functioning of the organization as a totality often tilts the balance toward surprises and emergencies due to lack of coordination of the elements of the organization); cut through "red tape" to arrive at solutions by reducing the complexity of hierarchial channels; take responsibility where formal leadership is nonfunctional or unaware of the problem due to its emphasis on technical competence in lieu of managerial competence; and perform a shepherding role, which is to say the problems are ushered through mazes to solutions without confronting the organization qua organization. Huddlers stay away from formalities and technical language; they have an instant rapport, see problems and solutions similarly, and know how to weave their way through the often complex and rigid structure of the organization. In a sense, they are a "mental health team" for the organization, performing "therapeutically," if you will, on the organizational corpus; they operate informally from the very inception of the problem, through the solution-proposing stages, out to action sequences that "get the job done."

A similar article by Boyd (1979) takes up where the above-cited article leave off, viz., by pointing up how the structure of organizations pits "regulation" and "innovation" against one another and at opposite extremes. If innovations cannot grow naturally out of an organization's makeup, then informal or huddling-type solutions have to surface if the organization is to maintain integrity and continue to function profitably. This is another example where the structure, the formal lines of control and regulation of an

27

organization or profession, harden so firmly that change, innovation and emergent problem-solving are precluded or vastly diminished. This hardening process is all the more lamentable when research efforts are at issue because, by its very nature research is supposed to be innovative as well as problem-solving. The article indicates that only one new product results from among a total of one thousand research efforts due to the interposition of "research management" between the inception of the idea and the end product. An incidental observation in the Boyd article corroborates a point made above: smaller organizations that cannot afford to spend time and money on a complex and awkward management structure operate more economically and efficiently.

These kinds of efforts to smooth out the pressure--stress points or stressors--in organizations and professions not only get the organization off the backs of the employees (including high level management) and thereby avoid or minimize tension at the employee level; they also help the organization itself to function better. One might proffer the generalization: Healthy organizations beget healthy individuals (insofar as their relationships to the organization is concerned); and anxious and tense individual status grow out of stress points in organizations. Upon even casual observation one can note how professional organizations (medical societies, law associations, departments in universities as well as the university itself) function similarly to large industrial and business organizations; the differences are not in kind but in the web of intricate detail that prevents innovation, involvement and problem-solving on the part of individuals, reflecting at the same time the tension/anxiety states of the individuals and the stress points in the organization.

Alternative to the discussion of how organizational stress can make for tensions and anxieties in and among individual members are discussions of how redesigning work and professional roles (making them more functional, thereby less frustrating and conflictful) can directly change behavior, improve morale (some say "rehumanize the person"), and promote additional organization changes (Kanter, 1977, p. 255; Ford, 1969; Walton, 1974). It is difficult for professions and organizations to see how the stress created by the way the organization itself functions ramifies into the lives of individuals and makes for tension and anxiety at the "lower" levels. The organization has its eye on the organization itself

28

(its profits, in the case of business organization, the integrity and structure of the organization in the case of professional societies) and tends to dichotomize the individual and the organization too rigidly. For sample professional societies such as medicine and law resist giving out information to consumers on fee structure, and consider this an intrusion into the rights of the professional organization; whereas any professional will doubtlessly reveal fees (when asked) on and about any service whatsoever. Why this dichotomy between the local medical organization and the individual practitioner, between the bar association and the practicing lawyer, when such a basic and simple matter as fee structure is involved? Professional societies put enormous pressure on individual practitioners to prevent them from revealing their fee structure when consumer groups in localities wish to publish such information; resulting in individual practitioners being caught in the middle between the stress caused by the professional society on the one hand and the tension and anxiety felt by the individual practitioner who wishes to comply with the consumer group request on the other hand. Similarly, historically public schools have resisted giving out information to parents about their children (achievement and other psychological and educational test scores) when this information might have been useful to parents in planning for their childrens' education. The rigidities of the professional organization put stress on individual, classroom teachers and guidance personnel, as well as create anxieties in the parents and the teachers who interact at a personal level in reference to the child's welfare. There are countless examples of "policies" that simply maintain themselves out of institutional rigidities, hardening into lumps of resistance against information sharing, thereby producing conflict (tension and anxiety) at the level of the individual participant (parent or teacher).

In all of the above examples of how organizational stress may filter down to produce individual tension and anxiety (the anxieties being the more or less enduring aspects of felt tension arising from contact with pressure points in the organization), the organization must be viewed as an entity in its own right, attempting to preserve its integrity without direct reference to the individuals serving the company (or the profession), and putting itself above the inerests of the individual members as well as the public served. First comes the organization or the professional association; then the individual members (management,

professional practitioners, who are supposed to
knuckle under the organization's pressures); and lastly,
the public served by the organization and the practitioners.

In observing another facet of this problem it is
important to note how it has taken enormous effort to
get businesses and industries tobe responsible for air,
water and ground pollution arising from putting noxious
and unhealthful chemicals into the environment. Business has taken the attitude that such pollutants were
possibly annoying but a natural--and uncontestable--
by-product of their manufacturing or other activities,
that complaining environmentalists were simply a source
of annoyance in drawing attention to the issues
involved. The entity--the corporation (similarly for
other organizations and professions)--was seeing itself
as being above the issues and not responsible to anyone other than itself for its own ends (profit, productivity). This is now changing with the advent of a
number of environmental acts to correct pollution
problems. One change that has taken place in the new
laws is to make the corporate executives responsible,
as individuals, for the pollutants their businesses
disperse into the environment. The stress points put
on the environment and on individuals by the corporations are now boomeranging back to the corporate
leaders, as individuals. Instead of the vicious circle
involving innocent bystanders--individuals in the
corporation who may sympathize privately with environmental issues and purposes--and the public, the
individuals and the public are screened out of the
circle and the circle returns to the perpetrators of
the problem in the first place. One way, then, of
correcting injustices and unnecessary pressures promulgated by organizations and professions is not only to
reduce the pressure--tension and anxiety--on the
individual members (and indirectly on the public), but
to turn the pressure or tension points back on the
organizational entity itself and make it directly
responsible for its actions and policies. Thus laws
have not only been passed to make corporations and
businesses responsible for environmental pollution,
laws might be passed to make organizations and
professions responsible for dispersing information
that is judged to be in the public interest.

A good example of organizational pressures on
individuals is seen in the book Working, by Terkel
(1974). Terkel interviews persons in a wide assort-
ment of occupational areas, from day laborers to

30

executives, in quest of information about the individual's emotional and other reactions to their jobs. One interview takes place with a corporate management consultant. Terkel quotes the interviewee: "The corporation is a jungle. It's exciting. You're thrown in on yourown and you're constantly battling to survive. When you learn to survive, the game is to become the conqueror, the leader." (Terkel, 1974, p. 530). Apropos of some of the discussion in the immediately preceding pages, Terkel has his respondent saying, "Corporations always have to be right. That's their face to the public. When things go bad, they have to protect themselves and fire somebody. 'We had nothing to do with it. We had an executive that just screwed everything up.' He's never really been his own boss." (Terkel, 1974, pp. 530-531).

The pervasiveness of stressful pressure points that impinges on the individual in the form of tension and anxiety are well captured in the same interview:

> Fear is always prevalent in the corporate structure. Even if you're a top man, even if you're hard, even if you do your job-- by the slight flick of a finger, your boss can fire you. There's always the insecurity. You bungle a job. You're fearful of losing a big customer. You're fearful so many things will appear on your record, stand against you. You're always fearful of the big mistake. You've got to be careful when you go to corporation parties. Your wife, your children have to behave properly. You've got to fit in the mold. You've got to be on guard (Terkel, 1974, p. 531).

And tieing up a number of points made previously about the rigidity of how large organizations appear, Terkel's respondent says,

> The older the corporation, the longer it's been in a powerful position, the more rigid, the more conservative they are in their approach. Your swinging corporations are generally the new ones... but as they get older, like duPont, General Motors, General Electric, they become more rigid...It's only when they get in trouble that they'll have a young upstart of a president come in and try to shake things up (Terkel, 1974, p. 531).

31

Many of the stresses promulgated, intentionally or not, by large organizations, including the ones Terkel's interviewee refers to, can have direct reference to illnesses and anxieties accumulated from the tensions:

> We always saw signs of physical afflictions because of the stress and strain. Ulcers, violent headaches. I remember one of the giant corporations I was in, the chief executive officer ate Gelusil by the minute. That's for ulcers...There's one corporation chief I had who worked, conservatively, nineteen, twenty hours a day. His whole life was his business (Terkel, 1974, p. 534).

However typical these tensions might be in large corporations, it is no wonder that there has been a move toward mid-career changes, "dropping out," or even "burning out" under such pressures (Travis, 1979). Nor is it to imply that large corporations are the only organizations that foster such tensions and anxieties. In fact, all of the above quotes from Terkel's book and the articles from the New York TIMES are instances of organizational behavior that is not confined to the giants but can be observed in the local medical or dental association, in departmental membership in universities and colleges, and, indeed, in the whole faculty bodies of higher institutions of learning. There are probably no organizations, as such, that escape the rigidities the pressures, the filtering down of tensions into the lives of individuals (Kanter, 1977; Terkel, 1974).

Stress and Health

The consequences for individual health from organizational stress can be documented in another way. Not only are ulcers and stomach upsets job insecurities and internecine hostilities, frayed temper and fatigue resulting from long working hours common, there are more profound changes insofar as coronary diseases are concerned. There is a growing literature that relates coronary diseases not only to diet and exercise but to generalbehavior patterns and stress in daily living (Glass, 1977; Knowles, 1977; Henry and Stephens, 1977; Harris, 1975; Illich, 1975; Mechanic, 1976; Holmes & Rahe, 1967; Friedman & Rosenman, 1974). One way of describing this stress, based on the way people live, and resulting in bodily tensions and anxieties, is to characterize it as "Type A Behavior." Type A Behavior consists of a number of tendencies to master stressful and frustrating situations, to see frustration or delay in reaching objectives as a threat to one's sense of control, toexperience more than the usual amount of frustration and psychological exhaustion, to be "time bound," (that is rushing and hurrying and feeling under time-related pressures to get somewhere or to achieve something), to value achievement and to strive for it, to be impatient with others and with delay, and to pitch one's behavior on a high activity level. Type B Behavior is described as behavior relatively lacking in such urgencies, although Types A and B are not so separated in reality that a person is wholly either Type A or Type B; most people are mixtures of the two with more or less slant in one or the other direction; pure types probably don't exist.

Keeping in mind that stress, as conceptualized in this chapter, arises from situational variables (the organization, the nature of work pressures, and the like), and tension and anxiety are seen as individual characteristics, one set of which would be Type A behavior, we can expect stress to result in some form of tension or anxiety. Additional stressful situations extant in one's work and profession are seen to be such factors as "status incongruity" (Glass, 1977, p. 6) and upward social mobility. These might be thought of in everyday parlance as pressures toward achievement and motivation for reaching higher (social, professional, organizational) status, with urgency and impatience as fueling conditions. The upwardly mobile person is unhappy with his/her level and seeks "improvement" in status. The manner in which this upward mobility is then pursued gives rise to tension, psychosomatic complaints, and more or less saturated collection of Type A behaviors. Type A behaviors, in turn, are related to coronary heart disease (Glass, 1977; Henry & Stephens, 1977; Knowles, 1977). Following a review of the relationship between Type A behavior patterns and coronary-prone diseases, Glass says, "Individuals in professional and managerial occupations tend to have a higher frequency of Pattern A (Type A) behavior than individuals of lower levels of the occupational hierarchy" (Glass, 1977, p. 25). Thus striving, upward mobility and efforts to improve status are correlated with Type A behaviors which in turn, are related to coronary disease. This series of events is the individual counterpart of stress arising in organizational settings, and pertains most often to men in managerial/ executive/professional roles who identify most strongly with organizational goals and practices.

Related to the "dropping-out," "burning out" or
mid-career change phenomena, Type A behavior persons
tend, under prolonged stress and tension to "give up,"
become exhausted, and develop a feeling of helplessness.
Glass says, in this connection, "These (i.e., Type A's)
active coping attempts eventually extinguish in the face
of uncontrollable stimuli, for without reward the
relentless striving and time urgency of the Type A individual leads to frustration and psychic exhaustion,
which culminate in giving-up efforts at control. An
almost ironic reversal of behavior is then observed
with Type A individuals showing greater signs of
helplessness than their Type B counterparts" (Glass,
1977, p. 7). Think back, now, to the passages above
from Terkel where his corporate official interviewee
said, "The corporation is a jungle...and you're
constantly battling to survive" (Terkel, 1974, p. 530)
as representing the striving of Type A persons; and
the following as an example of "dropping out," or
"calling off the game": "It was difficult, the transition of retiring from the status position...In the last
four, five years, people have come to me with tempting
offers...I realized what I'm doing is much more fun
than going into that jungle again. So I turned them
down" (Terkel, 1974, p. 540). And a further example
of possible Type A striving and the consequent Type A
throwing-in-the-towel, from Sarason's work which deals
heavily with mid-career (or mid-life career changes),
is his discussion of "The Santa Fe Experience," a
setting in New Mexico where can be found "...scores
of career changers and dropouts, almost every one of
whom had been a highly successful professional, e.g.,
embryologist, museum director. Santa Fe is a magnet
for such people..." (Sarason, 1977, p.9).

The act of dropping out or leaving the profession
is ultimately an individual matter, but there appear to
be enough similarities in the provocations of organizations to propel an increasing number of persons into
more or less sweeping changes. It is difficult to
know what stresses in the organization lead to what
tensions in the individual, and how much the resulting
personally felt tensions influence individuals to make
changes in their professional status. Some students
of stress and tension have attempted to develop rating
systems designed to bring some order into the variety
of stresses and tensions people experience. One such
proposal comes from Holmes and Rahe (1967) who asked
people to rate the stress associated with a collection
of life change events such as death of one's spouse,
divorce, pregnancy, in-law troubles, job stress,

sexual difficulties, and so on. Some of the items in the Holmes-Rahe list relate directly to work: Being fired, retirement, major changes in one's work responsibilities, difficulties with one's boss, and major changes in one's working conditions. While these are global categories and thereby fail to specify the exact nature of what "trouble with boss" means, there may be enough commonality in a list to suggest that peoples' experiences are similar and thus stress points are similar. In addition, trying to delineate a list of life event changes, some research has suggested that these events precipitate later health problems and that there is some correlation between these types of stressful events and later cardiac and other somatic illnesses (Rahe, 1972, 1974, 1976; Rahe and Arthur, 1978; Rahe, Romo, Bennette and Siltanen, 1974). Yet other studies shelter this stress-later-illness paradigm and suggest that if the stressed individual has social support, that person is less likely to succumb to serious illness (Denise, 1973). One of the observations of Terkel's interviewee was that corporate managers lack affiliation with peers who are supportive; that when the person is fired, he is completely ousted and loses his peer and friendship relationships, which hurts as much as the job loss itself. In a college level version of the Holmes-Rahe life change experiences by Anderson (1972), Marx et al (1975) found that among University of Kentucky freshmen men, a high life change category was associated with a significantly larger number of illness days compared with men in the low life change group; and freshmen women showed a similar directional change in illness days associated with high life change events frequency. In regard to the presence of social support in person's lives minimizing illness reactions to stress, perhaps college freshmen are particularly vulnerable, being away from home for possibly the first time over a considerable time span and not yet knowing others well or developing supportive peer or other social relationships. The presence of change in one's life may, however, change one's perspective leading to the impression that changes are more significant; or individuals showing illness may be more sensitive to changes, making it hard to tell which are the precipitating and which are the resultant events when cross-sectional and actuarial studies are performed.

The Social Stress Model of Disease and Illness

Although not totally convincing statistically, there is enough of a suggestion in the stress-and-later-illness paradigm to suggest more study. It is a link in the movement away from a total disease notion of illness to a social model of illness, where the social conditions of stress result in enough individual impact to create tensions and anxieties that may ripple on for months or years, precipitating illness, low morale, job dissatisfaction, adverse mid-career changes, and even the more complete act of dropping out altogether from one's profession. The interminglings of all these results of stress are hard to untangle, but a plethora of untoward reactions do characterize individual tension and anxieties, giving rise to a revised notion of some diseases as being more socially detrimental than heretofore thought.

Schematically the changes in the notion of disease being the sole cause of illness, to the notion that the social context is a vital precursor if not cause of illness, and the way this model extends to cover all kinds of job-related implications may be seen in Figure 2-1.

Such a schemata is not to suggest that there are no disease or germ models of illness, or that all health problems are caused by some vague social condition or work environment that cannot be specified. It is to suggest that as the more disabling diseases have changed in the last several decades from the purely infectious types (Tuberculosis, etc.) to those illnesses that reflect tension in the individual and in the individual's living/working environment (heart conditions, cancer, etc.); the nature of stress, itself, in the environment, and the tension and anxiety residues of stress are somewhat traceable and can be shown in at least a gross way to be related to some types of illnesses and to a vast range of malcontentment with one's life and occupation. The broad stress points can also be shown to relate to the proclivity to change one's life considerably away from the sources of tension, and to see the unhealthiness of professions as antithetical to sane and enjoyable living as well as professional contributions and productivity. (See Figure 2-2).

It is one thing to document a number of changes in the health status of professions and organizations and quite another thing to explain why these problems

36

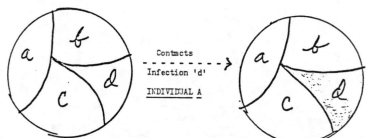

Schemata depecting how Individual A moves from a state of health to one of illness in some aspect of his psychophysiological functioning, due to contracting some disease or infection 'd'.

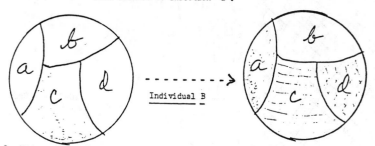

Condition of Work Stress   Condition of Illness and/or Professional Problems

Schemata showing work Stress in Individual B's life leading to Health Problems ('a'), low morale and job difficulties ('c'), and family problems ('d').

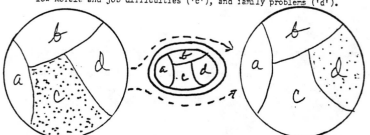

Condition of Work Stress   Condition of Illness and/or Professional Problems

Figure 1:Schemata showing Individual C under work Stress but sheltered (supported) by others, thus reducing impact of Professional Stress on various facets of C's life.

FIGURE 1

37

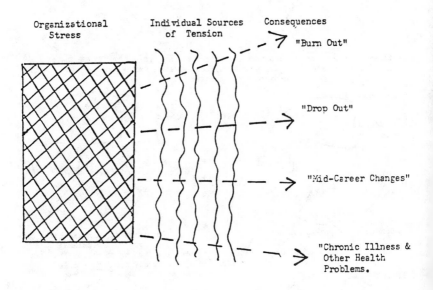

Figure 2-2. Showing possible outcomes from accumulated Stress at the Professional/Organizational level in the form of individual Tension & Anxiety.

exist. All societies have their health problems: susceptibility to pestilence, shorter-than-usual life span, the rampaging of certain illnesses, subtle connection between environmental health practices and the existence of diseases, and other connections between the health of individuals and groups and the surrounding physical and social environment (Dubos 1959; Dodge & Martin, 1970; Dingwall, 1976; Lilienfield, 1976). As Dubos said, "Each civilization has its own kind of pestilence and can control it only be reforming itself ...many of the diseases characteristic of our times have their origin in some faulty factor of the modern environment... (P. 164).

Nearly all of the present day authors of studies on epidemiology observe that all modern technological societies, irrespective of their particular political, social or economic organization, share common environmental problems that create health hazards. These common problems are shared not only at the level of the physical environment--handling human and industrial waste, managing pollution,etc.--but at the human social level as well, in the form of stresses from the social organizations themselves (crowded cities, poor working conditions, low morale, absence of proper health care distributed throughout the population, noise authoritarian governmental pressures on individuals, pressures from schools, churches, and organization)--the list is endless.

Documenting the shift from infectious diseases as the major causes of death in the early years of this century to the recent past, contrasted with current causes of death, it has been shown (Dodge & Martin, 1970) that whereas in 1900 the three major causes of death in the U.S.A. were pneumonia and influenza, tuberculosis, and diarrhea and enteritis; in 1960, the contrasting three major causes of death were heart diseases, malignant neoplasms, and vascular lesions affecting the central nervous system, this group accounting for 66% of all deaths. Several factors contribute to the change in the pattern of disease killers from infectious types to those emanating from stress and strain. An increased vulnerability to the latter owing to a generally older population, more successful medical treatment in the past few decades of infectious diseases, and perhaps better health and mortality records and statistics. The overwhelming contributor to this disease pattern change, however, is the stress and strain of modern living (Dodge & Martin, 1970, pp. 5-11). Within this shifting pattern of mortality from diseases is a higher arteriosclerotic heart disease increase among whites and more specifically among white males (Dodge & Martin, 1970, pp. 8-9), thus suggesting the differential influence of professional and organizational stress on white males (between 1900 and 1960, although there was an increase in non-white persons entering the professions and also an upgrading of professional opportunities for women of all ethnic backgrounds; this change has been gradual and has certainly not reached its peak by 1960, nor even by 1980!). White males have run the corporations, the major professions (except nursing), and have both contributed to and suffered from the rigidification of organizational and professional entities which attempt to preserve their integrity and influence individual participants in the profession. White males have, by and large, been the stress-producers and the tension-recipients, the ones holding the residues of anxiety, consequently the ones showing the effects in terms of mortality figures, professional disenchantment and other psychological and vocational problems.

But women have not escaped the pressures from professional stress. There has been both a direct and an indirect influence on women: indirect through the pressures from the anxieties, health and professional problems of their husband (Goodman, 1979); and directly on women themselves as they move more clearly into professional and organizational life (Kanter, 1977; Bernard, 1971; Seidenberg, 1973; Culbert and Renshaw, 1972; Whyte, 1951a, 1951b; MacPherson, 1975; Papanek, 1973; Terkel, 1974; Kanter, 1976; Golde, 1969).

Indirect pressures (by far the greatest) on wives, often leading to anxiety and depressive reactions, have to do with the informal relationships between men of corporate, organizational and professional societies and the roles imposed on their wives. The wives are expected to host parties, to appear chic, to have the right conversational slant on political/business/professional issues, to keep unpopular notions to themselves, to dress properly, to drink discretely, to appear supportive of their husbands (by appearing at the right times and places with them irrespective of their needs, preferences, committments, etc.), and to support the "family man" status of the husbands (Seidenberg, 1973). Many organizations and profession have wives' auxiliaries, the term really signifying the wives' roles of unofficial supporters. Wives "go along with..." the husbands in all matters pertaining to the profession or the organization, whether this i manifested in assuming auxiliary status or surfacing now and again at formal occasions, taking up causes for the husbands' profession or organization or corporation, or doing more conspicuous things such as raising money (sometimes for charities sponsored by the husband's affiliated organization).

These indirect roles represent pressures on the wives more than is usually supposed (Goodman, 1979), leading to women "dropping out", seeking career changes, and the like. Let a wife of a rising executive, or an aspirant professional who seeks a conspicuous office in a professional society, fail to "do the right things" and her husband will suffer as a result (White, 1951a, 1951b). One group of physicians was discussing a particularly respected and popular middle aged physician as the most likely candidate for presidency of the local medical society, when one member of the group said, "Well if John gets the nod for presidency, we'll have to put up with Nancy's chatter, drinking and frivolity, you know, for at least two years." Other members of the group averred, and one added, "It's too bad we can't have John without her!"

Womens' indirect roles are subject to pressures when the company or professional society's pressure tend to dictate where the family will live, whether the wife feels she can go to school, hold an independent position (part-time job, even), engage in a career of her own even though it is part-time or avocational (e.g., the artistic wife of a corporate executive found herself in frequent conflict between her own art-related activities, and dinners, meetings, out-of-town conclaves, and the like required of her husband in his professional role). It is not the case that wives refuse to share professional activities with their husbands or support the husbands in various ways, it is the way the organization takes for granted the wives' roles and acts as if the wives could have no independent interests in their own rights. Added to this taken-for-granted role that wives are often cast in is the impact the husband's progress in the corporation or organization requires in terms of out-of-town travel (the wives often cannot go along owing to caring for the children in the home), evening meetings, overworked and extra long days, and more.

Corporations and professional organizations may become even more articulate and formal in setting requirements for wives of men they anticipate employing (Whyte, 1951a, 1951b). The wives have to

41

fit into the corporate group, fostering what Whyte
called "groupmindedness." Wives are subject to various
conduct rules and constraints, have to support the
office or professional world of the husband yet have no
direct role in it, and end up being lackeys (Whyte,
1951a; Willett, 1972). Kanter observes that women,
under these "lackey roles," become involved in "alcoholism, unwanted pregnancies, divorce, and bouts of
depression... all having been ...attributed to features
of the managerial lifestyle" (Kanter, 1977, pp. 109-110).
The conflict wives find themselves in--often leading to
the types of complaints just cited--are between being
servile office helpers without salary or status on the
one hand and expert companions to husbands with whom
they share all the sophisticated corporate or organizational responsibilities and committments on the other
hand. Adding insult to injury, the wives in these
conflictful roles are seldom rewarded for their
efficiency or effectiveness but always expected to be
on hand at the right times and places fulfilling their
varied and conflictful roles without complaint. All
the effort goes to helping the organization--which the
husband is already committed to in terms of his career
line--and little respect or regard goes out to the
wives. Papanek (1973) calls this arrangement a "two-
person single career," which attempts to integrate the
formal and paid roles assigned to men with the informal
institutional demands placed on the wife. The corporation gets two people for the price of one!

These kinds of organizational (professional,
corporate) pressures on wives not only adversely affect
the wives but act back in a kind of boomerang fashion
to disaffect the husbands and families as well. Family
problems abound under these dual pressure conditions:
estrangement, separation, divorce, family members having
to go into psychotherapy to deal with their multi-
faceted problems, pressures on husbands torn between
commitment to the corporation and to the family, wives
equally split in allegiances, children suffering from
the lack of marital integrity in their parents, and
the threat of economic pressures if the husband's
private life keeps him from "doing well" in the
organization or profession. One lawyer who was a
corporate secretary with many pressures on him,
reflecting in therapy on his private life and its
effect on his functioning, said, "How can I deal with
the many problems I have daily in my job if I have to
have a fight each morning with Brenda over my time,
energy and commitments to my job? She makes both
matters worse by her complaining--the job and the

family both suffer." An executive complained that his
wife and family could not "...have it both ways--a
lovely home, pool, boat, three cars, travel...and not
leave me free to work to earn enough to support these
luxuries which they so much enjoy." As the pressures
on the male increase they ramify into the relationships
with the wife, the family and ultimately with the whole
lifestyle. It is difficult to determine what and where
something will yield, or break, or how much pressures
on can stand and still keep functioning. Often the
"solution" is seen in illness--as has been adumbrated
above--or alcoholism, or worse. The ripple effect of
the unhealthiness of professions and organizations
accumulates into near tidal waves of consequences in
the lives of the individual caught in the professional,
corporate, organizational network.

But there are also some small and healthful signs
of rebellion against such unilateral corporate use of
person's time, energies and talents. One such new group
on the scene is named "Inform" (Bergson, 1979). In an
article in the New York TIMES, Inform is depicted as
one that gathers and disperses information on ways in
which corporations affect workers, the working environment and consumers. Inform reviews the full spectrum
of corporate responsibility vis a vis the public, but
the public includes the workers and their environment
as well, not just people "out there." Jacking up the
corporation's responsibilities may include information
on issues as wide ranging as children's television,
auto safety, and foreign investments. Inform attempts
to integrate corporate responsibility with that of
society's needs, insisting that the two are basically
one. Although this is a belated move on the part of
corporations--consumer groups promulgated such activities in the early 1960s and labor groups preceded
even them, moving toward social activism and the
eaching of corporate social responsibilities early after
World War II--it is a good sign, and the more grass
roots efforts it generates and encourages, the less the
corporation should figure in the stress-related provocations discussed throughout this chapter. But the
corporation and other organizations and professions with
a corporate structure as their main posture--that is,
being primarily "out for themselves"--are slow to change
and the good signs are scattered far and wide over the
terrain.

We will pick up these matters again later in the
book and relate them to more general need for change at
all levels of corporate, organizational and professional

responsibility. Immediate attention will now turn to a variety of professions--medicine (physicians, dentists, nurses), lawyers, teachers, clergy, and others--as we examine their "health."

CHAPTER II

BIBLIOGRAPHY

Anderson, G.E. A schedule of recent experiences. M.A. Thesis, Dept. of Guidance and Counseling, Fargo: U. of No. Dakota Press, 1972.

Argyrus, C. The incompleteness of social psychological theory, *Amer. Psychol.*, 1969, 24, 893-906.

Bergson, L. The corporate world is her beat, *N.Y. TIMES*, Sunday, March 25, 1979.

Bernard, J. *Women and the Public Interest.* Chicago: Aldine, 1971.

Boyd, J. A. Research management stifles innovation, *N.Y. TIMES*, March 11, 1979, p. 7.

Crozier, M. *The Bureaucratic Phenomenon.* Chicago: U. of Chicago Press, 1964.

Culbert, S.A. & Renshaw, J. R. Coping with the stresses of travel as an opportunity for improving the quality of work and family life. *Family Process*, 1972, 11, 321-322.

DeGrazia, S. *Of Time, Work and Leisure.* Garden City, N.Y.: Doubleday, 1964.

Denise, T.C. The concept of alienation: Some critical notes, in Johnson, F.(Ed.) *Alienation: Concept, Terms, and Meaning.* N.Y.: Seminar Press, 1973.

Dingwall, R. *Aspects of Illness.* N.Y.: St. Martins Press, 1976.

Dodge, D.L. & Martin, W.T. *Social Stress and Chronic Illness.* Notre Dame, Ind.: U. Of Notre Dame Press, 1970.

Dubos, R. *Mirage of Health: Utopias, Progress and Biological Change.* N.Y.: Harper & Row, 1970.

Etzioni, A. (Ed.) *Readings on Modern Organizations.* Englewood Cliffs, N.J.: Prentice-Hall, 1969.

Ford, R.N. *Motivation Through the Work Itself.* N.Y.: Amer. Management Assn., 1969.

Friedman, M. & Roseman, R.H. <u>Type A Behavior and Your Heart</u>. N.Y.: Knopf, 1974.

Glass, D.C. <u>Behavior Patterns, Stress and Coronary Disease</u>. Hilledale, N.J.: Lawrence Erlbaum Assoc., 1977.

Golde, R.A. <u>Can You Be Sure of Your Experts?</u> N.Y.: Macmillan, 1969.

Goodman, E. <u>Turning Points</u>. N.Y.: Doubleday, 1979.

Harris, C. <u>One Man's Medicine</u>. N.Y.: Harper & Row, 1975.

Henry, J.P. & Stephens, P.M. <u>Stress, Health and the Social Environment: A Sociobiological Approach to Medicine</u>. N.Y.: Springer-Verlog, 1977.

Holmes, T.H. & Rahe, R.H. The social readjustment rating scale, <u>J. Psychosom. Res.</u>, 1967, <u>11</u>, 213-21

Illich, I.D. <u>Medical Nemesis</u>. London: Calder & Boyer 1974.

Jay, A. <u>Corporation Man</u>. N.Y.: Random House, 1971.

Kahn, R.L., Wofe, D.M., Quinn, R.P., Siroek, J.D. & Rosenthal, R.A. <u>Organizational Stress</u>. N.Y.: John Wiley, 1964.

Kanter, R.B. <u>Work and Family in the United States</u>. N.Y.: Russell Sage Fdn., 1976.

Kanter, R. M. <u>Men and Women of the Corporation</u>. N.Y.: Basic Books, 1977.

Knowles, J.H. (Ed.) <u>Doing Better and Feeling Worse: Health in the United States</u>. N.Y.: W.W. Norton & Co., 1977.

Levinson, H. <u>Emotional Problems in the World of Work</u>. N.Y.: Harper & Row, 1964.

Likert, R. <u>New Patterns in Management</u>. N.Y.: McGraw Hill, 1961.

Lilienfield, A.M. <u>Foundations of Epidemiology</u>. N.Y.: Oxford Univ. Press, 1976.

MacPherson, M. The Power Lovers: An Intimate Look at Politicians and Their Families. N.Y.: Putnam, 1975.

Marx, M.B., Garrity, T.F. & Bowers, F.R. The influence of recent life experience in the health of college freshmen, J. Psychosom. Res., 1975, 19, 87-98.

Merton, R. K. Bureaucratic structure and personality, in Complex Organizations: A Sociological Reader, by Etzioni, A. (Ed.) N.Y.: Holt, Rinehart, 1961.

Merrell, V.D. What makes companies work? Huddling? N.Y. TIMES, March 11, 1979., p. 1.

Miller, A. The Death of a Salesman. N.Y.: Viking Compass Books, 1958.

Papanek, H. Men, women and work: Reflections on the two-person career, Amer. J. of Sociol., 1973, 78, 852-872.

Presthus, R. The Organizational Society. N.Y.: Knopf, 1962.

Rahe, R.H. Subjects' recent life changes and their near-future illness reports, in Dohrenwend, B.S. & Dohrenwend, B.P. (Eds.) Stressful Life Events: Their Nature and Effects. N.Y.: Wiley, 1974.

Rahe, R.H., Romo, M., Bennett, L., & Siltanen, P. Recent life changes, myocardial infarction and abrupt coronary death. Arch. Intern. Med., 1974, 133, 221-228.

Rahe, R.H. Stress and strain in coronary heart disease, J. So. Car. Med. Assn., 1976, 72, 7-14.

Rahe, R.H. & Arthur, R.H. Life change and illness studies, J. Human Stress, 1978, 4, 3-15.

Sarason, S.B. Work, Aging and Social Change. N.Y.: The Free Press, 1977.

Schumacher, E.F. Small is Beautiful. N.Y.: Harper Torchbooks, 1973.

Seidenberg, R. Corporate Wives - Corporate Casualties? N.Y.: AMACOM, 1973.

Selya, H. Stress Without Distress. Phila: Lippincott, 1974.

47

Terkel, S. <u>Working</u>. N.Y.: Pantheon, 1974

Thompson, J.D. <u>Organizations in Action</u>. N.Y.: McGraw-

Travis, J. W. <u>The Wellness Workbook: Preventing Burn-Out in the Helping Professions</u>. Mill Valley, Calif.: Wellness Resource Center, 1979.

Walton, R.E. Innovative restructuring of work, in <u>The Worker and the Job: Coping with Change</u>. Rosnow, J.M. (Ed.) Englewood Cliffs, N.J.: Prentice-Hall, 1974.

Whyte, W.H., Jr. The Wives of Manangement, <u>Fortune</u>, October, 1951a.

Whyte, W.H., Jr. The Corporation and the Wife, <u>Fortune</u> November, 1951b.

Whyte, W.H., Jr. <u>The Organization Man</u>. N.Y.: Simon & Schuster, 1956.

Willett, R.G. Working in a man's world: The woman executive, in <u>Women in Sexist Society: Studies in Power and Powerlessness</u>. Gornick, U. & Moran, B.K. N.Y.: Basic Books, 1972.

CHAPTER III

THE MEDICAL PROFESSION

For many years, medicine has been regarded as the "best of all professions" (Becker, et al, 1961). Despite many growing disclaimers to the contrary, medicine is still a prestigious profession, but its prestige now carries more responsibilities and more vicissitudes. The state of health of medicine is increasingly in question. The Bible said, "Physician, heal thyself" (Luke 4:23), but the activities of the past few decades, more particularly in recent years, have cast doubt not only on medicine being the chosen profession, but on its own state of health and its own awareness of how deeply mired down medicine is in many facets of its operation. The organization and structure of medical services, the nature of the delivery of services to the populous, the multiply emotional and psychological problems of physicians, the rising incidence of suits against physicians, the prevalence of addiction, alcohol and suicide problems among physicians, and social image of not trusting the medical profession as implicitly as before, all attest to the growing embarrassment of medicine vis a vis the public. Medicine's integrity is suffering.

Medicine has been idealized in the past. It has been ranked as number one among the professions in terms of prestige and desirability. In earlier days, medicine and law were the two learned professions (the clergy may have challenged them on occasion), hence being a man of medicine meant not only the emphasis on humanitarianism and the care of the sick and wounded, but also meant the physician was a scholar, a gentleman as well as a healer. This was a hard package to beat, and few if any other professions--until recently--challenged the prestige of medicine. General W. C. Gorgas described medicine as "...the only profession that labors incessantly to destroy the reason for its own existence" (Gorgas, 1914; see Bartlett, 1955, p. 698).

The Becker, et al study (1961) made on entering medical fresmen at the University of Kansas tended also to idealize medicine and medical practice. Not only did these fledging physicians deem medicine the "best" of the professions (just what "best" meant was more a matter of halo than it was an enumeration of specific supportive items typifying medicine), they expressed a strong desire to help people, to enjoy their work, to uphold medical

49

ideals (The Hippocratic Oath), to earn a comfortable living (not a primary concern two to three decades ago and to engage in practice rather than in research. Tw< or three decades ago there were few medical malpractic< suits, so there was no foreboding facing the fledging physician. Also, a flourishing practice was assured, even if the physician settled in a small mid-western town (the students studied in the Becker, et all repor (1961), came mostly from small-town, mid-America to which they returned to practice medicine). There was not the opportunity for, nor pressure toward, speciali zation at the time of the Becker study that is present today; general practice would suffice, at least for a number of years.

But the problems noted by tyro physicians in the late 1950's and early 1960's began to grow and consti- tuted some of the factors that contributed to the present day status of medicine. Student attitudes in the Becker, et al study included prejudices against certain classes of patients: "Crocks" were disliked a patients who had no discernible medical problems but had what we today call "problems in living," personal problems, psychosomatic complaints, and just chronic malaise. Obese patients were not a challenge to the physician in the Becker study, since they were viewed as incurable, indolent, and probably not worth the attention they seemed to demand from the physician. Patients with dangerous communicable diseases were anathema to the young physician (and perhaps rightly so for, as we shall see below, some of the illness of physicians stem from incomplete or improper screening and diagnosis of patients with communicable diseases, especially tuberculosis, in the 1950's).

There were also many psychological problems posed by the patient and his/her illness for the physician to face: the likelihood of a patient's early death du to an inoperable tumor, the growing incidence of cance and the unpreparedness of the physician to deal person ally with such a patient or his family. When young physicians could not deal, as individual physicians, with the perplexing patients, the physicians fell back on what Becker and his associates called the "medical culture." This culture provided answers for the fledging physician when he was in conflict with ways and means of dealing with refractory, seriously ill, o perplexing patients. So-called psychiatric patients were likely to present problems baffling to the fledgi physician; as were pediatric patients, since children were often viewed as uncooperative and difficult to

examine. Since there were so many limitations on the
competence of the young physician, even when practice
was simpler in the 1950's and early 1960's than it is
today, the young physicians often gained the impression
that they were not a doctor after all (Becker, et al,
1961, p. 321). Adding to the technical problems of
providing help to refractory, seriously ill and communi-
cably diseased patients, those patients with "social
diseases," lead some of the young physicians to treat
the patient as he were "immoral" rather than in need
of medical help (e.g., women with gonorrhea). Charity
patients came in also for some dislike--they did not
seem to show their poverty sufficiently clearly (they
may have driven up to the clinic or hospital in a new
car, or appear to dress too stylishly, incommensurate
with their alleged welfare status)(Becker, et al, 1961,
pp. 323-325).

Sexual matters other than those associated with
veneral diseases also perplexed the tyro physician in
the Becker study. Young physicians spoke about their
avoidance of certain aspects of a physical exam
(examining external genitalia of a man, some embarrassment in gynecological examination of women, and the
questions of prudery and abnormal modesty on the part
of physicians examining, however routinely, women as
part of a general work-up.

The young physicians we are talking about,then,
preferred the "really sick" people, those with discernible organic conditions, and not the vaster range
of patients with psychosomatic complaints,sexual problems, culturally different attitudes, and the like.
The physicians were looking for "ideal patients" and
fell back on their own equally subjective culture to
explain their attitudes, to explain away the need for
services to these non-preferred patients, and perhaps,
in time, to drive them into specialities wherein they
would not need to deal with the more sordid side of
medicine. It should come as no surprise that physicians
with the attitudes described in the Becker study
covering the decade of the '50's, turned more and more
to specialization, developed a very preferred clientele,
settled in urban areas among the more affluent and
culturally acceptable patients. They may have also
taken risks on the nature of the care rendered patients
resulting, over the next two decades, in a growing
dissatisfaction with medical practice, a proliferation
of malpractice suits, the emergence of the physician
himself/herself as sometimes being a patient with
debilitating disorders; and the medical profession as

one looking for personal and financial gain in a manner and to a degree different from the previously prevailing view of medicine held by the general public.

One obvious adjustment of young physicians to these growing changes and increasing pressures was as already noted, that of moving toward specialties. A number of criteria were advanced by which a specialty could be judged (Becker et al, 1961, pp. 403-407 and 416-418); among which were money, hours of work required, the need for special personality traits, and the nature and length of the preparatory period. While these were essentially realistic criteria, the Becker study speculated as to why many young physicians chose specialties so early and firmly, and suggested that the specialty choice--surgery and psychiatry being among the most common--may have been related to the fact that these are specialties best known to laymen (future patients). These two specialty choices also made the choosers, relatively speaking, somewhat different from the other medical students (Becker, et al, 1961, p. 416).

Medical School Influences

Medical school certainly influences the attitudes of young to-be physicians. And, moreover, practicing medicine further strengthens the attitudes of physicians. It is unthinkable that as one practices a profession--be it medicine, law, the clergy, college teaching, or whatnot--that changes in attitudes would not occur over time. The interesting thing is the nature of such changes. Do professionals become inured to their early ideals, do they become more mercenary (or just practical in the sense of giving up on many or most of their earlier ideals)? We have seen in the previous chapters that professionals from all walks of life are questioning more and more the advisability of continuing their professions--they think of dropping out entirely, they sometimes "burn out" and are forced to choose alternatives (unless they have financial security already established and can retire), they make lateral transfers into related work that promotes refreshing changes in what they do, or they develop new and different specialties. In summary, they engage in second or even third careers (Sarason, 1977; Krantz, 1978), sometimes even "radical" career changes (Krantz, 1978).

The professional world is becoming increasingly vulnerable to attitude and career changes,owing partly to the individuals entering the professions (especially

medicine) with an overly idealistic viewpoint. For
example, in the Becker, et al study (1961), the
students were asked, "What is your idea of a successful
physician?" whereupon the freshmen answered this question overwhelmingly in what was classified as "medical
idealism" whereas the sophomores, juniors and seniors
were far less idealistic, and emphasized, in contrast,
such matters as respect of patients and community, a
comfortable living, and large practice (perhaps these
boil down to <u>economic</u> onsiderations). It may be this
emphasis on a growing concern for the economical and
financial aspects of medical practice--noted consistently during the medical school years--that leads to
even greater emphasis thereon as one enters into full
practice. Moreover, it may be the economic emphasis
that makes up the "rat race" of medical practice and
the untoward consequences (some of which we will see
below) in the form of stress, tension and anxiety that
builds up gradually and unrelentingly. The seeds of
what's to come in the way of mounting tensions and
disenchantment with many aspects of medical practice,
not to mention the health problems arising out of
prolonged stress, were noted even during medical
school days--and were in evidence as early as the
1950's (Becker, et al, 1961, p. 429).

The above background does suggest that physicians
might be expected to have their own health problems,
what with the entering attitudes toward the profession,
their goals, their attitudes toward certain classes of
patients, and the gradual increase in economic and
financial interests. Add to these more individual
reactions to medicine a number of characteristics of
the profession qua profession--the stress, tension
and anxiety paradigm cited in Chapter II--it is no
wonder that the health of the medical profession is up
for examination and even cries out for help. Some of
the ways in which the men and women of medicine, and
the profession they are integral to, evidence illness
will be elucidated below.

Tuberculosis. Most people would tell you that
tuberculosis (or T.B. as it is commonly referred to)
has all but been wiped out. However, T.B. is now and
has been an "occupational disease" of physicians and
other health care workers (Barrett-Connor, 1979).
While There were more tuberculin infected young men at
entry into medical school in the 1915 - 1935 period
than later, and the rate of infection during and after
medical school has declined consistently over the past
6-7 decades, "...the cumulative percentage of tuber-

culin-positive physicians remains at least twice the age-specific rate for the U.S. population" (Barrett-Connor, 1979, p. 36). Recent rates among medical specialties show the highest rates of infection among general medical practitioners, among pediatricians and surgeons, with less pronounced rates among obstetric and gynecological and orthopedic practitioners, and lowest rates among radiologists and psychiatrists (Barrett-Connor, 1979, p. 36). Although there were over 32,000 new cases of T.B. reported in 1976 in the U.S.A., there has been an active decrease in incidence. However, this general decrease in incidence of T.B. may have left physicians unwary of the risks they take --improved prognosis, better care, and lessened communicability, while true conditions, may mask the vulnerability the physician still faces in regard to tubercular infection (Sutherland, 1976). One report states that a single patient with unrecognized tuberculosis infected 45% of tuberculin-negative medical student and physician contacts (Barrett-Connor, 1979, p. 37; Ehrenkranz, et al, 1972). Students of medical and tuberculosis infection status among physicians state that the latter take too few precautions to prevent the disease. This behavior fits with the observation so often voiced that physicians try to treat themselves too often, do not consult physician-peers for fear of embarrassment or other inconveniences, and take undue health risks with their own lives and those of their patients and families.

Cirrhosis. It has been noted in this country and in England that mortality from cirrhosis of the liver is up to three-and-one-half times as great among physicians than among the general population (Cook, 1979, p. 156). Many have assumed that cirrhosis among physicians is due to alcoholism and that it signals conditions of living and practice such as overwork, emotional stress/tension, and anxiety. However, the cirrhosis might be of the micronodular or the macronodular type which is to say it may also arise in relation to Hepatitis B. infection, an infection also common among dentists, nurses, and other health professionals, compared to individuals outside the health field.

Hepatitis B. There has been an increase over the past two decades among physicians and other health workers of infection with Hepatitis B. virus (BHV), causing it to emerge as an "occupational disease" among these professions. Various studies have identified high risk areas of HBV exposure: hemodialysis

units, oncology wards, and in clinical laboratories
(Denes et al., 1978, p. 210). The study on which a
nationwide survey was conducted consisted of over one
thousand participating physicians (at AMA conventions)
who gave a 10-ml specimen of nevus blood, answered a
consent form and responded to a brief questionnaire.
The study reports that 18.5% showed serologic evidence
of previous Hepatitis B infection (positive anti-HB),
that women had a somewhat higher prevalence than men,
that Oriental physicians had a higher incidence rate
than whites, but no regional nor geographic differences
were found save for the fact that those physicians
practicing in large urban areas (over one million
people) were more likely to have positive results than
those from small communities. The significant matter
was that the prevalence among physicians of Hepatitis
B infections was over five times that of a comparison
group of volunteer blood donors from a national survey
(Denes, 1978, p. 210). The specialties harbouring the
greatest frequency of Hepatitis B were anesthetists,
surgeons, internists, and family practitioners
(Carstens, 1977, Editorial, 1975). Physicians in non-
patient care (administrative work, public health work,
etc.) had one-fiftieth theincidence of Hepatitis B
found among surgeons and family physicians (Denes et
al., 1978, p. 211). This would appear to be an area
of health care important to physicians in order to
prevent occupationally acquired HBV infection, perhaps
through immunoprophylaxis (vaccine induced active
immunity). For physicians (and other health care professionals) to ignore this prevalence is to risk
increasing the problem and further advancing the image
of physicians as not healing themselves. Routine
examination for physicians, similar to those they
expressly recommend for others, would be desirable
antidote to this problem.

    Hodgkin's Disease. Hodgkin's disease problems
among physicians have been noted and examined by
Brody (1975) and by Vianna et al. (1974). Not too
well-known, this disease is characterized by progres-
sive, chronic inflammation and enlargement of the
lymph nodes of the neck, armpit, groin and mesentery;
sometimes also by enlargement of the spleen and occasionally of theliver and kidneys. The disease has
been known for over 100 years after having been
described by the original discoverer, Thomas Hodgkin,
an English physician. Brody suggests that evidence
exists for the transmissibility of Hodgkin's disease
which might account for physicians having it often;
and he recommends extreme care in laboratories where

neoplastic tissues are handled. Following on the same reasoning, Vianna et al. suggest that physicians are a high-risk group for Hodgkin's disease. They examined all upstate New York hospitals for deaths due to this disease during a period of time, 1960-1972. They found that physician mortality rate was greater than that for dentists, the general population, or for higher socio-economic controls of the same age and sex distribution as physicians. The relative risk physicians encounter for Hodgkin's disease amounted to 8:1, according to their findings. While Hodgkin's disease may bring on considerable stress owing to curtailment of activities among physicians, the initial causes seem not stress-related as far as present evidence goes. However, the need to guard against exposure necessitates a vigilance on the part of physicians and is thus possibly stress-inducing.

Emotional Problems and Stress

Not only do physicians have a much higher percentage than the general population of certain organic diseases--Hepatitis B. Cirrhosis of theliver, Tuberculosis--but they have a plethora of other (psychological) disturbances growing out of a number of factors in their lives, observed from the beginning of the medical career (even including the selection process as to who enters medicine), throughout their careers, and even ramifying into their families and personal lives (Duffy & Litin, 1967).

Suicide. Although suicide records for all segments of the population have some inherent unreliability (all suicides are not reported, hence there is bias probably in favor of better known people being reported as having committed suicide rather than picking up the same fact among less conspicuous members of the community), it is generally regarded that suicide rates among physicians is three times that of people in general, and among psychiatrists suicide rates are five to six times as common as they are among the population at large (Wolfgang, 1975). Biases regarding the lives of physicians and especially psychiatrists suggests they have more stress and strain than other people, in both their training and in their practice. Personality types are said to exist among the suicide-prone individual (including the physician). Psychiatric practice is not founded on the same scientific basis as most of the rest of medicine, hence their status is less secure, their self-image less positive, and so they are said to be prone to lack of success in their

56

practice which does not have the precision and cut-and-dried features found in some areas of medicine (a bone has knit, or it has not, a broken arm has been set correctly or not, one is recovered from an appendectomy or not, and so on). While all of these beliefs may have some faint validity, the value of them in understanding suicide among physicians and especially among psychiatrists is moot. The general fact is the suicide rate is higher, as stated,and at this time only speculation abounds as to why these facts exist (Wolfgang, 1975, pp. 24-26).

Ross (1971, 1975) studied suicide among physicians and did a literature review covering 75 years (Ross, 1971). He reports that knowledge about physician suicides is spotty and incomplete; that the rate of suicide among physicians, as well as among people in general, varies from country to country; that suicide rates among physicians is higher in such diverse geographic areas as England and Wales, South Africa, Denmark and the U.S.A. Over a considerable period of time, the suicide rates among physicians in the U.S.A. has been at least double that of people (males) in general. Female physicians also have a high suicide rate in the U.S.A., up to four times as high as females in general among age groups over 25. In the Ross study, psychiatry had a higher suicide rate than any other medical specialty. There has been too little work done, even among physicians, in regard to suicide prevention, early detection of the suicide-prone physician. The organization of medicine itself has not risen to support the needs of the potentially suicidal physician.

Related to the last point, Lipsitt (1975) observes that the doctor is not usually a good patient. As we have seen above, the Bible exhorts the physician to cure himself (Luke 4:23); yet folklore attests to the fact that the physician is not a good doctor, nor a good patient, for himself. Neither do physicians put themselves under the care of other physicians, especially about stress, anxiety, emotional and other psychological problems. Converting the proposition that physicians do not make good patients--either for themselves or for other physicians--the following humorous, but valid folkloric version captures the spirit of the matter:

> If a doctor is doctoring a doctor,
> Does the doctor doing the doctoring
> Doctor the doctor being doctored
> The way the doctor being doctored

57

Wants to be doctored?
Or does the doctor doctoring the doctor
Doctor the doctor being doctored
The way the doctoring doctor usually doctors?

Facetiousness aside, there are inherent limitations on one physician treating another: Friendships
get in the way and candidness is sacrificed; the
doctor-patient is treated more as a colleague rather
than as a patient; examinations may be superficial
and cursory; follow-up treatment may be lacking, thus
allowing a chronic problem to persist, or the
"doctoring-doctor" may assume that his doctor-patient
"knows what to do and will take care of himself once
started on the right track." Perhaps the better plan
for treating physicians would be for medical societies
to set up review boards, develop referral systems, and
monitor the progress of the "sick doctor" in order to
protect all concerned: the doctor-patient him/herself,
the treating physician, the "sick doctor's" own
clientele, and the profession as a whole (Pinner &
Miller, 1952; Grotjahn, 1964; Valliant, et al, 1972;
Crosbie, 1972; Eron, 1955; Shur, 1972; Scheiber, 1978).
These strictures are particularly important where the
disturbed physician--general practitioner, psychiatrist, or other--is potentially suicidal, since the
shock of suicide probably ramifies more broadly and
profoundly among the friends, acquaintenances and
patients of the victim than death by any other means
(Sargent, et al, 1977).

While many versions exist as to why physicians
commit suicide in such large proportions compared to
comparable general populations, some features seem to
stand out as relevant (Sargent, et al, 1977). Sargent
et al, aver that the presuicidal physician comes from
a disturbed family, has had a "barren childhood,"
probably excelled in school, is an older physician, is
more often a psychiatrist and more often a woman
(Pasnan and Russell, 1975). Sometimes related to suicide, especially among older physicians, are failing
health, problems with marriage or medical practice,
aging and attitudes toward retirement, and overwork
often engaged in compensatorily to ward off signs of
profound changes in one's life. But other people in
other walks of life have to contend with the same
vicissitudes, so why the differences in suicide rate?
Perhaps it is because physicians consider themselves
(allegedly) as invulnerable; they often appear narcis-
sistic and vain and unassailable in the face of life's
ordinary problems. They are slow to recognize the nee

58

for help, hence may let minor or correctable conditions
fester and grow beyond their own self control. They
are used to telling others how to live and not to
applying their wisdom to themselves. Being members of
the favored profession (Becker, et al, 1961), the
"best of all professions" (so they believe!) ill equips
them to be mere mortals like the rest of us and
observe the telling signs of disease, conflict,
emotional deterioration, and other calls for help.
Some authors--Sargent, et al, (1977)--carry this matter
even further and involve the wife and family:
"Frequently, a doctor's wife has married a god-like
figure with whom she can establish a child-parent
relationship...the doctor is more worshipped than
loved..." (Sargent, et al, 1077, p. 144). The wife
may remain, in such cases, oblivious to the physician-
husband changes and impending problems, or she may
rise to become a "superwife" intent on protecting her
husband from whatever might ail him and sheltering him
from himself, his colleagues and his patients, all to
wake up one morning and find the holocaust his hit!
Peers, too, protect other physicians as we have seen,
whether they are treating the "sick physician" or not.
Peers also scoff at weaknesses among fellow physicians
and feel a good game of golf, or a few stiff drinks,
or laying-a-broad will rectify the momentary ills.
Many practical problems abound, too, in deterring the
physician from receiving help for emotional problems:
the cost of psychotherapy (especially without
insurance support), the exposure to others in the professional community as "needing help," theproblem of
choosing a therapist who will be candid, helpful and
competent (just a buddy-buddy won't do), and the
willingness to trust, self-disclose and admit the need
for help with emotional problems (Finseth, 1977; Pallis,
et al, 1976; Ross, 1975; DeRosis, 1974; Steppacher and
Mausner, 1974).

The impression should not be gained that only male
physicians experience the stress, tension and anxiety
leading to suicide. As noted above, female physicians,
although their gross number is far less than male
physicians, have a higher suicide rate than male
physicians (Finseth, 1977; Notman, 1975; Steppacher
and Mausner, 1974). There appears to be a higher
suicide rate among young women physicians--whereas men
tend to rank higher as suicide victims in mid-life--
and single women constitute a larger percentage than
married women (this appears to be true among other
professional women as well (Notman, 1975)). It is
claimed that the role of women in conflict between

professional status and the usual female role of house
wife and mother constitute a greater stimulus to suici
In competing with men in professional roles, women ten
to ignore normal frustrations, role conflicts, and try
to build super confidence and skill, consequently they
develop stresses and tensions that overload them. Pus
ing one's self too far and too hard leads to breakdown
feelings of helplessness and depression; the outcome m
be suicide.

The female role conflicts cited above apply not
only to physicians but to other professional women as
well (Steppacher and Mausner, 1974; Craig and Pitts,
1968). Women chemists have a higher suicide rate tha
women in general; nurses, too,tend to commit suicide,
especially in the younger age groups, at a higher rate
than women in general; and the suicide rate among female psychologists was about three times that of the
general female population (but male psychologists show
no higher suicide rate than found in the general popul
tion) (Steppacher and Mausner, 1974).[1]

Generally the suicide rate among physicians reflects the stress, tension and anxiety motif addressed
in the preceding chapters. Especially among the young
er women physician suicide victims, there is the stres
of medical school, conflicts over marriage, pregnancy
and bearing children, as well as the extent to which
commitment to medicine absorbs their time and preclude
the development of broad, culturally interesting and
socially rewarding activities. Many young women feel
trapped in their pursuit of medical degrees and career
yet even if disenchanted would consider dropping out
embarrassing, humiliating and a sign of failure. The
one-life-one career motif dominates their thinking, ye
at the same time they know what else in life they are

[1] Data for suicide rates among physicians were de
rived from AMA records and obituary columns (see Steppacher and Mausner, 1974, p. 325). All students of
suicide rates -- among professionals as well as the la
population -- recognize that published reports of suicide, causes of death on death certificates, coming as
they do from over 3,000 counties in the U.S.A. vary
widely and may be unreliable underestimates. Protecti
of the suicide act of the individual and/or his/her
family as well uncertainty concerning actual causes
of death (e.g., death from a car veering off the road
may be a massed suicide) affect the reported or publish
cause of death.

missing, thus the ensuing conflict may be so gripping
that only a gradual sinking into helplessness and ultimate suicide seems the way out. With men the course of
events may extend over a different time and age trajectory yet encompass some of the same features. Over-
devotion to work, restriction of family and social life,
the monotony of seeing dozens of patients daily many
of whom have complaints and problems other than those
treatable by medical means, can injure the male physician to the glories of medical practice (Barclay, W. R.,
1978). The glow of being a "doctor" fades perceptibly
under such conditions; the physician feels trapped (what
else can he do vocationally?), helpless and depressed.
Relief through alcohol, drugs and affairs may assuage
him momentarily, but only contribute in the long run to
his ultimate downfall. Sometimes the only way out is
suicide.

Curious as it may seem, physicians (except for
psychiatrists who specialize in treating suicide-prone
individuals) do not like to deal with patients who are
suicidal (Bradshaw, 1978, p. 89). Bradshaw cites a
study in which 44 percent of "junior doctors" and 25
percent of "senior doctors" in a hospital felt hostility
toward suicidal patients whereas none felt this hostility
toward patients admitted with coronary related heart
conditions. Physicians have also been known to abhor
working with alcoholic paitents (unless they develop
this as a specialty), with drug addicts, and with youth
who experiment with various means of obtaining "highs".
Whether these medical biases are more culturally or
individually inspired, no one can say; perhaps to some
extent the physician's sensitivity to the fact that
"... there but for the grace of God go I..." leads him
or her to dislike working with patients who present
other than standard disease problems (especially those
who baffle all of us with suicide threats, inane drug
usage, alcoholic excess and the like--they all seem to
lack what we naively call "will power" and hence do not
submit readily to treatment-- medical, psychological,
or otherwise --very well).

Drug Addiction. A number of factors contribute to
the overuse of drugs among physicians (Korcok, 1977;
Borsay, et al, 1977). These factors include easy access
to drugs which is a continuous opportunity. Add stress
and tensions and anxiety from daily pressures, and drugs
may seem an easy way out; especially if, as some authors
say (Korcok, 1977), that the drug using physician had
unusual stress during his/her early life, sometime had
prolonged childhood illness (this condition not infre-

61

quently sensitizes bright but sickly youngsters to wanting to enter medicine), academic overachievement, sexual
inhibitions and emotional hypersensitivity. This set of
characteristics, while not typical of physicians in general, may nonetheless be potent enough when they do occur
to tip the stressed physician toward drug use.

Drug use among physicians is ten times that among
the general population-- 1:400 vs 1:4000 in the general
population (Korcak, 1977, p. 89).

Once started, drug usage among physicians tends to
continue because the style of living that gives rise to
the stress and tension seem not to abate with age, but
may actually increase at least until the physician
tapers off in his/her work after age 60 or 65. Peers who
know of a given doctor's drug use are reluctant to report
it to other medical authorities, to the medical associations, or to approach the physician drug user him/her as
a drup user as most physicians are taught to handle drug
users who are non-physicians, and the drug abuse literature emphasizes the physicians as healer, not as user wh
has, himself, to be healed. Physicians who are appre-
hended as drug users are detected by audits of regulator
boards, not be peers. Peers are simply not sensitive
enough to the fellow physician drug user, have no ready
tactics to put into operation to arrest the condition,
and generally remain silent and hope for the best (Borsa
1977).

Nor has treatment, when undertaken, been decisely
helpful to the drug-using physician. Drug therapy programs (usually manned, in part at least, by other physicians) tend to treat the drug using physician as a VIP
who really knows all he/she needs to know, and must the:
fore simply stop the use of drugs. The life styles of
the drug using physician are often not seriously ques-
tioned-- that is,the reliance on overwork, long hours,
lack of relief via vacations or travel or a warm home
life-- by other physicians who are often caught up in
the same overwork treadmill. Although the reported improvement rate for drug using physicians is higher tha
for people in general (27-92% for physicians vs 5-15%
for people in general), the comparison is hardly an equ
or controlled one, as physicians constitute a much high
educated group with many alternatives in life, economic
ly, socially and vocationally, compared to the average
drug user who may also be a "street person," usually
unemployed and often unemployable, a drifter and a was-
trel.

The physician as a drug user typically began drug use in adolescence or early adulthood, and has become an habitual user by the mid-30's. Physicians introduce drugs to themselves--again, growing out of stress and tension-- rather than by peers as is more often true among the general population. Further, the physician tends to use Demerol, in contrast to the use of heroin among the general population.

Treatment has its vicissitudes as well. Just arbitrarily stopping the use of drugs by physicians is not a promising prospect (Korcok, 1977). When the physician is put in a hospital in another community, sheltering him/her from localsuspiciousness or rumor, this is a more comfortable therapeutic medicine and a better protected procedure. Withdrawl takes from one to 14 days depend ng upon a host of variables associated with drug use. This short a period of withdrawl can often be covered as a "Vacation" period by the physician, hence helpful rehabilitative measures can take place unvitiated by the daily medical practice activities of the drug using physician. Help, then, by peers, can often aid in sustaining the non-use of drugs, and friends can monitor the progress in non-use of their physician colleague. Continuing psychotherapy, once begun in the hospital, can be a potential benefit and help correct the over-extended work schedule where indiciated. Treatment must look tothe larger value system of society as well--medical values concerning the use of drugs for therapeutic purposes abound, and we are a nation of drug users for almost any and every ailment. Since the physician "thinks drugs" so often, and has demands made on him or her by patients for relief via drugs, it is part and parcel of the physician's own thinking about his/her own difficulties to include drugs as an aid. This whole recourse to drugs has to be questioned, and questioned seriously and long if the drug using physician is to be helped and if the whole matter of drug use by physicians as a professional group is to be challenged effectively.

Emotional Problems. These types of problems abound as well among physicians. Some contend that one of the primary motivations for entering medicine (along with high intelligence, good scholastic records, an interest in human functioning, and other virtues and assets) is that the prospective medical student has experienced emotional problems in his/her growing up an views medicine as a aid in self-correctionas well as a profoundly important way to help others (Becker, et al, 1961; Illich, 1976; Bradshaw, 1978). Motivation for any occupation or profession is probably a complex mixture of selfish and altruistic goals, hence medicine is not unique in this respect. However, the preponderance of other broad problem areas among physicians--drug use, alcoholism, suicide, etc.-- all attest to the fact that serious emotional problems may underlie, or be integral to, these conditions.

One of the distinguishing characteristics among physicians with serious emotional problems is that they are often unwilling to accept the fact that they have emotional problems (Murray, 1977; Jones, 1977). Furthermore, the treating psychiatrist, since his/her patient is also a physician, taking an overly optimistic view of the corrective process, allocating to the physician-patient more self-knowledge, motivation and capacity to change (without additional effort) than often seems warranted. The physician-patient may also discharge him/herself on his/her own recognizance, sometimes precipitously from treatment, thus truncating the entire treatment effort (Murray, 1977).

Characteristics common to emotionally disturbed physicians reads like the characteristics associated with other health problems such as suicide, addiction and alcoholosm: High levels of compulsivity to detail, high aspirations, overwork, deferred gratification (fits nearly with the overworked syndrome), and when in emotional crisis tend to turn against themselves and become hypochondriacal (which, in turn, may lead to taking relief via drugs and alcohol).

Since "emotional disturbance" is a catch-all category, some more specific nosological references must be made. Depression is often associated with the general state of emotional disturbance (Blachly, et al, 1971; Duffy and Litin, 1964). Hypochondriasis is also noted. If compulsivity associated with overwork is part of the emotional disturbance syndrome, then obsessive-compulsive traits are also to be found. Their perfectionism (supported by compulsivity, high aspirations, etc.) may lead to over-commitment and to resentment against patients who do not progress well; having exigencies arise that add new burdens to their already oversubscribed programs, thus adding anger and resentment to the whole picture, may also be part of the syndrome. These reactions often form a vicious cycle, leading the physician to feel trapped or boxed-in. The whole cycle may look like this: over-aspiring (from earlier motivations to succeed, achieve highly be conspicuously successful) --over-commitment (overwork) -- lack of relief (due to absence of recreation or leisure time) -- per-

64

sistent tension -- resort to artificial forms of relief
(drugs, alcohol, etc.) -- continuance of the cycle
leading to breakdowns, excess in use of drugs or alcohol or suicide -- perhaps momentary relief from treatment -- repeating the cylce, perhaps worsening the
outcome. Sometimes, of course, the visious cycle can
be overcome through a reduction of work load, inter-
spersing days off, taking up hobbies, stopping reliance
on drugs or alcohol, thereby softening the whole pressure cycle they work under. Sometimes, too, the vicious
cycle grinds on and a final explosion or demise ends
the tragedy of living with the tragedy of premature
death (Cray, et al, 1977; Greenson, 1966).

Family Pressures. It is only to be expected that
the above-cited array of problems would ramify into the
physician's family. The overwork schedule alone would
rob the family, especially the wife, of time due; but
when the problems in living escalate into other areas
of addiction and habitual drinking, the impact on the
family is even more profound (Cray, 1977; Greenson,
1966; Ottenberg, 1975).

There is first a dimunition of communication with
the family. The physician father (or mother) is gone
a lot; when home, fatigue, reading journals, making
reports, desk work and the like supervene. The psychiatrist, especially, has spent his/her day listening to
patients and has had enough of this passivity, wanting
now, at home, to get away from the talk...talk...talk.
Perhaps these are times when drinking, or sleeping, or
being away to play golf or go fishing take the place
of available family activities. Also, the physician
is always "on call," via phone, an emergency trip to
the hospital, or some other demand by patients which
take precedence over family matters. After all, the
family can wait; the patient is needy and demanding.

At home, the physician, perhaps more so the psychiatrist, is just the husband or "daddy" (similarly
for the mother if she is a physician), but to the patient the doctor is God. This extra high regard is not
conducive to adjustment to the family routine; father
(or mother) get contexted at home and their extraor
dinary status accorded them by adoring patients (or even
their critical status by complaining and demanding patients) does not obtain elsewhere.

The physician suffers from the same marriage
idealism that plagues our whole culture; the "married
and lived happily ever after..." slogan is a shibboleth

that is just as inapplicable to the physician as it is
to to people in other walks of life. But if the physician is God to start with, then the disenchantment
growing out of poor or infrequent communication, absen-
teeism, pressure from overwork, and readiness to set
aside the family in favor of patient demands, all add
more disenchantment to the family circle and its smooth
and loving functioning. Marriages and family relations
suffer in the wake of these activities and commitments.

Being close to the male physician-husband and noting his moods and peculiarities, the wife may be the
first one to sense important changes in her physician-
spouse (Chester, 1973). Of course, a marital breakdown
(if there is one) may be a result of the overwork and
consequent problems cited above, or it may help to precipitate and/or exacerbate them. The implication should
not be gained that changes in the physician-husband's
status (or the wife-physician's status) are always long
and drawn out; they may be crisis-oriented, or take place
over relatively short periods of time, yet be lasting
in their implications, and be difficult to change because they become interwoven with one's whole style of
living (Chester, 1973). Some of the signs that the
spouse can pick up that suggest that stress is mounting
to the point where it may signal important changes in
the physician-husband's health status, the marriage and
family relationships, or even more serious consequences
are: serious weight changes, changes in amount or pattern of sleep, lack of energy, occasional readiness to
cry or unexplained weeping, inability to concentrate
(being overly absentminded, not following conversations
in the usual manner), neglect of one's person (cleanli-
ness, shaving, slovenliness of clothiers), increased
smoking, increase in use of alcohol or moving from social drinking to inebriation even without apparent
increase in consumption. Sometimes, too, these changes
in health status may follow marital breakdowns (following separation, divorce, or ambivalence concerning
whether the couple will continue to live together). The
family condition may be as accurate a signal of impendin
crisis as the physician's conduct in professional matter
or in personal habits; sometimes the physician's relationships to his/her patients, needed for economic, pres
tige and professional reasons, may be the last to falter

The "Physician's Disease." There are so many intertwined symptoms and syndromes of the ailing physician's
status that one author wrote about the "physician's
disease" (Ottenberg, 1975). Pointed up here as important are the facts of "treadmill living," and excessive

66

ambitiousness to get ahead financially and professionally. Devotion to medical practice, as we have seen above,
puts exact and compelling time limits on the physician.
Breaks and respite are hard to get and even they are
grabbed on the run. Ottenberg thinks that extraordinary devotion to work signals an attempt to ward off
other threats, perhaps feelings of insecurity or worth-
lessness, all too often exposed to the physician if he/
she has a less-than-demanding practice, and the failure
to have hobbies or other leisure pursuits (including
time with family) to relax the pace. Trying to reach
coveted goals, then relaxing, seems not to lead to the
relaxati-on. The overly busy physician has no time to
be disappointed, to cry,to fail, to meet exigencies that
cannot be solved in haste, to need and accept assistance,
and to know the joy of recovering from a problem.

In the backgrounds of many overworked and overly
ambitious physicians -- the most unhealthy ones -- are
probably several factors that help to drive the person
into more and more trouble. One of these is the possibility that his/her childhood was based on evaluations
of the person for what she/he did not for what she/he
was. Acceptance, then, was a matter of achievement
(you were loved if you achieved, not on just being a
person, accepted and appreciated in one's own right).
Another contributing factor to the health status of
physicians is the fact that they tend to be future oriented: there is always some pot of gold down the road
apiece, and one is rushing to this illusory gain, never
stopping to enjou the scenery along the way. Even before one has gotten close to this illusory goal, being
illusory, it has vanished, only to be replaced by an
equally grandiose and distant goal, perhaps more entic-
ing and more worthwhile. Being "time bound" is yet
another motivational characteristic of the overworked
physician (or the "workaholic" in any field of endeavor).
This is a corollary of the future-oriented-goal syndrome.
There is not only no time now to enjoy and savor, one
must rush on to other, more important, goals; time is
wasting, there is so little of it! The overly busy
physician cannot enjoy a dinner party without frequent
interruptions from urgent phone calls from the office,
the hospital, or from patients having learned to be too
dependent (thus making the physician feel even more like
God), or too demanding (placing the physician in conflict
between putting the patient in his/her place vs losing
the patient out of anger, then suffering the consequences of a reputation for being too impatient and nonunder-
standing). Under these circumstances, how easy it is
to fall into the use of drugs and alcohol, the "occupa-

tional hazard" among medical people (Valliant, 1970; Valliant, et al, 1972; Pearson, 1975); how easy it is to contribute one's own behavior to the generalization that the single largest social group incidence of narcotic dependence is that of physicians (Modlin and Montes, 1964); to add one's own habit to the observation that three to six thousand physicians (1-2 percent of all doctors in the U.S.A.) were narcotics addicted (Modlin and Montes, 1964). (The percentage may have increased since 1964). The problem of drug dependence has been so noticeable in some states that disciplinary action has been taken against nearly 1% of the physicians in Connecticut, nearly 2% in Arizona and Oregon (Modlin and Montes, 1964). Drug abuse has also grown among medical students.

The "physician's disease" is further elaborated upon by Modlin and Montes (1964) who say that the etiology is based on life-long personality traits (masochism, addiction to work, overachievement motivation, life without pleasure, feeling indispensable, compulsivity, perfectionism, rigidity, over conscientiousness) and current stress and steering factors in their professional and personal lives. Apropos of earlier discussion of stress/tension/anxiety (see Chapter II), it can be said that the background of personality characteristics may represent stress from the family and interpersonal lives of the physicians when young (achievement emphasized out of proportion to general, healthful living), that tension would arise in connection with all the professional practice, peer competition, reputation-seeking but essentially abiding aspect of the stress and tension factors. All these, in turn, push the physician to relief through a variety of temporizing activities without changing his/her basic orientation or lifestyle.

When therapy is called for. In all of the above instances of problems among physicians, therapy is advisable. Although physicians, as we have seen, are not themselves good patients and are reluctant to admit the need for help, they are more frequently today submitting to both institutional forms of therapy (e.g., medical societies doing something about helping the addicted or alcoholic physician into treatment) and to individual therapy on their own (Shreiber, 1978). Also, husband-wife (either or both being physicians) therapy is becoming more common, along with family therapy.

As we have seen, physician's wives may have a toug' go of it in trying to deal with the male physician's emotional problems, and may often have to join her hus-

68

band in conjoint therapy (Goldberg, 1975). Therapists of (especially) male physician husband-wife patients find the physicians nearly exclusively professionally oriented and tend to neglect wives and families. This attitude grows out of the factors cited above such as high ambition, long work hours, and achievement motivation. The wives feel the physician-husbands are non-communicative, respond neither to the good or the bad in their behavior ("he's always indifferent to me whether I cook an unusually good dinner, or leave the house sloppy for a week, yet I don't feel he doesn't love me," one wife averred), and are unreceptive to the wife's efforts to engage the husband in household or family plans.

The physicians, on the other hand, feel the wives are too preoccupied with the family and children and feel inferior and inadequate compared to the physician's other friends and peers. These two opposing sets of attitudes put the husband-physician and his wife at odds and constitute the second most common reason for hospitalization of male physicians (Jones, 1977) when the tensions lead to a breakdown. These discords also account for many of the cases where the physician's wife is propelled into therapy "in order to learn how to cope with my doctor-husband." It does not seem that the female physician wife with a non-medical husband encounters the same kinds of difficulties; most of the findings in this pairing suggest the difficult roles the female physician has to play in being both doctor and wife (and mother) and do not suggest the non-medical husband's role is one of exacerbating the wife's problem.

As with many young couples, marriage is entered into in typical American middle class idealized ways. This is probably not a good beginning for the physician-husband and his wife since their condition of strain is, from the beginning, more likely greater than that of the average couple for reasons already cited. The physician in his practice is confronted with a problem of emotional balance between himself and his patients; being interested but not too involved; being compassionate but not letting the patient become dependent. The male physician tends to bring home a high proportion of these problems about his patient and can well bore the wife with details, especially if demanding and dependent patients are attractive women. The psychiatrist is particularly vulnerable to the interpersonal aspects of the doctor-patient relationship (Rogow, 1970; Greenson, 1966) since that is his stock-in-trade (Greenson, 1966). Chronic distress placed on the marriage in this manner strongly suggests the need for psychotherapy for the male physician and his wife (Goldberg, 1975) or possibly considering a career change (Krantz, 1978).

Women Physicians. Not only do male physicians chalk up a number of health problems, but women physicians demonstrate their share of these problems as well. While the number of women physicians is small compared to males, the number of women evidencing health problems in various areas is apparently on the increase, particularly among younger women (where there is, of course, the greater number of participants since the population of women in medicine is of relative recent vintage and on the increase).

The woman's role in medicine is complex for several reasons. First, it appears hard for women to get into medicine based on undergraduate work, compared to men. The liberation movement in the last few years has resulted, in part, in getting more women of capability accepted into medical school. There seems still considerable bias against women in medicine -- they are more stereotyped as being nurses, physician's aides, physical and occupational therapists, and in other ancillary roles -- and as recent as 20 years ago, it was unusual to consider women even for psychiatry. For example in the Holt and Luborsky volume (1958), there was virtually no discussion about women throughout the study of male psychiatrists in training at the Menninger Clinic. In an Appendix to Chapter 19, Volume 1 of this series, the authors say,

> A good a priori case can be made for the proposition that women should make good psychiatrists. Qualities of patience, kindliness, sensitivity, gentleness, and intuition are commonly associated with femininity in our culture. Thus, women should do well in an occupational role that demands such qualities (Holt and Luborsky, 1958, p. 397).

The women's movement had, of course, not caught on in 1958. This quotation shows some sensitivity to the potential of women but also clearly states that their role in medicine, especially in psychiatry, was severely limited as recently as 20 years ago. A footnote on the same page of this reference indicated that in 1950, only five percent of physicians were women, yet women made up about 40 percent of employed professionals and semi-professionals in the U.S.A.

Even upon entry into medical school, women do not have easy going. The competition is severe -- as it is, of course, for men -- and the biases against women, especially among older men physicians, can be noted during the woman's progress through medical school and into practice (Forbes, 1977). Even though the liberation movement has made women freer today, no long stressing wifehood and motherhood, the taking on of other roles (such as profressional ones, especially in medicine) makes the choice all the more crucial for the young woman. She is foraging a new role for herself and she must suceed or look bad to her competitors as well as to her peers in other roles in life, hence failure becomes unacceptable, even unthinkable. Several books purporting to orient the fledging physicians to medicine, psychiatry and general (or special) practice fail to have references in the indexes to women and the role of women in medicine, especially the role of women in medicine's problem areas (Viscott, 1972; Rogow, 1970; Bradshaw, 1978), thus attesting to still notable peripheral roles played by women in medicine.

The Background of Medical Choice

Why and how people choose to go into medicine is made up of a complicated network of ideas, motivations, family and social circumstances, financial considerations, and stereotypy. As we have noted above, the work of Becker (1961) on the University of Kansas freshmen medical students, indicated that many medical students come from upper middle class, well-educated families and many of them come from families already engaged in medical practice. Very often medicine is part of a legacy handed down by the family culture.

Schafer (1974) examined the attitudes of approximately 21,000 college seniors toward medicine as well as other careers. As expected in the survey, the general stereotype of medical practice of affording opportunity to be one's boss, to contribute to the welfare of others, an interest in working with people, devotion to work and security (meaning financial security) loomed large. On the less positive side and more suggestive of the stressful and health-related problem cited above, many seniors saw medicine as taking one away from his/her family to a great extent, as being demanding of one's time and devotion to work, as being

71

stressful and requiring long hours, and as having an unwritten but rigid code of behavior (Schafer, 1974, p. 85). These are the factors -- assessed here as attitudes toward medicine -- that, indeed, turn out to be the _facts_ about medical practice, and that from the backdrop too many of the health problems evidenced by physicians. In a sense, medical people know what they are getting into -- if initial attitudes are a guide -- and it should come as no surprise that these examples of foreknowledge and anticipatory attitudes turn out to be self-fulfilling prophesies: the tensions are great, the pace and demands of medical practice are unrelenting, and the potential for health problems abound. There is, then, considerable selection in terms of attitudes and expectations as to who goes into medicine and as to what they anticipate will be their roles as medical practitioners. These selective factors may be as important in setting the lifestyle, hence the health problems, of medical practitioners in later life as are the childhood background factors and the factors current in the practice of medicine itself. In a very real sense three sets of factors contribute to the health problems of physicians, if we are to believe the literature: the problems related to high achievement, ambition, high expectations learned during childhood and youth; the attitudes toward medicine in young adulthood (college years) which stress its service to humankind but also note the stresses and strains and rigidities inherent in medicine; and the actual tensions of medical practice over the adult years that culminate in the many health problems noted above. The latter are exacerbated by the nature of the medical organization in which medicine is practiced.

The anticipations of college seniors about various attributes and characteristics of medical practice (as well as other professions), are largely borne out in actual medical school studies. Coburn and Jovaisas (1975) studied the perceived sources of stress among 52 first-year medical students, at the University of Toronto. Findings by these authors are essentially coroborated in studies by McGuire (1966); Adsett (1968); Gottheil et al (1969); Boyle and Coombs (1971); Rosenburg (1971); and Becker, et al (1961). The noted stress during the first year of medical school is matched by the incidence of dropouts from school and by the incidence of illnesses among the students. Their largest reported areas of stress are related to entering the final exam in an important course, apprehensions lest they not absorb all the knowledge needed, fear of doing poorly and getting bad grades, and the number of hours of study required. These are all academically related fears and tensions. Inaddition, a group of stresses emanate from restricted social life, from sexual problems, and from feeling they are in helpless and limited roles as students. Clinical sources of stress are also noted: apprehensions concerning errors in diagnosis, dealing with chronically ill patients, fear for own personal health from coming into contact with ill patients, carrying out examinations, and discussing personal and sexual matters with patients. Everywhere they turn, then, the beginning medical student is best with stress and tension (keeping in mind our earlier definition of stress as arising from the external nature of the circumstances in which one finds him/herself, and tension being the impact these sources of stress have on the individual, with anxiety being the more or less abiding and recurrent characteristic of both, and also leading to anticipatory tension as one becomes anxious about future events, future tests of one's adequacy, and the like). While the tensions may subside somewhat as the student progresses beyond the first year of medical school, some of the damage is already done, and the adjustment to the stress of further training is always up for test. The stress and tension that relate to the dropout rate from the first year of medical school is not a "natural selection" process of weeding out the less able or less motivated. Coburn and Jovaisas observe that "Evidence from a number of studies suggests that the stress of medical school may have undesireable consequences ... studies ... report that dropouts do not differ inability (measured by Medical College Admission Test scores and/or college grades) from those who graduate; that is, it is not necessarily the intellectual capacity of the student that decides whether he will continue or drop out" (Coburn and Jovaisas, 1975, p. 589). Adsett (1968) noted that at the University of Oklahoma thirteen percent of the medical students received psychological counseling for emotional problems each year (italics added), and many more consulted about their somatic problems. Hunter, et al (1961) found at McGill University that over 18 percent of medical students sought help for emotional problems. The impression from this study was that over 60 percent of the problems were due to the pressures of medical education rather than to prior problems.

Evidently the unrelenting pressures in medical school take their toll. The students' fears concerning their own inadequacy rank high in promoting tension. Rosenberg (1971) concluded from his study of first-year medical students that "the violence done to the self-

73

image of the medical student is the most serious consequence of his educational program." This is a serious
indictment of medical training and it is an indictment
that seems amply supported by a variety of studies in
a number of schools starting at least 20-25 years ago
(Becker, et al, 1961; Hunter et al, 1961). Given this
kind of stressful start in medicine, it is no wonder
that the health status of the medical profession over
the adult years can be seriously criticized and the
public served by these medical practitioners can hope
for, even demand, a change; for the consequence of such
a high order of health problems among physicians bodes
poorly for the profession as a whole, for the patients
they serve, and for their own comfort and well-being.
If pressures and grades and stress tolerance were unrelated to medical expertise or competence inlater
years, perhaps the rigors of medical training would be
understandable and useful, but there is no evidence that
the sheer emphasis on stress, resulting in so many personal tensions, plays any constructive role in who makes
a good physician. In fact, the evidence is to the contrary: stressful training years may make the fledging
physician more vulnerable to tensions and anxieties
over time and may help precipitate -- yes, even make
chronic -- later problems which, as we have seen, contribute to breakdowns, alcoholism, addiction, family
conflicts and suicide.

The Medical Profession As An Organization

The practice of medicine is not simply a matter
of thousands of physicians plying their trade. As professions gather momentum, structure and purpose, they
take on a life of their own, over and above that of the
individual practitioners. This is true of all professions. The profession qua profession may not, however,
operate in the best interests of the practitioners or
the public (King, 1972; MacKay and Mylander, 1978:
Bradshaw, 1978; Illich, 1976; Gurin, Veroff and Feld,
1960; Twaddle and Hessler, 1977; Olesen and Whittaker,
1968; Friedson, 1961; Hughes, Hughes and Deutscher,
1958). Helping along this process of a profession becoming an organization or an institution is the develop
ment of what some sociologists have called the "professional self-image" (Merton, Bloom and Rogoff, 1956;
King, 1962). The development of a professional self-
image is a kind of matching role between the individual
physician and the profession as an extant entity. The
latter stereotypes roles, defines behavior, sets standards, promotes a public image; the individual fits
into these role definitions and subscribes to them more

74

or less. A process of identification between the individual physician and the profession takes place. Training and schooling, of course, help to promote this identification, but the important matter is that the two -- practitioner and the profession -- join forces in creating an extant, public image that speaks for itself. Moreover, there is pressure for the individual to engage in this identification process. Can you imagine many physicians not belonging to the American Medical Association (or dentists not belonging to the American Dental Association, and so on throughout all the major professions). One's credentials are set in part by these professional organizations, and changes in professions are ushered in and out by the organizations with individuals more or less going along. Professional organizations among other things protect the individual members against unfair criticism, or explain the attitudes of individual members or practitioners, and promote the causes felt to be important by individuals. There is a fair exchange on most issues between the individual practitioner and the professions as a profession, especially in medicine, which plays such a conspicuous role in society (Eron, 1958; Bradshaw, 1978; Twaddle and Hessler, 1978). The function of the professional organization is to promote the well-being, security and purposes of the profession. Sometimes these objectives supersede those of service to the general public; sometimes there is conflict between the two commitments. And sometimes the profession goes tooling along without regard to the consequences to the individual members, their welfare, as well as being unmindful of the impact the profession is having on the public through its influence on the individual practitioner. The point of view expressed in the remainder of this chapter is that the medical profession errs in putting tensions on physicians to the detriment not only of the physician but, indirectly, to the detriment of the public at large which is to be served by the physician directly and the professional organization indirectly (Scharr, 1970).

Some physicians say that staying in the profession of medicine is harder than getting there (Barclay, 1978). We have seen that getting into medicine is an arduous task, and one that appears to ill equip the fledging physician for assuming an emotionally and professionally mature role that evidences undistracted interest in the services to society he/she can perform. Rather, the emphasis in medicine has shifted to the profession itself (Traska, 1978; Powles, 1973; Wecht, 1975; Hall,

75

1976; Thompson, 1977), and this emphasis has been inimical to the public image of medicine and the public's acceptance of medicine (Illich, 1976; Bradshaw, 1978; King, 1962).

What impact does the profession qua profession have on the young practitioner? One of several likely answers is continued on into the practice of medicine (King, 1962, pp. 196-197). The idealism characterizing the first-year medical student gives way to cynicism by graduation. As one author says, "When he leaves (graduates) he is more interested in bodies than people, as aloof and often indifferent to suffering, and concerned with making money rather than serving mankind" (King, 1962, p. 196). Eron (1958, 1959) studied what he called "cynicism" among students of law, medicine and nursing, and found that as law students progressed through school their cynicism decreased, whereas cynicism increased between the freshman and senior school years for medical students. Cynicism was defined by Eron as "a contemptuous disbelief in man's sincerity of motives or rectitude of conduct, charterized by the conviction that human conduct is suggested or directed by self-interest or self-indulgence." While these attitudes certainly do not characterize all physicians, their presence in even a small number of physicians tends to set up stereotypes and to provoke a reactive cnynicism toward the practicing physician (Gurin, 1960). Overcrowded waiting rooms, delayed schedules, "quick-and-dirty" or cursory concern for the patient are practices that contribute to criticism toward practicing physicians and a turning of the cyncism toward them.

Medicine emphasizes death and disease; it is pathology oriented. A modern trend called "social medicine" (not to be confused with socialized medicine) stresses health and more fulfilling living (King, 1962; Twaddle and Hessler, 1977). Medical practice which emphasizes illness tends to make the patient dependent upon the physician, to recommend and carry out more operations than are needed, to rely excessively on drugs, and to keep the patient coming again and again for check-ups and examinations. This kind of practice continues what the student learns in medical school and tends to narrow the vision of the physician while at the same time increasing medical practice and augmenting the pressures on him/her for ever-increasing services which may not be needed.

Medicine as a profession is an "in-group." That

is, the physicians tend to come from families with high percentages of physicians and, perforce, from higher socio-economic groups (Twaddle and Hessler, 1977). This in-breeding is not only a phenomenon found in the U.S.A., it is equally true in the Soviet Union, Poland, East and West Germany, Bularia, Frances, The Netherlands, and the United Kingdom (Twaddle and Hessler, 1977, p. 170). With so much in-breeding as to who becomes a physician, it follows that the attitudes and practices relating to medicine are "inherited" (socially speaking) from the young physician's family mentors and that many attitudes toward medicine are "givens" in the lives of young physicians. They are already "organizational men (or women)" before they practice medicine. Supporting this notion of the culture of medicine from an organizational standpoint is the fact that in the U.S.A. and many western nations, most physicians are men. Women comprise only about eight percent of the total number of physicians as recently as 1972 (Martin, 1973) in the U.S.A. Some have suggested this male-dominated status of medicine in the West springs from identifying medicine with science (hence it is "masculine") whereas in the Soviet Union and in the East, it is more identified with nurturance and considered to be "feminine" (over 75 percent of physicians were female in Poland and over 80 percent were female in Russia, in 1970 (Twaddle and Hessler, 1977, p. 170). Young physicians, male or female, then are not just numbers added to the local medical society list of practitioners; rather, they enter a cult, and a culture that exerts pervasive influence, and they submit to a set of structured pressures, rules, standards, and expectations that govern a large part of their behavior.

The latter point is further corroborated by statistics on attrition in medical school. Only about 40 percent of freshmen premedical students return to the program in their sophomore year. There is of course great preparation for acceptable academic work and a strong effort to avoid being weeded out. Following this trend, Twaddle and Hessler (1977, p. 171) observe, "By the junior and senior years, premedical students have not become much more sophisticated about the nature of medicine but they have become significantly more committed to a _medical_ _career_ (italics added). This medical career emphasis stresses certain preparatory academic areas: biology is first in importance, chemistry is next, and the humanities are last. This particular structuring of important information and value systems (these knowledge areas are _both_ informational and value-ridden) slants the thinking of future medical practitioners away from the patient as a human being and put the emphasis on technology and instrumentation. It is little wonder then that persons who later become the patients of these physicians often complain about perfunctory treatment that excludes the person as a person from prime consideration. It is also no wonder that medicine seen only as a technology and supportive of economic and big practice motives gives rise to the stress that accumulates into the tensions and anxieties that are so replete among medical men and women.

We have noted that medicine as a profession arises from many in-group influences, i.e., young men (less so, women) get into medicine through family and other informal influences. Once in the profession, relationships among physicians are also regulated by many kinds of informal pressures and influences. Among the informal influences as to who gets patients referred to him (or her) are friendship patterns, where one went to school and/or interned, and who one knows among older physicians. Hospital appointments come by the same informal process, often accounting, over time, as to who gets into a lucrative practice and who hobbles along less ably. If one is part of the inner fraternity, the small group of physicians who control appointments, elections and other prestige matters, then one is well set (Hall, 1946; 1947; 1949; 1951; 1954; 1976; Twaddle and Hessler, 1977). The acceptance of the young physician informally into the inner circle means that the former has to be affable, be competent, know the right people, give some time and service to charity patients, and to extend uncompensated services to the medical community itself. There is pressure, also, to be "correct" ethnically and religiously (preferable white and protestant) and to have a "good personality."

Persons not accepted into the inner circle of influence have to fly it by themselves; they're called the "individualistic career pattern" types and are often intensely competitive, strive for a high income, and less often specialize. They tend to receive referrals from physicians not in the inner circle of influence and from lay persons. Although it is not clearly known, this group of more individualistic physicians may be the ones most subject to the stress of medical practice because they are outside the mainstream of colleague associations and referrals and therefore are subject to more pressures in order to function optimally (Twaddle and Hessler, 1977, pp. 178-179).

78

Wherever there is an informal structure, there is also a formal structure. As expected the informal and formal structures inherent in the medical profession overlap. The formal structure -- the American Medical Association -- tends to be the political arm of the whole organization and also tends to be more conservative and usually more influential than the informal organization. The AMA's role has been vigorous since its inception in the middle of the nineteenth century (to protect the interests of "allopathic" physicians faced with threats from allegedly "irregular" practitioners). In time, the AMA became the more official platform of policy making and enforcement for all of medicine; it sponsored the original and influential Flexner Report, initiated and politically sponsored licensing laws and medical training standards (Twaddle and Hessler, 1977, p. 179; Harris, 1966).

The formal organization of the AMA, in turn, has yielded much power over medicine, although its (now waning) influence continues to be more pronounced in the case of general practitioners, surgeons and family physicians, and less pronounced among the more specialized. Within the broad practice of medicine, then, there is the more conservative wing represented by the AMA and the more liberal wing composed of specialty groups such as the American Academy of Pediatrics (Twaddle and Hessler, 1977, pp. 179-180; Miller, 1977; pp. 233-234). The AMA is hardly a democratic organization and its operation depends partly upon physicians with political interests, with smaller practice (hence time for political activities) and upon older, semi-retired men who no longer need to depend upon a lucrative practice. The private opinions of physicians, especially the more liberal ones, are disagreed with by the AMA which has long opposed national health service and any model of delivery of health service that isn't an individual private practice model. Younger and more liberal physicians experience pressure from the formal organization to submit to the official line, the "inner fraternity" if they are to get along well with referrals, hospital appointments, and be accepted in the informal circles that overlap the formal structure.

Medicine, then, has grown into a complex structure over the last 100 years owing to a variety of causes. Chief among the causes of a move toward greater complexity -- hence greater tension on the individuals practicing medicine are: The rapid and still accelerating increase in medical technology and knowledge, carrying with it a movement toward specialization (in 1930, about 20% of the active practitioners considered themselves specialists, whereas in 1970, 82% so considered themselves) (Miller, 1977, p. 234); the rising importance of the hospital as the center of medical care due to the cost of equipment and technology and to the size and variety of the staff, all combining to take over the role of "the physician" in the private sense; and the spread of available medical practitioners to the suburban areas of large cities to an extent greater than population growth in the suburbs over the past two decades, thus promoting competition among medical practitioners, and changing the overall distribution of physicians for private care away from the inner city or other areas where the poor may be served. Newly graduate physicians submit to these changes, willingly or not, and are thereby ushered into a predetermined mode of practice that may add tension to their lives and contribute to some of the anxieties and health problems noted above. These changes in the character of medical practice and in the distribution of physicians available widely for health care delivery tend to accumulate problems for the patients and contribute to the growing negative attitudes toward doctors and medical practice (Illich, 1976; Knowles, 1977; Dodge and Martin, 1970; King, 1962). The stratification of the practice of medicine and the delivery of health services to the population has contributed a multitude of problems for medicine as an institution, for the profession as an organization, locally and nationally, and for the populace. These conditions could not help adding to the stress and tension experienced by the individual physician (Miller, 1977; Twaddle and Hessler, 1977; Dodge and Martin, 1970; Knowles, 1977; Ginzberg, 1977; Wildawsky, 1977; Bennett, 1977; Saward, 1977).

If the organization and structure of medical practice are such that they create or contribute to the many health problems noted above, then there must be some characteristics of medical practice that also help account for the multitude of health problems. The health practice of the individual practitioner are midway between the background of schooling and indoctrination, the structure of medicine as an organization, on the one hand, and the day-to-day practice of medicine on the other. One set of conditions influences the other. As a result of the enormity of stresses laid or the individual practitioner, we have the tensions and anxieties they evidence, and the consequent impact on the profession as a profession (Illich, 1976; Bradshaw, 1977; Freidson, 1970). In the words of Dr. Bradshaw, doctors are now on trial (Bradshaw, 1977). How is this so?

The most trenchant criticisms of current medical practice are noted in the books by Bradshaw (1977) and by Illich (1976). Illich contends that the medical profession has become its own worst enemy, a threat to its own purported concern for health. He has emphasized the word _Iatrogenesis_ to describe this condition; a word meaning physician-caused or physician-initiated illnesses (_iatros_ Greek for physician, and genesis, of course, means origin, hence physician-caused illness). There are several ways in which, according to Illich, Iatrogenesis is manifest.

Medicine is power-centered, political-minded and self-aggrandizing. Medicine cannot cure its own ills, Illich avers; it can only assert its political acumen to maintain what it has already abrogated and only and aroused public can cure the ills of medicine. He feels that our health problems are worsened by excessive dependence on mechanized and technological sciences and because we correspondingly overlook the normal healing powers of the body. "Health levels can only decline when survival comes to depend beyond a certain point on the heteronomous (other-directed) regulation of the organism's homeostasis. Beyond a critical level of intensity, institutional health care -- no matter if it takes the form of cure, prevention, or environmental engineering -- is equivalent to systematic health denial" (Illich, 1977, p. 7).

Medicine is caught up in the same technological morass as other facets of our modern life. Medical technology threatens health in a manner comparable to the way the volume and intensity of traffic hinders mobility, the way formal education and the media hamstring learning, and the way urbanization deprecates homemaking and family life. All of these purported ways to aid our health, help our learning and living, are counterproductive, and the practice of medicine is a glaring example of this counterproductivity.

Other than allowing for the progress in handling specific infectious diseases (polio, diphthereia, tuberculosis), Illich doubts that current medical practice has muted many illness; in fact, as we have seem earlier, illnesses today are stress-induced illness, not specific infectious illnesses, and medicine, if anything has added to the plethora of stress-induced illness and has by its very nature and practice few effective ways of coping with these stress-related illnesses. Illich says, "...an expanding proportion of the new (italics original) burden of disease of the last fifteen years is itself the result of medical intervention in favor of people who are or might become sick. It is doctor-made or "iatrogenic" (Illich, 1976, p. 14).

Doctors are not as effective in curing illness as they claim, Illich says. Even before Koch produced the cure for TB, the death rate in New York from TB had already declined from 700 to 10,000 population to 370 per 10,000 between 1812 and 1882 (the year of Koch's discovery). "Cholera, dysentery and typhoid... peaked and dwindled outside the physician's control. By the time their etiology was understood and their therapy had become specific, these diseases had lost much of their virulence..." (Illich, 1976, p. 16). Supportive of this is the report by the World Health Organization (van Zijl, 1966) that diarrheal type diseases are controlled by better water supply and sanitation, not by curative medical intervention. Diseases peak and decline, Illich says, not so much due to medical discovery, therapy application and social control (social changes may decrease or exacerbate the occurence of many illnesses wholly apart from medical applications). Replacing the older diseases, modernity has produced an increase in coronary heart disease, emphysema (in relation to smoking, certainly a "social" disease), hypertension (modern living induced and exacerbated), cancer (particularly lung cancer, related to smoking and to the exhaust fumes produced by modern technology), arthritis, diabetes, emotional problems and so-called "mental" disorders.

Consonant with Illich's thesis ofiatrogenesis (physician caused illnesses) are injuries and illnesses incurred in the hospital setting as well as under the doctor's aegis. Illich says, "The pain, dysfunction, disability, and anguish resulting from technical medical intervention now rival the morbidity due to traffic and industrial accidents and even war-related activitie and made the impact of medicine one of the most rapidly spreading epidemics of our time" (Illich, 1976, p. 26). (In this connection, see also: Moser, 1969; Spain, 1963 Bradshaw, 1978; Wildawsky, 1977; and MacKay and Mylander, 1978). It has been reported that on a daily basis from 50 to 80 percent of adults in the U.S.A. and in th United Kingdom take medicines of one type of another; many of these may be unnecessary, are often combined with other drugs in ways that may be harmful to patient or may have harmful after effects. In addition, surgery is often done unnecessarily, being borne out by the fact that the rates for surgery for men and women in Canada in 1968 were nearly twice the rates found in England during the same period (Vayda, 1973; Lewis, 1969). Many of these problems arise from what Illich calls a de-personalization of diagnosis and therapy in the physician's office and in the hospital.

One consequence of these forms of clinical iatro-genesis is the rapid increase of malpractice suits (Illich, 1976, p. 31; Fox, 1977, p. 13). When suits are settled in favor of the patient-plaintiff, s/he gets little of the malpractice insurance (perhaps as little as 20 percent, with the rest going to lawyers, physicians as medical experts, and court costs) (Illich, 1976, p. 31). Some of these suits are based on injuries received in the hospital setting. For example, accidents are reported more frequently in hospitals than in any other industries but mines and high-rise construction. During hospitalization, one in fifty children require specific treatment due to injury (Lowrey, 1963; McLamb and Huntley, 1967; Illich, 1976, p. 32). Over 20,000 malpractice suits are brought yearly against physicians, with awards multiplying many times over in the past decade (Fox, 1977, p. 13).

Arising out of carelessness or indifference in hospital settings is what some call "Iatrogenic Mal-nutrition" (Butterworth, 1974; Illich, 1976, p. 31) wherein the providing of balanced and nutritious diets for in-patients is treated carelessly (Mayer, 1971).

Illich takes his thesis of Iatrogenesis a step further in his criticism of medicine and medical practice. He speaks of "social iatrogenesis" as "...a category of etiology that encompasses many forms. It obtains when medical bureaucracy creates ill-health by increasing stress, by multiplying disabling dependence, by generating new painful needs, by lowering the levels of tolerance for discomfort or pain, by reducing the leeway that people are wont to concede to an individual when he suffers, and by abolishing even the right to self-care. Social iatrogenesis is at work when health care is turned into a standardized item, a staple; when all suffering is 'hospitalized' and homes become inhospitable to birth, sickness, and death; when the language in which people could experience their bodies is turned into bureaucratic gobbledygook; or when suffering, mourning, and healing outside the patient role are labeled a form of deviance."

(Illich, 1976, p. 31).

Although some would claim (Knowles, 1977) that
Illich's case for social iatrogenesis is overdrawn,
it would still be admitted that our preparation for
healthful living is lacking in vigor and specificity.
Knowles (1977, p. 60) calls for better health care
based on better education in schools, including colleges, getting away from superficials such as ad-
monishments to brush one's teeth daily and other health
bromides. Society, instead, instructs, allows, or
even encourages youngsters by age sixteen to know how
to drink beer (sometimes excessively), to drive cars
riskily, to eat junk food, to smoke, and to gain social
status by and through these participations. These
social pressures take the place of instruction about
exercise, information about sex, eating regular and
balanced meals, holding down weight, sleeping sufficiently, and using alcohol moderately or not at all.
Matching these poorly directed forms of health instruction by society are TV and other media glorification
of medicine as being able to cure any illness (usually
instantly;) -- the "Marcus Welby" syndrome -- and
encouraging people to temporize with their lives,
their health and their habits.

Underlying the social iatrogenesis is the observation that what Illich calls "the medicalization of
society" stems from industrial, urbanization, and
mechanization changes rampant in Western society. As
society through its industrialization produces more
stress, tensions produce illnesses and more medical
attention is presumably required. Of course, the resulting medical problems are pseudo problems in the
medical sense; they are problems arising from stress-
full living. Calling these problems by medical names
("diagnosis") and prescribing more and more medicine,
more and more drugs, requiring more and more hospitals
and physicians are simply wrong approaches to the
social iatrogenesis so rampant.

Literature from clinical psychology, sociology
and anthropology support Illich's thesis, although
from a different vantage point. In discussion the
importance of social skills as an alternative to psychopathology, and social skills training as an alternative to traditional psychotherapy, Phillips (1978)
pointed out that when the more primitive or as-yet
developing societies begin to change toward industrialization, they take on the neuroses of Western societies (Phillips, 1978, p. 27). These developing

societies, industrially speaking, formerly had none of the western neuroses; the advent of stress and strain associated with modernization caused social and other problems in living "...and gave rise to symptoms and syndromes which, in our society, we would 'diagnose' as neurotic..." (Phillips, 1978, p. 27). Originally, the diagnosable symptoms were not indigenous to persons in the developing society, or to the society itself, but resulted from conflicts and pressures of industrialization (Carothers, 1953; Page, 1975; Tooth, 1950; Wallace, 1966).

Reliance on drugs and pharmaceuticals exacerbate the social iatrogenesis about which Illich speaks. Nearly everyone would agree, whether or not they are critical of medical practice and the health of medicine, that our populace relies too much on drugs. Since physicians prescribe drugs and look to chemical means as the chief, or as a highly important way, to regain and maintain health, physicians bear a serious responsibility to critically survey the use of drugs. We have already noted earlier in this chapter how much physicians themselves become addicted to drugs; the psychology of drug usage, then, permeates not only the medical profession but society as a whole.

Illich contends that physicians not only rely too heavily on recommending and prescribing drugs to their patients, physicians are often subservient to the pharmaceutical companies (McCleery, 1971; Mintz, 1967; Burack, 1970; Goddard, 1969).

Illich says that the Hoffman-LaRoche drug company spent two-hundred million dollars over a ten year period to promote valium; they commissioned two hundred physicians yearly to publish (scientific) articles about the properties of valium (Illich, 1976, pp. 71-72; Holdan, 1979; Greenberg, 1971). Such behavior on the part of physicians and pharmaceutical companies constitute ethical problems, treatment problems, and a thorough misuse of confidence in the physician's efforts to help patients via drugs. Such conduct is another strike against the image of physicians and adds to the impression cited above that interest in economic gain is a prime motive behind these actions. The pharmaceutical companies use the physicians in ulterior ways and the same behavior then characterizes the physician's behavior toward his patients.

Perhaps many aspects of social iatrogenesis or other forms of physician-induced illness would be toleraable if the outcome were a generally improved health status and improved longevity of the population. However, this seems not to be the case: Iatrogenesis, in whatever form, according to Illich and to other authors as well (Knowles, 1977; Bradshaw, 1978; Szasz, 1961, 1972). has contributed little if anything, to longevity (Forbes, 1967). Longevity has remained essentially constant over a two-decade period, 1945-1965 for industrialized countries, with the U.S. rate dropping for both men and women. The Forbes study concluded that the money spent on health care was, in 30 countries studied, unrelated to longevity of the population.

So-called mental illness, pain, anguish, suffering, and other forms of ill-health are byproducts of a society that does not teach its members how to live or care for themselves. The more the society builds up stress, the more its members succumb. Succumbing to stress in the form of anxiety and tension abound among members of the medical profession itself, but also generally in society. Paraphrasing Illich who says that"...an increasing portion of all pain is man-made, a side effect of strategies for industrial expansion" (Illich, 1976, p. 135), we can say that tensions and anxieties which may take a multitude of forms among the medical profession as well as the laity, accumulate into the need for drugs and nostrums, for more medical services, for more hospitals and physicians, for diagnosis of illnesses that do not exist in the physical/medical sense, and for a vast organization called "medicine," the health of which is open to question from the inception of the desire to be a physician all the way through medical school, into practice; it is woven into the society which structures the medical establishment in a way that allows it to grow more costly, less effective, and more self-centered with each passing year.

Bradshaw (1978) attacks the problems of medicine and medical practice in as trenchant a manner as Illich Bradshaw, however, is a physician and speaks from the "inside" of medicine. His book, "Doctors On Trial" is written in the style of a court hearing on medical practice. Bradshaw deals with a number of specific medical problems in various chapters -- obesity, coronary heart disease, drugs, and stress (although some of these are more due to cultural factors and the way medicine is practiced and not due to medical practice or knowledge, per se) -- and also discusses in one chapter "The Medical Institution." In a mock dialogue, "Hunter," one of the participants in the discussion on the medical institution, says to a member of the medical establishment:

I put it to you that the medical institution is a tightly-knit body, run mainly by and for doctors, and that in many ways it is not merely unrelated to health, but is now often antagonistic to health in the widest sense; that it is rigid, narrow in its outlook, hierarchical, self-satisfied, self-regulating, self-perpetuating, paternalistic and monopolistic (Bradshaw, 1978, p. 209).

In another passage, "Hunter," the inquirer comments:

Do you know how many specialities there are in the United States?--There are 65[1], and it could well be 85 (or even 105) in another decade. Not self-perpetuating? And 90 percent of American medical graduates try to specialize.[2] Are you aware that it has been said again and again by doctors that this corresponds, not with the needs of the American people, but with the desires of the American doctors? Are you not aware that there are, for example, far too many American heart specialists, both physicians and surgeons, but a gross shortage of family doctors -- men who will look at the whole person, be friends and counselors as well as technicians? (Bradshaw, 1976, p. 210).

And the most trenchant of all comments in Bradshaw's book; with "Hunter" again speaking:

"...it (the Medical Institution) has been accused of being over-friendly with the Pharmaceutical Manufacturers' Association, has it not? And now the

[1]Chase, R. A. Letter to the Editor. New England J. of Med., 1976, 295, 292.

[2]Levit, R. J., Sabshin, M., and Mueller, G. B. Trends in graduate medical education and specialty certification. New England J.of Med., 1974, 290, 545-549.

last and fourth element in the
medical institution... is the hugh
miscellany of societies, associations, unions, clubs, journals,
nursing homes, private hospitals,
and clinics, insurance organizations,
councils -- advisory, research,
consultative -- boards, panels,
committees... You do not think
that the medical institution--
which began, reasonably enough,
as a loose organization devoted
to doing what it could to help
people through sickness and even
death (if that was inescapable)--
that it got bigger and bigger,
just as industrial society and
other institutions, within it,
have, and more and more interested
in itself and the scientific approach, and less and less interested in what happened to the people to whom it ministered until
what it deprived people of, directly or indirectly, began to outweigh
any benefits it brought to them?...
And that now it has completely out-
grown its usefulness? (Bradshaw,
1978, p. 215).

In reply to the quoted passage, "Sir Guy," the medi
cal institution representative, retorts simply that
the medical profession has its defects, but also its
virtues, the latter being the greater, thus, or course,
differing with "Hunter".

A miscellany of other accusations against the
medical institution follows in Bradshaw's book, summarized briefly in the following items: Great Britain
has approximately two to three times as many family
doctors or general practitioners as does the U.S.A.;
physicians refer Medecaid patients to many doctors so
all may claim giving attention to the patients (and
bill accordingly); physicians' claims for attention
given many Medicaid patients in a hospital when only
cursory notice was given each patient; that the number
of doctors in the U.S.A. over the past few decades has
been increasing up to three times the base growth in
population; that there were as many attendances as out-
patient and accident and emergency departments in
England, in 1973, as the total population of England

(over 46 million in each case); and the medical profession is accused of being "A church, a religion, a
way of life and a way of death" (Bradshaw,1978, p. 216-
223).

An even more radical stand regarding medicine has
been taken by Carlson (1975), a lawyer-turned-social-
science-critic, in his book, The End of Medicine.
Mustering evidence for his renouncement of current
medical and health professions, and their alleged
failure to improve the health of the nation, Carlson
points up a number of contributions to this lamentable
state of affairs. He argues that current medical technology and practice have little or no relevance for
the health status of the public. Even the benefits
that might accrue to the public with current medical
practices will wash out in 20-25 years, he claims,
while social costs and damages propogated by the medical establishment will oppressively increase; medicine
will thereby dig its own grave. All this change will
be hastened if not initially caused by medicine's preoccupation with professionalism and its own narrow and
specialized technologies, neglecting the larger social
and health realities extant. Specifically, Carlson
(1975, p. 6-29) sees medicine as providing services
generated through their own interests and competencies,
unrelated to the actual outcomes of care to the patient.
He further charges medicine with a paucity of research
on the impact of medical care on the health of populations; medicine is too individual centered, thereby
avoiding responsibilities for large health and social
issues. Other factors that bear on health are neglected by medicine: noise and pollution of the environment;
the influence of education, housing, air, water, even
seat belts and Muzak on health (and related problems
of safety). Preoccupation with the individual after
she/he is ill is medicine's traditional role; prevention, another neglect of medicine's, is overlooked or
given short shrift. Much medical care is given that
is not needed, or at least its needs are not amply
demonstrated, Carlson asserts: e.g., statistics regarding elective operations for tonsils, hemorrhoids
and varicose veins, as well as hernia repair, vary
widely over several regions in a given state in the
U.S. Variations in the average rate of surgery in
various locales ranged from a low of 75 operations per
10,000 population to 240 operations per 10,000 persons.
Some regions of the state studied varied as much as
two to three times in rate compared to other regions.
These rates do not,then, reflect medical problems and
solutions but predispositions by available surgeons

to do surgery. He adds in this same connection: "In
the United States, there are twice as many surgeons
in proportion to population as in England and Wales"
(Carlson, 1975, p. 9; Lewis, 1969; Vayda, 1973).

Medicine ought to examine more closely the role
of placebos where, for example in the treatment of
warts, chemically inert dye may be used to gain the
disappearance of warts as reliably as surgery. Frank
(1961) early examined the role of placebos in medicine,
in his book, Persuasion And Healing, and concluded that
placebos gain their potency by being symbolic of the
physician's healing powers. It is as ifmmedication
and healing were one, similar to the power of the sha-
man in primitive society operating as healer and user
of symbols. Of course, advertising also uses symbols
and may on occasion be placeobic in inducing people
to "feel better" after having followed the "prescription" advertised. Pointedly, the value of placebos
is important in the practice of medicine and bears a
significant relationship to all medical technology,
one that needs a lot of further examination and one
that may become more useful in public health measures
in the future. And, of course, medicants and pharmaceuticals may have the opposite effect to that intended, depending on the nature of the instructions
accompanying the use of medicants. Healing occurs,
then, without technology and sometimes in spite of it;
the relationship between the physician or other medical specialist (nurse, for example) may go a longer
way in promoting cure or amelioration. In summary,
Carlson says: "In combination, then, theempirical evidence and the theory seem convincing; medical care has
a limited impact on health and is most effective when
applied to certain identifiable conditions where there
is evidence about its effectiveness. But when contrasted with all the other factors that demonstrably
affect health, medicine plays a minor role, despite
being cast for lead (Carlson, 1975, p. 29).

Medicine, then, is conspicuous among the professions in demonstrating its greatest strenghts--power,
prestige, and money-- to be its greatest weaknesses.
While other professions, as we shall see, are infected
with the same maladies -- even serious illnesses --
medicine is more obviously a failure because its role
in society is so clear and so commanding. Medicine
may be leading other professions into social chaos
because it is -- and has been - a model profession.
It is now modeling not appropriate, salient and positive aims, but selfish, neglectful and negative

90

purposes. If medicine does end -- as Carlson predicts--
it will end because society has moved beyond the need
for medicine. If medicine ends, it may well take other
professions with it; the conspiracy against the people
will also have ended.

CHAPTER III

Adsett, C.A. Psychological health of medical students in relation to the medical education process, J. Med. Educ., 1968, 43, 728-734.

Barclay, W.R. Staying is harder than getting there, JAMA, 1978, 239, 53.

Barrett-Connor, E. The epidemiology of tuberculosis in physicians, JAMA, 1979, 241, 33-38.

Bartlett, J. Bartlett's Familiar Quotations, 13th Ed. Boston: Little, Brown & Co., 1955

Becker, H.S., Geer, B., Hughes, E.C., & Strauss, A.L. Boys in White. Chicago: U. of Chicago Press, 1961.

Bennett,I.L. . Technology as a shaping force, in Knowles, J.S. (Ed.) Doing Better and Feeling Worse: Health in the United States. N.Y.: Norton, 1977.

Blachly, P.H., Disher, W., and Rodnner, G. Suicide by physicians, Bull. of Suicidology, 1968, 1, 1-18.

Borsay, et al. Physician drug addiction - a challenge to medical education, Ohio State Medical Journal, 1977, 73, 740-742.

Boyle, B.P., and Coombs, R.H. Personality profile related to emotional stress inthe initial year of medical training, J. Med. Educ., 1971, 46, 882-888.
Brody, J.I. Letter: Hodgkins disease in physicians, Lancet, 1975, 1, 790.

Bradshaw, J.S. Doctors on Trial. New York: Paddington Press, 1978.

Burack, R. The New Handbook of Prescription Drugs. New York: Pantheon, 1970.

Butterworth, C. Iatrogenic Malnutrition, Nutrition Today, March-April, 1974.

Carlson, R.J. The End of Medicine. N.Y.: Wiley,1975.

Carothers, J.C. The African mind in health and disease. Monograph No. 17. Geneva: World Health Organization, 1953.

Carstens, J. et al. Hepatitis B virus infections in anesthetists, Br. J. Anaest., 1977, 49, 887-889.

Chester, R. Health and marital breakdown: Some implications for doctors, J. Psychosom. Res., 1973, 17, 311-321.

Coburn, D. and Jovaisas. Perceived sources of stress among first-year medical students, J. Med. Educ., 1975, 50, 789-795.

Cook, R. Cirrhosis in Doctors, Lancet, 1979, Jan. 20, p. 156.

Craig, A.G. and Pitts,F.N. Suicide by Physicians, Dis. Nerv. System, 1968, 29, 763-772.

Cray, C. et al. Stress and rewards within the psychiatrist's family, Amer. J. Psychoanal., 1977, 37, 337-41.

Crosbie, S. The doctor as patient, Rocky Mtn. Med. J., 1972, 69, 49-52.

Denes, A.E. et al. Hepatitis B. Infection in Physicians, JAMA, 1978, 239, 210-212.

DeRosis, H. Suicide among psychiatrists, Amer. J. Psychoanal., 1974, 34, 97-98.

Dodge, D.L. & Martin, W.T. Social Stress and Chronic Illness: Mortality Patterns in Industrial Society. Notre Dame, Ind.: U. of Notre Dame Press, 1970.

Duffy, J. C. & Litin, E.M. Psychiatric morbidity of physicians, JAMA, 1964, 189, 989-92.

Duffy, J.C. & Litin, E.M. The Emotional Health of Physicians. Springfield, Ill.: C.L. Thomas, 1967.

Editorial: Hepatitis B - an occupational risk, Med. J. Australia, 1975, 2, 853-854.

Ehrenkranz, N.J. & Kicklighter, J.L. Tuberculosis outbreak in a general hospital: Evidence for

airborne spread of infection, Ann. Inter. Med.,
1972, 77, 377-382.

Eron, I.D. Effects of medical education on medical
students, J. Med. Educ., 1955, 10, 559-566.

Eron, I.D. The effects of medical education on
attitudes: A follow-up study, J.Med. Educ.,
1959, 33, 25-33.

Finseth, F. Suicide among women physicians, JAMA, 1977,
237, 19.

Forbes, L.M. Mental stress and the changing role of
women, J. Amer. Med. Women's Assn., 1977, 32,
376-379.

Forbes, W.H. Longevity and medical costs, New England
J. of Medicine, 1967, 277, 71-78.

Fox, R. The medicalization and demedicalization of
American society, in Knowles, J.H. (Ed.) Doing
Better and Feeling Worse: Health in the United
States. New York: Norton, 1977.

Frank, J. Persuasian and Healing. N.Y.: Scholsen
Books, 1961.

Friedson, E. The Sociology of Medicine: a Trend
Report, Current Sociology, 1961a, 10, 123-192.

Friedson, E. Patients' Views of Medical Practice.
N.Y.: Russell Sage Fdn., 1961b.

Ginzberg, E Health Services, power centers and deci-
sion-making mechanisms, in Knowles, J.H. (Ed.)
Doing Better and Feeling Worse: Health in the
United States. New York: Norton, 1977.

Goddard, J.L. The drug establishment, Esquire, March,
1969.

Goldberg, M. Conjoint therapy of male physicians and
their wives, Psychiatric Opinion, 1975, 12, 19-23.

Gottheil, E., Thornton, C.C., Corely, S.S., Jr. &
Cornelius, F.S., Jr. Stress satisfaction and
performance: Transition from university to
medical college, J.Med. Educ., 1969, 44, 270-277.

Greenberg, S. The Quality of Mercy: A Report on the
     Critical Condition of Hospital and Medical Care in
     America. New York: Atheneum, 1971.

Greenson, R.R. That impossible profession, J. Am.
     Psychoanal. Assn., 1966, 14, 9-27.

Grotjahn, M. On being a sick physician, in New Dimen-
     sions in Psychosomatic Medicine, Wahl, C. (Ed.)
     Boston: Little, Brown & Co., 1964.

Gurin, G., Veroff, J. and Feld, S. Americans View
     Their Mental Health. N. Y.: Basic Books, 1960.

Hall, O. The informal organization of the medical
     profession, Can. J. of Economics - Pol. Sci.,
     1946, 12, 30-46.

Hall, O. On the stages of a medical career, Amer. J.
     of Sociol., 1947, 53, 327-337.

Hall, O. Types of medical careers, Amer. J. of Sociol.,
     1949, 55, 243-253.

Hall, O. Sociological research in the field of medicine,
     Amer. Sociol. Rev., 1951, 16, 639-649.

Hall, O. Some problems in the provisions of medical
     services, Can. J. of Economics - Pol. Sci., 1954,
     20, 456-466.

Hall, O. A sociological view of medicine as a profes-
     sion. J.R. Call, General Practitioners, 1976,
     26, 102-106.

Harris, R. A Sacred Trust. New York: The New American
     Library, Inc., 1966.

Holden, C. Pain, dying, and the health care system.
     Science, 1979, 203, 984-986.

Holt, R. & Luborsky, L., Personality Patterns of
     Psychiatrists. N.Y.: Basic Books, 1958.

Hughes, E.C., Hughes, H. & Deutcher, I. Twenty-Thousand
     Nurses Tell Their Story. Philadelphia: J.B.
     Lippincott, 1958.

Hunter, R.C.A., Prince, R.H. & Schwartzman, A.E.
     Comments on emotional disturbances in a medical
     undergraduate population, Can. Med.Assn. J.,

1961, _83_, 989-992.

Illich, I.D. _Medical Nemesis_. London: Calder & Boyers, 1974.

Jones, R.E. A study of 100 physician psychiatric in-patients, _Amer. J. Psychia._, 1977, _134_, 1119-1123.

King, S. H. _Perceptions of Illness and Medical Practice_. N.Y.: Russell Sage Fdn., 1962.

Knowles, J.H. _Doing Better and Feeling Worse: Health in the United States_. N.Y.: Norton, 1977.

Korcok, M. Addiction among physicians--the problems may not be what you think, _Can. Med. Assn. J._, 1977, _117_, 89-90.

Krantz, D.L. _Radical Career Change_. N.Y.: The Free Press, 1978.

Lewis, C.E. Variations in the incidence of surgery, _New England J. of Med._, 1969, _281_, 880-884.

Lipsitt, D.R. The doctor as patient, _Psychia. Opinion_, 1975, _12_, 20-25.

Lowrey, G.H. The problem of hospital accidents to children, _Pediatrics_, 1963, _32_, 1064-1068.

Mackay, W. & Mylander, M. _Salesman Surgeon: The Incredible Story of an Amateur in the Operating Room_. N.Y.: McGraw-Hill, 1978.

Martin, B. Physician Manpower, 1972, in Vahovich,S., _73 Profile of Medical Practice_. Chicago: American Med. Assn., 1973.

Mayer, J. Iatrogenic Malnutrition. _New England J. of Medicine_, 1971, _284_, 1218.

Merton, R.K., Bloom, S. & Rogoff, N. Studies in socio-logy of medical education, _J. of Med. Educ._, 1956, _31_, 554.

Miller, A.E. The changing role of the medical profes-sional in urban and suburban settings, _Social Sci. & Medicine_, 1977, _11_, 233-243.

Mintz, M. Prescription Only - A report on the roles of the United States Food and Drug Administration, the American Medical Association, Pharmaceutical Manufacturers and others in connection with the irrational and massive use of prescription drugs that may be worthless, injurious, or even lethal. 2nd Ed. Boston: Beacon Press, 1967.

Modlin, H.C. & Montes, A. Narcotic addiction in physicians, Amer. J. Psychia., 1964, 121, 358-365.

Moser, R.H. The Disease of Medical Progress: A Study of Iatrogenic Disease, 3rd Ed., Springfield, Ill.: Thorias, 1969.

Murray, R.M. Psychiatric illness in male doctors and controls: An analysis of Scottish hospital in-patients, Brit. J. Psychia., 1977, 131, 1-10.

McCleery, R.S. One Life-One Physician - An Inquiry into the Medical Profession's Performance in Self-Regulation. Washington, DC. : Center for the Study of Responsive Law, 1971.

McGuire, F.L. Psycho-social studies of medical students: A critical review, J. Med. Educ., 1966, 41, 424-445.

McLamb, J.T. & Huntley, R.R. The hazards of hospitalization, Southern Med. Journal, 1967, 60, 469-472.

Notman, M.T. Suicide in female physicians, Psychiatric Opinion, 1975, 12, 29-30.

Olesen, V.L. & Whittaker, E.W The Silent Dialogue: A Study in the Social Psychology of Professional Organizations. San Francisco: Jossey-Bass, 1968.

Ottenberg, P. The "physician's disease": Success and work addiction, Psychia. Opinion, 1975, 12, 6-13.

Page, J.D. Psychopathology: The Science of Understanding Deviance. 2nd Edit. Chicago: Aldine, 1975.

Pallis, D.C. et al. Effect of junior doctor's action on self-poisoning. Br. Med. J., 1976, 1, (6005) 342.

Pasnan, R. & Russell, A. Psychiatric resident 'suicide'
--an analysis of five cases, Amer.J. Psychia.,
1975, 132, 402-406.

Pearson, M.M. Drug and alcohol problems among physicians. Psychia. Opinion, 1975, 12, 14-18.

Phillips, E.L. The Social Skills Basis of Psychopathology: Alternative to Abnormal Psychology and
Psychiatry. N.Y.: Grune & Stratton, 1978.

Pinner, M. & Miller, B.F. When Doctors are Patients.
N.Y.: Norton, 1952.

Powles, J. On the limitations of modern medicine,
Sci. Med. Man., 1973, 1, 1-30.

Rogow, A.A. The Psychiatrists. N.Y.: Putnam's Sons,
1970.

Rosenberg, P.P. Students' perceptions and concerns
during their first year in medical school, J.
Med. Educ., 1971, 46, 211-218.

Ross, M. Physician suicide risk - a practical recognition and management, South. Med. J., 1975, 68,
699-702.

Ross, M. Suicide among physicians, Psychia. Med.,
1971, 2, 189-198.

Ross, M. Physicians who commit suicide. The deck
is not stacked, Psychia. Opinion, 1975, 12, 26-29.

Sargent, D. A., Jeresen, V.W., Petty, T.A. & Raskin, H.
Preventing physician suicide, JAMA, 1977, 237,
143-145.

Saward, E.W. Institutional organizations, incentives
and change, in Knowles, J.H. (Ed.) Doing Better
and Feeling Worse: Health in the United States.
N.Y.: Norton, 1977.

Schafer, A.M. Medicine as a career--as viewed by
college seniors, J. Med. Educ., 1974, 49, 83-86.

Scheiber, S.C. Emotional problems of physicians: II
current approaches to the problem, Ariz. Med.,
1978, 35, 336-337.

98

Schoor, D. _Don't Get Sick in America_. Nashville: Aurora, 1970.

Shur, M. _Freud: Living and Dying_. N.Y.: International Univ. Press, 1972.

Spain, D.M. _The Complications of Modern Medical Practice_. N.Y.: Grune & Stratton, 1965,

Steppacher, R.C. & Mausner, J.S. Suicide in male and female physicians, _JAMA_, 1974, 228, 323-328.

Sutherland, I. Recent studies in the epidemiology of tuberculosis, based on the risk of being infected with tubercle bacilli, _Adv. Tuberc. Res._, 1976, 19, 1-63.

Szasz, T.S. _The Myth of Mental Illness_. N.Y.: Harper & Row, 1961.

Szasz, T.S. _Manufacture of Madness: A Comparative Study of Inquisitions and the Mental Health Movement_. N.Y.: Harper & Row, 1972.

Thompson, W.T., Jr. Society and Medicine: Four origins of current dissatisfaction, _Va. Med._, 1977, 104, 425-429.

Tooth, G.C. _Studies in Mental Illness in the Gold Coast_. London: Her Majesty's Stationary Office, 1950.

Traska, M. R. Hospitals build more doctors' offices despite certificate of need-uncertainty, _Modern Health Care_, 1978, 8, 46-49.

Twaddle, A.C. & Hessler, R.M. _A Sociology of Health_. St. Louis: Mosby, 1977.

Valliant, G.E. Physician cherish thyself, _Medical Insights_, 1970, 2, 46.

Valliant, G.E., Sobowale, N.C., & McArthur, C. Some psychological vulnerabilities, _N. Eng. J. Med._, 1972, 287, 372-375.

Van Zijl, W. J. Studies on diarrheal diseases in seven countries, _Bull. of the World Health Organization_, 1966, 35, 249-261.

Vayda, E. A comparison of surgical rates in Canada and

in England and Wales, <u>New England J. of Med.</u>,
1973, <u>289</u>, 1224-1229.

Vianna, N.J., Keogh, M.D., Polan, A.K., & Greenwald, P.
Hodgkins disease mortality among physicians,
<u>Lancet</u>, 1974, <u>2</u>, 131-133.

Viscott, D.S. <u>The Making of a Psychiatrist</u>. N.Y.:
Arbour House, 1972.

Wallace, F.C. Anthropology and psychopathology, in
Page, J. (Ed.) <u>Approaches to Psychopathology</u>.
N.Y.: Columbia U. Press, 1966.

Wecht, C.H. The interface of law and medicine, <u>Amer.
J. Law Med.</u>, 1975, <u>1</u>, 89-101.

Wildawsky, A. Doing better and feeling worse: The
political pathology of health policy, in Knowles,
J.H. (Ed.) <u>Doing Better and Feeling Worse:
Health in the United States.</u> N.Y.: Norton, 1977.

Wolfgang, S. L. Physicians who commit suicide: A
stacked deck, <u>Psychia. Opinion,</u> 1975, <u>12</u>, 24-29.

CHAPTER IV

DENTISTS

The dental profession is somewhat less ridden with stress than the medical profession but the qualitative signs of stress are similar in both professions. Both of them face the public which makes many demands on their services. And both professions count among their members those that have evidenced in a number of ways various psychosomatic and other signs of stress. This tend has been noted particularly over the past few decades.

The dental profession, compared to medicine, may have begun to recognize its plight more fully and to have begun to do something constructive about stress and its ramifications, among both dental students and practitioners. Also, since there are fewer dentists in the U.S. than there are physicians, there are, per-force, fewer factions, complications, insurance (third party payment sources) issues, and training issues. In its training and practice dentistry has been a more homogeneous and cohesive professional organization than medicine, although the stresses extant for demtistry today are increasing and they are beginning to look more and more like those affecting medicine.

One author -- Dunlap (1977) -- wrote about "sur-viving" in the practice of dentistry; his writing shows concern about the sources of stress. He asks, "What is this thing called stress?" (among dentists) and hastens to answer in the following quotation:

> "Good morning, Doctor, I'm afraid we've both a few little problems. There's been a water leak in the second opera-tory and the whole room is flooded. And the compressor won't turn on. Mrs. Smith called and said one of her front caps has broken. I looked that up -- it would be part of the eight-unit bridge we seated four months ago. Af-ter you left Friday, there was a call from an attorney about the trouble with Mr. Harris. He wants you to call him this morning. The number is on your desk. Joe Stark is in the wait-ing room. His face is swollen. He thinks it's the tooth that had the

101

root canal treatment. I had to schedule a denture adjustment and a
toothache for the lunch hour. Patty
called and said she couldn't be here
today. She has the flu. So I'll
have to be the assistant and the
receptionist. Oh, your wife called
about five minutes ago. She said
she had had a little accident taking the children to school. She
said for you not to worry -- every-
body is all right -- but the car
is sort of a mess."

Now _that_ is stress! (Dunlap, 1977, p. 9)

No doubt all professions and many skilled trades
run into stretches of bad luck, comparable in stress to
the above citation befalling the dentist. But if these
stresses are highly repetitive and unrelenting, they
can assumulate the bodily and psychological _tensions_
spoken of in preceding chapters, and make way for the
continuing _anxiety_ that puts a cloud over one's head
and leaves one in a state of foreboding -- a what-will-
happen-next feeling?

Dunlap (1977) thinks that much of the stress in
dentistry is due to myths that have been passed along
by dentists and by the public, thus making the dentist
more vulnerable to stress. The irrealitis of these
myths make facing daily life in the practice of dentistry harder than would otherwise by the case. One
myth Dunlap discusses is the "Myth of 100 percent,"
meaning that dentists feel they have to be perfect,
they cannot fail, there is no room for fault or error
or mishap. Given this unrealistic attitude, it is
no wonder, Dunlap avers, that

Many dentists literally hate their
work but they are so locked in financially they are compelled to
stay with it and remain silent about
their feelings. (Dunlap, 1977, p. 15)

The "feeling silent" about their tensions and concerns contributes, undoubtedly, to personal stress and
anxiety which, as we have seen, gnaw away at their
psychological and physical health and give rise to the
work-related attitudes that are as negative as Dunlap
states.

102

Nor is this "100 percent myth" the whole story. There are, in addition, clinical myths and social myths about dentists. Dunlap (1977) says the clinical myths (unfortunately believed by dentists and the lay public, alike), due to their unreality are correspondingly vulnerable to disconfirmation. The clinical myths include: The notion that dentistry is painless (preparing a patient for discomfiture, being realistic about procedures hurting, and answering normal questions posed by the patient is much more realistic); promoting the notion that false teeth are superior to natural teeth (people tend to think that false teeth, not developing cavities or otherwise prone to hurting, will provide a welcome relief to the vicissitudes of their own, natural teeth); caps are the answer to many problems of unevenness in "bite" and comfort (this notion could be invalidated for the same reasons cited above in regard to false teeth); X-Rays are supposed to reveal all there is to know about the condition of one's tooth or teeth (X-Rays provide important but limited knowledge, still have to be "interpreted" or "read"); good dental preventive work should lead parents to having all children under 12 get their teeth cleaned twice a year (the dentist should make the estimate on the frequency of teech cleaning among youngsters, upon knowing the child, the family's health and eating habits, and the like); and the notion that fluoride can be expected to prevent all cavities (this being a gross over-exaggeration can lead to otherwise careless or indifferent care of teeth and even failure to consult the dentist when it would otherwise be necessary or advisable). These myths are part of the "propaganda" advanced by dental ads, loose talk and writing about dental hygiene, and an overly optimistic view of what the dentist does or can do to prevent dental illhealth or keep the individual from suffering.

Additional myths, those related to the dentist's social status, also contribute to unrealistic notions of dentistry. They put unnecessary pressures on the dentist, or teach unrealistic expectations to the dental student or the pre-dental aspirant to the practice, and overemphasize the financial aspects of dental practice. These myths include the following: All dentists are rich (statistics show that dentists throughout the country do have high median incomes, but this is not tantamount to being "rich" or does it meet the stereotype of the rich person who does not have to work). Moreover, dentists do not have the highest incomes among the professions. An additional myth discussed by Dunlap (1977) is that there are not enough dentists in

practice. He observes that there were at the time of
his writing (1977) about 110,000 active dentists; with
our national population of 220 million people, this is
one dentist for each 2,000 members of the population.
As with the practice of medicine, the distribution of
dentists throughout the country, concentrated in urban
areas as they are (and as physicians are) makes for
disproportionately small numbers of dentists in rural
areas, among the poorer areas of the city and in sparsely
populated towns and villages. Apropos of the matter of
income and location, dentists and physicians tend to
charge more in urban settings--rent, utilities, professional help, and other expenses are higher--and so the
notions that dentists are rich may be easily fostered
in such settings. People forget how much it costs to
go through dental school, the financial and other
risks involved, and how much it costs to set up practice.
This is all "up front" expenditure, and while the
dentist does make a "good living" there are many slips
along the way and it is often several years before the
dentist's income can be considered secure. This, again,
is why Dunlap stated, as quoted above, "Many dentists
literally have their work but they are so locked in
financially..." (Dunlap, 1977, p. 15).

     The sources of tension cited by Dunlap have been
noted and reacted to in a report by Canfield, et al,
(1976), in which these authors report on the pressures
of dental training and how they might be ameliorated.
Not only reducing the tensions felt by the dental
students, but developing more positive attitudes was also
an objective of Canfield and his associates. They
observe that dentistry requires more courses than pre-
professional school (undergraduate training), in that
dental students are in classes and labs eight hours a
day. Study time comes on top of the basic course/lab
time. This unrelenting pace adds to the dental student's
stress and the tensions felt. Some schools have adopted
the practice of taking dental students, early in their
careers, on "retreats" to reduce their fears and apprehensions about their scholastic work and their professional future. Intended, too, was the encouragement of
the students talking about their expectations, their
relationship to faculty, the difficulties with course-
work, and other academic and professional matters.
When given the opportunity, the students elected to
continue with the practice of retreats; the faculty
felt students were encouraged to become more professional
in their outlook, and to be less tense and more open in
regard to their dental training. This is a forward
looking practice by some dental schools, especially when

conducted early in the student's academic career. Such measures help prevent some of the overly competitve, stressful and anxiety-ridden attitudes often unwittingly encouraged by all professional school training, especially in dentistry and medicine.

As we have seen in the chapter on medicine, characteristic changes take place in the student's attitude as s/he progresses through medical school. The medical student seemingly cares less about patients and patient care and more about economics and professional striving for notice and advancement. Early recourse to more relaxed contacts between dental students and faculty may help preclude in the dental profession the kind of rampant striving (with its attendant tensions and anxieties) found so commonly in the medical profession.

Early on, students of dentistry should be appraised of the stresses inherent in the job of dentistry (Howard et al, 1976). These authors did not take to the "retreat" method of acquainting students of the pitfalls of dental training and practice, but they have written in professional journals on these issues. Howard, et al aver that dentistry may be unusually subject to stress. Dentistry is physically hard work, with the dentist having to stand for long periods of time, having to assume strained and unnatural positions in order to work on the patient, and having to be physically and psychologically strong enough to withstand some of the tediousness of dental work, especially precision work. There is also a strain in building long-term dental practice. This pressure induces dentists to stay in the same community for long periods of time when they might otherwise want to move to more geographically convenient, or more modern quarters. These authors found in a survey of 33 practicing dentists with an average of 10 years professional work, that 70% had stayed in the same community all their professional life, and 85% had confined their professional work to no more than two communities.

Dentists work under unrelenting time pressures, as well. In a survey of their momentum in doing and finishing assigned work, Howard, et al found that 60% of the dentists "fell behind the clock" in their daily routines. Not a puzzle to understand, the dentists who stayed ahead of the clock experienced what they rated as "high stress," (based on a 40-item stress inventory) and those who fell behind also experienced the same. Only those who paced themselves equitable with the clock experienced less stress. Influencing "high pacing of activities" might stem from economic considerations, giving the patient the impression of an unusual level of skill and demand so as to influence the patient to come back again.

In the Howard et al study (1976), the average dentist worked about 9 hours a day, typically had one or two assistants, and engaged in general, rather than specialized, practice. The general practice emphasis in dentistry is different from the same tendency in the practice of medicine which, over the past few decades, has moved more and more physicians into specialized practice. This occurs partly due to the desire to reduce stress arising from general practice, and partly to economic considerations. Dentistry has not followed the same routes to reduce tension that medicine has followed. There are sufficient differences in the practice of dentistry to account for tension on a different basis from medicine, and the solutions dentists tend to follow to minimize stress are somewhat different from those found in medicine. For example, the psychology of the stress/tension/anxiety patterns in dentistry and medicine are knowably different and remedial efforts and practices have correspondingly taken different routes in the two professions. This is not to say, however, that financial considerations, strenuous years of training and the vicissitudes of professional practice show no similarities between dentistry and medicine.

Stress is often a very general matter. It is hard to point to sources of stress in daily life, among professionals or the laity, that equal the specificity of tubercular infection, measles, broken bones, or an abcessed tooth. However, now and then specific measures of stress on a professional population are made that are convincing. These are measures of stress and tension of a direct nature (in contrast to other more indirect measures of stress and tension and anxiety such as prevalence of heart attacks, suicide, job changes, and the like). A direct measure of tension among individual dental practitioners was taken at an American Dental Association meeting in 1973 (Cutright, Carpenter, Tsaknis and Lyon, 1977). The report says that under the conditions of the survey, dentists tend to show higher average systolic and diastolic pressures than the general population (p.919). The report says further that twenty-seven percent of the entire group of 856 dentists showed a diastolic hypertension, and 22.6 percent showed a systolic hypertension (p.919). Catching these many dentists at a convention may be somewhat atypical of how they would show up under blood pressure tests in their natural environments (although what is their "natural environment" may be moot: they would probably appear less hypertense on the golf course than in the office or in their homes). Allowing for sampling biases, perhaps atypical age distribution, and other factors, these data do contribute materially to the notion that dentists are a tense group of professionals and that the state of health of this professional group is to some measurable extent one characterized by tension and stress.

Public Scrutiny of Dentists

Having established that there is, indeed, considerable tension and stress in the dental profession, at least from indirect measures, but also some from direct measures of stress, we turn attention now to some professional and social circumstances that affect the health of this profession. These matters relate to professional stance vis-a-vis the public, the risk of suits, and the liabilities one encounters in the practice of dentistry. As we saw in the opening paragraph by Dunlap, the tensions of the day may be based on causes ranging from ill-done technical work, through office and mechanical mishaps, out to personal matters in the lives of dentists. Add to these sometimes indirect and general sources of tension, broad professional practice issues relating to malpractice, insurance, and the like, and we have another set of influences affecting the health of this profession.

Komensky (1978) writes that the Dental Association Council on Insurance is receiving more complaints from patients about dental work than in the past. Patients charge they have not been fully informed of the risks associated with dental procedures used on them. Komensky's point is that dentists need to ward off these types of complaints (which may be genuine) by receiving from the patients before the work is done informed consent agreements, thereby reducing the risks to the patient as well as decreasing the professional liability against the dentist. Komensky says that prior to treatment the dentist should: Inform the patient of the probable cause of his/her complaint or dental condition, the treatment plan proposed, how alternate plans would work, and the risks involved in each instance. The dentist should avoid technical language and speak in sentences the patient can understand and follow. The patient should also be informed in the presence of the dentist's assistant so a witness is available were

there to develop a court suit. In the case of dental
work on children, parental or guardian consent, following the same procedures should be obtained. The patient
is to sign the consent form after receiving the dentist's
explanation, so there is little or no dispute as to
what the dentist said or what s/he meant. The consent
form should be filed with the patient's record, kept in
safety for possible future use. Not mentioned by
Komensky is the possible fact that the patient would
have more confidence in the dentist taking this kind of
care, and a basis for better dental work would be
arrived at; hence, both parties would profit from this
explicit, formal procedure of risk protection--it is not
simply a mechanism to safeguard the dentist from malpractice suit. The dentist's tension, following such a
procedure, especially when we multiply it manyfold, as
Komensky does, would seem to be lessened, and a basis
would be laid in this aspect of dental practice for a
more wholesome and a more healthful professional practice. Komensky' comments are timely.

Collett (1978) recognizes the same problem and
calls dental malpractice "...an enormous and growing
problem." It is certainly a threat hanging over the
dentist to recognize that any patient who walks into
his/her office and sits in the dentist's chair could be
a potential plaintiff. Dentists know of extant suits
against other practitioners and, wondering what and
when something of a similar nature might happen to
them, feel the stress more than they might recognize
(Solomon, 1978).

Following a review of some legal decisions and
their impact on dentists, Gamer (1978) discusses and
quotes from published legal decisions that emphasize
the importance of the professional practitioner giving
written information to the patient about the type and
course of treatment anticipated, Gamer's play-on-words
includes the phrase: "Inform before you perform" and,
recommends as do other writers, a signed consent form
prior to the offering of treatment.

It should be clear, however, that signed consent
does not mean that the patient will not sue if s/he
feels negligence is an issue in dental treatment
(Collett, 1978). More devices need tobe considered suc
as legislation that would control the amount of damages
from various types of negligence; perhaps some type of
no-fault coverage might be considered. Also, compulsory arbitration might work in some cases (Collett,
1978, p. 224). Law schools are beginning to introduce

108

courses in medical (including dental) jurisprudence, often conducted by people with degrees in law and medicine; medical and dental institutes are run for attorneys, and vice versa. The value of these collaborative efforts will be to work fair and equitable solutions where damage to a patient has resulted from negligence and not give opportunistic advantage to lawyers and plaintiffs (patients) who are looking for a "fast buck" at the expense of the practitioner and the profession (Collett, 1978, p. 224).

Dentists' Contributions To Problems

Dentists may inadvertently contribute to their own problems by implying to complaining patients that other dentists (or another dentist) has done improper treatment (Artz, 1976). This gives the opportunity for an alert plaintiff's attorney to accept and pursue contingent fees. Such suits damage the reputation of the dentist in question in a general way (even if the dentist has not been negligent), induce patients to sometimes be critical beyond a reasonable basis for complaint, raise the cost of insurance, and ties up peoples' time needlessly in court actions that might be handled more economically and with less damage in other ways.

The problem of whether professions such as dentistry, medicine and law should "advertise" fees and other costs of their services has loomed large in recent years. Generally the professions have reacted negatively against the new emphasis on publishing information on fees, saying that such practices smack of "hucksterism" and make professional service a marketplace commodity comparable to groceries and other items of daily exchange (Solomon, 1978). The move to assemble and disperse information on professional fees to the public is a legitimate consumer issue and one pursued by consumer groups throughout the nation. There is a real difference between "advertising" and giving information; clients or patients of professional practitioners ought to be able to know in advance what a given service will cost (or at least a range of possible costs), how long it might take, and so forth. Even though one cannot be exactly sure of the costs, the attempt to publish fees and openly disclose matters related to fees, is a professionally responsible route to take. It is also commensurate with the recommendations cited above (among dentists themselves) imploring dentists to get signed informed consent from patients before services begin. If the dentist (the professional) needs protection against capriciousness, ignorance or misunderstanding on the part of patients (consumers), the latter need the same protection in regard to fees. One might say that a vigorous, healthy and responsible profession would take self-disclosure measures seriously and consider them an essential part of their practice. The accusation often leveled that dentists overchange their patients would be broungt under control (if it is true); or the issue would be settled out of court, so to speak, and consumers (patients) would feel better about their dental services.

Attitude and Emotional Factors

Dentists have personal and emotional histories; they have exercised choices to go into dentistry as a part of their career development; they undergo rigorous and demanding training, and they develop attitudes and predispositions toward dentistry as a profession. They also evidence attitude changes as they pursue dentistry from their first year in school tothe time when they become practitioners. Vinton (1978) studies by a questionnaire method the learning environment of 109 dental students over a four-year period. Among his findings are the following: The dental school "learning environment" is highly teacher-centered; authority is vested in the faculty and students are subservient to the faculty; the activities of the dental student-- classes, laboratory experiences, clinical experience-- are highly structured and communication between student and faculty is essentially one-way (from faculty to student). As a result of this kind of structuring of the educational experiences of the dental student, the student him/her self changes in attitude over the four years: The amount of learning from and sharing among peers is downgraded; communication and close relation- ships with others are valued less over time by the students; and value is increasingly placed on each student's own interests and goals (Vinton, 1978, p.251) With this kind of structuring and slanting of dental school experiences, it is not difficult to see how dentists as practitioners may place extremely high value on individual career goals, money, resistance to community responsibility and disclosure in matters of fees, dispersing information about dental hygiene, or influence their attitudes toward community health problems that impinge on dental care and health and the need for dental service (Sherlock & Morris, 1972; Dimarco and Pearlmutter, 1976; Hutton, 1968). If one

110

wanted to change the course of dental school graduate attitudes, one might opt for some refinements in the selection process as to who get accepted to dental school (place more emphasis on values, attitudes, community service, for example), or opt to change the curriculum in important ways in order to slant the four-year education more toward community-related goals and less toward individual goals. Or, one might pursue both methods of change. At any rate, what Vinton calls "...a process of clarification of values..." would be required of the faculty and administration; changes are not likely to come about in dental practiioners' attitudes without a curriculum emphasis change (Vinton, 1978, p. 256).

But not all want to change the attitudes of dentists (Isman, 1977). Some aver that a reevaluation of dentists' attitudes, their schooling, the emphasis that schooling takes, and the quality of dental services among practitioners are not needed for the profession. Isman states that most dentists object to evaluations of their skills and services, feeling that such evaluations deprofessionalize dentists and make them comparable to assembly line workers (Friedman, 1972).

Not surprisingly the dental profession has undertaken more inquiry into the nature of its educational process than has medicine. Being a smaller number, the dental profession is less unwieldy than medicine; and the smaller number of specialties (although they have been increasing in dentistry) reduces the amount of internal conflicts growing out of proprietary interests. It is not to be implied that the dental profession is thoroughly self-conscious and given to disclosure about its operations--that is not the case--but there appear to be more articles, research studies, and opinions expressed in writing as to how the profession can better its purposes and improve its educational stance. We are reminded by one author--(Johnson, 1976)--that dentistry meets more health problems than any other profession, that the most common diseases of mankind are those occurring in the teeth and surrounding bone and soft tissue (Johnson, 1976, p. 699). Dentistry, then, is not a minor health area, hence its professional stance is of consequence for the profession itself and for the delivery of services to the consumer.

A special dental education evaluation committee was established at the Washington University's Boyne School of Dental Science (Tamisiea et al, 1977). This group surveyed 244 recent graduates, receiving replies

111

from 166 deliverable questionnaires, in order to ascertain what the graduates thought of the curriculum they had experienced during dental school training. The graduates were asked to rate the "quality" of their education, meaning the amount of time spent on a subject in relation to its usefulness in later dental practice, among other issues about their education (in all, 32 subjects were evaluated by the questionnaire, including such categories as clinical dentistry and basic science). The study was not intended to form the basis of a new curriculum, but only to point to new directions for rethinking the curriculum. One area of particular weakness was that of "practice administration," which refers to how the consumer of dental practice is dealt with ("administered") and how smoothly one's dental practice progresses. In addition to surveying recent dental graduates, as did the Tamisiea et al study (1977), dentists with 5 - 25 years of practice might well be surveyed with a similar questionnaire. The first years of dental practice, while significant for sole problems, are hardly representative of all of dental practice. Presumably successful dentists would improve in their "practice administration" over time and/or define the problems more clearly.

Dentists were surveyed in one geographic area of the State of New York on their opinions concerning issues facing the profession (Goldberg, et al, 1976), and on the extent local dental groups agreed with the official policies of the American Dental Association. Considerable agreement was found among local dentists in matters relating to licensure and peer review, and in the choice of favored courses as a part of continuing education and licensure (without additional examinations). Peer review was favored by this local dental group of practitioners. Reminiscent of some problems noted above, fee posting (not called "advertising" in this report) brought indecisive replies by the group; the pressures exerted by the official policies of the American Dental Association seem not to be decisive in affecting the opinions of this local dental group. Perhaps in the field of dentistry, tensions felt by individual practitioners resulting from stress produced by the profession as a profession, seem less formidable than in medicine.

The cost of dental education looms large as a stressful factor, however (Adams, 1976). This author says the cost of dental education ranged from over $6,000 to over $16,000 per year, in 1975, and thereby ran the risk of screening out minorities, and the poor from consideration as dental applicants. In addition, once in dental school the continuing and mounting financial obligations put stress on students and perhaps slant them toward considering the financial returns from dentistry as overwhelmingly important (at the expense of dental care, the delivery of services to the total population and other socially-related matters). Adams says, "The upshot of the matter then is that membership in the dental profession is fast becoming limited to the well-to-do" (Adams, 1976, p. 263). The financial situation is one set of not-so-subtle stress factors (or "stressors," as they are sometimes called) that "lock in" the dentist to his occupation, perhaps being so strenuous as to make the dentist hate his work (Dunlap, 1977, p. 15). During schooling years, scholarships and loans (ranging from eight to fourteen percent in 1975) hardly suffice to relieve the financial plight of students. In addition, tuition rates and the costs of books and instruments has accelerated beyond the general rate of inflation. Adams' comment that only the well-to-do can now qualify for dental school takes on real significance, and even these students are financially stressed.

Self-Examination and Peer Review

Despite these financial pressures, the dental profession continues to attempt to monitor its own performance (Milgram, et al, 1978). Milgram and his associates look at dentists' self-evaluation in relation to their clinical performance. They note that most standards of practice are set by individual practitioners. Improving upon this self-evaluation are the practices of dental schools which try to teach the student how to evaluate his own work accurately. The Milgram, et al study included nearly 1,200 general practitioners in their study, and they concentrated on 102 general practitioners working on 2,753 patients, on whom performance ratings were accumulated. The dentists' self-evaluations were high: ratings of 5.8 to 6.3 on a number of performance items, based on a 7-point scale (maximum self-evaluation rating). While self-evaluations are important, they cannot stand alone. A study of this type should have included independent ratings (anonymously given) by peers; comparing, then, these peer ratings with self-evaluation ratings. Since dental practitioners, like other professionals, balk at evaluative procedures generally, self-evaluations are a first approximation to constructive self-criticism; perhaps in time more objective

113

standards of evaluation will be developed and followed.
Although evaluations are considered by the profession
as stressful--and, indeed, they are, especially if the
practitioners are adamantly opposed to such procedures--
gradual acceptance of the need for evaluation will
reduce stress and improve services. A little stress may
sometimes be a good thing! (Selye, 1974).

Peer review procedures in dentistry, as in medicine,
have functions to perform that are vital to the public
image of the profession (Martin, 1977). In recent years,
dental practitioners have experienced an increase in
documented complaints and malpractice suits, as has
medicine. Peer reviews are set up to handle these
complaints and suits. Peers are usually other dentists;
some peer review groups are also composed of other
professional persons, and lay persons. The Social
Security Act of 1972 established PSROs (Professional
Standards Review Organizations), designed to monitor all
medical services provided through the Social Security
Act. These PSROs, or peer review groups, evaluate the
quality of services performed, reasonableness of
procedures used, and a decision as to whether the
services were performed according to high professional
standards. Although many dentists object to these peer
reviews, citing fear and anxiety as common consequences
(the ways in which tensions are felt by the dental
practitioners); and although peer review can also
increase competition and beaucratic constraints among
dentists, the general outcome of peer review seems
salutary. Peer review will doubtlessly continue, nay
increase and, as with other professional monitoring
systems, become an integral part of the practice of
dentistry. Peer reviews are needed for the health of
the profession and for the protection of the public.

Some of the dental profession's self-examination
includes, as one might expect, concern for the
selection of students to become practicing dentists.
We have already seen how financial considerations
preempt choices in selecting dental students (Adams,
1976). There are other motives--more psychological--
that influence the selection of students, the attitudes
of dental practitioners and those of faculty as well
(Whittemann and Currier, 1976). This report, as well
as earlier studies, point out that, among other attributes, the interests of dental students on the Strong
Vocational Interest Blank are found to be in the
biological and physical sciences and in business and
technical service. In addition, personality features
of entering dental students include preferences for

114

autonomy, a desire to work with one's hands, preferences in working with people (as distinct from ideas, or things), and to gain prestige (Mann and Perkin, 1960; More, 1961). Also, dental students tend to identify with practitioners rather more than with peers or with faculty in terms of interests and attitude toward dentistry. Over the years of dental school training, students tend to converge in their attitudes and become more similar (Heist, 1960). These and other findings were derived from a questionnaire--the Professional Motivation Ranking Scale (PMRS) (Speir, 1972)--administered to all four classes of dental students at the Virginia Commonwealth University during the 1972-1974 academic years. The study asked individuals why they chose dentistry as a career. The 12-choice answer range included the following: To advance in the professional respect of my peers; to make full use of my present knowledge and skills; to earn a good salary; to learn and develop to my full potential; to work on difficult and challenging problems; to have congenial associates as collegues; to work in association with persons of high technical competence; to grow and learn new knowledge and skills; to contribute to broad technical knowledge in my field; to advance in administrative authority and status; to have the freedom to carry out my ideas; and to build my professional reputation in the community.

Sometimes the "old hands" think that the young professionals are not carrying on the traditions of the profession, that the new generation is less professional and not as devoted to techical objectives as the oldsters. The Whittemann and Currier study disavow this stereotype of the young-comer to the profession:

> The dental student and the private
> practitioner are motivated primarily
> by nonmonetary factors: 'freedom to
> carry out one's ideas' and 'to develop
> to one's full potential.' These are
> characteristics of an individualist.
> Earning a good salary is a priority,
> but so is growth in new knowledge and
> skills. The desire for growth is a
> necessary motivational factor for con-
> tinuing education for both the dental
> student and the practitioner. This
> similarity of motives should ease the
> minds of practitioners who believe

that contemporary dental students have
perceptions of the profession radically
different from theirs." (Whittemann
and Currier, 1977, 267-268).

One question that naturally arises from the
Whittemann and Currier study is whether the dental
student should harbour the same values and attitudes as
the experienced practitioner. Is there not room for
growth and change of attitude from student days to
experienced professional? If the students are cut out
of the same mold as the professional, where is there
opportunity for change,especially in the direction of
more socially conscious use of one's skills and expertise? Moreover, the 12-item set of questions advances
only professional and/or individual goals (including
earning a good salary) and includes no references to
public or community service. As with medicine, there
is a considerable bias built into the selection, education and eventual professionalization of dental
practitioners. It is little wonder,then, that the
pressure from the profession slant the attitudes and
opinions of the practitioners. The extent to which the
practitioner is beholden in these respects to the
profession is the extent to which stress from the
profession is easily transmitted as tension and anxiety
to the practitioner. The one divergence from this
generalization is that the "dental educators" (the
professors in dental school) considered the factors
of interrelationships with others, high technical
competence, and the development to full potential, as
being of considerable importance.

The professors naturally consider economic factors
of less importance or they would not have chosen to be
educators instead of practitioners, the latter earning
the greater income.

We have noted that change in attitudes among dental
students is an important matter for study. Steinberg
(1973) used a questionnaire survey among students in a
longitudinal (four year) study at Loyola University.
He says of his results: "In the current study, marked
changes occurred in some of the attitudes of students
during the period of their professional education.
The greatest change was in the students' increased
concern for gaining a monetary reward." (Steinberg,
1973, p. 41). Steinberg relates his results to the
decade-earlier study by More (1962) who, on the basis
of a questionnaire administered to all entering dental

students in the United States in 1958 obtained 99 percent returns (3,578 students were represented). Findings from the 1958 sample were compared with 2,400 paired returns from the same questionnaire in 1962. More concluded that dental schools appear not to nurture cynicism or "dollar-minded dentistry." However, the dental students reported on the questionnaire that they desired a lucrative practice and expected high incomes.

Another way to examine the attitudes and opinions of dental practitioners and students is through what some researchers call "role perception". All professionals engage in various roles: practitioner, researcher, health care provider, public service role, student of the profession role, etc. Rosen et al (1977) examined the changes in roles perceived by first-year dental students at the University of California, Los Angeles. They observed that "role identification" starts early in the student's training, first being more closely related to that of older students than to practitioners (the freshmen observe and often know first-hand the older students but do not as yet have a chance to know and observe the practitioner). Correspondingly, patient roles are more distant and not clearly perceived. These authors say "...the student is (somewhat) inclined toward the patient (clinic patients, video-taped patients) but does not observe or conceive of close identification between doctor models and patients" (Rosen, et al 1977, p. 510). Faculty at dental schools and dental educators are often puzzled by the role perceptions of beginning dental students (sometimes by more senior dental students as well) and their lack of sensitivity to patient plight and patient roles, but there is far less exposure to patients than to the curriculum, far less emphasis on the delivery of services than on science, technology and the passing of exams. If role perceptions of the beginning dental student--even the senior dental student--are to change in the direction of patient care, community responsibility, and related roles, then the curriculum will have to be shorn up in this respect and an emphasis on interpersonal relationships (doctor-patient relationships) will have to emerge.

Roles are related to personality characteristics, and vice versa. When personality traits among dental students are studied, they are found also to change: Rosenberg (1965) studied 47 male dental students on

the California Personality Inventory before they
entered dental school and again four years later.
Beginning with no differences between the freshmen
dental students and students in general on this inventory, the same students as seniors were found to exhibit
a change: They were less self-reliant, less independent,
their potential for leadership was less, and initiative
and ambition had declined. Students had become more
stereotyped, again showing evidence of the effects of
dental school pressures, attitudes, and emphasis. This
study may also show the need for questioning many
aspects of dental education as it appears to slant the
student away from those attributes that would make for
more resourceful, community-oriented, patient-oriented
and versatile practitioners (Rosenberg, 1965; Steinberg,
1973; p. 36 and p. 41).

Stress From Health Problems

Dentists, like physicians, come in for their share,
proportionally speaking, of infectious conditions.
Hepatitis may be the main offender among dentists.
Feldman and Schiff (1975) studied hepatitis in the
dental profession. They sent 434 questionnaires to
dentists and 787 to attorneys (acting as controls), in
one county in Florida. Dentists reported more hepatitis infections among themselves than did attorneys
(6.7 percent for dentists vs. 2.4 percent for lawyers);
the highest rate for the dental group was found among
oral surgeons (21 percent). Further, the highest
incidence among dentists of hepatitis was associated
with their treating drug addicts. These findings were
not one year statistics but, rather, included a thirty-
year span. These findings call for more education
regarding drug abuse among youth, but also more education among dentists so that the latter are more fully
acquainted with the risks they are taking in their
practice. I t would appear that the dentists' plight
is a matter of general exposure to hepatitis found to
be on the increase among persons practicing in the
health professions (Glazer, Spat, and Catone, 1973).
It is felt that dentists do not take adequate safety
measures, some having been found not to use gloves
even with surgery (Feldman and Schiff, 1975).

Glenwright (1974) studied 500 Australian dentists.
He found serum hepatitis in dental surgeons to be more
than seven times as common as it was among the general
population (1:166 cases among oral surgeons as against
1:1,100 for people in general). Again it was conclude

that oral surgeons must exert more care of a preventive
nature in regard to hepatitis when they treat patients
with "high carrier rate"--prisoners, the mentally
handicapped in institutions, especially mongols,
patients born in equatorial countries, and drug addicts.
He concluded that wearing rubber gloves was obligatory
as a preventive measure. Overlooked often among dentists is the potentially serious nature of hepatitis
infection; it can cause death, a long period of in-
capacity, and the risk of being a carrier.

A more forceful statement of hepatitis infection
among dentists could not be found than that proffered
by Weil et al (1977). They state, after studying 512
dentists in a survey in New York: "Hepatitis B (serum
hepatitis) infection is an occupational hazard for
dentists" (Weil et al, 1977, p. 587); and, further,
"...dentists are a risk to their patients during the
high contagious incubation period before onset of
clinical disease and during the carrier stage which
follows clinical illness (Weil et al, 1977, p. 587).
These authors emphasize proper care by the dentists
treating suspect hepatitis cases by more careful
history taking which should cover instances of organ
transplants, hemodialysis and blood transfusions.
Particular on guard should be oral surgeons and orthodontists who tested highest in the Weil et al study
for hepatitis B.

The international nature of the problem of hepatitis among dentists is further corroborated by a
survey among Auckland dentists by Nicholos (1977).
He states: "A survey among Auckland dentists has
shown a high exposure of viral hepatitis occurring
during practicing years (Nicholos, 1977, p. 413).
He further states that viral hepatitis infections are
common throughout the world and may in many cases
constitute a serious health problem and consequently
an economic problem. Nicholos found that Auckland
dentists showed a higher rate of viral hepatitis than
American dentists, that general practitioners and
orthodontists yielded the highest proportion of this
infection. This surveyor agreed with other studies
in concluding that the nature of the dental profession
puts them at a higher risk than people in general, and
that preventive measures are mandatory. Despite these
generalizations, Spearman and Bader (1977), studying
380 dentists in the Seattle, Washington area found
that dental offices were not a significant source of
hepatitis transmissions. However, Spearman and Bader

did not address the problem of the incidence of hepatitis among dentists or oral surgeons.

Waste anesthetic gases are also a problem for dentists. These gases are found in hospital dental operating rooms (Cohen et al, 1975). The study performed by Cohen and others was based on a mail survey of 4,797 dental practitioners and 2,642 oral surgeons, asking them about their exposure to waste anesthetic gases. The survey results showed that 20.2 percent of the general practitioners and 74.8 percent of the oral surgeons had anesthetic exposures exceeding three hours per week. The survey further turned up the finding that there was a sizeable increase (78 percent) of spontaneous abortion in the spouses of exposed dentists, and an even more significant increase (156 percent) in liver disease for exposed dentists. Earlier work (Vaisman, 1967) on 303 Russian anesthetists indicated a reported high incidence of headaches, fatigue, and irritability among members of this population. Similarly, a high percentage of pregnancies among female anesthetists in the Vaisman study ended in spontaneous abortion. Other studies on smaller populations in the U.S., the United Kingdom, and Denmark confirm the already stated findings by Vaisman, and show an increased incidence of congenital abnormalities for exposed pregnant physicians, and the occurrence of cancer among exposed nurse anesthetists. A more recent and larger study of operating room personnel in the U.S. has corroborated the findings from other studies and shown a significant increase in spontaneous abortion, congenital abnormalities, cancer, and hepatic disease among women who are employed in operating rooms and who are also exposed to waste anesthetic gases (Cohen et al, 1975). Jones and Greenfield (1977) develop further the points made in the Cohen et al study (1975) and differ with the study-report by Spearman and Bader (1977) cited above, in that Jones and Greenfield assert measurable trace quantities from sedative/anesthetic agents and equipment are found in the air of the dental office. They say that epidemiologic and animal studies corroborate the notion that exposure to trace quantitie of inhalation agents may present health hazards among dental office personnel.

Virgilio (1971) cites a number of health hazards associated with the occupation of dentistry. He points out that the income, the health status, and the continuance of a stable practice depend upon the dentist being aware of the hazards of practice. Among Virgilio's listing of occupational hazards are the

the following: The <u>hands</u> (Dermatoses: contact and
infectuous dermatoses); the <u>eyes</u> (subject to injury from
routing operative procedures, high speed drills, water
spray, dirty hands, tooth fragments, filling materials
and bone particles); the <u>ears</u> (the high pitched whine
from high speed instruments may cause acoustic trauma
that may be chronic and go undetected for years);
<u>internal organs</u> (extrogenital syphilis resulting from
infection (through the dentist's open wounds or cuts)
from patients carrying veneral disease, contamination
via water and air spray from patient's mouth, inhalation of mineral oil used in lubricating high speed
instruments and equipment, and circulatory and digestive
diseases); injuries to the <u>feet</u> and strain on <u>body
posture</u> (standing long periods of time may induce
slowing of circulation, placing ligaments and muscles
of feet, pelvis and spine under strain, and may result
in flat feet and varicose veins); and stress on the
<u>nervous system</u> (anxiety, frustration, worry, stress
from practice demands and obligations as well as handling
refractory or "problem" cases, meeting financial and
professional demands, etc.). Numerous articles cited
by Virgilio address ways to cope with and/or prevent
these and other occupational hazards in dental practice.

Women in Dentistry

The presence of women in dentistry is a source of
stress to the profession as a whole (i.e., to men) and
to the women themselves who become dentists (Symposium,
1975; Austin, Maher & LoMonaco, 1973; Rosenberg &
Thompson, 1976). These problems seem to have an
international flavor, especially in countries in the
western world which have a low percentage of women
dentists and dental students. A symposium (1975) was
held at the Royal Society of Medicine in Great Britain
in which the women dentists and students asserted belief
in the rights to greater time in dentistry and for more
money. The issue of conflict in roles related to
family (wife and mother) vs the practice of dentistry
were aired. The amount of time women need toget back
into the practice of dentistry after having children
or meeting other family obligations should be extended,
review courses were suggested and recommended,and there
should be fewer and less rigid demands on women who
want to reenter the practice of dentistry. A need was
also expressed in the symposium for more career counseling during undergraduate as well as during graduate
training in dentistry.

In the early 1970's, less than two percent of the

population of dentists in the U.S. were women (Austin, et al, 1973; whereas in the U.S.S.R., Finland, Greece, Denmark and Cuba, women outnumbered men as dentists. In 1973, in the U.S., women comprised 7.1 percent of the physicians, and less than 2.0 percent of the dentists, but the figures began to show an increase of women about the mid-1970s and has increased since. Nationally, the class of 1975 included 3.2 percent women dental enrolles and in 1978, 11.2 percent women dental enrollees (Rosenberg & Thompson, 1976). Despite the good signs associated with the stated increase in the proportion of women in dentistry, women themselves did not feel accepted, reported a sense of isolation (from men dental students) and saw themselves in role conflicts that put pressure and stress on them. Negative attitudes and discriminations against the women were reportedly felt by the women dental students from faculty and male peers alike (Rosenberg & Thompson, 1976, p. 676). These authors also report a need for more counseling and advising of women dental students when they are candidates for dental school as well as upon admission to dental school. Dentistry appears to be moving in the direction already noted among physicians where women are concerned, viz., more formal acceptance of women into professional training but an increase in stress and tension (at the professional and individual levels, respectively) as women take up training and practitioner roles.

Dentists, then, are beset with an abundance of health and related problems. Similar to physicians, dentists' problems range over physical health, psychological, social and professional issues in profusion. Some of the many ways in which these issues are noted in the dental literature are summarized briefly as follows:

1. Dentists moving out of traditional offices into shopping centers, becoming "department store dentists" (Bailey, 1979); which belies their emphasis on professional status, resistance to consumer requirements regarding information on fees and services, and in contradiction to their traditional stand represent a bowing to pressures to advertise in the pejorative sense.

2. Becoming more like medicine in that the profession is promoting specialists as a growing trend (Consumer Reports, 1975); thus yielding their role as general practitioners and separating themselves further from families and from their traditional clientele.

3. Promoting the notion in the dental literature that dentistry is a "hazardous profession" (Hermanson, 1972); not simply one with stress, tension and anxiety (Howard et al, 1976).

4. The presence of a number of physical health problems, noted as follows: Hearing loss, Von Krammer (1968); Herpes simplex virus in dentists' fingers, Miller (1976); radiation hazards from x-ray exposure, Hicks (1967); dangers arising from trace anesthesias in the dentist's office, Jones & Greenfield (1977); the presence of bacterial infections, mercury poisoning, and related issues, Royd-house (1977); air pollution in dental offices, Miller & Micik (1978); tinnitis, Gullickson (1978); eye injuries, Colvin (1978); various anesthetic health hazards adversely affecting different organ systems, Cohen et al (1975); heart disease susceptibility, Editorial (1966); and more.

5. Noting the presence of psychological health problems includes the following: Acute anxiety, "Letters to the Editor," (1979); stress and dentistry, Selye (1968); Cassell (1977); the need for stress management awareness and training, Jackson & Mealiea (1977); the recognition of suicide, alcoholism and divorce problems among dentists, Shankle (1977); problems with personal satisfaction in dental practice, Klein (1978); and many more.

Considering the relative narrowness of dental
practice compared to medical practice, dentists evidence
a considerable range of problems, but their intensity
and chronicity may not approach that presented by the
medical profession. Dentists appear to recognize some
of their problems more readily than do physicians, but
this observation may simply reflect certain attitudes
extant in the published literature of the two professions, not the real life practices of members of each
profession. Dentists do not have as much to live up to
as do physicians in terms of public stereotypes, being
"the chosen profession" and other similar notions that
are highly vulnerable to discreditation. Dentists
also appear to accept the need for help more readily
than do physicians, but data on such trends are not
highly reliable, and no one in either profession has
apparently sought information on various treatment and
preventive programs for their respective professional
membership. This last fact, alone, is a strange one,
in view of the central position of both medicine and
dentistry in the healing professions; but the facts are
that both professions are more poised to represent themselves as being necessary to the health of others, and
at the same time systematically leaving self-examination
in any explicit sense out of the picture. The point
here, again, is one raised many times in this volume,
viz., that the professions are more bent on their own,
selfish causes, on preserving public stereotypes and
images, and on maintaining economic advantages, than on
carrying out their supposed missions to the public.
Illich et al (1977) call the health professions and
some other professions (law and teaching, for example)
"disabling professions," and state in this connection:
"There is a growing awareness that during the past
twenty years or so, the professions have gained a suprem
ascendency over our social aspirations and behavior by
tightly organizing and institutionalizing themselves.
At the same time we have become a virtually passive
clientele; dependent, cajoled and harrassed, economicall
deprived and physically and mentally damaged by the
very agents whose raison d'etre it is to help" (Illich
et al, 1977, p. 9). The observations of Illich and his
co-authors hit well enough at the professions as profes
sions--and this is an important matter, dealt with
extensively in this book--but the erosive effect of suc
a unilateral and self-serving stance on the part of
professionals--dentists, physicians and others, alike--
is that they are injuring themselves in this process
and it may take this kind of erosion of confidence,
health and viability to awaken the professions to their

124

plight; moreso than simply point out to them how they, as professions, are influencing society and misserving public need (although the latter is certainly true and well-documented throughout this book). We will see in the following chapters, especially the one on nurses and on allied health professionals, how the professional position, as a profession, on the part of medicine and dentistry influence other related professions and contribute to their stress, tension and anxiety.

CHAPTER IV

BIBLIOGRAPHY

Adams, C.V. The dental profession. Where it is
    going and where it is now, J.Dent. Educ., 1976,
    40, 263-264.

Artz, A.H. Letter: Cause of malpractice suits, J.
    Amer. Dent. Assn., 1976, 92, 856.

Austin, G.B., Maher, M.M., and LoMorraco, C.J. Women
    in dentistry and medicine: attitudinal survey of
    educational experience, J. Dent. Educ., 1973, 37,
    11-17.

Bailey, E. The department store dentist, Forbes, 1979,
    March 19, p. 112.

Canfield, R.C., Powell, G.L., and Weinstein, P.
    Facilitating the transition to dental school,
    J. Dent. Educ., 1976, 40, 269-271.

Cassell, D. The stress factor, CAL, 1977, 41, 6-9.

Cohen, E.N., Brown, B.W., Jr., Bruce, D.L., Cascorbi,
    H.F., Corbett, T.H., Jones, T.W., and Twitcher,C.E.
    A survey of anesthetic health hazards among den-
    tists, J. Amer. Dent. Assn., 1975, 90, 1291-1296.

Collett, H.A. Dental malpractice: An enormous and
    growing problem, J. Prosthetic Dent., 1978, 39,
    217-225.

Colvin, J. Eye injuries and the dentist, Aust. Dent.J.
    1978, 23, 453-456.

Consumer Reports. How to judge a dentist, July, 1975,
    pp. 442-448.

Cutright, D.E., Carpenter, W.A., Tsaknis, P.B., and
    Lyon, T.C. Survey of blood pressure of 856
    dentists, J. Amer. Dent. Assn., 1977, 94, 918-919.

Dimarco, N. and Perlmutter, K. Impact of class enviror
    ment on Machiavellianism and Leadership, Inter-
    personal need and Lifestyle Orientations, J. Dent.
    Educ., 1976, 40, 340-343.

Dunlap, J.E. Surviving in Dentistry: The Sources of

Stress. Tulsa, Okla.: Dental Economics/PPC Books, 1977.

Editorial. Heart disease and the dentist, Tic, 1966, 25, 7-10.

Feldman, R.E. and Schiff, E.R. Hepatitis in dental professionals, J. Amer. Med. Assn., 1975, 232, 1228-1230.

Friedman, J. W. A Guide for the Evaluation of Dental Care. Los Angeles: U. of Calif., 1972.

Gamer, S. Recent legal decisions and their effects on dentists, J. Prosthetic Dent., 1978, 39, 106-107.

Glenwright, H. D. Serum hepatitis in dental surgeons, Brit. Dent. J., 1974, 136, 409-413.

Goldberg, J.J., Cafferata, G.L., Roughmann, K., and Fox, R. Survey of dentists' opinions on issues facing the profession, J. Amer. Dent. Assn., 1976, 93, 348-354.

Gullikson, J.S. Tinnitus and the dentist, J. Oreg. Dent. Assn., 1978, 47, 8-9.

Heist, P. Personality characteristics of dental students, Educ. Rec., 1960, 41, 240-252.

Hicks, H.H. Hazards of radiation from X-ray exposure, J. Amer. Dent. Assn., 1967, 75, 1194-1195.

Howard, J.H., Cunningham, D.A., Rechnitzer, P.A., and Goode, R.C. Stress in the job and career of a dentist, J. Amer. Dent. Assn., 1976, 93, 630-636.

Hutton, J. G. Attitudes of dental students toward dental education and the profession, J. Dent. Educ., 1968, 32, 296-300.

Illich, I., Zola, I.K., McKnight, J., Caplan, J., and Shaiken, H. Disabling Professions. London: Boyars, 1977.

Isman, R. Appraising the performance of dentists, J. Pub. Health Dentistry, 1977, 37, 224-234.

Jackson, E., and Mealiea, W.L., Jr. Stress management and personal satisfaction in dental practice, Dent. Clin. North Amer., 1977, 21, 559-576.

Johnson, V.S. Dentistry as a profession, <u>J. Amer. Dent. Assn.</u>, 1976, <u>93</u>, 699-700.

Jones, T.W. and Witcher, C.E. A survey of anesthetic health hazards among dentists, <u>J. Amer. Dent. Assn.</u>, 1975, <u>90</u>, 1291-1296.

Jones, T.W. and Greenfield, W. Position paper of the ADA Ad Hoc Committee on trace anesthetics as a potential health hazard in dentistry, <u>J. Amer. Dent. Assn.</u>, 1977, <u>95</u>, 751-756.

Klein, A.J. Personal satisfaction for the dental practitioner, <u>Dent. Clin. North America</u>, 1978, <u>22</u>, 187-196.

Komensky, A.M. Dental profession liability prevention: Part one: Council on insurance, <u>J. Amer. Dent. Assn.</u>, 1978, <u>96</u>, 1054-1057

Letters to the Editor. Dentist's acute anxiety--and a call for help, <u>Dent. Survey</u>, 1969, <u>45</u>, 67-68.

Mann, R. and Perkins, G. The dental school applicant, <u>J. Dent. Educ.</u>, 1960, <u>24</u>, 16-21.

Martin, J.L. Dental peer review--a conceptual model, <u>New York State Dental Journal</u>, 1977, <u>43</u>, 76-79.

Milgram, R., Weinstein, P., Ratener, P., and Morrison, K. Dentists' self-evaluation relative to clinical performance, <u>J. Dent. Educ.</u>, 1978, <u>42</u>, 180-185.

Miller, J.B. Herpes simplex virus infection of the fingers of a dentist, <u>J. Dent. Child.</u>, 1976, <u>43</u>, 99-102.

Miller, R.L. and Micik, R.E. Air pollution and its control in the dental office, <u>Dent. Clin. North Amer.</u>, 1978, <u>22</u>, 453-476.

More, D.M. The dental student, <u>J. Amer. College of Dentistry</u>, 1961, <u>28</u>, 5-94.

More, D.M. The dental student approaching graduation-- 1962, <u>Amer. Col. Dent. J.</u>, 1962, <u>29</u>, 115-208.

Nicholos, N.K. Viral hepatitis among practicing dentists, <u>New Zealand Med. J.</u>, 1977, <u>85</u>, 413-416.

Rosen, A.C., Marcus, M., and Johnson, H. Changes in

role-perception by first-year dental students, J. Dent. Educ., 1977, 41, 507-510.

Rosenberg, J. L. Attitude changes in dental and medical students during professional education, J. Dent. Educ., 1965, 29, 399-408.

Rosenberg, H.M. and Thompson, N.L. Attitudes toward women dental students among male dental students and male dental faculty members, J. Dent. Educ., 1976, 40, 676-680.

Roydhouse, R.H. Occupational hazards for dental personnel: a review, Gen. Dent., 1977, 25, 53-58.

Selye, H. Stress and dentistry, Amer. Inst. Oral Biol., Annual Meeting, 1968, 25, 131-140.

Selye, H. Stress Without Distress. N.Y.: J. B. Lippincott, 1974.

Shankle, R.J. Suicide, divorce, and alcoholism among dentists, fact or myth? N.C. Dent. J., 1977, 60, 12-15.

Sherlock, G.J. and Morris, R.T. Becoming A Dentist. Springfield, Ill.: Charles C. Thomas, 1972.

Solomon, C. The hucksters of dentistry (letter), J. Amer. Dent. Assn., 1978, 96, 383.

Speir, M. The Professional Ranking Scale. Indianapolis, Inc.: Eli Liley, 1972.

Spearman, J. and Bader,M. Dentistry and hepatitis, J. Amer. Dent.,Assn., 1977, 94, 25.

Steinberg, D.N. Change in attitudes of dental students, J. Dent. Educ., 1973, 37, 36-41.

Symposium - Women in dentistry, Brit. Dent. J., 1975, 139, 153-156.

Tamisiea, P.E., McKercher, C., Mattson, A., Blankenau, J.J. and Trumm, A. Emphasis and quality of a dental education: A survey of graduates, J.Dent. Educ., 1977, 41, 575-577.

Vaisman, A.I. Working conditions in surgery and their effect on the health of anesthesiologists (See Cohen et al. 1975, p. 1291).

Vinton, J.C. A four-year longitudinal study of the
    impact on learning structure on dental student
    lifestyle values, J. Dent. Educ., 1978, 42, 251-
    256.

Virgilio, J.P. Occupational hazards of dentistry,
    Dental Student, 1971, 49, 77-78.

Von Drammer, R. High speed equipment and dentists'
    health, J. Prosthet. Dent., 1968, 19, 46-50.

Weil, R.G., Lyman, D.O., Jackson, R.J., and Bernstein,
    B. A hepatitis sero-survey of New York dentists,
    New York State Dent. J., 1977, 43, 587-590.

Whittemann, J.K. and Currier, G.F. Motives to enter
    the dental profession: students, practitioners,
    faculty, J. Dent. Educ., 1976, 40, 265-268.

CHAPTER V

NURSING

The nursing profession may come in for more stress --with fewer offsetting compensations--than any other health profession. Nurses have traditionally been subordinate to physicians and to the hoary tradition of medical practice. The fact that nurses have been beholden to physicians for jobs, for notice and appreciation, for salaries and for advancement,has kept them from seeing their own professional role in true perspective (Reich & Geller, 1976). More recently, and along with some power from the "woman's movement," nurses, being mostly women, have begun to rise up and ask for more professional status. Their struggle in this direction over the past decade or two has given direction and meaning to their many areas of stress, tension and anxiety (Powell, 1976).

The sources of stress in the nursing profession stem, as they do in medicine and dentistry, from both "outside" and "inside" the profession. Nurses have been self-conscious about their status for a long time, but have only recently begun to become constructively active in overcoming difficulties with the medical profession, with hospital administration, and with their own self-image (Hughes et al, 1958). Possibly the first far-reaching and thorough study of nurses came from the study of twenty thousand nurses by Hughes et al (1958). This study inquired into why nursing was chosen as a profession, the expectations entering nurses held, and changes in nursing attitudes as they matured into the profession and gained life experiences in the common settings in which nurses are employed.

Choosing Nursing

Most nurses chose nursing--so they said in retrospect--early in life. Many idealized nursing as children and appeared to have strong motivation to help others (Thompson, 1968). Some had considered no other profession, and those who did consider other professions had ranked teaching, other health professions and service professions fairly high on their list (Hughes et al, 1958). Nursing, then, has appeared to be a highly self-selected occupation based on motivation for service to others, on endurance of adversity, on subordinate roles,and on gaining satisfactions from

131

personal as contrasted with scientific, economic or prestige factors. Nurses have been ideally set up to be the "fall guys" in the medical and health professions; it is no wonder that they have suffered considerable stress and have absorbed many of the ills of the medical profession. Powell says that for too long nursing has turned its attention inward on its patients and its "good works," neglecting issues related to how the profession appears to society and to other, related professions (Powell, 1976). Remarking further on this subordinate role of nurses, Powell observes that nursing education has often been taken away from nurses themselves and given to physicians, hospital personnel and education administrators. Unfortunately until recently, nurses have allowed other professionals to dominate not only their job settings but their education and their organization as a profession.

As with medicine and dentistry, nurses upon entering professional training idealized their roles as helpers, typically leaving out references to skills, to tasks, and to scientific preparation. But as senior level nurses in training they had changed to a more realistic outlook: they saw the hard and menial work in nursing practice, the unfairnesses in medical and hospital administration, and the subordinate role in which nurses were often cast. "The outlook of senior students was task-centered; the outlook of freshmen humanitarian and personal" (Hughes et al, 1956, p. 54). Pursuant to the reporting of attitude changes over time among nurses, the Hughes et al study reported one investigation of attitude changes toward physicians, indicating that freshmen nurses typically (63 percent) replied "good" to the relationship with physicians and did not qualify this opinion, whereas senior nursing students qualified their answers more and only 44 percent felt the relationship with physicians to be "good."

How can a profession grow and develop its own integrity if its members are explicitly taught to be deferential? Hughes et al (1956, p. 63) discuss studies of nurses' attitudes toward physicians in hospital and in social situations. In one investigation of nearly 2,500 licensed nurses in Pennsylvania, 77 percent of them answered "Yes" to the query: "In hospital situations, should nurses rise when the doctor enters the room?" Fifty percent of these nurses concurred on separate dining facilities in hospitals, thereby separating them from physicians; and even 16 percent of the nurses felt they should rise in the

132

presence of the physician in _social_ situations! While these attitudes represent those extant in the late 1950's, some semblance of them still exist today. How detrimental to both the nursing and medical professions are such attitudes! No wonder both nurses and physicians experience ramifying changes in attitudes over time, attitude changes that are related to the stress they experience as professionals, and to the seemingly abnormal demands the profession, qua profession, places on them.

Nurses subdivide themselves at the professional level as do other professions. In addition to specialties such as surgical nursing, pediatric nursing, geriatric nursing, and so on, there are also variations in the ways in which nurses are oriented to their profession. Habenstein and Christ (1955) delineated several "types" of nurses extant in the 1950's, likely current today to an even greater extent: Those described as "professionalizers" (they emphasized knowledge, arenot idealistic, tend tobe rational, task oriented); "traditionalizers" (idealistic, following the orientation of Florence Nightingale, fit the stereotyped and venerated public notions of nursing); and "utilizers" (lack long-term goals, are oriented to the immediate task, lack dedication). Whether these orientations are equally productive professionally, whether they are schooled into nurses during training, or whether they represent more basic personality orientations (which might obtain irrespective of the particular profession these women enter such as school teaching, physical or occupational therapy) are all moot. The members of the nursing profession who are motivated to induce change in the profession toward greater independence, assertiveness, and who seek higher professional status, probably come from the "professionalizers" and not from those more acquiesing types (Reich and Geller, 1976; Carlson, 1976).

Self-Attitudes of Nurses

We have seen that traditionally nurses have been subordinate to physicians to a considerable extent (some would say to an astonishing and detrimental extent). This subordination, as one might expect, psychologically, has not fostered respect for nurses among physicians; in fact, it has bred the opposite attitude among physicians: one of down-rating the nurse. Hughes et al (1956) report that patients of nurses and the personal friends of nurses tend to rate nurses higher in esteem; compared to physicians who

133

rate nurses lower than do men-in-general (Hughes et al, 1956, p. 194), with younger physicians rating nurses lower than older physicians (above age 60). Physicians tend to think of the "hospital system" as requiring a hierarchy of authority, subordinant and superordinant roles in order to preserve order in the system, and tend to rate nurses in accordance with this conception. In crisis, especially in the operating room, the doctor's orders are law; the nurse must move quickly, efficiently and obediently. Attitudes developed in this setting then seem to generalize to all, or most, physician-nurse relationships; the hierarchy is maintained even in social settings to some extent--as we have seen, above--even though it is not in any way functionally related to medical or nursing care. Physicians criticize nurses mainly for giving medication and/or treatment not prescribed by the physician--less than for failing to give those measures which had been prescribed--and for assuming roles of independence which, even in the 1950's the physicians thought to be a recent development in the nursing profession. Maybe physician-nurse attitudes have not changed much qualitatively over the last several decades, but the move toward independence on the part of the nursing profession has kept pace with similar changes extant at large in society, especially among women and more particularly among women in professional roles.

Physicians also criticize nurses for emphasizing more wage and hour matters that concern them and neglecting thereby professional nursing care (physicians are not supported in this attitude, however, by patients who have been under the care of nurses); and wanting professional status and respect on the one hand but pursuing organized labor-type demands on the other hand (Hughes, et al, 1956, p. 197). More recent information however (Washington POST, December 3, 1978) indicates that governmental wage scales nationally for janitors and other blue collar workers affords them higher wages than are paid to nurses. The areas of wages, hours and professional status have been an issue with nurses for a number of years, and their surfacing now and again in nurse-physician relationship is not surprising.

The matter of patients' attitudes toward nurses and nursing care is the one area--if there is just one--which unites nurses, which sets them off from physician (and dentists) and gives them a feeling of prestige and reinforcement for their labors that has not been forthcoming from any other source. As far back as data have

134

been accumulated, patients have rated nurses high (Hughes et al, 1958, pp. 198-199). These authors report, after surveying several studies in different parts of the U.S., "More than 90 percent of the patients offered unqualified approval of nursing service" (Hughes et al, 1958, p. 198). They go on to report that unbearable criticism of hospital routine, visiting hours, hospital food, and so on were offered freely. These authors say, additionally, "Offered 10 statements about nurses and nursing, the patients disagreed with all the unfavorable statements and agreed with all the favorable; for example, 99 percent agreed that most nurses are respected" (Hughes, et al, 1958, p. 198). It is understandable that nurses have traditionally emphasized that part of their role that dealt with patients. Nurses have "looked inward" to improve their lot and to earn reinforcement for their efforts; they have turned away from the more tension-provoking stresses extant in the nursing profession and in relationship to their "bosses," the physicians. All of us need support for our efforts, some understanding of our position, be it about professional or personal matters; we go where the "goodies" are - and nurses have turned to their relationships with patients and the personal satisfactions they reap from care and caring.

Stress - External and Internal

Stress has continued to mount from outside the profession; and from inside by those nurses seeking better acclaim, more recognition in terms of material benefits, and more independence. The two sets of forces--from inside and outside--have combined in recent years to increase the stress on the profession, as a profession, and to increase tension on the individual nurse. The recognition of the latter has resulted in studies to increase the assertiveness of nurses vis-a-vis physicians and to challenge nurses to revise some of their old notions about themselves and their work (Carlson, 1976).

Carlson worked with recently graduated RNs (Registered Nurses) to help them assert their newly found roles of leadership and responsibility, by holding eight weekly sessions of 1.5 hours each on such behavioral objectives as rehearsal of role assignments, modeling, coaching, and the carrying out of homework assignments between sessions. Various tests of assertiveness and self-appraisal were used before and after training, and an audiotaped role-played

135

nurse-physician interaction was used. Carlson reports
that the nurses learned more assertive behaviors,
increased their self-esteem and their self-acceptance.
Personality characteristics of exhibition, autonomy,
and dominance increased significantly; irrational ideas
abasement and nurturance decreased. The Carlson type
of study works, of course, on individual nurses in
small groups, and in particular settings; such a study
does not address the matter of how the whole profession
of nursing appears to physicians, to hospital administrators, to nursing educators (especially those who
are not nurses), or to the public. But each small
effort, in however limited a way, that increases nurses
self-esteem and assertiveness, goes some of the distance
toward enhancing their roles and their effectiveness
as nurses, and demonstrates openly that significant
change is possible.

One of the essentials of nurses' improvement of
their plights vis-a-vis stress is to admit that they
have problems with their self-esteem and with some of
their professional relationships, especially with the
medical profession (Davis & Fricke, 1977). Reich and
Geller (1976) studied the self-images of nurses using
the Gough and Heilbrun Adjective Check List. On this
inventory nurses portrayed themselves as more assertive
and self-confident than the norm suggests, rejecting
also the image of themselves as timid and submissive.
Either some nurses are coming out of their coccoons
or they are putting up a front that assumes roles and
strengths which, in fact, they do not possess. Also,
differences in the findings of studies investigating
self-assurance and assertiveness speak to the ferment
in the profession--some nurses in some settings have
gone a long way toward improving their professional
lot; others are lagging behind and commiserating with
themselves over their subordinate roles.

Tawes, Corwin & Haas (1963) studied nurses' self-
concepts and satisfaction with their profession, sayin
that people identify themselves and are identified, by
their vocations. Their self-images (self-evaluation
and evaluation of the profession) was influenced by
dissatisfaction with salaries (25%), by poor advancement opportunities (22%), and by complaints regarding
the distribution of duties (17%) (p.7). Self-satisfaction and self-image are not ethereal or wispy
concepts, but spring from the daily duties people
engage in, and from how much these images conflict
with their idealized notions of professional and
humanitarian activities, and with fair and equitable

136

treatment.

Economics is usually a source of stress among professional groups, nursing being no exception. As far back as the Hughes et al study(1958), nurses were complaining about their salaries (25% so reported) and, together, hours/pay/job grievances made up 70 percent of their complaints in a group of 2,425 RNs (Hughes et al, 1958, p. 219). Younger nurses tended to complain more about salary than older, more experienced nurses. Pressure for more income is increased when nurses are obliged to spend more time than they deem productive in record keeping, and in dealing with student nurses and auxiliaries (Hughes et al, 1958, p. 219). These activities take nurses away from their care-taking roles and since these roles are the most reinforcing for nurses, other duties are seen as distractions which yield no compensations for them at the personal level; more income, then has been the only recourse they have.

Self-Esteem and Assertiveness

Despite changes in the growth of self-esteem and assertiveness among nurses, there is still much ferment within the profession. A number of studies and articles address this issue (Schoenmaker, 1978; Hott, 1976; Simpson and Green, 1975; Ziegler, 1977; Anderson,1978; Hopping, 1976; Shabecoff, 1979). Issues relating to broader base from which nursing applications are received, and a greater openness to male nurses are noted by Schoenmaker (1976). Hott (1976) points out that nurses as a profession are politically naive, that nursing has allowed itself to become a "woman's profession" and thereby has allowed itself to suffer the vicissitudes confronting women in society. Nurses have not settled the issues of where and how nursing education should be carried on: in hospitals or in institutions of higher learning, or both. Nurses are pressured on all sides as has been noted above--by medicine at the technical and patient-care levels, by hospital administrators at the administrative and professional qualifications level, and to some extent by patients who suffer neglect at the hands of the medical profession and/or the hospital administration. Although all nurses sit for the same qualifying exams, some arrive at this point through 2-year associate degree programs, some through a 3-year hospital school diploma, and some via a 4-year baccalaureate program. Even though male nurses are far from popular and not yet integral to the profession, they generally merit

137

higher salaries at all levels than do females (Hott, 1976, p.304). It is no wonder that nurses feel an isolation in their jobs and in the profession at large. In response to some of these problems within the profession of nursing, nurses are admonished to pay more attention to the "maleness" in their make-ups (this will help offset the tendency for them to practice "feminism" to the extent that they assume subordinate and inferior roles), to supporting one another, to attempt to control their fate more vigorously, and to emphasize leadership traits more fully and openly (Simpson and Green, 1975; Ziegler, 1977). These and other problem areas associated with the role of nursing in hospitals has gotten into the literature of novels and into the popular press (Anderson, 1979). Anderson's book cites the very caring and care-taking role so prominent in the nursing profession and allows that peoples' lives are saved by nurses, not physicians. What the patient in a hospital needs is a good nurse, just as a child in the school setting needs a good teacher who can function well and interestedly despite administrative problems and complications of educational philosophy and technology.

Nurses' striving for a place in the sun has led them to take on some of the tactics of trade unions (Hopping, 1976). Hopping deplores the movement toward trade unionism in the nursing profession which may appear necessary in order for nurses to secure their rights more ably vis-a-vis the medical profession and hospital administration. It is pointed out that nursing will lose its time-honored role as a caring profession and nurses risk being seen more as "hospital workers," comparable to "steel workers" or "auto workers," if these tactics do not abate. Hopping states that unions come about because individuals are (or feel) powerless; the union gains power through group cohesiveness and agreement on purposes, using this power to coerce others into the group's viewpoint. Professionals, on the other hand, Hopping avers, come together in order to enhance their professional status (their training, their expertise), in order to gain new knowledge and to respond to solving the unknown, to pool existing knowledge and information, and to improve services of a professional calibre. The apparent inimical nature of professional motivation vs trade union motivation is part of the dilemma of nursing. On the one hand, nurses are rendered less able, given less recognition, and not rewarded at a level comparable to their actual service, expertise and extant attitudes; yet on the other hand

138

they have available to themselves as a group the types
of cohesiveness characterized by trade unionism and
they are more and more prone to using these tactics
to gain the ends they feel are merited by virtue of
their professionalism. Ferment within nursing, then,
is as active as it is between nursing as a profession
and other medical professions.

Independence

Besides concentrating to some extent "inside"
the nursing profession to enhance self-esteem and
assertiveness vis-a-vis other professions, nurses are
also taking on the role of independent health care
professionals. They are assuming some of the roles
traditionally assigned to physicians (Shabecoff, 1979)
such as using the stethoscope, examining a child,
checking eyes/ears/motor reflexes, and even assuming
some of the psychologist's role by examining mental
ability, verbal skills and developmental status.
Nurses performing these wide-ranging roles are not
physicians, nor are they under the direct supervision
of physicians, although they may have physicians to whom
they refer in case of need. They are "nurse practitioners." They are registered nurses. Along with the
upsurge in feminism, they are assuming a greater role
in health care delivery and are setting up independent
practice. They are following the roles already laid
down by psychologists and social workers in freeing
themselves from physicians' supervision (and domination)
and, like the forerunners' examples from social work
and psychology, becoming more professional as they
become more independent. Nursing as a profession is
moving more toward autonomy in many ways, although
they are·not yet able to receive third-party payments
(Medicare/Medicaid/Blue Cross and other insurers) for
their services, a matter still strongly resisted by the
American Medical Association. It is interesting to
note that medicine as a profession becomes most articulate vis-a-vis nursing (and perhaps in relation to
other allied professions such as social work and
psychology) when economic issues are at stake and not
with other professional issues related to growth,
maturity and responsibility. The same stress that
characterizes medicine as a profession trickles down--
yes, even rushes down--to other professions, causing
them the same stress and anxiety at the individual
level that physicians experience as individuals. The
physicians are weakening (and losing?) their case,
however, for as they relinquish interest in the poor,
in family care, in the populace in the inner city,

these slacks are taken up by the nurse practitioner, by
the social worker and psychologist; the medical professions' dominance of health care may be weakened by their
desire to control the more lucrative aspects of health
care at the same time they give up on those matters of
care less economically inviting to them. Shabecoff
(1979) points out, for example, that Memphis' indigent
population of about 200,000 receives its health care
from public health nurses through a system of clinics,
with city hospital backup when needed. Further, nurses
are caring more and more for pregnant women, from conception through delivery, the number of such patients
having doubled in the last decade nationwide. The
medical profession acts as if it were a feudal lord,
dominating what it wants and throwing the crumbs of
discarded practice and uninteresting (to them) clientele
to other professions in the health area. Not only are
the other health professions rebelling at this kind of
unilateral treatment, the public is becoming increasingly aware of medicines' unilateral stance, accelerating costs, and often too shoddy treatment.

Mental Health Problems

It is a short step from the ills of the nursing
profession, as a profession, to the problems of individual nurses, including mental health, physical health
and attitudinal issues. Ellis (1977) observes that the
organization of nursing care in hospital settings
contributes materially to many of the ills presently
felt by the nursing profession, and by individual nurses
Hospital organization brings about stresses on nursing
roles, on matters of responsibility for patient care,
and often promotes conflict between physicians and
nurses. The nurses are the "work horses" of the
hospital; they know this and are increasingly resentful
of their plight.

Nurses evidence the same kinds of professional
pressures as physicians but for some reason do not have
as high rate of some diseases as physicians. For
example, Balinger et al (1978) found that the exposure
and disease frequencies for nurses are about equal to
frequencies found in the general population, ages
30-55. There has been more self-consciousness among
nurses attempting to control their health problems. In
a survey of over 238,000 nurses (122,000 returned
questionnaires), prior to 1978, the percentage of
female nurses using oral contraception declined from
43.0 percent to 5.5 percent; the number smoking decline
from 34 percent to about 24 percent; and the number

using hair dyes declined by 50 percent (Ballinger, et al 1978). Nurses have apparently been more successful in stopping smoking than physicians (Burgess, 1978); which may, in turn, be related to less stress among nurses, or may relate to more nurses being female and thereby perhaps less under the pressure of prestige motivations often associated with smoking. Nurses, along with physicians, evidence narcotic addiction problems, especially in the use of Demerol; however, the extent of Demerol usage among nurses is not known (Garb, 1965).

Nurses do a lot of hard work. They carry and move about heavy equipment, have to physically move obese patients who lie inert in bed, are on their feet long hours, and rush from one critical service to another throughout the day and night. Back pains and injuries are an occupational hazard of nurses (Cust et al, 1972; Cust, 1976). Most back injuries sustained by nurses occur on duty; sometimes back pain arises from sudden, unknown onset. Perhaps nurses learn to adjust to the physical requirements of their profession, since back injuries are most common in the 21-25 year old group and tend to occur less frequently with later age (Hershey, 1967).

The incidence of cancer among working in anaesthetists' role is noted (Corbet et al, 1973). Nurses, then, suffer exposure to many hazards--both subtle and obvious--and this constant vulnerability to disease and injury combines with job dissatisfaction to produce great stress (Anderson, 1979; Gunderson et al, 1977; Winsted-Fry, 1977; Blinderman, 1977).

Nurses meet crises as do their patients (Davis et al, 1975). Davis thinks that nurses are more prone to crisis situations than is necessary, and that the education of nurses overlooks the often-crisis nature of their work. Nurses are known to make strong demands on themselves for conscientious work, striving for achievement, setting high goals and, through the occasional failure of these motivations, are subject to personal disorganization and emotional crises. They are similar to physicians in these respects but seem not to present equal vulnerability to tension and anxiety.

Role Preparation

One consistent source of stress among nurses is that they are often poorly prepared for some of the roles they have to assume. While nurses may attempt to specialize in operating room nursing, in emergency room nursing, in general nursing, in special duty nursing, and so on, they often range widely in their first years over many specialities before deciding on where to concentrate. As a result of fluctuating demands on their skills, they are often found to have been poorly trained in handling certain kinds of problems such as alcoholism, drug abuse, drug addiction (Burkhalter, 1975) which lacks then submit them to undue pressures and anxieties. Burkhalter asserts that nurses receive too little information and instruction on drug dependence problems, that this puts extra stress on these nurses, and that preparation for roles dealing with drug dependence, being on the rise, will continue to make increasing demands on nurses. It appears to Burkhalter that training in psychiatric nursing is the only source of instruction in drug dependency problems for the fledging nurse; whereas such training should also obtain in pediatrics, in medical-surgical practice, in obstetrical-gynecological practice, and in the newborn nursery. We are to be reminded in this connection that nurses have recently complained that too little of their education is in their own hands and too much in the hands of physicians and hospital administrators and educators. Perhaps if nurses gained more control over their own destinies they would exercise good professional judgment and prepare for roles now fraught with stress and anxiety owing to faulty preparation (Koehne-Kaplan & Tilden, 1976; Kohnke, 1973).

One might surmise that the extent to which nurses deal with death and dying would place them in a particularly vulnerable position in this regard. Nurses are, of course, sensitive to death-related issues in life, particularly with their patients (Denton, 1977 Gow & Williams, 1977), but they appear not to be any more vulnerable to stress than are other health professions. The impact that death among patients under the charge of the nurse has on the nurse depends on a host of factors: The age of the nurse, experience with death, the nature of the patient's death (whether violent, unexpected or a matter of resignation), the frequency of experiences with death in the nurse's family, and the person (patient) seen die. It is an important part of nursing training, however, to train the student in the problems s/he will encounter in regard to death and dying. The fact that our society is today more accepting of the problems related to dea and dying than previously helps to enlarge the nurse's

142

grasp of the problem and to lessen the specific stresses encountered by the nurse.

Perhaps more stress on the nurse is found in ways other than from death and dying (Welch, 1975). Registered nurses in 111 hospitals in New York were studied in regard to the events in their practice that were particularly satisfying and/or stressful. The research looked at such experiences of nurses in terms of their physical status, their psychosocial status and relations in their families. Stressful and/or satisfying experiences were not particularly related to family or job characteristics. Most satisfactions came from improving (or improvements in) the patient's well-being and the patient's long-range potential for recovery. This finding corroborates the age-long observation that nurse's are strongly motivated to help patients and invest most of their energies in this direction. Consonant with the emphasis on the patient's well being as a derivative of nurse satisfaction, the most stress on the nurse came when the patient did not progress well.

It has been indicated that the organization of the hospital itself is, or can be, a source of stress for the nurse. Oberst (1973) observes that crises among nurses and other staff in hospital settings are on the increase. This author thinks that this crisis-prone condition is related to the bureaucratic structure of the hospital (continued frustration at not getting needs met, problems solved), to a lack of consensus about goals in relation to patient care, and to the conflict between salary on the one hand versus patient care, teaching and research on the other hand. Under these stressful conditions, nurses resort to calling in sick, refusing to work overtime when needed, arriving late for work and leaving early, shifting workload to peers and especially those less experienced, and appealing to peers for support. Some of the main stressors giving rise to these individual crises (stress in the larger organization giving rise to individual tensions and anxieties) are disapproval and criticism of physicians, having to deal with terminal patients, coping with increasing patient demands and criticism, dealing with faulty equipment, and poor supervision and supervisory support. Faced with these multiple and often intense problems, nurses do look outside their immediate situation for relief in terms of more independence as a profession, more influence on the organization of hospitals and more peer-like relationships with physicians. These latter "remedies" may, however, provoke additional tensions,not necessarily produce solutions. Physicians, as we have seen, tend to reply to the nursing profession's demand for more independence as a lack of "professional motivation" and regard independence as a "trade-union" type of action. The nurses are faced, then, with stress at the level of daily dependence on physicians for support and approval, but this role keeps them subordinate; more action and assertiveness on the nurses' parts entail risks of more disapproval from physicians but an increase in opportunity for professional growth, independence and future development.

Nurses say that stress is an interference with the functioning of the person in his/her daily activities and, further, tends to create a situation which one seeks to avoid (Dossett, 1978). Stress for nurses is particularly potent in intensive care (therapy) units, or in what the British call "high dependency areas," meaning nursing care where the patient is totally or near-totally dependent on nursing care. Work in intensive care units should be more carefully regarded by hospital administrators, physicians and nursing supervisors (Hay and Oken, 1975), in order to modulate the stress on nurses. Intensive care units are glamorized in movies and television and may appear dramatic and inviting to the viewer of such hospital scenes. But the routine nature of the intensive care unit, the repetitive checking for vital signs for each patient and the general monitoring--which may occur several times per hour per patient--add considerable stress to the nurse's daily routine. The intensive care unit spells conflict for the nurse--they are called on to save lives, yet many patients die. Intensive care nurses ban together in pride over their work and the unusual nature of their duties, yet they are ready to shift to other duty when possible; only the youthful nurses have the stamina (most are in their 20's, yet older nurses look back with pride on their period of intensive care service)(Hay and Oken, 1972).

Stress in the intensive care unit can be reduced if there is more cohesiveness among the nurses, sharing with each other their concerns; if special recognition is given nurses in such units (special patches, badges or uniforms to signify distinction); if there is interspersed a limited tour of duty with some time in other units with less pressure; if there are frequent brief vacations; and if there is good physician backup

administrative support, and close nusing supervision.
Too often nurses are drawn into intensive care units
out of an initial challenge that later turns out to be
far less appealing and far too pressureful.

Ellis (1977) gives a lot of consideration to the
plight of nursing practice and the problems of intensive care. Ellis points to a need for better
organization of nursing activities and services in the
hospital. Nurses are held down and held back from
professional progress due to the way hospitals are
organized, their economics and their hierarchy of
administrative power and control. It remains unfair
to nurses--and ultimately to the patients receiving
care--to put the physician at the top and the nurse at
the bottom of the hospital as an organization. Moreover, this hierarchical stratification leads to poor
self-images among nurses, a resentment against the
system that demeans them, and hostile feelings directed
against physicians. Recourse for the nursing profession would include: More varied roles for nurses in
hospital organization, better feedback on their
services from physicians and hospital administrators
(they already get good feedback from patients but
approval here does not improve their general plight as
professionals in the health delivery system), and
perhaps putting a "price tag" on their services by
billing the patient according to the needs met (as
physicians and hospitals already do).

Legal Aspects

The problem of nursing control over nursing
education has invited legal battles (Powell, 1976),
thereby increasing the stress in the profession and
the tension and anxiety among nurses. The outcome of
a suit in Texas discussed by Powell (1976, p. 343)
appears to be a case where decisions were made about
nursing education without nurses participating in the
decision, resulting in a "put down" of the nursing
profession. Powell further discusses the trials of
nursing education and the definition of nursing in
New York (Powell, 1976, pp. 343-344), such delibera-
tions resulting in some concurrence as to who and what
is a registered professional nurse, and updating an
early law (1938) to reflect the practices of nursing
as it is carried on today. When the venerated profession of nursing has so many problems with state legis-
latures, with licensing boards, with the profession of
medicine and with hospital administrators and educators,

it is time to look more closely at the health of professions and to ponder the conditions that give rise to so much professional confusion, back-biting and tension (Fagin, 1976; Jackson and Cumbie, 1976; Lewis, 1976; Kinlain, 1977; Beland, 1970; Claus & Barley, 1977).

When stress in a profession or in an organization reaches a given level, the effects ramify in a variety of directions. The more stress, the more spread of effect. The stress, as we have seen above, is experienced as tension in the lives of individual practitioners and anxiety states that are more or less permanent (or at least recurrent). Dealing with the stress takes one into several directions: Work on the profession itself here and now, especially in its relationships with other professions; and considerations of how the profession can be improved by better selection of its members, making education for the profession more efficient and less stress-ridden, and by better methods to usher fledging members of the profession into full practice. The nursing profession faces all of these problems, as do medicine, dentistry and other professions in the health field. We have already noted how the profession of nursing, as a profession, impacts and is impacted by medicine; we now turn to more consideration of how training and education in nursing might contribute to a better health status for nursing.

Training and Education

There is felt to be a need for better recruitment and better selection of candidates for nursing training (Sobol, 1978). We have already observed that nurses enter the field as freshmen with high expectations and idealistic notions of what nursing is about. Sobol calls for more early realism, more education of the nursing candidate about the realities of nursing as a profession. Coupled with less idealism and more reality on the part of nursing educators and recruiters is a need for more study of the personality characteristics of nursing candidates (Sobol, 1978, p. 243; Koehne-Kaplan & Tilden, 1976). More nursing candidates are looking for opportunities for self-actualization, for independence, and for self-direction Candidates with these motivations are focing forward new considerations for nursing educators; the nurse candidate is no longer being groomed for a subordinate, highly "feminine" role as a lackey or underling (Lewis, 1976). Since the number of nursing candidates is increasing, this gives schools of nursing more choice in whom to select and with this greater choice range, more responsibility for making open and wise choices of candidates. Those who sit at the gateway to nursing school can let in the more independent, assertive and self-directed candidates and thereby change to some extent over time the characteristics of the profession. These types of candidates full-fledged in nursing expertise would, in five to ten years, challenge even more the previous roles of nurses, especially as they have been subordinate roles. Or the gatekeepers could maintain a traditional set of criteria and select only those candidates who were less assertive and less self-directed, hoping that as mature professional practitioners they would "rock the boat" less and fit in more readily and harmoniously with existing medical, hospital, and allied health professional practices. The latter is not likely to happen, however, and Sobol and others are opting for the more assertive and self-directing types of candidates. These kinds of nursing candidates, once selected, would put pressures on nursing schools to rely less on lecture methods and more on audiovisual laboratories that would nurture self-directed and independent learning. Emphasized, too, would be student-led as well as instructor-led groups focusing on solving nursing problems. There would be an accent on the cultivation of assertiveness and self-awareness groups as part of personality development of student nurses and as a way to cultivate the development of attitudes that later make the nursing profession a more viable and independent profession (de Tornyay, 1977; Kramer, 1969; Meleis and Farrell, 1974; Williamson, 1972; Wilson, 1974). In these respects--i.e., the general development of independence and assertiveness among nurses--the nursing profession is changing remarkably. These changes may bode well for the future of nursing but they will churn up a number of problems at the professional level as well as at the individual level for some time to come. Fledging nurses have to be prepared for the change and for the stress, tension and anxiety brought on as a result.

Male Nurses

Male nurses have begun to appear on the employment scene in increasing numbers of late (Garvin, 1976; Bush, 1976). While the backgrounds of male vs female nurses may differ slightly--male nurses are somewhat older, more likely to be married, and evidence on tests more theoretical and less religious values--they

147

tend to be very similar on tests of vocational interest and on personality characteristics (Garvin, 1976). Both male and female nurses have strong social values and interests and appear to be similar insofar as they value patient care. Male nurses may interject a stronger theme supporting professional nursing due to the sheer fact they are male, thereby shoring up the professional image among physicians and hospital administrators. That's on the positive side--the side that seeks to foster greater independence in the nursing profession--but on the less positive side a movement toward male domination of the nursing profession could spell invidious sex comparisons and an appropriation of power by male members of the profession. Only time will tell which way the trend will develop or how strong an influence males will ultimately exert within the nursing profession, and at the juncture points between nursing and other professions.

In summary it is to be noted that the nursing profession is moving toward greater independence. While this professional movement may be considered a mixed blessing by some, most nurses feel they have been too long endentured to medicine and are looking to a variety of ways in which they can be independent and self-determining. The traditional status of the nursing profession has had a negative influence on nursing and this condition has indirectly and unwillingly contributed to poorer service to patients and to the fostering of a unilateral position by the medical profession. Some authors have observed, in commenting on nursing and their relationship to other professions as follows: "For the physician, personal distress and career satisfaction may be independent dimensions... this is probably not the case in nursing, and to a lesser extent, pharmacy, where more job dissatisfaction exists, particularly in hospital settings. In these professions unmet needs for recognition and self-esteem and a greater disparity between career expectations and the reality of work are cited as causes of considerable dissatisfaction...(Stone et al, 1979, p. 421). Attempting to change the status quo of nurses has led, as one might expect, to inner turmoil within the body of the nursing profession, and also in the posture nursing has taken vis-a-vis other professions. How the nursing profession handles these multifarious problems in the upcoming decades will have a lot to do with nursing as a profession and with the delivery of health services on a deep and increasingly broad scale Nursing may become the nexus between the health professions and the public. People entering the profession of nursing should realize that there is great ferment within the profession and a clear struggle to move forward in its relationship to medicine and to the public. The health of the nursing profession will depend upon how well the members handle these stresses over the next decades. The tensions on the nurses, and anxieties connected with change and ferment will doubtlessly increase; fledging nurses will experience more of these conditions than in the past and more than likely will be experienced by the seasoned nurse.

CHAPTER V

BIBLIOGRAPHY

Anderson, P. Nurse. N.Y.: St. Martin's Press, 1978.

Balinger, C.F., Rosner, B., and Speizer, F.E. The
nurses' health study, Amer. J. Nurs., 1978, 78,
1039-1040.

Beland, I.L. (Ed.) Clinical Nursing: Pathophysio-
logical & Psychosocial Approaches. N.Y.: Macmillan,
1970.

Blinderman, A. In praise of my nurse, Amer. J. Nurs.,
1977, 77, 1463-1465.

Burgess, A.M. Cigarette smoking by Rhode Island
physicians, 1963-1973; comparisons with lawyers
and other adult males, Amer. J. Public Health,
1978, 68, 63-65.

Burkhalter, P. Alcohol, drug abuse, and drug
addiction: A study of nursing education. J. Nurs.
Educ., 1975, 14, 30-35.

Bush, P.J. The male nurse: A challenge to traditional
role identities, Nurs. Forum, 1976, 15, 390-405.

Carlson, B.C. The effects of an assertion training
group on the assertiveness and the self-concept
of student nurses, Ph.D. Dissertation. Ann
Arbor, Mich., Univ. of Michigan M-Films, No. 76-
19749, 1976.

Claus, K.E. and Bailey, J.T. Power & Influence In
Health Care: A New Approach To Leadership.
St. Louis: C.V. Mosby, 1977.

Corbet, T.H., Cornell, R.G., Lieding, K. and Endres,
J.L. Incidence of cancer among Michigan nurse-
anesthetists, Anesthesiology, 1973, 38, 260-263.

Cust, G., Pearson, J.C., and Mair, A. The prevalence
of low back pain in nurses, Intern. Nursing
Review, 1972, 19, 169-179.

Cust, G. Low back pain in nurses, Queens Nurs. J.,
1976, 19, 6-8.

Davis, C.R., and Fricke, N. Crises in nursing students
Nurs. Forum, 1977, 16, 56-70.

Davis, M.A., Kramer, M., and Strauss, A.L. Nurses in
Practice: A Perspective on Work Environments.
St. Louis: C.V. Mosby Co., 1975.

Denton, J. A. Death experience and death anxiety
among nurses and nursing students, J. Nurs. Res.,
1977, 26, 61-64.

de Tornyay, R. Changing student relationships, roles,
and responsibilities, Nursing Outlook, 1977, 25,
188-193.

Dossett, M. Stress 1: Nursing staff in high dependency areas, Nurs. Times, 1978, 74, 888-889.

Ellis, B. Nursing profession undergoes intensive
scrutiny and adjustment, Hospitals, 1977, 51,
139-140.

Fagin, C. Can we bring order out of the chaos of
nursing education, Amer. J. Nurs., 1976, 76,
98-101

Garb, S. Narcotic addiction in nurses and doctors,
Nursing Outlook, 1965, 13, 30-35.

Garvin, B.J. Values of male nursing students, Nurs.
Res., 1976, 25, 352-357.

Gow, C.M., and Williams, J.I. Nurses' attitudes toward
death and dying: A causal interpretation, Soc.
Science & Medicine, 1977, 11, 191-198.

Gaunderson, K., Percy, S., Canedy, B.H., and Pisani,S.
How to control professional frustration, Amer. J.
Nursing, 1977, 77, 1180-1183.

Habenstein, R.W. and Christ, E.A. Professionalizer,
Traditionalizer and Utilizer. Columbia, Mo.:
U. of Missouri Press, 1955.

May, D. and Oken, D. The psychological stresses of
intensive care unit nursing, Psychosom. Med.,
1972, 34, 109-118.

Hershey, N. When the nurse is injured, Amer. J.
Nursing, 1967, 67, 1458-1460.

Hopping, B. Professionalism and unionism: Conflicting ideologies, Nurs. Forum, 1976, 15, 372-383.

Hott, J. R. The struggles inside nursing's body politic, Nurs. Forum, 1976, 15, 325-340.

Hughes, E.C., Hughes, H.Mac G., & Beutcher, I. Twenty Thousand Nurses Tell Their Story. Philadelphia: J.B. Lippincott, 1958.

Jackson, B.S. & Cumbie, C. Getting nursing education and service together, Supervisor Nurse, 1976, 7, 25-33.

Koehne-Kaplan, N.S. & Tilden, V.P. The process of clinical judgement in nursing practice: the component of personality, Nursing Res., 1976, 25, 268-272.

Kramer, M. Collegiate graduate nurses in medical center hospitals: Mutual challenge or dual, Nursing Res., 1969, 18, 196-210.

Lewis. F.M. Nurse as lackey: a sociological perspective, Supervisor Nurse, 1976, 7, 24-29.

Meleis, A.I. & Farrell, K.M. Operation concern: A study of senior nursing students in three nursing programs, Nursing Res., 1974, 23, 461-468.

Oberst, M.T. The crisis-prone staff nurse, Amer. J. Nurs., 1973, 73, 1917-1921.

Powell, D.J. The struggles outside nursing's body politic, Nurs. Forum, 1976, 15, 341-362.

Reich, S. & Geller, A. Self-image of nurses, Psychol. Reports, 1976, 39, 401-402.

Schoenmaker, A. Nursing's dilemma: Male vs. female nursing admissions choice, Nurs. Forum, 1976, 15, 406-412.

CHAPTER VI

ALLIED HEALTH PROFESSIONS

An important part of the health industry as it is
cometimes called is the work of allied health professionals. These include pharmacists, social workers,
physician's assistants, various technicians, all those
other than physicians, dentists, and nurses, who are in
some way an expert and necessary in the delivery of
health services to the public.

The entire health field has grown enormously since
World War II, and more particularly in the last decade
or so. According to Fein (1976), up to about 13 percent
of all new jobs in the United States between the 1960-
1970 decade came from the health field. This area of
expertise has grown so rapidly standards of preparation
and licensing have probably not kept pace with public
demand for services. In the clamor to provide allied
health professionals and practitioners, there may have
been feeble efforts to see that these workers were well-
screened, well-prepared and somewhat exemplary in their
health practices and knowledge. Getting into the
particulars of the health of allied health professionals
we do come upon some lacks, some similar to those found
among physicians, dentists and nurses. It appears
strongly that the same problems that plague the major
health professions also disaffect the allied practitioners. This may be due to the fact that allied
practitioners, too, need to have good relationships
with their clients or patients, need to be stable
persons themselves, and are required to possess adequate
technical knowledge and competence. In their eyes they
need to be competent to face the public well and to
relate to fellow professionals, especially to physicians,
dentists and nurses, under whose scrutiny they usually
come. Also the allied health professional has to
satisfy the consumer, since the consumer often judges
the adequacy of his/her care by the way the provider
behaves rather than on the basis of some expertise that
shines through (Doyle & Ware, 1977; Stone, Cohen &
Adler, 1979; Rutter, 1980; Melhuish, 1980).

The work of the health professional is very
demanding and constantly up for criticism. When there
is considerable pressure (stress) from work, work may
kill (Berman, 1977). Berman's study suggests that the
conditions under which many work, particularly in the
health area, may be adverse. This refers to the

physical environment, to the interpersonal environment that produces stress, to the hierarchial structure of the occupation or profession for which people are trained and in which they spend a considerable amount of time, and the equally hierarchial structure of the setting in which people work (hospitals, clinics, etc.)

Organizations, professions and occupations are formed and function to get jobs done, not in most instances to provide a healthful climate for work. Over time, occupations and professions have been structured to meet a limited set of demands--productive work, enough pay to employees to live satisfactorily, some considerations for safety on the job, and other matters --all pretty recent and usually hard-won gains. But little has been done to actively study professions and occupations; and to alter them so that they are not psychologically damaging to the practitioners. The considerable problems of the health professional in the form of reported statistics on their need for psychological referral, admission and help testify to the fact that there is an inordinate amount of stress on these professionals.

Stress and Mental Health

Colligan et al (1977) studied nearly 4,000 workers in thirty fields of endeavor, including allied medical fields and found that health technicians were more often referred to or admitted to a mental health facility than were other occupations on the list, and more often than people in general. Following the highly frequent referral of the health technician, others frequently referred for mental health reasons were practical nurses (third in frequency), clinical laboratory technicians (seventh in frequency), nurses' aides (in tenth place in occurrence), and dental assistants (twelfth in frequency). Thus among the first twelve occupations in frequency of referral or admission to a mental health facility, five were medically allied health occupations. The contribution of the medical setting to the stress underlying these referrals is more than noticeable, it is appalling. One could argue that people entering the allied health fields are somehow flawed in regard to mental health problems, but this is hardly tenable. In each of these five allied health fields the members' referral and/or admission came far more frequently than comparison to people in general would predict. In the Colligan et al study, women were represented in the

mental health admissions or referrals less than .8 the
expected number. These authors assert "...it is felt
that the...study provides a rational basis of identifying specific occupations warranting intensive study
regarding job stress and mental health" (Colligan et al,
1977, p. 39). While all occupations and professions
that are apparently stress-prone need study and correction, the fact that five of the first dozen come from
allied health fields bodes poorly for them in this
respect. These authors add, "The disproportionate
number of female workers, especially those in the
health-related occupations, seeking treatment in the
community mental health centers warrants further study.
This finding may reflect the operation of traditional
sex roles..." (p.39). The fact that such a goodly
number of health practitioners are the subjects for
referral for mental health services suggests that they
may not be able to meet the public well and thus not
serve their function. It also suggests that hospitals,
clinics and other medically related facilities should
develop stress-reduction programs on their own premises,
such that the facility itself would improve in its
mental health stance vis-a-vis the practitioners and
absorb some of the tension that goes with being a
practitioner in a health field. We have already seen
in the chapter on nurses how their roles and maturing
professional stance are conflicting with traditional
medical notions of how nurses ought to function; it is
possible that similar conflicts are being generated
between the various allied health practitioners and
physicians (and insitutions that reflect the way
physicians want them to run).

Results from this study of allied health professionals suggests findings regarding the amount of
stress associated with general practitioners versus
specialists among physicians, dentists, lawyers, and
security analysts and traders (Russek, 1965). Russek
says that most of the lethalness associated with high
fat diets may actually pivot more on stressful living
and the proneness to coronary disease caused thereby.
Among medicine, dentistry, law and securities, the
least stress was associated with specialties such as
dermatology, periodential, patent law and analysts in
the securities field, whereas general practitioners in
all fields were said to suffer more stress. The allied
health practitioners are more akin to general practitioners than they are to specialists in their daily
routines, hence may suffer more stress as a result.
Mechanic's report (1977) suggests that medical techno-
logy--which would include the areas of employment for

most allied medical health practitioners--results in
bureaucracy and has negative implication for medical
care.

Pharmacists

Among allied health professional workers, pharmacists come into consideration. Research reports tend
to indicate they gain less individual recognition than
they feel they need, especially in hospital settings
(Johnson, et al, 1977) and that career expectations
and eventual reality of work are disparate conditions
that trouble pharmacists. It will be remembered that
nurses, physicians and dentists all tend to begin
training with high aspirations and that as they mature
into the professions other goals and values begin to
be more important. Pharmacists do not have as many
degrees of freedom to influence their vocational
destinies as do physicians and dentists, and their
earnings are considerably less on the average, hence
they do not have the recourse leading to alternative
satisfactions in their work compared to physicians and
dentists. Knapp & Knapp (1968) discuss disillusionment
in pharmacists and pharmacy students; as do Knapp, et
al (1969), and note that as pharmacists engage in more
clinical work and utilize their expertise, they enjoy
their work more and reveal more job satifaction. Also,
as they engage in clinical work they are using their
training largely outside the medical bureauracy, hence
they satisfy their own professional needs and are less
beholden to the medical hierarchy.

Pharmacists have a higher suicide rate than any
other allied health professionals (Powell, 1972), and
only chemists appear to have an over-all higher suicide
rate than pharmacists. Perhaps the availability of
drugs is a contributing factor in the suicides of both
pharmacists and chemists. The use of drugs in one form
or another, to the point of addiction, is found among
all professional groups that prescribe or make drugs:
physicians, dentists, pharmacists, nurses, chemists
(Sherlock, 1967). Sometimes addiction comes on gradually, arising out of experimentation with drugs but
when tensions increase and persist, the easy access to
drugs among these professional groups invites continuec
use, occasionally leading to strong addiction. More
characteristic of pronounced use appears to be associated with professional role strain and role deprivatio
(Sherlock, 1967, pp. 195-197). In contrast to the
allied health professions other, non-medical helping
professions--school teachers, clergy and social worker

--tend to have relatively low drug usage rates. There must be some factors as yet unclearly identified in relation to medical practice (broadly conceived), stress, the availability of drugs, and the assumption of an independent role that eschews help with personal problems, that contribute to the high incidence of drug use among medical and allied medical workers.

Although reputed by some to be a profession with high anxiety manifestations, the literature on anxiety in relation to the practice of pharmacy appears inconclusive. We have seen that pharmacists do experience considerable stress in their work, feeling they lack professional acceptance, not being allowed to make decisions appropriate to their level of training, being beholden to physicians, and other complaints. The attrition rate from pharmacy practice appears to be moderate--about 10 percent--compared to (say) nursing which can run as high as 40 percent (Thurlow, 1974). In addition, the "turn-over" rate among pharmacists has been reported to be high (Powell, 1972). Along with similar characteristics among other medical and health related practitioners, suicide rates have been substantial among pharmacists (Rose & Rosow, 1973; Murray, 1974). It seems reasonable that the presence of anxiety in such a stressful profession as pharmacy would be noticeable. In a study by Curtiss and Johnson (1977) based on the responses of 741 individuals (out of a solicitation group of 1,115 graduates of eight widely selected colleges of pharmacy) to a mailed questionnaire (the Spielberger State-Trait Anxiety Inventory), the anxiety ratings of these young pharmacists was not appreciably high. Scoring higher were both male and female undergraduate freshmen students, male school teachers,and general medical patients (especially depressives) (Curtiss & Johnson, 1977, p. 159). Several reasons may explain these results: First, the young pharmacy graduates may have wanted to project a good, solid, non-disturbed image of themselves; second, they may have been in the practice too short a time to accumulate the stress cited above in connection with turn-over, drop-outs from the profession, or suicide; and third, they may have not reported thoughtfully or thoroughly on themselves via a questionnaire. Mass solicitations of these sorts, based on hundreds of replies, may be fair screening or trend-suggesting devices, but as to the actual state of affairs in regard to personality characteristics, anxiety, and the like, may leave much to be desired.

159

Psychologists are allied health practitioners only
in some settings. Usually psychologists are found in
university settings, perhaps next often in mental health
settings and counseling centers, many of which are not
medically run. The clinical psychologist is more
likely than any other type of psychologist to work in a
medical setting (hospital, community mental health
clinics, in teaching and research settings in hospitals
and medical schools). Their roles as allied health
personnel are not as likely to reflect states of stress
as much as those professions more subordinate to medicine. However, female psychologists are more often
suicide victims than women in general, and they approach
the rate of suicide found among female physicians
(Mausner & Steppacher, 1973). It may be that the
greater nurturing role of females, especially as
deliverers of health services, leads them into more and
more stress, sometimes resulting in suicide. Coupled
with this tendency is the fact that women psychologists
and women physicians play heavily dual roles with
family and career sometimes splitting them, their
loyalties and allegences. Perhaps women psychologists,
too, along with physicians and dentists hold to an
ambitious, striving,materialistic set of goals which
puts them under more stress, unlike the clergy who
view the work in less materialistic/competitive/striving
terms (Cartwright, 1979, p. 426). (See Chapter X for
more detail) Interesting, too, but not often emphasized
in the study of professional stress is the clergy's
belief in a superior being, one to whom they defer, so
to speak; physicians, are known to eschew personal help
for emotional, addiction, drinking and other personal
problems, arising out of their unilateral stand
regarding being "helpers" and their long-standing
perfectionism. Perhaps allied health workers assimilat
some of the standard medical attitude and accept stress
take risks, and fail to get help soon enough, all
contributing in time to the greater need for help as
shown in the study by Berman (1977) and by Colligan, et
al (1977).

Drop-Outs

One of the major professional concerns among
workers in health and service fields is the rate of
drop out from the profession. This is sometimes known
as "burn-out" since the person experiencing a loss of
motivation, caring and ability to use formerly acquire
skills seems to reach impasses in daily work and often
in sudden and overwhelming ways (Freudenberger, 1975;
Garte & Rosenblum, 1978; Maslach, 1976; Maslach &

Pines, 1977, 1978; Shelton & Warnath, 1976). These students of burn-out have detected its presence among medical workers, among allied health professionals, and among other mental health workers such as counselors, rehabilitation counselors, social workers, and even in such settings as prison guards. Wherever there is continued vigilance of the health worker for the receiver of the help (counselee, client, patient, inmate, etc.), there is a risk toward the helper going into a burn-out phase.

Burn-out arises from a variety of causes. One is the early high expectation that the counselor or health worker will always relish the helping role and she/he cannot wait to get out of graduate school in order to become a full-fledged practitioner. This is called the discrepancy between graduate school idealism and on-the-job reality (Shelton & Warnath, 1976) and has been observed among nurses, physicians, dentists, and other professionals. Sometimes the professional health worker fails to see in his/her own behavior the kinds of stress reported by the client or patient, and thus goes on and on, offering service to a myriad of people refusing to stop until an impasse has been reached (Maslach, 1976; Maslach & Pines, 1977, 1978).

As burn-out takes over, the professional worker tends to distance himself from the client or patient; this is harmful to both the client and the worker, and remedies should be instituted as soon as the distancing is noticed. One ameliorative measure is to have professional health workers find more time to talk with each other about their respective cases and the problems they present. Sometimes changing therapist or counselor might help, with the permission of the client. More frequent breaks in the day's routine, short vacation periods, and change in the type of client served, may all be helpful antidotes to the build-up of stress that leads to burn-out. Above all, the health worker should know that she/he is limited in the capacity to give service and should avoid setting too many appointments, receiving calls at home (except in dire emergency), and should try to accumulate a variety of patients/clients so that there is not a build-up of seriously disturbed or demanding patients going to one counselor/therapist/rehabilitator all of the time. Nurses have to be spelled when the work in intensive ward units becomes too demanding; so, similarly, mental health workers are in a kind of boiler factory of care and concern and, they too, have to build in respite.

The apathy, cynicism and anger that builds up as part of the burn-out syndrome have to be dispelled (Garte & Rosenblum, 1978); it won't just go away. Workshops can often be helpful, based on the fact that counselors, therapists, and other dispensers of mental health and physical health measures can become disillusioned; they are not perfect human beings who never falter or become depressed. Their limitations have to be recognized and addressed in group confabs where these workers reveal their emotional states in order to move toward resolution. Remedial measures are not only of value to the burnt-out counselor but to the recipients of his/her services. Maslach (1976, p. 16) says "...burnout plays a major role in the poor delivery of health and welfare services to people in need of them." Thus the recipient of services is injured by being in the hands of a burntout and disinterested counselor, therapist or other health worker. Overwork, which is to say a too high ratio of clients to professional worker tends to be associated with burnout; relief on that score is likely to reduce the instances of burnout and may be achieved, as cited above, by a variety of measures. Burnout may also be reduced by teaching the counselor or health worker to actively express his/her feelings toward the client--in a constructive way-- rather than sit silently while the patient or client drones on in ways inimical to change as the counselor or therapist sees it. In this way both therapist/ counselor and patient/client engage in a more open and feedback-controlled exchange that keeps both from miring down in emotional slush and slop that precludes both objective solution and emotional understanding.

If the burnout syndrome includes other complaints than those cited above--anger, resentment, distancing, apathy, criticism, which it might, depending upon particulars--these may have to be treated in individual instances. Sometimes headaches may be treated by relaxation procedures, exhaustion by some plan for short rest periods daily and/or a vacation respite. Gastrointestinal disturbances may be treated by relaxation practice, together with recognition of the causes of anger in the health worker; sleeplessness by schedule adjustments, exercise and some change of the pace of work; boredom by changes in the types of clients seen and in altered schedules. A faulty and non-helpful reaction to burnout would be to consider the counselor/ therapist/health worker as "through," or as lacking motivation for work (often the burnout victim is an unusually hard and conscientious worker and burns out owing to lack of satisfactions commensurate with

162

expectations and previous experience). It must be
ascertained that the burnout health worker is not using
client relationships to replace a personal and social
life; recreation and judicious socializing are, then,
prerequisites to effective and rewarding work.

Psychosomatic Complaints

Some of the psychosomatic complaints which are
often associated with the burnout syndrome among health
workers are described in common terms: tiredness,
fatigue, bone weary (Criswell, 1979; Valle, 1979);
fear of taking on the problems of the patient, especially
those who relieve stress through alcoholic consumption
(Emener, 1979); work with long-term patients who seem
to fail to progress well (Lamb, 1979); pressures on the
health worker from the organization she/he works in to
keep up an economically determined pace rather than
serve clients appropriately (Hall, et al, 1979); special
problems arising from the patients's family making care
of the aged or dying patient far more stressful (Allen,
1978); and other signs.

An interesting twist in the study of burnout and
psychosomatic complaints comes from a study of 162
"helping professionals" in 11 agencies treating
childrens' problems (Armstrong, 1977). The burnout
syndrome among these professionals was related most
closely to management processes, and to the youth and
inexperience of health workers. While encouraging
workers to improve their own mental health status,
this study strongly suggested that "...it appears that
quality of management and the work environment" are
critical variables in the occurrence of burnout
(Armstrong, 1977, p. 258). As burnout progresses more
lasting psychosomatic complaints often ensue.

Thus, no matter where where we look in the health
and helping professions we are likely to encounter
burnout: day care centers, clinics for children,
community mental health facilities, university
counseling centers, hospital in- and out-patient
services, hospices for the dying, rehabilitation
centers, schools for the handicapped, and so on. All
health professionals are included in the burnout
syndrome: psychologists, counselors, rehabilitation
workers, child care teachers and supervisors, nurses
in a variety of settings, and classroom teachers. The
consuming public is the chief loser if the burnout
syndrome is not discovered early on and remedied; and
the health workers are vulnerable to the continuing

stress associated with burnout and may take to a number
of compensatory behaviors intended to ameliorate the
stress: irregular work, dropping out of the profession,
use of drugs and alcohol, the development of antithetical attitudes toward clients, becoming so pessimistic,
cynical and apathetic as to offer inferior or harmful
services and to reflect badly on themselves, their
institution and profession. Remedial measures are, of
course, those antithetical to the burnout syndrome:
Early recognition of the burnout attitude, dispatchful
measures through peer contacts, personal therapy,
improving institutional support, respites and other
planned changes in the work schedule, alterrations in
the client load and other measures tailored to suit the
situation and persons involved. Important, too, are
remedial measures that not only act as stop-gaps in
particular settings and/or with particular individuals,
but measures are needed that relate the allied health
professions more maturely and fairly and equitably to
medicine and dentistry. If the stronger and more
established professions such as medicine and dentistry
take a negative stand against nursing, social work,
psychology, pharmacy and other allied professions, the
stress will negatively influence the professional
relationships at points where the delivery of services
to the public will be adversely influenced, and all the
helping professions will lose in the competitive aftermath that follows. It is important that the public
realize that the helping professions are to be kept
to their mission of helping, irrespective of individual
professional preferences and precedences; and that
administrative boards, consumer interest groups, and
professional peer review bodies will act to keep all
the helping professions honest, responsible and open.

CHAPTER VI

BIBLIOGRAPHY

Allen, H. J. Aspects of "burn-out" among medical social workers, Arch. of the Fdn. of Thanatology, 1978, 7, 156.

Armstrong, K.L. An exploratory study of the interrelationships between worker characteristics, organizational structure, management process and worker alienation from clients, Dissertation Abstr. Intern., Ann Arbor, Mich.: Univ. Of Mich. M-Films, No. 7812458, 1977.

Berman, D.M. Why work kills; a brief history of occupational safety and health in the United States, Intern. J. of Health Services, 1977, 2, 63-87.

Calligan, M.J., Smith, M.J., and Hurrell, J.J. Occupational incidence rates of mental health disorders, J. of Human Stress, 1977.

Cartwright, L.K. Sources and effects of stress in health careers, in Stone, G.C., Cohen, F., and Adler, N.E. (Ed.) Health Psychology. San Francisco: Joseey-Boss, 1979.

Criswell, G.E. Dead tired and bone weary, Voices, 1979, 15, 49-53.

Curtis, F.C. and Johnson, C.A. Assessment of anxiety among young pharmacy practitioners, Amer. J. of Pharmacy, 1977, 149, 157-161.

Doyle, B.J. and Ware, J.E. Physician conduct and other factors that affect consumer satisfaction with medical care, J. Med. Educ., 1977, 52, 793-801.

Emener, W.G., Jr. Professional burnout: rehabilitation's hidden handicap, J. of Rehab., 1979, 45, 55-58.

Fein, R. Health manpower: some economic considerations, J. of Dent. Educ., 1976, 40, 655-661.

Frendenberger, H.J. The staff burn-out syndrome in alternative institutions, Psychother., Theory,

Research and Practice, 1975, 12, 73-82.

Garte, S.H. and Rosenblum, M.L. Lighting fires in
     burned out conselors, Pers. and Guid. J., 1978,
     158-160.

Hall, R.C. W., Gardener, E.R., Perl, M., Stickney, S.K.,
     Pfefferbaum, B. The professional burnout syndrome
     Psychiatric Opinion, 1979, 16, 12-13, 16-17.

Johnson, C.A., Hammel, R.J. and Heiner, J.S. Levels of
     satisfaction among hospital pharmacists, Amer. J.
     of Hosp. Pharmacy, 1977, 34, 241-247.

Knapp, D.E. and Knapp, D.A. Disillusionment in
     pharmacy students, Soc. Science and Medicine, 1968,
     1, 445-447.

Knapp, D.E., Knapp, D.A., and Edwards, J.D. The
     pharmacist as perceived by physicians, patrons and
     other pharmacists, J. of the Amer. Pharmaceutical
     Assn., 1969, N59, 80-84.

Lamb, H.R. Staff burnout in work with long-term
     patients, Hosp. and Community Psychiatry, 1979,
     30, 396-398.

Maslach, C. Burned-out, Human Behavior, 1976, 5, 16-22.

Maslach, C. and Pines, A. The burn-out syndrome in the
     day care setting, Child Care Quart., 1977, 6,
     100-113.

Maslach, C. and Pines, A. Characteristics of burn-out
     in mental health settings, Hosp. and Community
     Psychiatry, 1978, 29, 233-237.

Mausner, J.S. and Steppacher, R.C. Suicide in profes-
     sionals: a study of male and female psycholo-
     gists, Amer. J. of Epidemiology, 1973, 98, 436,
     445.

Mechanic, D. The growth of medical technology and
     bureaucracy: implications for medical care,
     Milbank Memorial Fund Quarterly, 1977, 55, 61-78.

Melhuish, E.C. An approach to teaching doctors social
     skills, in Singleton, W.T., Spurgeon, P., and
     Stammers, R.B. (Eds.) The Analysis of Social
     Skills. N.Y.: Blenum Press, 1980.

Murray, R. M. Psychiatric illness in doctors, <u>Lancet</u>, 1974, <u>1</u>, 1211-1213.

Powell, M. Occupational problems of professional men: dentists and pharmacists, <u>Occup. Psychol.</u>, 1972, <u>45</u>, 52-66.

Ross, K.D. and Rosow, I. Physicians who bill themselves, <u>Arch. Gen. Psychia.</u>, 1973, <u>29</u>, 800-805.

Russek, H.I. · Stress, tobacoo, and coronary disease in North American professional groups, <u>J.A.M.A.</u>, 1965, <u>192</u>, 89-94.

Rutter, D.R. A programme of interview training for medical students, in Singleton, W.T., Spurgeon, P., and Stammers, R.B. (Eds.) <u>The Analysis of Social Skills</u>, N.Y.: Blenum Press, 1980.

Shelton, J.L. and Warnath, C.F. The ultimate disappointment: the burned-out counselor, <u>Pers. and Guid. J.</u>, 1976, <u>55</u>, 172-175.

Sherlock, B.J. Career problems and narcotic addiction in the health professions: an exploratory study, <u>The International J. of the Addictions,</u> 1967, <u>2</u>, 191-206.

Stone, G.C., Cohen, F., and Adler, N.L. <u>Health Psychology</u>. San Francisco: Jossey-Boss, 1979.

Thurlow, R. M. Pharmacists who've said, "To hell with it," <u>Drug Topics</u>, 1974, Mar 8.

Valle, S.K. Burn out: occupational hazard for counselor, <u>Alcoholic Health and Res. World</u>, 1979, <u>3</u>, 10-14.

CHAPTER VII

PSYCHOLOGISTS

One of the fastest growing professions in recent decades is that of psychology. The American Psychological Association, the official head of the profession reports a gain in membership from a few thousand after World War II to over 50,000 at the beginning of the 1980 decade. Departments of psychology in universities and colleges have also proliferated, as have divisions of hospitals, public health and mental hygiene centers in the direction of including ever more psychologists. Popular magazines, such as <u>Psychology Today</u> and <u>Human Behavior</u>, attest to the "pop psychology" movement, the public's interest in psychology, and the tendency, ever growing, for people to ask "why?" about their own behavior. People observe themsevles more readily today than ever before and try to get a handle on how and why they and others behave as they do. Nearly everyone knows about popular movements in psychology such as Behaviorism, Gestalt psychology, Humanistic Psychology and, of course, the ubiquitous Freudian Schools of Psychology. Nearly all major businesses and industries employ psychologists to help with the marketing and promotion of products, and advertising, as well as to smooth out the internal workings (interpersonal relationships) of such organizations. Psychology underlays education; in fact, education is applied psychology. Psychology figures ever larger in medicine and has given rise to two or three recent developments linking psychology and medicine: Behavioral Medicine, Behavior Therapy (especially in its application to overcoming bad health practices such as over-eating, over-smoking, drug usage), the burgeoning field of Health Psychology and various areas of Psychosomatic Research delving into the etiology of somatic complaints that have psychological implications or origins, that ramify in relation to one's style of living, and that need the therapy of "talking it out" to ameliorate such conditions. Now and again psychology seems to offer treatment to replace drugs (especially tranquilizers), but the issues of whether to use primarily one or the other, or to use in combination, forever surfaces and re-surfaces. Psychology has a kind of fascination for some in the case of hypnosis which has not only grown in scientific credibility recently but has also experienced a popularization; nearly everyone is curious about hypnosis, even to the point of doubting that it really "exists" as a legitimate phenomenon. Psychology has collaborated, perhaps even more seriously, with other scientists in the study of thinking in relation to computers, and in a number of ways that regard "how the mind works."

With all this growth psychologist--some would say--have become "heady", even arrogant about their knowledge, power and expertise. As research on most topics accumulates, however, most psychologists are made more humble about what they know or don't know. But there are always a number of them up front extoling their virtues while at the same time overlooking their liabilities and limitations. "Pop" psychology presents probably the best example of this tendency. Many feel that psychology is in danger of emulating medicine in its use of its power, wealth and public acclaim, and further in minimizing its role in regard to social concerns and human welfare generally (Patterson, 1972). As we have seen, professions such as medicine, law, dentistry and executive roles have loosened themselves considerably from social purposes; it may be that one inherent problem in the growth of professions is early recognition of the tendency to insularity and in trying to minimize it or at least offset its more dire consequences. Psychology may be a fledging "test case" for just this kind of constructive inter- vention. Being attuned to what is coming from studying the professions of law and medicine, psychology can be placed on alert, so to say, to try to maintain its earlier genuine interest in human functioning without regard to profit to psychologists themselves or to an elitist attitude on the part of the profession qua profession.

A psychologist with a keen perspecitive on psycho- logy's role vis-a-vis social concerns, mental health, and the delivery of services to all people regardless of their economic plight, is Albee (1980). Albee is fearful that psychology--especially in its clinical aspects--will simply become a profession of "fat cats" who innure themselves to larger concerns and responsi- bilities. He says,

> As clinical psycholgists-psychotherapists
> become more numerous and more affluent,
> especially if they win the battle of
> reimbursement, I can see the whole pro-
> fession tilting down that runway. Gold
> is a powerful reinforcer. We are in
> danger of becoming like the AMA and other
> fat-cat guilds--self-serving and manipu-

170

lative. The health care industry is
growing richer all the time, but there
is no improvement in our health (Albee,
1980, p. 2).

Recent reports by the surgeon general of the United
States indicate that Americans are living somewhat
longer and experiencing somewhat better health than
before (e.g., more people are stopping smoking, except
for youthful persons who seem to be taking up smoking
in larger numbers than a decade ago), but there are
still vast pockets of inadequate health care such as
among those living in rural areas,and among the inner-
city poor. Albee's point,however, is well taken,
because the nations health can improve somewhat in
average figures while at the same time the health
professions are growing disproportionately richer and
also disproportionately failing to rise to the challenge
of the exceptions to our health care systems' record
of improvement.

Mental Health Issues

Psychologists have not come in for a great deal of
study of their own personalities which is surprising
considering how much psychologists have studied others
and how introspective and self-observing many
psychologists are (and are taught to be). But psycho-
logisits have never been of one mind about the subject
matter of psychology (some say psychology is the study
of behavior, some regard it primarily as studying human
nature, and others aver that it studies the mind); thus
it is not surprising they have not studied themselves
as much as might be desirable or informative (Hardy,
1978).

Psychologists have evidenced some reasonable job
satisfaction, at least in the clinical/counseling/
personality areas of practice and teaching (Randolph,
et al, 1977). These authors studied 125 doctoral
students in counseling psychology in 20 southern universities by way of the Personality Research Form, and
followed them up 3 years later when performing on jobs.
They were a satisfied lot, on the whole, and their job
satisfactions appeared to be related to personality
need satisfactions offered by their jobs. While three
years is a very small amount of time on which to base
both the stability of personality needs and job satisfaction, results based on this short period of time

171

are at least encouraging. Counseling psychologists are more likely to function in personnel settings, in university or college education or psychology departments, and in some businesses. They are not as likely to work in medical settings, in out-patient clinics, hence do not come in contact as much with medical personnel. Counseling psychologists, while they often are trained in the same--or nearly the same curriculum--as the clinical psychologist, do not apply their skills in the same settings, and may avoid some of the more traditional clashes between clinical psychologists and psychiatrists, which might affect job satisfaction. Super (1977) seems to think that counseling psychologists look for and stress the personal strengths in their clients more than the clinical psychologists, with the latter stressing the weaknesses of their clients/patients and veering more in medical directions by treating more obstinate cases, more often psychotic cases or other refractory conditions. The tougher load of the clinical psychologists--if this be a truism--may reduce job satisfaction for the clinical psychologist in comparison to some other psychologists and throw him or her into more direct medical competition. We simply do not have the data today on a wide variety of psychologists--clinical, experimental, counseling, child, social, educational, etc.--working in varied settings--colleges and universities, hospitals, out-patient clinics, businesses, research institutions--to say which groups are having their personality needs most adequately met and/or how job satisfactions are correlated with such personality needs (Weigel, 1977).

Internal Stress

Cleavages within psychology, not only between clinical and counseling psychology, but between experimental and applied psychology abound. All of them affect job orientation and satisfaction. The growth of various areas of applied psychology in recent decades has strained the credibility of academic departments in colleges and universities, and has made many people wonder what psychology is. However, as Hilgard pointed out (1980), concerns that clinical and counseling psychology heed mostly the marketplace and not research and scholarly (or even social applied interests) is not uncommon, as Albee as already noted. Psychology in its experimental vs. clinical aspects is not vastly different from Business Schools and Economics Departments in universitites in their respective concern for applied vs. basic research; or

172

in Engineering vs. Physics and Chemistry; or in relation to Chemical Engineering and Chemistry; and so on. The growth of psychology as an applied scientific area and as a profession has brought about problems not dreamed of by psychology's founders a hundred years ago (although they, too, had their applied and human/social concern interests--they were not all structly academic or pure science oriented).

As already stated, job satisfaction for clinical psychologists working in medical settings may be less than for other psychologists working in non-medical settings. Brandsma (1980) has recently written of his experiences in trying to gain full medical staff membership in a hospital setting, when Ph.D. trained individuals in physics were granted such full medical staff privilege. The matter of "certifying" Ph.D. physicists comes partly from hospital convenience and economic support in third party billing for nuclear medical services, a type of service not within the province of psychologists, but at the same time disallowing the same importance to psychologist-rendered services of a diagnostic or therapeutic nature. Brandsma says, "This and other incidents make it painfully clear to me that doctors do not conceive of a hospital as part of a health care delivery system which is for the benefit of consumers; rather, hospitals are their territory where they exercise economic and political control to maintain and enhance their own interests" (Brandsman, 1980, p. 13). Making the case for clinical psychologist job satisfaction matters important in medical settings is the further fact that Ph.D. Physicists have no licensing, no clinical training, no professional scrutiny (National Register, e.g.)., or any other credentials other than their academic training in physics. The problems faced by Brandsma and other clinical psychologists in medical settings ramify into relationships with the medical profession, as is the case with nurses and with allied health professionals from other professional backgrounds (Sapor, 1970).

Psychologists, like psychiatrists, are encouraged to undergo personal therapy as part of their training and as part of their self-awareness in relationship to people (clients/patients) who are looking to them for help in sometimes crucial and life-threatening ways. Garfield and Kurtz (1976) found in a survey of 855 clinical psychologists that 63 percent of them had undergone personal therapy (more common among female than male clinical psychologists). Most of the clinical psychologists studied--62 percent--felt undergoing personal therapy was important or moderately important, but as "not important" by about 16 percent; only 1 percent considered personal therapy "detrimental." Those undergoing personal therapy regarded it as beneficial to a greater extent than those not having undertaken such therapy. Separating types of clinical psychologists--the fractination of psychologists is forever with us!--those with a behavioral/learning theory orientation regarded personal therapy as less important than did respondents with a humanistic or psychoanalytic orientation. Job satisfaction among psychologists, especially among clinical psychologists may be enhanced by adequate self-knowledge to which personal therapy may be a contributor.

Social and Ethical Matters

Along with the growth in personal therapy as responsible preparation for human services, recent years have also shown a growth of interest in the personal conduct of psychologists. They are seldom sued for illegal or unethical practices, but problems of an ethical nature in relation to psychologists(and psychiatrists) having intimate sexual relationships with patients (usually of the opposite sex) have arisen (Butler and Zelen, 1977). The same topic has surfaced several times in recent years during national meetings of the American Psychological Association. Butler and Zelen interviewed 20 psychologists and psychiatrists who admitted to sexual contact with their patients; 18 were male, 2 female therapists. The interviews with the clinicians yielded information leading to the impression that the therapists were at a particularly "needy" time in their personal lives when sexual relations with patients occurred. The sexual contact between therapist and patient was not viewed as particularly therapeutic for either, nor was the contact planned or systematically pursued. What may be more alarming is that the Butler and Zelen reports indicates that the professional psychotherapists did not seek personal help or particularly feel the need for it; and these clinicians were not discouraged from continuing these practices by their respective professions. Psychologists--and this would include academic psychologists having intimate relationships with students in college and university settings--may ultimately come hard onto ethical problems related to personal/sexual conduct more than in relation to other ethical issues such as too high fees, misdiagnosis, poorly executed treatment, and the like. All of these ethical problems seem to arise from the power status

174

of the therapist (or teacher) vis-a-vis the patient
(or student), and from the fact that this power can
easily be misused (Pope, Levinson, and Schouer, 1979;
Stricker, 1977; Maffeo, 1979; Hare-Mustin, et al,
1979; Holroyd and Brodsky, 1977).

Sanders and Keith-Spiegel (1980) have reported on
ethical complaints against psychologists, their report
being the second published account of similar ethical
issues (Sanders, 1979). The Sanders and Keigh-Spiegel
report is based on over 200 cases presented to the
Committee on Scientific and Professional Ethics and
Conduct (EXPEC) between the period January 1977 and
June 1980; represented in 19 illustrative cases. The
presented cases stem from violations of various ethical
principles found in the American Psychological Association's Ethical Standards of Psychologists (1979), and
can be subsumed under such rubrics as responsibility,
competence, moral and legal standards, public statements, confidentiality, welfare of the consumer,
professional relationships, utilization of assessment
techniques, and pursuit of research activities. The
fact that the American Psychological Association has
gone on record so strongly in quest of high ethical
principles bodes well for the profession, but does not
mean that heads are lopped off at will or indifferently.
In fact, the censorship might appear mild to many since
in only one case did the APA's Board of Directors
formally vote to expel the member from the Association,
and in two additional cases the members agreed to resign
with reapplication eligibility coming five years later
(Sanders and Keith-Spiegel, 1980, p. 1105). Other, less
severe, dispositions were made of other cases of ethical
infractions. The open concern and the publication of
ethical issues infractions by the Association are good
signs of social awareness and professional responsibility; perhaps this frankness will generalize to other
professions and also act as a deterrent to psychologists
who might otherwise be careless about ethical issues.

Research

Another trend among psychologists is their failing
to live up to their reputation and potential as
researchers (Pasework, et al, 1973). The vigorousness
of a profession--if not its health--is seen in its
research. Most research among psychologists is done in
university and college settings, particularly among
universities who heavily fund and support research.
Clinical psychologists as a population do not do much

research (Pasework, et al, 1973). And Cohen (1979) reports that many do not even read research articles to any appreciable extent. He found that academic psychologists and medical school psychologists read over 4 research articles per month; whereas other psychologists read about two research articles a month. Cohen's research was based on 50 psychologists listed in the National Register, and were chosen from VA hospitals, medical schools, state mental hospitals and community out-patient clinics. Others have noted that many mental health workers, including psychologists, fail to find that research contributes to or influences their practice (Larsen and Nichols, 1972). While research involvement is not a health problem, per se, the status of psychologists has long been built on their research prowess, and all would agree that research undergirds practice even though obvious connections are not always noted between the two. Job satisfaction often depends upon people being able to see problems and work on them, the most sophisticated example of which is that of research. The scientist-professional model is the one most commonly espoused among psychologists, especially clinical and counseling psychologists, and one that aims to set and maintain a balance between service, societal concern, and scientific responsibility (Weins, 1969; Hoch, et al, 1966; Bardy, 1972).

One reason that psychologists have not encountered more ethical problems than they have, and a reason they seem to be ahead of most other health-related professions in this regard, is that the American Psychological Association has been highly conscious and articulate about ethical issues (1965, 1968a, 1968b; Shah, 1969; Fisher, 1964; Zenoff, 1962).[1]

_____

[1]The reference to self-consciousness about ethical issues among psychologists should not be taken as representing a homologous viewpoint among psycholgists (Klockars and O'Connor, 1979; Reynolds, 1979). Indeed, the more ethical issues are pursued, the more intriguing, conflictful and puzzling problems appear; as regards conflicts between research/scientific interest and those of the subjects, between scientific obligations and scientist-citizen responsibilities, and between the scientist's responsibilities as an investigator after knowledge vs. the application of such knowledge to society, among other issues.

Cost of professional liability insurance for psychologists is one of the best indicators of how well a profession is doing vis-a-vis suits for various offenses; the liability insurance for psychologists has risen only about what one would expect from inflation over the past 5 - 10 years, whereas many other professions have found such liability insurance soaring over the same time span owing to suits against them for various alleged offenses. Professional groups--other than psychologists--in some regions of the country have found liability insurance costs so oppressive that they have set up their own insurance plan.

In the chapter on Women (Chapter IX), we have already seen that women professionals have a more difficult time--given the same training, experience, and professional expertise--than male professionals. That is, women evidence more suicide and personal problems than men in some professions--medicine, psychiatry, as examples, but are surprisingly healthy in some other professions (nursing, for example). Among psychologists, women have a higher suicide rate than male psychologists (Mausner and Steppacher, 1973). These authors obtained from the American Psychological Association a list of all psychologists who died during the 1960-1969 decade, being able to locate death certificates for 80 percent of the listed deaths (684 people, from a grand total of about 855). Through secondary resources, these authors were able to obtain reliable information on 10 percent more, making a coverage of 90 percent of the original 855 persons; all under 65 years of age. Suicides among this group totalled 58 people (39 males, 19 females), with 50 of the 58 classified as suicide on the death certificate (34 males, 16 females). The remaining 8 cases were judged to be "probable suicide" cases or cases for whom there was secondary information pointing to death by suicide. Compared to the total population of expected deaths by suicide, male psychologists as a whole--based on the figures from the decade cited above--showed an expected frequency of suicide in the age group 25 - 65 only about three-fourths that found in the general population (34 observed compared to 46 expected). Female psychologists, on the other hand, showed a frequency of suicide in the decade cited and in the same age range (25-65) about three times that expected in the population at large (16 observed suicides vs. 5.7 expected). Thus generalizations about suicide along psychologists must, as with medicine and dentistry, be broken down into male/female categories, in order to bring out the true nature of the phenomenon of suicide. By far--55 percent--of the female psychologists commit suicide by poisoning (Analgesics, spororifics and other solid and liquid substances), whereas male psychologists use this method only 25 percent of the time. Male psychologists use firearms and "all othermethods" equally often--about 37 percent of the time in each classification. Female psychologists commit suicide only 15 percent of the time by firearms and used "all other methods" (Unspecified) about 30 percent of the time.

Although there are doubtlessly many errors in suicide statistics, at this time in our accumulation of knowledge we are obliged to go with present figures. Existing figures may be wrong in two major ways - they may be underestimates of the total number of suicides (anywhere from 10 - 50 percent underestimates), and the exact determination of suicides in subject populations may also be in error owing to imcompleteness of data, misinterpretation of same, or outright error in the figures.

In the figures provided in the study by Mausner and Steppacher (1973) women surface as the major suiciders in the psychologists population,as was true in these authors study of suicide among physicians (Steppacher and Mausner, 1973). These authors see the phenomenon of suicide among psychologists as fitting in with similar data among physicians, although the rate of suicide of the former is less,on the whole, than among the latter. These authors say: "Although the study reported here focuses on psychologists, its implications can best be interpreted in conjunction with our study of suicide in physicians. The major findings of both studies were high suicide rates among female professionals in comparison with rates for females in the general population" (Mausner and Steppacher, 1973, p. 441). The role conflicts of female psychologists, while not as intense as that of female physicians, and certainly not as long-standing, are similar to those of other highly committed professional women. Male psychologists,on the other hand, seem not to suffer any appreciable role conflicts and, unlike male physicians, have a lower-than-expected suicide rate. Matters, then, relating to suicide among psychologists must not be interpreted as cutting across the profession (as is more likely true in medicine) as much as showing differential effects on adult/gender/ role considerations that separate male and female psychologists in the matter of suicide. To date, other

178

data relating to longevity, death from different causes, statistics covering divorce, dropping-out from the profession and other signs of professional malaise or ill-health, are unfortunately not available to us from published sources on psychologists. One considerable research need, then, is the accumulation of broad-based health and psychological well-being matters among psychologists, as well as among other professionals, especially among members of the "newer professions" such as communications, to data-processing, to transportation, tothe broad range of health professionals, and to politicians, governmental officials, and middle-level managerial groups.

The most important lesson to be learned from the study of psychologists in matters relating to the profession per se and to health considerations, is that psychologists stand at the crossroads of becoming an influential profession, playing an ever-increasingly important role in society and in public health. If psychology as a profession becomes insular and self-servicing (which some signs now point to), they will not only tend to arouse suspicion, mistrust, and disrespect from society--as have many older professions --but will injure themselves by turning inward too much over their own concerns for money, prestige and power. The latter turn will carry with it, if the message in this book is accurate and valid across professions, a deterioration in the training of psychologists, more bias in their selection, and less rewarding personal lives in the service of science and society. If psychologists as a profession are sufficiently aware of the choices before them--and the consequences of their choices--perhaps they can act altruistically before it is too late and before they have gone the way of far too many professions to date.

CHAPTER VII

BIBLIOGRAPHY

Albee, G. Editorial, APA, Monitor, 1980, 11, #9/78, p.2.

American Psychological Assn. Special issue: Testing a public policy, American Psychol., 1965, 20, 857-993.

American Psychological Assn. Ad Hoc Committee on Ethical standards in psychological research. American Psychol., 1968a, 23, 689-690.

American Psychological Assn. Ethical standards of psychologists, American Psychol., 1968b, 23, 357-361.

American Psychological Assn. Ethical Standards of Psychologists. Washington, D.C., 1979.

Butler, S. & Zelen, S.L. Sexual intimacies between therapists and patients. Psychotherapy: Theory, Research and Practice, 1977, 14, 139-145.

Brandsma, J.M. One month in the life of a medical center psychologists. The Clinical Psychologist, 1980, 23, #1, p.13.

Fisher, R.M. The psychotherapeutic profession and the law of privileged communication, Wayne Law Rev., 1964, 10, 609-654.

Hardy, A.G. The rising of clinical psychology, Psychiatry, 1978, 41, 194-201.

Hare-Mustin, R.T., Marecek, J., Kaplan, A.G., & Liss-Levinson, N. Rights of clients, responsibilities of therapists, American Psychologist, 1979, 34, 3-16.

Hilgard, E.R. Preparations for the future, APA Monitor, 1980, 11, #11, p.3.

Hoch, E.L., Ross, A.D., & Winder, C.L. (Eds.) Professional Preparation of Clinical Psychologists Washington,D.C.: Amer. Psychological Assn., 1966.

Holroyd, J.C. & Brodsky, A.M. Psychologists' attitudes and practices regarding erotic and nonerotic physical contact with patients, American Psychologist, 1977, 32, 843-849.

Klockars, C.B. & O'Connor, F.W. (Eds.) Deviance And Decency: The Ethics Of Research With Human Subjects. Beverly Hills, Calif.: Sage, 1979.

Larsen, J. & Michels, D. If nobody knows you've done it, have you? Evaluation, 1972, 1, 39-44.

Maffeo, P.S. Thoughts on Stricker's "Implications of research for psychotherapeutic treatment of women," American Psychologist, 1979, 34, 690-695.

Mausner, J.S. & Steppacher, R.C. Suicide in professionals: a study of male and female psychologists, American J. of Epidemiology, 1973, 98, 436-445.

Pasework, R., Fitzgerald, B., Thornton, L., & Sawyer,R. Icons in the attic. Research activities of clinical psychologists, Professional Psychology, 1973, 4, 341-346.

Patterson, C.H. Psychology and social responsibility, Professional Psychology, 1972, 3, 340.

Pope, K.S., Levenson, H., & Schover, L.R. Sexual intimacy in psychology training, American Psychologist, 1979, 34, 682-689.

Randolph, D.L., Caston, E.E., & Wright, T. Prediction of job satisfaction of psychologists via personality needs, Southern J. of Educ. Research, 1977, 11, 229-239.

Reynolds, P.D. Ethical Dilemmas And Social Science Research: An Analysis of Moral Issues Confronting Investigators In Research Using Human Participants. San Francisco: Jossey-Bass, 1979.

Sanders, J.R. Complaints against psychologists adjudicated informally by APA's Committee on Scientific and Professional Ethics and Conduct, American Psychologist, 1979, 34, 1139-1144.

Sanders, J.R. & Keith-Spiegel, P. Formal and informal adjudication of ethics complaints against psychologists, _American Psychologist_, 1980, 35, 1096-1105.

Saper, B. Psychology, power and the power structure. _Professional Psychology_, 1970, 1, 105-114.

Shah, S. Privileged communication, confidentiality and privacy, _Professional Psychology_, 1969, 1, 56-69.

Steppacher, R.C. & Mausner, J.S. Suicide among male and female physicians, _J.A.M.A._, 1973.

Stricker, G. Implications of research for psychotherapeutic treatment of women, _American Psychologist_, 1977, 32, 14-22.

Vardy, M. Role of the mental health professional: Therapist-Healer or agent of social change? a historical perspective, _Professional Psychology_, 1972, 3, 277-280.

Weigel, R.G. I have seen the enemy and they are us-- and everyone else, _Counseling Psychology_, 1977, 7, 50-53.

Weiss, A.N. Scientist-professional: The appropriate training model for the mainstream of clinical psychology, _Professional Psychology_, 1969, 1, 38-43.

Zenoff, E. Confidential and privileged communication, _J.A.M.A._, 1962, 182, 656-662.

CHAPTER VIII

TEACHERS

Teachers are everywhere. Not everyone has been to a physician or dentist, heard a preacher, or been attended by a nurse, but there is hardly a person who has not had contact with a teacher. Teachers influence us, moreover, when we are most impressionable, when we form lasting attitudes toward learning, toward school, toward teaching as an occupation or profession, toward ourself and our relations with the world.

G. B. Shaw said "Those who can, do - those who can't, teach." This is an unfair statement, prejudicial to teaching and teachers. Informally, everyone is a teacher: the older child teaches the younger child in ways of the world at the child's level; newspapers teach us attitudes about our society and how to regard what is transpiring in politics, religion, business and human affairs; preachers teach us about religion, belief, faith, charity, and attitudes toward God and the cosmos. We learn all the time; if we learn, perforce someone teaches us. Teaching is ubiquitous.

There are more teachers than any other professional group - two million plus, at last count, compared to about 110,000 dentists, 360,000 physicians, 150,000 ministers, and about 450,000 lawyers. To the young child the teacher is the most important person in his/her life - after the parents and immediate family members. If asked what impressed one most in young life, many people will say they remember most fondly (or most unsavorily) a teacher; teachers make impressions, for good or evil.

Teachers and schools, therefore, come in for lots of criticism. Teachers are beholden to school boards (who hire and fire them, set salaries and working conditions), to school administrators, to parents, to social critics who check teachers' attitudes, their work, their style of life, their very being - from the pulpit, in the newspapers, among gossipers, and from scholars who study teaching as a profession and schools as social institutions (Brenton, 1971; Lortie, 1975; Knoblock and Goldstein, 1971; Biegeleisen, 1969; Lieberman, 1956; Adams and Garrett, 1969; Moore, 1970; N.E. A., 1968a, 1968b, 1971; Marsh, 1973; Fisk, 1973; Combs, 1974). While all the professions are coming under increasing public scrutiny and criticism -- and rightly so -- the teaching profession has had to live in a glass house for decades... even for centuries.

183

All of the professions have come a long way toward self-development in recent decades, especially since World War II. Teaching is no exception. A look at some of the practices that influenced teaching and teachers might be considered, especially in terms of the stresses they experienced long before stress, tension and anxiety became an impelling and fashionable study. Teachers were _early_ stressed, as they are today.

Background

In Colonial times, teachers were licensed by school boards one year at a time (Lortie, 1975, p. 19; Moore, 1970). Teachers were chosen not on the basis of general criteria, but on an individualistic bases by ministers, or by leading citizens in the community. Teachers "boarded around," living a week or two as the guests of parents in part-exchange for their teaching. Uncertainty about living conditions, about requirements for teaching, about whether one would even have a position, plagued the early-day teacher. Brenton observes: "Some two hundred years ago schoolteachers were sent to American shores along with pigs and cattle and general cargo; less than a decade ago a former schoolteacher became President of the United States: (Brenton, 1971, p. 13). (Brenton is referring to President Lyndon Johnson who succeeded to the Presidency in 1963 upon the assasination of President John Kennedy.)

Teachers have mostly been "she's" in recent decades, although in early American history teachers were male as they were better able to cope with the vagaries of living, pay and self-keep; still more recently, males ha' again populated the ranks of teachers (generally at high er salaries than females in corresponding roles). Now teachers are a cross-section of the general population; perhaps a bit higher in intelligence and education, more demuring socially, and more given to values related to learning, scholarship, love for children, and social awareness than the average person (Brenton, 1971; Robert 1973).

Teachers experience stress and react to it in a variety of ways. Until recently when teachers began to strike (N.E.A., 1968a), they seemed to remain for many decades intimidated by society and by restrictions put on their lives. Some of the pressures on teachers have made them conservative politically (this attitude being associated with security factors in their jobs, not wit' siding with monied and therefore conservative elements in society, as is associated with the conservative atti tudes of physicians, dentists and lawyers). Similarly, teachers have been believers and purveyors of middle-class attitudes; conventional in beliefs, socially retiring, appearing publicly as spectators, physicially inactive (with respect to sports), and tending to select activities that make few intellectual demands (and with a corresponding tendency to select escape activities when not at work) (Brenton, 1971, pp. 30-31; Ziegler, 1967). Teachers early had a lower social position than they do now, had to sweep up at the local school, ring the school bell, teach Bible lessons, and engage in educational activities that often subordinated them to ministers who held sway over the teacher's job as well as teaching activities (Lortie, 1971, pp. 10 - 11). Later teachers became subordinate to school administrators and principles, replacing the subservience originally given to ministers. Like nurses, teachers have been the workhorses of their profession, demuring in regard to status, money, and promotional possibilities to those "above" them (Lortie, 1971; Knoblock and Goldstein, 1971).

Mental Health Issues

Teachers' mental health has been affected by the practices cited above (Lortie, 1975; Kaplan, 1959; Bard, 1969; Knoblock and Goldstein, 1971; Berman, 1954; Eisner, 1961, 1961; Ringness, 1968, 1968; Robert, 1973; Combs, 1974; Volliner and Mills, 1966); and not only recently with the ferment in education, but over the decades as these scholars indicate. The mental health of teachers has long been a consideration of teachers themselves, of school administrators, and of society. There has been noted enough mental health problems among teachers to make this an extant issue. Articles are written about how to prevent mental health problems among teachers, what to do about these problems when they are discovered, and how to make schools into more hospitable work and social climates for teachers as well as for students. Some stresses on teachers are as follows:

Kaplan (1959) reported long ago that teachers typically work under strain and nervous tension. Emotional disturbances are said to underlie the commonly observed complaints of teachers and their absence from the classroom (Randall, 1965). Teacher turnover is related to their state of emotional health (Stirdivant, 1957). A UNESCO report (UNESCO, 1954) revealed that a Mayo Clinic study of professionals (who applied there for medical treatment based on physical complaints) found a higher

185

percentage of teachers (54 percent) showing "neurotic complaints," compared to other professionals: clergy, 42 percent; lawyers, 36 percent; dentists, 30 percent; farmers, 19 percent. In the 1950s, however, the bias against women and their adjustment problems may have slanted these percentages against teachers, compared to lawyers, dentists, farmers, and clergy all of whom are (or were) mostly men.

Many of the results from stress in the environments of teachers lead to the symptoms cited above. One important area of chronic stress is the number of hours that teachers work. Whereas, industry and business and goverment long ago achieved the 40-hour work week, teachers in 1959 worked between 45 and 50 hours per week (Kaplan, 1959, p. 402). Included in this extended time which is still typical of teaching activities today are such extra-classroom duties as grading appers, preparing lesson plans, writing examinations, attending professional meetings, continued schooling for higher degrees, and various other extra-curricular activities. In recent years, some time has been allowed teachers from classroom duties in order to complete clerical, grading and other professional activities; however, they continue to work more than a 40-hour week and perhaps more than many other professionals they are expected to "keep up" with further developments and education in their respective fields of expertise.

Teachers, like nurses and physicians and dentists, tend to enter the profession with high ideals and expectations (Kaplan, 1959, p. 407). In their early years, teachers are humanitarian and liberal in their thinking after 10-15 years they become more traditional, dogmati authoritative, and tend to stress subject matter over personality characteristics of their students.

As has been and will be noted in this chapter, teachers, like nurses, are expecting a greater "say" in their professional lives. Much sought is more relief from non-teaching clerical duties, more help with disturbed and problem children, more participation in decision-making regarding how schools are run, more autonomy in their instructional duties, support for their professional advancement, better relations with school administrators, better pay, more advancement opportunities, and greater security (Shipley, 1961; Solomon, 19 Randall, 1965; Delp, 1963; Bowen, 1978; Metz and Fleis man, 1974; Wilson, 1973; Gibson, 1976; Marsh, 1973; Fi 1973; Berger, 1974; Eddy, 1973; Stinnett, 1970).

If suicide and various social/emotional/family problems are common complaints among physicians and dentists, then "loneliness" and "anxiety" may be two of the leading characteristics of emotional difficulty among teachers (Coates and Thoresen, 1976). Brenton asks "what's happened to teachers?" (Brenton, 1970), observing that changes in the profession, the problem status of teachers, their mental health, and the impact of schools upon teachers, have all proliferated into formidable anxiety-provoking problems in the last two or three decades. Knoblock and Goldstein (1971) have noted and written about the "lonely teacher" in a book by that very title, observing that the teacher is more sustained by the somewhat one-sided relationships with children (where teachers get their most reassuring social and psychological reinforcements) while at the same time they eschew or aresomewhat restricted from general social contacts inthe community on a level commensurate with other professional, managerial and better educated groups (Robert, 1973). Several of these broad issues concerning teachers' mental health, emotional well-being and community-relatedness will be taken up topically below.

Loneliness. Knoblock and Goldstein observe that "... one of the core concerns teachers experienced was that of loneliness" (Knoblock and Goldstein, 1971, p. 5). Why are teachers lonely? They feel squeezed between their duties and obligations to do their best with children (helping children being their prime motivation from the incipiency of their desire to teach onward intheir lives) and the largeness, the insensitivity, and the actual impediments in the school environment (Robert, 1973). Schools as organizations are large, over-crowded, heavily oriented toward administration; they are bureaucratic, and open to increasingly frequent and intense attacks from the public. The teacher is caught in the middle of an oppressive triangular set of pressures: Dealing with and teaching the extremely great variety among the children they meet, coming from lower, middle and upper class families with extremely heterogeneous backgrounds; dealing with the administration which sets all manner of salary, promotional, professional and even personal-life criteria for the teacher to follow (and willingly!); and the onslaughts of society that see schools not during their jobs well, not educating children, not handling disciplinary problems constructively, yet asking for more money, more personnel benefits, more status, and for more teacher power in the organization and maintenance of schools as institutions.

While the classroom may be "the teacher's castle",
it is an area of relative isolation; few outsiders know
what goes on in a classroom. Administrators are too
busy and perhaps not well prepared to visit the classroom and make useful suggestions to the teacher. Parents do not know what to observe in the classroom --
except their own little "Jonnies" and "Mary" -- and
can be more disruptive to the teacher and the children
than constructive if they visit the classroom often.
Parents make demands that the classroom teacher "get
results" with children, but the parents are most often
the ones who fail to attend PTA meetings where they can
learn more about the classroom, the school and the
teacher and, while throwing the educational torch to
the teacher do not themselves support the school's effort to educate their children. Many parents expect
the schools and the teacher to "fix up" the child
educationally speaking, the way they expect an auto
mechanic to adjust their car's carburetor or fix a
flat tire. Understanding the classroom and the schools
as "educational milieus" is difficult for the parent
even as it is for the teacher and the educational
administrator.

The relative isolation of the classroom allows --
even forces -- the teacher to get his/her "kicks" from
dealing with the children. If administrators don't know
who makes good teachers, and parents have little or no
perspective, and the classroom is so demanding that outsiders can hardly ever get a proper view of things, the
teacher, like the nurse with her patient, is beholden
to the specific ones she/he is serving and the teacher's
world is narrowed accordingly. Children know their
teachers better than anyone else - but who listens to
the children in such cases? But children can seldom
help a teacher "improve" - children and teachers are
caught, as it were, in little life rafts afloat on an
uncharted sea. The people in the big boats and on the
shore cannot see, or they care little, what is going on
in the isolated raft, the classroom.·

Teacher loneliness would be helped if teachers
could communicate more with peers and if the school wer
organized to allow more explicit communication with
other adults. Some teachers have said that they go day
without a real conversation with other teachers during
the school day - they have to make appointments after
school to get to socialize and communicate fully with
peers (Jackson, 1968). Teachers' lounges may help, and
the office may sometimes be a temporary meeting ground
for teachers, but these transient states do not offer

188

the teacher much surcease against the pressures of the
classroom, the phone calls from parents, the committee
meetings, the clerical work, and more that make his/her
day 9 - 11 hours long ("from 7:00 A.M. if you want to
get something done before the hullabaloo starts, to
5:00 or 6:00 P.M., if you need to wind down, think over
what's happened, put yonr experiences in perspective,
and have a little composure"), as one teacher expressed
it.

Anxiety. Anxiety must be the second compelling
problem area of teachers, if it is not the first one
(Randall, 1951). If anxiety is thought of as a hypothetical cause, or summary statement about physiological,
psychological and social signs of tension, its ubiquitousness is clearly manifest (Coates and Thoresen, 1976).
In the Coates and Thoresen review of anxiety problems
among teachers, they found that the literature revealed
anxiety problems irrespective of the teacher's range of
experience. Beginning teachers were apprehensive about
how they might perform, about pupil and peer and administrator acceptance of their presence and their work,
and about organizing and presenting themselves in the
classroom setting. More experienced teachers had their
anxieties as well: About their acumen in understanding
stndents and student problems in behavior and with efficient learning, to separate their own -- the teacher's
-- responsibilities from those of the student and the
school, and to evaluate their own (teacher's) contributions to the student's progress. One could say from
those studies that the teacher's role remains unclear.
The teacher's role appears to have changed considerably
over the years but its definition does not remain reliable or predictable. If one does not really know what is
expected of him or her, role execution -- no matter the
skill level or experience -- can be very perplexing
(Moore, 1970). This perplexity, expecially in the face
of criticism, can lead to expressions of anxiety on the
physiological level (somatic complaints), on the psychological level (depression, nervousness, self-doubt), and
on the social level (withdrawl from others, expressions
of lack of self confidence, absences from work and rapid
teacher turnover,and even "burn-out") (Freudenberger,
1975).

The review of published research by Coates and
Thoresen (1976) found that the incidence of anxiety manifestations among teachers was high. As far back as 1933,
Hicks (1933) found in a survey of 600 teachers that 17
percent were "unusually nervous" and those having suffered from "nervous breakdowns" amounted to 11 percent.

189

These figures put more than one-fourth of these teachers
in a category comparable to "nervous impairment of
(their) capabilities and functioning" occasioned by
anxiety. Other studies (Randall, 1951; N.E.A., 1938;
N.E.A., 1967) covering more recent decades indicate
from 16 percent to 37 percent of teachers suffer from
varying degrees of "nervous anxiety" or report symptoms
categorizable in this manner. The number of teachers
in these studies range from 600 (Hicks, 1933) to 2,200
(N.E.A., 1951), to 2,290 (N.E.A., 1967), to 5,150   ,
(N.E.A., 1938), based on nationwide samples (Ringness,
1968; Kaplan, 1959; Marsh, 1973; Rubin, 1973; Beale,
1936). Further studies along anxiety-prone lines point
to the vulnerability of single teachers, student teachers, single female teachers, and blacks (Powell and
Ferraro, 1960; Singh, 1972; Carter, 1970). As has been
noted repeatedly in studies, beginning teachers are not
the only ones displaying (or reporting) anxiety; experienced teachers have their share as well, since the
concerns they have, while differing with experiences,
nonetheless signal conflicts, concerns, stresses and
tensions in the profession. While not doubting the
prevalence of anxiety conditions and feelings among
teachers, the research literature does not tell us in
specific details what anxiety reactions are brought
on by what stresses and strains in the daily lives of
teachers. On-the-spot observations of teacher and
student behaviors in the classroom would be needed
in order to tie down the specifics of anxiety reactions,
feelings and self-reports by teachers. It is not as
easy to pin down the sources of anxiety reactions
among teachers, sequestered in a classroom of 30-40
children, young, restless and energetic as they are,
compared to the office of a physician, dentist or
lawyer who is tending mostly adults in short bursts of
time over a 3 - 4 hour period before rushing off to the
hospital, a meeting, or pleading in court.

Discipline. A general source of anxiety experienced
by teachers is related to establishing and maintaining
discipline among students. Some teachers -- even among
beginners -- appear not to have a large problem with
discipline, but most do. In a review of studies conducted on beginning teachers' reports of causes of anxiety, nearly every study reported by Coates and
Thoresen (1976, pp. 162-164) mentioned discipline as
a major factor. Other sources of anxiety were, of
course, noted: motivating students, being approved of
by supervisors, good faculty relations, stimulating
student interest in learning and achievement, handling
cheating, establishing and maintaining classroom

routine, liking students and having them like the teachers, noting and dealing with individual differences
among students, maintaining academic standards, feeling
adequacy and satisfaction with efforts expended and
with outcomes, having students do well on standardized
exams, one's students getting into coveted colleges or
other programs in higher education, and knowing and
keeping up with one's subject matter field. Nearly
everything a teacher does, then, can be a source of
anxiety. There is probably no other occnpation that
depends as much on immediate feedback of results,
vagaries of which can occasion anxiety, unless it is
the ministry. Nurses gain feedback on their activities
from appreciative patients; physicians and dentists
on administering what they think will be helpful efforts or techniques, plus the money they typically earn;
executives from influencing others, and in terms of
direct and indirect financial rewards. But the teacher is wedged between the children and the outside
(professional and other) world and the nature of feedback often has to come from the teacher, himself or
herself, knowing that a best effort has been made, with
positive results far off in the distance, or negative
criticism close at hand. This is one reason why the
teacher must be a "whole person" (whatever that means!)
and be enough self-contained to be secure against the
onslaughts of criticism, conflict, stress on the job
and tension in their own makeup. What the teacher
can't obtain in terms of rewards and benefits from
others, she/he has to secure within the daily confines
of teaching in the classroom with children, knowing,
loving and stimulating the children despite the vicissitudes in the out-of-clazsroom world (Brenton, 1971;
Lortie, 1975; Knoblock and Goldstein, 1971).

Articles continue to appear which link teachers
with anxieties and with other psychological problems
such as suicide (Brehant, 1972), although suicide among
teachers is rare. Part of the problem has been the
shortage of teachers in the 1950s and 1960s, giving part-
time and ill-prepared teachers responsibilities in the
classroom and for children's health and education far
beyond the surrogate teachers' capabilities (Shipley,
1961). The poor preparation of such a large number of
substitute teachers -- up to 15% in some localities --
has also given teaching a further blow in reputation.
Teachers respond with anxieties, with absences (hence
the high rate of substitutes), and with eventual discouragement and illness when they received too many
stresses from the environment. These include: Too
many surprises (arising from assignments to accept or

191

to keep unruly children); to put on programs for special PTA and/or administrative meetings; excessive
interruptions with the classroom routine; extra duties
that interfere with the smooth functioning of the day's
schedule or after-school composure (yard duty, hall duty,
bus duty, after-school detention); and an excess of
paper work. Over against these vicissitudes, Shipley
calls the teacher "...one of the hardest-working members
of the community" (Shipley, 1961, p. 8). Devotion to
purpose that is easily frustrated and placed in conflict
with other motives can create tensions and anxieties;
the teaching profession has many examples of this state
of affairs.

One of the earliest studies on mental health problems among teachers was reported over 50 years ago
(Mason, 1931). At the time of this study, three-fourths
of the disturbed teachers were single (60% of the men
and 82% of the women), a much larger number than was
true of the general population at the time and far more
than would be the case today. These single individuals,
while they would be atypical today, were doubtlessly
subjected to many social pressures and anxiety provocations. While the point of view of the Mason article
puts an emphasis on hereditary causes or predispositions
in the disturbed teacher population, the actual data
presented as to the known contributing cause of psy-
choses among the 700 maladjusted teachers referred
primarily to environmental (or experiential) precipi-
tants: financial troubles, love affairs, unemployment,
death of relatives, school (job) troubles, and worry
over sexual diseases. As stress, tension and anxiety
have been studied more over the past decades, causes
have been located more and more in the environment and
diagnostic predelictions have given way to descriptions
of environmental stresses such as those cited (but not
properly recognized) in the Mason study.

Considering teaching one of the most stressful
occupations, Brodsky (1977) investigated long-term work
stress among this population (and among prison guards).
Teachers (N = 16 females, 15 males) were selected for
study who, among 1,200 persons, had filed industrial
accident claims or applied for service-connected disabilities. They claimed injury due to pressure on their
jobs. All had good health histories and had been on th
job nearly 18 years on the average; malingering was not
a factor. Brodsky observes that the teacher's plight
vis a vis illness has much to do with conflicting roles
society now wants teachers to equip children with

192

independence, initiative and objectivity, yet again it wants children to merely fill roles in the economic structure with teachers preparing the children for this simple role. Long-term teacher conflicts were with the children (especially older ones, where disciplinary and even violence were concerned), with peers, and with superiors. Stress in these situations was defined as a discrepancy between the demands of the (teaching) situation and the capacity of the individual to meet the demand (Brodsky, 1977, p. 135). This definition will probably meet the generalized notion of stress found throughout this book. The onset of stress was judged to be occasioned by repeated, daily demands and by the teacher's inability to express emotions of anger, fear, guilt, etc. arising from these unmet demands. Thus the teachers were caught in unresolvable conflict. In short, they were trapped. Over the long haul, this trapped state of affairs caused and sustained long periods of tension; as the teacher moved into each day's duties with the unresolved ones of the past still present, anxiety supervened. The study found superiors and subordinates among the teaching profession in much the same state of affairs. Triggering events may occur in the school--with students, administration, parents, or several of these--which pose indelibly the teacher's plight, revealing his/her vulnerability, isolation, and absence of recourse. Prolonged states of this type result in somatic problems which may not only persist but may become more severe in time (Kiritz & Moos, 1974). Brodsky goes further than simply describing stress among teachers and the untoward consequences associated therewith. He feels they should be prepared for the likely stress as an when they become teachers. He points out: "We insist that those working with radioactive materials or with x-ray machines wear badges that will reveal exposure to excessive radiation. We should inform teachers...and others who are subject to long-term stress about the early indicators of overexposure" (Brodsky, 1977, p. 138).

We have indicated that stress arises from a discrepancy between what is expected (demanded, required, integral to given roles) and what actual performance yields. Teachers, along with other professionals have a good dose of this discrepancy; and have to be sensitive to the unresolved role tensions, and be prepared to find ways to cope. One way to help all professionals cope better with their stress is to observe the good things they do and separate these contributions from the public stereotypes that professions often exhibit for themselves.

Although teachers are often criticized for not educating their pupils - and there is some truth in this accusation - it goes far beyond the classroom teacher; there are probably many instances when teachers might be appreciated more. Sylvia Ashton-Warner (1979) wrote a book about her teaching career in New Zealand in the early 20th Century. Many of the features of her early life with her itinerate school teacher mother are similar to those cited earlier about the plight of teachers in America in the early days of this country. She conflicted with the teaching establishment and never received much credit for her ideas and contributions. In giving proper credit to Ashton-Warner's ideas and contributions, Osborne (1980, p. 36) says, "...teachers of language and reading are the ones who are primarily responsible for the vast growth of the reading public...teachers, more than any other profession, have energized the development of... information service industries. Teachers, who despite their own self-denigration, are the ones who help nourish each generation of writers, poets, dramatists..."

Teacher Effectiveness

More empirically based judgements of the effectiveness of teaching comes from the Lazar and Darlington (1979) report on the longitudinal effects from the "Head Start" program which began over a decade ago during the Johnson Administration. This report summarizes the preschool's effects on later school performance (age 10) in regard to three quantitative variables: the number of children assigned to special education; and/or those who were retained in grade; and achievement test results.

The results showed that a statistically significantly larger number of controls (those children not experiencing the enrichment of the "Head Start" program), among six separate projects, were assigned to special education classes, compared to the "Head Start" children. Moreover, the children experiencing the enrichment programs (eight separate programs) were far less often held back in school than the controls. In eight separate programs the percentage of treatment children (those receiving the enrichment curriculum) who turned out to be underachievers were statistically far less in occurrence than the controls. Statistical analyses revealed that at the beginning of the program the "treatment" and control groups were equally matched in I.Q. and other socially related variables (age range 3 months to 5 years upon entry into the program, 92% black children, average level of mother's education was 10.5 years, 40% without fathers in the home, and one-half of the children had three or more siblings) (Lazar & Darlington, 1979, p. 1). Summarizing the results overall, these authors say, children who participated in preschool intervention programs were more likely than control children to meet at least the minimal standards of their schools (Lazar & Darlington, 1979, p. 8) (Emphasis original).

Qualitative signs and cost-effective results also eminated from the preschool educational enrichment programs. Attitudes and values were improved: Mother's aspirations for their children improved; children became more achievement oriented; children's self-evaluation and self-concepts improved; and children's social relations and social participation show gains; all comparing the "treatment" group with the controls. Cost effectiveness was studied by Weber, et al (1978) who found that the costs attributable to the preschool enrichment programs paid off in terms of economics brought on by reducing the number of children referred to costly special education programs. These results show in a modest but encouraging way that mobilizing efforts among teachers and educators to enrich the educational and personal/social lives of disadvantaged preschool children and infants does reap benefit; and that such benefits are not at the expense of the tax-payer, the school system, or biased comparisons with other children. While the enrichment of the "Head Start" programs was confined to the early years of life, there is reason to think that continuing such enrichment throughout the child's school life, would bring on equally encouraging benefits (Jenck, 1979).

What are relevancies for the teaching profession qua profession in these preschool enrichment program findings? First of all, the implications are only suggestive, not conclusive nor final. When teachers are supported with technical skills appropriate to their tasks, they flourish; they are more interested in their work, and the feedback from prospering children is exciting and highly rewarding. Thus, the basis for teacher reinforcement in the lives and progress of the children is materially enhanced. Parents are involved in integral ways; the parent learns to cooperate with the school and the teacher in the child's interest, not to maintain a stand-off, critical posture that sees teaching the child a one-way street, expecting enormous effort and sacrifice on the part of the teachers. The evidence from the enrichment programs eminating from "Head Start" show that disadvantaged children can learn and, in cooperation with parental effort, can often overcome much of the educational bias against them. The old saw of the ones who "have" getting more and the "have-nots" suffering even greater losses is fully contested and partially reversed. Resentment against the school as non-democratic (Farber, 1970) and as not interested in the child's welfare is challenged and shown to be faulty. Although most of the "Head Start" work is still new, and older children have not been the subject of as much intensive study as the preschoolers and early elementary age child, there is hope that some of the adverse reactions of junior high school and high school students to school can be ameliorated if the "Head Start" lessons are amply and carefully replicated at the higher educational levels (Project Talent might be a starter in this direction). Finally, the "Head Start" philosophy puts ginger in the schools when they have been languishing due to too many conflicting educational philosophies (Fitzgerald, 1979); to too rapid expansion and overcrowding; to confusion arising among teachers as to their professional future, economic position and related issues; and due to the emergence of drop-out, burn-out, career change and other attritional factors among teachers. While "Head Start" is no end-all or be-all, it does portend a better future if it is continually implemented and moved in principle to the higher grades. No other profession has within its own professional structure generated as much constructive and prospectively encouraging change as the teaching profession. Perhaps here the more adverse aspects of professionalization, of rigid organizational and bureaucratic structure that sets itself against its original purposes, can be overcome and the profession can again assume the role it needs to have in a democratic society.

Discipline

The discipline problem appears to be looming larger and larger for teachers. The New York Times (October 28, 1979) recently reviewed a series of discipline problems that have impacted teachers mightily. The author, Dena Kleiman (1979), quoted recent Gallup Poll results as indicating a "lack of discipline" to be the top-rated problem for parents, teachers, legislators and others who were involved in some way in public education. Some of the findings from the TIMES report place the discipline problem in the following perspective: Student misbehavior is a nationwide concern; inner cities report the highest level of school violence against person and property; vandalism, drug abuse, alcohol abuse, smoking, theft and truancy are common in both suburban and rural areas; over 400 secondary school teachers are attached during any given month (in N.Y. City); all combining to make school teaching above the elementary level a dangerous occupation (Eddy, 1973; Berger, 1974; Fisk, 1973; Marsh, 1973). Supporting the last point, the TIMES article quoted some appaling statistics describing violence in New York City schools: 1,856 assaults, 1,097 robberies, 310 fires, 1,243 cases of disorderly conduct, 69 cases of sexual abuse, and over 300 incidents involving deadly weapons, in one year. What profession, then, is more dangerous than teaching?

Methods of handling these grave concerns are legion and so far none has worked too well. The banning of corporal punishment is common, although, incomprehensibly, the U.S. Supreme Court ruled two years ago that the practice of corporal punishment was constitutional (they required that paddling must be administered only after a youngster has been put on notice of such a possibility, and if administered, paddling has to be in the presence of another teacher or school official). How such a climate of opinion regarding teacher and pupil roles vis a vis discipline could possibly lead to other than additional confusion, resentment and retaliation, is hard for anyone to comprehend who understands the present atmosphere of misbehavior in schools. Unfortunately the word discipline in this context is often used to mean punishment (Phillips & Wiener, 1972) rather than the act or condition of submitting one's self to another to learn (as a disciple). As long as the use of the term discipline connotes punishment rather than positive

197

efforts, conditions and intentions, it will continue to have untoward effects on schools, teachers, parents and students (Shapiro, 1979; Henry & Brown, 1979; Phillips & Wiener, 1972).

The classroom teacher suffers the greatest harm in these instances of violence and abuse. Administrators are often a lengthy hallway removed from the classroom, can resort to dismissing the student from school (hence do not deal with the problem in depth), and can confine their efforts to legalistic and administrative measures. Some more positive means of dealing with school violence are, encouragingly, under way: group counseling of students, group sessions for teachers, increasing student involvement in school government, in-service training programs for teachers, consultation on a more regular (and preventive) basis with parents, and work-incentive programs for teachers, aides and school administrators.

O'Toole (1978), also writing a popular article in the N.Y. TIMES, pointed up the length and breadth of student attacks on teachers in schools. O'Toole stated that National Educational Association statistics indicated over 60,000 attacks on teachers occurred in the U.S. during the 1977-78 academic year; up to 3 percent of the nations over 2 million teachers have suffered some kind of physical or psychological casualty. Similarly a study by the Department of Health, Education and Welfare on the problem of school safety and violence revealed that 17 percent of all teachers work in fear of physical violence, that about 12 percent of the nation's high school teachers are threatened annually with attack, that teaching in urban high schools is nine times as likely to bring an assault as rural teaching, and once a teacher is targeted for attack (and attacked) that teacher is more likely to be attached again. Assailants, studies show, may not only be students with chains, chairs, fire extinguishers, handguns, files, steel combs, ice picks, lead pipes--anything with which to assault--but may also include intruders into the school.

Few professionals or people in business and industry face the potential violence teachers face in schools. At the time of this writing, a number of newspaper accounts cited violence in metropolitan area high schools. In one instance a gang sought out a high school student in the crowded cafeteria at noon and drew guns on the victim; and exchange of shots left injured three of the four participants in a Western-type "shoot-out" drama. The sixteen year old victim defended himself by drawing his own handgun, carried on his person for "protection" (Weisskopf & Saperstein, 1979). The news report indicates that students regularly carry weapons at this school.

The attack on teachers is all the more devastating when teachers are trying to see themselves as compassionate, and engage in activities that are loving, caring, idealistic, touched up by traits of passivity, indulgence and restraint. If the teacher loses these roles of compassion and interest in the student's welfare, what will be the incentive to teach? What will be reinforcing for teachers? Teachers' rage and fear turned on themselves owing to the stress from classroom disorder and violence coupled with administrative callousness will de-motivate teachers and lead to greater and greater tension among them (Stinnett, 1970; Berger, 1974; Eddy, 1973; Robert, 1973; Bower, 1973; Wilson, 1973; Metz & Fleischman, 1974; Myers, 1973).

Permissiveness

Some would say that decades of tauting permissiveness in child rearing and education have their natural consequences in these instances of violence in schools and classroom with a consequent injury to the teaching profession as well as to children (Phillips & Weiner, 1972; Wiener & Phillips, 1972). Misbehavior, from the standpoint of the permissive doctrine, usually (or most always) stems from allegedly "deep" psychological causes. This doctrine, then, discourages the teacher from calling a spade a spade, and causes him or her to demure in the face of misbehaviors of all sorts, not only violence, attack and threat. The doctrine of permissiveness plays into the already passive roles of teachers and disables them further, discourages action, and passes the responsibility for correcting the student's maladaptive behavior on to others (such as therapists, school psychologists, school nurses, and other professionals). Unfortunately--or fortunately--the permissive viewpoint is untenable, but it has nonetheless contributed materially to the present plight of schools and teachers vis a vis student misbehavior, all the way from "naughtiness" out to violence. As teachers are taught in their group discussions to act early and clearly at the first signs of misbehavior in their

199

classrooms--and--this is important--get administrative
back-up and respect from school authorities--they will
learn to forestall the milder forms of misbehavior and
be better prepared to deal with the grosser acts as
well. This is not just a matter of suppressing student
misbehavior or squelching maladjustment and psychological difficulties in pupils. It is a more positive
thrust toward meeting maladaptive behavior head-on
and toward developing constructive alternatives for
students to follow. Student participation in classroom and school governance are entirely compatible with
a more active role by teachers, and more likely to gain
the student's respect, encourage self-control, and
produce better learning (Phillips & Wiener, 1972;
Wiener & Phillips, 1972).

The effect of school violence and the public mistrust of teachers has many consequences for the
teachers and for the profession. Like the nurses who
are struggling for a greater place in the sun, teachers
will be struggling more and more for protection, for
rights, for administrative support, for better salaries,
for insurance support in the event of medical and hospital needs and costs associated with violence, and so
forth. Teaching will soon be known as a hazard
occupation if things do not change materially in the
next few years, especially in large urban settings and
in inner city areas. One teacher of special education
students captured the spirit of teacher discouragement
when she said, "I'm tired of being called all the dirty
names, being spit at, getting no support from families,
and hearing only criticism from the administrators
about classroom discipline--that's why I'm getting
out."

Also affecting school violence and misconduct
is the attitude of courts. They are too often lenient
with children and pass responsibility back to the
school to "maintain discipline," when the school is
already over-taxed and needs the court's support.
The TIMES report by O'Toole (1978) avers that kids feel
free to act as they impulsively do because they know
they will not be punished. Children, especially
belligerent adolescents, overturn one after another
person of authority--the classroom teacher, the parents,
the school administrator, the court social worker, the
juvenile court judge, the probation officer--and run
amok in the process. "They are so heddy, they are hell
bent for trouble and only violence will stop their
violence," one school probation officer testified in

200

a panel discussion on juvenile crime in the schools. Many of the violent youngsters come from violent homes where the only authority is physical punishment; they are attuned to solving problems by physical means and they carry this predisposition into the schools, taking their hostilities out on the greater passivity of teachers and school authorities. As the TIMES article recommends, schools, police, courts, welfare agencies, parents and others should work together, but they seldom coordinate their efforts in forceful and effective ways.

Teachers who do not drop out in the face of these and other onslaughts to their personage and integrity are demanding supplemental insurance benefits for possible injuries sustained "in line of duty," requiring better administrative support, improved school security, and more widespread psychological support from peers (Stinnett, 1970). Time will tell whether these measures will prove encouraging and effective.

Other Conflicts. The anxieties of teachers are based on conflicts between what is expected of them and how they perform. We have seen that the types of anxieties, or content thereof, differ between novice and experienced teachers. We have seen also that disciplinary problems exist in great abundance for teachers. These, too, represent conflicts between teachers and the standards they and the schools and society set for youth versus the differences between these standards and the unruliness of students, their different ethnic and social backgrounds, home based discipline and standards, and related issues. Now we look at some other conflicts encountered by teachers, perhaps some of them on a smaller scale than those cited above, but nonetheless compelling at times.

Teachers are supposed to "teach" the students who are sent to them, but teachers do not (usually) invent curricula (except occasionally within a specialty area). Curricula are devised by supervisors, specialists in various fields such as math, English, geography, etc., and by the authors of textbooks (Gibson, 1976; N.E.A., 1971; Guthrie & Craig, 1973; Bolton, 1973; Trachtenberg, 1973). Teachers are held responsible for what students learn but they are often unwilling participants in a contract for which they had no special training and in which they did not

originally participate. If students don't learn math,
it is often regarded as the teacher's fault; yet
teachers for example did not invent the "new math" and
the teaching of the new math, so-called, often conflicts
with the more traditional concepts and operations of
math learned a generation or two before by the teachers
and parents. Similarly with teaching reading: Teachers
are often forced into adopting particular theories,
procedures and routines regarding reading when they may
not "get into" such a viewpoint; yet they are held
accountable for the child's progress in reading. The
teacher cannot say to the complaining parent, "Why, you
know, I don't believe in the method of teaching reading
I (we) use." The teacher cannot say, even if she/he
thinks privately, "I think the new math stinks."
Teachers are on their own at the level of accountability
--accountability for the student's progress--but not at
the level of making the original decisions about
teaching methods to suit their own best judgements as
to what students will most profit from (Knoblock &
Boldstein, 1971; Jackson, 1968; N.E.A., 1968a; Fisk,
1973).

In the classroom, too, there are conflicts with
students. Common are power struggles as to how classroom order, procedure and an orientation toward
learning can be kept. Often enough to perplex and
annoy anyone, students come to school with a chip on
the shoulder, an attitude that says, "I dare you to
try to teach me anything;" and similar postures.
Parents often remark that this or that subject is
"useless"; they make derogatory comments about the
teacher, the school, the purposes of education, and
particular subject matter areas. There has never been
a curriculum at any educational level that the whole
of society has agreed is important, useful and to be
taught with certain procedures and objectives in mind.
Given the task of teaching recalcitrant children from
opposing backgrounds, is it any wonder the teacher's
life is beset with conflict, anxiety, stress and
tension? The nurse or physician can say to their
respective patients that if orders are not followed,
the patient's health may be harmed or put in jeopardy;
and the patient is allowed to choose. The same laise
faire attitude cannot be maintained in the classroom
or in the school. The teacher faces far more accountability than does the nurse or physician (unless, of
course, they do things that actively harm a person or
are life-threatening).

Teachers, like nurses, are in conflict with their traditional roles when and as they join unions to try to get better salaries, working conditions, broader benefits, and the like (Fisk, 1973; N.E.A., 1968b; Ziegler, 1967). Teachers for many years were reluctant to join unions because of their considerable passivity, because they received their "kicks" in the successes and relationships they had with students in the classroom (similar to nurses' satisfactions with individual patients who improved), and because they were so used to being told what to do, how to think, when and what to feel, that when initiative was suggested to them, they were disbelieving and largely unable to take up the cudgle for themselves. Teachers have begun to emerge from this cocoon but only slowly and haltingly, experiencing much conflict in the process.

Teachers receive the brunt of conflict between the school system, it's philosophy and standards on the one hand and reformers of the educational system on the other hand--such as John Holt, Jonathan Kozol, Herbert Kohl, Ivan Illich, Lewis Silverman and others. While these reformers are well-intended and often point to inadequacies in the prosent public school system, the classroom teacher is powerless to make very many of the changes recommended by the reformers. The reformers are, at best, piecemeal in their allegations and prescriptions for improved schools, and often only succeed in heightening the awareness of the public in the less admirable aspects of our schools while ignoring how the schools reflect society at large especially in relation to public attitudes of indifference, carelessness, procrastination and defeat. These reformers often center accusations on the classroom which is far from an independent entity within the school system, only reflecting, as it does, the confusion in the system at large.

The System At Large

Funding for reform and improvement are at issue here. Funding for schools has probably increased some in recent years, yet teachers' salaries have long lagged far behind the incomes of skilled workers and others less well-prepared in terms of formal education and skills. In the early 1960s, public school teachers on the average, nationally, earned about $5,000.00 per year, at a time when the average city worker needed to earn $6,700.00 to maintain an accepted standard of living. Lynn, et al, (1967) quoted the National Science Foundation review of funds for major areas of the U.S. Treasury between 1961-63 as follows:

$ 17.6 million for the U.S. Office of Education

$ 16.3   "   "   " Bureau of Commercial Fisheries

$ 23.2   "   "   " Agricultural Research Service

$ 660.6   "   "   " Public Health Service

$7,371.3   "   "   " Department of Defense (Lynn, et al, 1965,p.109).

While funds for such services and agencies may fluctuate from decade to decade, the allocations cited above reflect the low value we place in our country on formal support for education, hence on teachers' salaries. These figures, even if they changed markedly in the last 10 - 20 years (which they have not) would have set a standard and a precedence unsupportive of education which feeds back into the body politic and further casts education in poor light (teachers being the principle cogs in the educational wheel suffer from these low funding habits and from the attitudes they imply toward education) (Keyserling, 1967). Moreover, if spending money on education, funding research in new and better classroom teaching methods are important in directing the future of education and teaching, the low level funding will preclude the building of educational equity for the future; the longer these habits persists --like poor eating habits--the more adverse their effect will be over the years. We cannot have good schools, good teaching, good teachers and educated children a decade hence if we do not support these objectives today.

Lynn and associates sum up the last-cited conflict area for teachers with the following observation:

> The question is raised, what function does a school teacher first and foremost fulfill-- that of an instructor, of a custodian or of a social worker? The professional status of the school teacher is altogether questioned on the grounds of his limited autonomy, of his restrictions in decision-making concerning what and how

he teaches, and of his position as a
strictly supervised employee (Lynn, et al,
1967, p. 93).

Schools and the educational institution, nationally
considered, are like other large organizations. It is
hard to locate responsibility in large organizations;
it is difficult to tell how they function and how the
public good, allegedly of first importance, is properly
met. The fact that the drop out rate of high school
students has reached a significant proportion (somewhere near 40%) can be blamed on who, what? (N.E.A.,
1967). Where would one start if he sought to decrease
this dropout rate? Primarily with the classroom teacher?
Hardly. With local school administrators at the County
or city or state levels? Perhaps. But, if so, how
would a reform program be implimented? Would the Office
of Education figure largely in such reform?--it is
difficulty to see how, other than through publicizing
the problem and urging local school systems to respond.
The garguantian organization called "education" could
hardly respond effectively to a request to lower the
drop out rates of high school students. Likely,
responding would be confined to a series of inconsistent grassroots (more or less abortive) efforts through
curriculum change, more vocational education, closer
ties between the school and the community, more parent
involvement, and so forth. Like a huge serpent with a
thousand legs, the "school system" would respond first
by wiggling one leg, then another, hopefully in time
moving the beast a bit forward.

If the classroom teacher is going to be in any way
responsible for the education of children--other than
performing a daily ritual which is supposed to be
educational--means will have to be found to translate
this alleged responsibility into concrete terms.
Allinsmith and Goethals (1962) observe that teachers
have little understanding of how schools make policies
which affect them--the teachers, as well as the children
--and how seldom school practice are under the control
of teachers. Supervisors rule the day, as they do with
nurses in hospitals. Supervisors are often principals,
but they leave the classroom teaching roles to get into
better paying and less tension-provoking jobs. Principals assign students to classes, set schedules, exercise authority in terms of student promotions, student
problems and parent-school relationships. Most principals know very little--and probably care less--about
what goes on minute by minute in the classroom. Lynn,

et al, observed the following: "Lack of democratic
administration procedures and a share in policy-making
were among the main causes of poor teacher morale
recorded in a survey made by the George Peabody College
for Teachers..." (Lynn, et al, 1967, p. 94-95).
"Responsibility without authority...and without support
--that's our big problem", stated on teacher in a
seminar discussing how classroom teaching could improve
the school system's mission to educate children.

Teachers are often in conflict with their communities, especially small and compact ones. Teachers are
often chosen more on their looks and physical appearances than on qualifications, proven skills, and good
work histories. Teachers with physical disabilities or
limitations may receive low consideration for posts.
Lynn, et al, state: "Of primary importance (in hiring
and promoting teachers) is the teacher's conformity with
existing standards. The code of ethics of the National
Education Association demands that a teacher accept the
community's pattern of behavior" (Lynn, et al, 1967,
p. 95). One can easily imagine how these community
standards can constrict the lives, the morale and the
stability of teachers in small towns throughout the U.S.
as well as preempt and preclude the hiring and cultivation of teachers with handicaps, unorthodox outlooks
and even some socially nonconforming behavior patterns.
One teacher summed up the plight of teachers in this
regard: "Communities want teachers to be models of
behavior for children but the parents and the communities fail to be models for the children, and adults
in other professions and occupations fail to model
acceptable values and standards for teachers." Perhaps
more than any other profession than the clergy, the
teacher is in the public eye and this eye scrutinizes
the teacher's behavior in a variety of ways that create
anxiety for the teacher lest she/he violate standards
not imposed on other public servants.

The teacher's role in the community might be
characterized as having responsibility without authorit
(except in the classroom). Martin Luther judged the
teaching role to be equal to, or next to, the ministry.
The teacher has been at times glorified as the "fashior
of souls" (Thomas Carlyle in Sartor Resartus) and as a
person who should be ranked with political leaders,
generals and field marshals (it is interesting that
glorifying teachers in this example ranked them with
defenders of, rather than promoters of liberty, justice
and equality such as reformers, writers, philosophers

and moralists). Over against these laudatory views of
teachers one finds in history contrasting views of
teachers. In early Greece, teachers were barely
respected, receiving scant pay for teaching children to
read and write and memorize. In early Chinese schools,
teachers were those who had failed in other intellectual
pursuits, unable to pass examinations for more intellectually demanding jobs. In Russia, early Germany
(Prussia) and China, teachers were often gleaned from
invalids and misfits, another example of relegating the
teacher to inferior social and intellectual status.
The laudatory views of Carlyle and others might have
been pivoted on what teachers ought to be, how they
ideally should be regarded in an equalitarian society;
but, alas, there have been few if any equalitarian
societies, hence the way teachers have been treated
is more instructive of the respect offered them than
visionary poetic expressions of how they might be
treated. If society is judging what the teacher should
do in the classroom, the results on the child's
learning and behavior, the teacher comes in for much
scrutiny and responsibility; but when it comes to
giving the teacher a role in society and particularly
in his/her profession, the teacher gets little attention
and is mostly regarded as a servant. Aspirant young
teachers, idealizing their roles in helping children to
learn and grow, do not know what is lurking backstage
for them nor how soon their idealization will be
exposed for the emptiness it often holds in the view
of the public at large. If teachers in time gain more
respect in and from society they will have to fight
for their rights and for respect; it will not be
accorded them because they are teachers of the young!

Children And Teachers Of Doubtful Value

It is highly likely that the low value placed on
teachers reflects in part the relative value also
placed on children (Piers, 1978; Giovannoni & Becerra,
1979; Finkelher, 1979; Brady, 1979). If teachers are
to educate children but children are not intrinsically
important, then how can teaching them be more than a
cursory matter? It has been only in the last few
decades that children have been regarded as other than
small adults to be tolerated until they could be
economically productive and capable of sharing responsibility with others older and more skilled. Even as
recent as the end of the 19th century and the beginning
of the 20th century, as important an educational
leader as Stanford's E.P. Cubberly regarded schools as

207

similar to factories where raw materials were shaped
into finished products to meet the various demands of
life and the economy. It is true that children have
to "fit in" to society and assume a productive role,
but this is a more reciprocal role--we are learning
more each day--not simply a matter of shaping raw
materials into some rigidly fashioned object (Lynn,
et al, 1967, pp. 96-98). The striking similarity here
between treating children and education as marketplace
commodities is too great to escape notice. This view
denegrates children, but also it denegrates teachers--
sets them up to run a stencil-replicating machine--and
further places a low value on education if it serves
any purposes other than preparing the individual for
the giant industrial machines that so able dominate our
lives today.

One of the subtle and far-reaching influences on
the classroom teachers is that arising from business
and industrial attempts to influence the curriculum
and classroom teaching (Harty, 1979). Harty's publication, Hucksters In The Classroom, documents how well
public education can--and often does--become a vehicle
for indoctrination by business and industry--for, of
course, profit motives. Business knows the strengths
and weaknesses of the classroom environment, the value
and availability of equipment and supplies, and knows
how to cajole teachers into using their products.
Schools and classroom teachers are particularly
vulnerable: schools spend only 1 percent of their
budget on instructional materials, yet more than 90
percent of classroom time is spent using such materials
(Harty, 1979, p.2). The need is therefore great.

The classroom is an easy "grab" for business and
industry getting, as they do, substantial charitable
and educational contribution deductions from their
corporate tax payments (these deductible figures have
risen from $252 million in 1950 to $1.35 billion in
1976). Yet business is not giving itself away, since
their charitable and educational contributions have
represented less than one percent of their profits
(Harty, 1979, p.2). The cost/benefit ratio for
business in this connection is decidely favorable to
business. Children--and teachers (but they may not
know it)--are the pawns.

The review of industry's propaganda in the schools
includes many basis industries, and touches the lives
of children in salient ways in regard to food, energy
and power, chemicals, films, books and pamphlets, and
visual and auditory aids. Not a new problem, however,
is the attempted influence on the schools and classrooms by industry. In 1929 a report on how propaganda
was used in the schools was presented at the Atlanta
meeting of the National Education Association. As a
result of this 1929 presentation, a series of questions
were posed school systems which included the following:
What outside sources are trying to use the schools
for propaganda purposes? How have school boards,
executives and teachers attempted to meet the propaganda onslaught? Is further action on the part of
schools needed or desirable? And how can the schools
be guided by their acceptance and/or rejection of
privately supplied materials? Doubtlessly these
questions have not been satisfactorily answered in the
ensuing 50 years since the 1929 report. The enormity
of the problem nationally cannot be fully appraised
by even present data. Several decades ago one New
England city classroom was inundated with a list of
82 commercial items from companies seeking to influence
the children thereby, ranging widely from advertising
for cereal to insurance.

Reactions have set in and will continue to be
heard. Various educational committees on local and
national levels are mobilizing attention to the
educational hazards of product dispersal in the classroom. One strong opinion was voiced as follows:
"I would underscore the need for vigilance, the need to
question...I am most concerned with ideological propaganda which promotes corporate values in subjective
presentations, as well as promotional efforts to sell
products" (Harty, 1979, pp.104-105).

The dishonesty of the matter is apparent even in
this brief presentation of how hucksters operate in
the classroom. Under the guise of information, propaganda and advertising are snuck in, and without due
regard to opposing ideas, to the health and welfare
of the children, or to the consequences of such
materials and their long-range influence on the
classroom. No more dastardly view of the misuse of
corporate power--unless it is the capturing of
children's minds via TV advertising--can be envisioned.

The problems presented by classrooms used for corporate purposes lines up with many other corporate abuses of our environment. It constitutes serious ethical problems for teachers and for their concern as to how the classroom is used. It is another set of stressors impinging on teachers.

Will teaching become more and more stressful? Will trained people abandon the profession in favor of lessor trained, because only with not caring and with cavalier attitudes can one stand the on-slaughts of stress, tension and anxiety arising from the classroom, the playground and the administrative office? Will the web of social interaction and support (reinforcement) arising from teaching children be worn so thin by economic, professional and personal stress that few capable persons will be able to continue in teaching? It is entirely possible that this deterioration is already advanced and that we have but a few years to correct the ills of the teaching profession, or witness its demise along with other professions suffering a similar plight.

CHAPTER VIII

BIBLIOGRAPHY

Adams, S., & Garrett, J.L., Jr. To Be A Teacher: An Introduction to Education. Englewood Cliffs, N.J.: Prentice-Hall, 1969.

Allinsmith, W., & Goethals, G.W. The Role of Schools in Mental Health, Monography Series No. 7. Joint Commission of Mental Health. New York: Basic Books, 1962.

Ashton-Warner, S. I Passed This Way. N.Y.: Knapf, 1979.

Asborne, L.B. The Organic teacher, review of Sylvia Ashton-Warner's book, I Passed This Way, Wash. POST, Jan. 6, 1980.

Bard, B. The blackboard. New York POST. March 15, 1969.

Beale, H.K. Are American Teachers Free? New York: C. Scribners" Sons, 1936.

Berman, L. The mental health of the educator, Mental Hygiene, 1954, 38, 422-429.

Berger, M. Violence In The Schools: Causes & Remedies. Bloomington, Ind.: Phi Delta Kappa Educational Foundation, 1973.

Biegeleisen, J.I. Careers and Opportunities in Teaching. N.Y.: E.P. Dutton, 1969.

Bolton, D.L. Selection and Evaluation of Teachers. Berkeley, Calif.: McCutchan Corp., 1973.

Bowen, H.R. Academic Compensation. New York Teachers Insurance & Annuity Assn., 1978.

Bower, E.I. Teachers Talk About Their Feelings. DHEW Publ. No. (HSM) 73-9032. NIMH - Center For Studies In Child & Family Mental Health, 1973.

Brady, K. Father's Days: A True Story of Incest. N.Y.: Seaview, 1979.

Brehant, J. Pourquoi les enseignments si suicide-ils? Nouv. Presse Med., 1972, 1, 1312-1313.

Brenton, M. What's Happened To Teachers? N.Y.: Avon, 1970.

Brodsky, C. M. Long-term work stress in teachers and prison guards, J. of Occup. Med., 1977, 19, 133-138.

Carter, V.L. Anxieties of White and Negro elementary and secondary student teachers in biracial participation. Dissertation Abstracts Intern. North Texas State University, 1658A-1659A; Univ. of Mich. M-Films No. 70-17972, 1970.

Coates, T.J. & Thoresen, C.E. Teacher anxiety: A review with recommendations, Rev. of Educational Res., 1976, 46, 159-184.

Combs, A.W. The Professional Education of Teachers. Boston: Allyn & Bacon, 1974.

Delp, H.A. Mental health of teachers still a problem? J. of Teacher Educ., 1963, 14, 142-150.

Eddy, J. The Teacher and the Drug Scene. Bloomington, Ind.: Phi Delta Kappa Educ. Fdn., 1973.

Eisner, E. Situation potentials and personality needs in teaching, J. of Teacher Educ., 1961.

Farber, J. The Student As Nigger, N.Y.: Pocket Books, 1970.

Finkelher, D. Sexually Victimized Children. N.Y.: Free Press, 1979.

Fisk, L. A Survival Guide For Teachers. N.Y.: Wiley, 1973.

Fitzgerald, F. America Revised, History School Books In The Twentieth Century. N.Y.: Little, Brown, 1979.

Freudenberger, J.J. The staff burn-out syndrome in alternative institutions, Psychotherapy: Theory, Res. and Practice, 1975, 12, 73-82.

Gibson, J.T. *Psychology For The Classroom.* Englewood Cliffs, N.Y.: Prentice-Hall, 1976.

Giovannoni, J.M. & Becerra, R.M. *Defining Child Abuse.* N.Y.: Free Press, 1979.

Gutherie, J.W. & Craig, P.A. *Teachers and Politics.* Bloomington, Ind.: Phi Delta Kappa Educational Foundation, 1973.

Harty, S. *Hucksters In The Classroom: A Review of Industrial Propaganda In The Schools.* Wash.,D.C. Center For The Study of Responsive Law, 1979.

Henry, N. & Brown, C. Students accused of high school classroom rape, Washington POST, p. D-1, Dec. 14, 1979.

Hicks, F.P. *The Mental Health of Teachers.* N.Y.: Cullman and Ghertner, 1933.

Jackson, P.W. *Life in Classrooms.* N.Y.: Holt, Rinehart & Winston, 1968.

Jencks, C. *Who Gets Ahead.* N.Y.: Basic Books, 1979.

Kaplan, L. *Mental Health and Human Relations in Education.* N.Y.: Harper & Bros., 1959.

Keyserling, L.H. *Goals For Teachers' Salaries In Our Public Schools: A Vital Test of the Sincerity of our Great National Purpose.* Wash., D.C. Conference on Economic Progress, 1967.

Kiritz, S., & Moos, R. Physiological effects of social environments, *Psychsom. Med.*, 1974, 36, 96-114.

Kleiman, D. Keeping discipline in the schools is the No. 1 educational headache, N.Y. TIMES, Oct. 28, 1979.

Kohl, H.R. *The Open Classroom.* N.Y.: Vintage Books, 1970.

Kohl, H.R. *Half The House.* N.Y.: Dutton, 1974.

Knoblock, P., & Goldstein, A.P. Boston: Allyn & Bacon, 1971.

Lazar, I. and Darlington, R. Lasting Effects After Preschool. Washington, D.C.: DHEW No. OHDS 79-30179, 1977.

Lieberman, M. Education As A Profession. Englewood Cliffs, N.Y.: Prentice-Hall, 1956.

Lortie, D.C. Schoolteacher: A Sociological Study. Chicago: Univ. of Chic. Press, 1975.

Lynn, K.S., & the Editors of Daedalus. The Professions in America. Boston: Beacon Press, 1967.

Marsh, L.G. Being A Teacher. New York: Praeger, 1973.

Mason, F.V. A study of Seven-Hundred Maladjusted School teachers, Mental Hygiene, 1931, 15, 576-599.

Metz, A.S. & Fleischman, K.L. Teacher Turnover In Public Schools. U.S. Dept. of H.E.W. DHEW Publ. No. (OE) 74-11115, 1974.

Moore, W.E. The Professions: Roles & Rules. N.Y.: Russell Sage Fdn., 1970.

Myers, D.A. Teacher Power: Professionalization and Collective Bargaining. Lexington, Mass.: Lexington Books, 1973.

National Education Association. Fit To Teach: A Study of the Health Problems of Teachers. Washington,D.C. Nat'l. Educ. Assn., 1938.

National Education Association. Teaching load in 1950, Research Bull., 1951, 29, 3-50.

National Education Association. The American Public School Teacher, 1965-1966. Research Report, R-4, 1967. Washington, D.C.: Nat'l Educ. Assn., 1967.

National Education Association. School Dropouts (by Sherrell E. Varner). Washington, D.C.: N.E.A., 1967.

National Education Association. Teacher Strikes and Work Stoppages, January 1940 to July 1968. Washington,D.C., Nat'l Educ. Assn., 1968.

National Education Association. Careers In Education. Washington,D.C.: Nat'l Educ. Assn., 1968.

214

National Education Association. Schools For The 70's and Beyond. Washington,D.C.: Nat'l Educ. Assn., 1971.

O'Toole, P. Casualties in the classroom, N.Y. TIMES, Magazine Section, Dec. 10, 1978.

Phillips, E.L. & Wiener, D.N. Discipline, Achievement and Mental Health. 2nd Ed. Englewood Cliffs, N.Y.: Prentice-Hall, 1972.

Piers, M. W. Infanticide - Past and Present. N.Y.: Norton, 1978.

Powell, M., & Ferraro, C.D. Sources of tension in married and single women teachers of different ages, J. of Educ. Psychol., 1960, 51, 92-101.

Randall, H.B. Health is for teachers, too, Nat'l Educ. Assn. J., 1951, 40, 467-468.

Randall, H.B. Twenty-Year report on teacher absences. Paper, Amer. School Health Assn. Chicago, Oct. 1965.

Ringness, T.A. Mental Health In The Schools. N.Y.: Random House, 1968.

Robert M. Loneliness in the Schools. Niles, Ill.: Argus Communications, 1973.

Rubin, L.J. Facts & Feelings In The Classroom. N.Y.: Talker, 1973.

Shapiro, M. Mother enters P.G. classroom and publicly whips daughter, Washington POST, p.1, Dec.15,1979.

Shipley, J.T. The Mentally Disturbed Teacher. Phila.: Chilton Book Co., 1961.

Singh, A.J. Incidence of anxiety among teachers under training and teachers in service, J. of the Indian Academy of Applied Psychol., 1972, 9, 61-64.

Solomon, J.C. Neuroses of school teachers, Mental Hygiene, 1960, 44, 79-90.

Stinnett, T.M. (Ed.) The Teacher Drop-out. Itasca, Ill.: F.E. Peacock, 1970.

215

Stirdivant, L.E. Teacher turnover due to ill health, Calif. Teachers' Assn. J., 1957, 53, 20-22.

Trachtenberg, P.I. Testing The Teachers: How Urban Schools Districts Select Their Teachers and Supervisors. N.Y.: Agathon Press, 1973.

United Nations Education, Scientific & Cultural Organization. Highest neuroses found in teachers, UNESCO Courier, 1954, 5, 25.

Volliner, H.M., & Mills, D.L. (Eds.) Professionalism. Englewood Cliffs, N.J.: Prentice-Hall, 1966.

Weber, C.U., Faster, P.W., & Weikart, D.P. An economic analysis of the Upsilanti Perry Preschool Project, Monogr. of the High/Scope Educ. Res. Fdn., #5, 1978,

Weisskopf, M. & Saperstein, S. Gun battle jolts school in Baltimore, Washington POST, p. C-1, Dec.4,1979.

Wiener, D. N. & Phillips, E.L. Training Children In Self-Discipline and Self-Control. Englewood Cliffs, N.J.: Prentice-Hall, 1972.

Wilson, E.C. Needed: A New Kind of Teacher. Bloomington, Ind.: Phi Delta Kappa Educational Foundation, 1973.

Zeigler, H. The Political Life of American Teachers. Englewood Cliffs, N.J.: Prentice-Hall, 1967.

CHAPTER IX

WOMEN

No writing today on the consequences of social stress, health and personal problems would be complete if it failed to include women. Women are the largest minority and one of the most conspicuous examples of a population under stress. Much of the stress, tension and anxiety women suffer comes not so much from the intended hands of men--although bias is certainly ever-present--but from the "system", i.e., from the economic and professional constraints that meet women on every corner of development, achievement and service.

Many aspects of the "woman's problem" have surfaced in recent decades, many features of which are economic. The economic matters appear to be ubiquitous, to infiltrate all walks of life (professional, blue-collar and non-specialized); and to inhibit the progress of women in the form of bias against them even being considered for many professions and posts, out to screening them out as part of selection procedures (for job, for training, for higher professional education), and even in the executive of their jobs as they move through life as mature contributors.

A paradox in the lives of professional women and women high in the business world is that as they compete with men for positions of rank, they tend to take on the worries, health problems and career issues generally associated with men. In order to take advantage of what has heretofore been a man's world, they move in the direction of being more like men, perhaps in unwelcome and unsavory ways as well as in matters of achievement, earnings, status and prestige. As one observer said, "As women become more like men in the outside world, they also become more like men in personal ways--they can't remain women and still be like (compete with) men." Perhaps this dichotomy is too strong and too severely drawn; only time will tell. But as women achieve comparably to men, they must bend to the system (the professions, the organizations, ultimately the stresses, tensions, anxieties); in so doing they cannot help acquiring unasked-for characteristics.

217

The way most writers characterize women in the professional world is to say that women have "role conflicts." This means something very simply: They try to be women in the traditional sense (homemakers, child-rearers, social secretaries and supporters to their husbands, and the like) as they also move into professional fronts. Balancing both of these roles is no easy matter. Men have seldom if ever had to do it, being given pretty much carte blanche access to their worlds, with women as supporters if not wholly yoken-in (see chapter on The Clergy). At every juncture women face the role conflict motif: As and when they try to apply for many professions, in the actual training required by a profession, in serving intern and/or other advanced specialty roles, in carrying out the duties of a mature member of a profession, and in sharing the professional role with other aspects of womanhood (family, child rearing, domestic responsibilities and more).

Not only are the dual and often uncomplementary roles of women unharmonious, they may also be openly conflictful. Winter et al (1977) studied 51 undergraduate members of the class of 1964 and followed up on them ten years later, observing matters relating to the husband's roles and motives and the wife's career line. The more men were power oriented (and this motive looms large in men of business and in some professions like law and medicine) the less the wife's career accomplishments later in life. More positively correlated with wife's career level were the husband's affiliative interests, his selfhood being articulated, the husband's college grades and satisfaction with college. Business executive husbands and those politically conservative tended to live and act in ways that were inhibitory to the wife's career development. Of course, people who are somewhat alike choose each other (part of the conservatism of men is shown in selecting wives who are conservative, traditional, hence less likely to rock-the-boat), and perhaps other circular matters tend to cooperate in producing this kind of husband-wife-career outcome.

Sex Role Changes

The loosening up of sex roles, career lines and stereotyping is currently in evidence in some research among youngsters even as early as the ninth grade. Westbrook (1976) studied 279 ninth graders of both sexes as to their career choices and competencies,

218

testing in the process some models of how youngsters mature with respect to careers. Among older students as well (Quaranta, 1976), covential sex roles were less rigidly adhered to in matters of vocational or career choice, and women were found to explore and select widely among opposite sex-typed career choices (i.e., chose occupations and professions heretofore dominated by men). Quaranta studied 334 college freshmen, males and females. Up and down the educational ladder, women are sampling wider career prospects whether they follow through on them or not. However, "sampling" career choices widely is not tantamount to entering any career without bias or limiting conditions. Perhaps the fact that many new occupations and wider professional choices are open to women bodes well, but it is only a starter.[1]

If young women have experienced undue constraints upon trying to enter a profession, older women wishing to return to the world of work find even more deterrents to their aspirations (Vriend, 1977). Women who give up the primary occupation of family and household care at mid-age find trouble being admitted to programs even where the need for new workers is great, such as in nursing. These re-entry women need counseling in order to grapple with the stubbornness of the professional work, in regard to training and re-education problems, and in overcoming sex role stereotypes. Their own confusion and lack of purpose, aligned with the prejudices of professions and the vicissitudes of the marketplace all combine to make the woman's role very trying during mid-life changeovers. Preparing younger women for these possible role changes (McLaughlin, et al, 1976) may be an important part of their general education as well as being pointed to later ease in career re-training and re-entry.

---

[1]Two comprehensive bibliographies of women in relation to sex role stereotyping and in relation to work are seen in the American Psychological Association's Journal Supplement Abstract Service, specifically one by Nieva and Gutek (1976) on Women and Work: A Bibliography of Psychological Research, and one by Baer and Sherif (1974), A Topical Bibliography (Selectively Annotated) On Psychology Of Women . In connection with this chapter and the one on Executives, one might also consult the publication, Women as Managers Scale (WAMS): A Measure Of Attitudes Toward Women In Management Positions (Peters, Terborg and Taynor, 1974).

Attempts to offset the biases of sex role stereotypes are not always successful. Rohfeld (1977)
studied 290 high school female students on how they
rated career planning resources available to them.
They placed high value on concrete experiences: Field
work trips, having workers visit schools, and talks by
teachers and other instructors on specific job-related
skills. Counselors, often unthinkingly, tended to
steer women into traditional sex role professions and
jobs, thus causing more ambivalence among women in
regard to career matters, and doing them a disservice
when it came to helping them sample widely and
convincingly among the many career choices available.
Again, the "system" tends to push women into traditional
roles and even to actively discourage them from
entering the major professions (except teaching and
nursing) or sampling non-professional jobs widely.
The "system" is the vast network of education, career
guidance, selection procedures, training and educational
programs, economic benefits and constraints, and
progess in a profession, or occupation, once entered.
At all junctures women meet more career hardships than
men, and sometimes the crossroads are dimly marked,
rough and circuitous (Burlin, 1976; Quarantana, 1976;
Vriend, 1977; Westbrook,1976).

At some higher levels of achievement--those with
the Ph.D. in physical, biological and social science
areas--women tend to gain more equality of opportunity
and salary commensurate with men. Cole (1979) reports
on how women fare in science in universities and in
other settings, concluding that it is basically "fair,"
but allowing as to how it was not fair in the past.
Viewed in terms of quantity and quality of publications
women equal men in status and reputation. A demure to
Cole's findings was voiced by Mason (1980), indicating
that women probably make more contributions to science
than their rewards acknowledge; and that greater
rewards in science do not come to women because they
are often denied access to the various means of production of scientific contributions: research facilities, graduate assistants, professional sponsorship,
secretarial help, and more. Many people associated
intimately with various departments in universities
will often attest to the fact that department
committees have to be reminded that "women and
minorities" must be given high consideration for jobs,
for research opportunities, for assistants, and other
means of support. It is not a reminder that comes

easily in many university departments, but one that
has to be goaded and proded. Women are not fully
equal with men in the university/scientific setting
although they do better here than in many other professional settings and better than they did decades ago.
Much of the problem in these settings is local--the
particular university, the particular department, and
the men (and women) making up these departments.

Women And Business

The situation with women in business, industry
and professional life in general bodes less well.
Women make up 51% of the total population in the
U.S.A., but only 40% of the work force. Most women
among the 39 million in the work force in the U.S.A.,
are employed in five major (predominantly "female")
occupations which include: secretary-stenograph,
household workers, bookkeepers, elementary school
teachers and waitresses. Fewer than six percent of
employed women work in managerial, administrative or
professional jobs (Biles and Bryatel, 1978). Men out-
number women 600 to 1 in executive level positions!
The highest salary and bonus and stock earnings are
afforded men; only one woman appears on the Fortune
500 list as a chief executive officer (CEO). Barriers
and myths abound Biles and Pryate (1978) assert, as
to why women are accorded a lesser position in the
professions. One myth is that women do not make good
managers, tending to be too emotional; as economic
risks they rank high, according to the myth, because
they are ill too much, with marriage and children
further cutting into their work-a-day life. Factually,
women between ages of 20 and 40 do work about 7 hours
less per week than men (Ruby, 1976). Another myth
holds that women have less training and education in
general than men, whereas the fact is that the
average female worker has completed 12.5 years of
school, males 12.4 years. The language of work
predisposes favor to men: <u>Man</u>power planning, work<u>mens</u>
compensation, <u>man</u>-hours of work, right <u>man</u> for the
job, and so on. Our mentality is masculine. Our use
of words tells us a lot about biases and prejudices,
not only among men and women but in all walks of life.
Do women lack achievement motivation? Myths assert
yes. In high school young girls achieve better on
the average than boys; most college Phi Beta Kappa
elections are to women. But the more youth partici-
pates in life-in-general, the more male dominance
begins to assert itself, resulting over the mature

years in decidely higher male accomplishments. But
is this not primarily cultural, i.e., not integral to
the biological beings, men and women? Our best evidence
seems to say the biases are indeed, cultural.

What will bring changes in opportunities for
women? More women being made available for jobs
through their need to support themselves due to
divorce or to never having been married. Better
training and more advanced degrees won by women will
increase their pressures on the job market. Overcoming
the myths cited above will let men and consumers know
that some can do as well as men in providing most if
not all professional services. Finally, federal
legislation, such as the Equal Pay Act, amended in 1972,
Title VII of the Civil Rights Act, as amended by the
Equal Employment Opportunity Act of 1972, make it
illegal for employees to discriminate against hiring
women qualified for positions. It is further important
for women to know they are being treated fairly and
equally with men, however this equality is established.

Health And Fairness Issues

Although nearly a decade has passed since some of
the fair employment victories have been won by and for
women, only a decade earlier people like Friedan were
vigorously pounding their way into the male citadels
(Friedan, 1963; Millett, 1970). Much of the movement
for women's rights derived from medical care and
health matters, notably areas that most directly
affected women such as gynecologic examinations, birth
control knowledge and measures, abortion, sexuality,
childbirth and psychotherapy (Ehrenreich & English,
1973; Masters & Johnson, 1966; Firestone, 1971). In
these areas the woman's life was touched most
saliently. Despite the vigor of the feminist's movement for personal health gains, women seldom occupied
the upper echelons of the medical establishment,
although women represent the vast majority of health
workers (Fee, 1975). Womens' gains were won from
the outside, so to speak, because women have not
traditionally had much power in the medical establishment, although there are now signs that this is
changing. The gains, however, are not unilaterally
good. As women move into men's roles in medical and
health sciences, they become more like men, take on
their health and emotional stress problems, and for
example are found to rank high in suicide rates and in
other debilities. Whatever areas have afforded women

222

greater opportunity in professional life in recent
years have also had the unasked for and sometimes hidden
cost of poorer health, more stress, family problems,
divorce increase, and the like (Walsh, 1977). This
set of complex circumstances has led to what Fee (1975)
describes as liberal, radical and Marxist feminism.
The former type of feminism has asked only to be
included in the male establishments (professions, for
example), the more radical types have asked for
transformation of existing social institutions, and
the Marxist variety has pointed out that sexism (which
is equivalent to feminism in most respects) has been
useful to capitalism and that this should change if
women's roles are permanently to improve. Woman's
disadvantage in the capitalist system, it is held, is
seen as oppressing women as both patient and worker.
Fee observes, "If capitalist medicine fragments the
organization of work, it also fragments the delivery of
health care. First it provides multi-level services
based on a patient's ability to pay. It affords very
high quality service to the wealthy; shoddy, assembly-
line care for the poor. Specialization makes it
difficult, at almost any level, to find comprehensive
care" (Fee, 1975, p. 129). Women suffer more than
men in this fragmentation. Women are the recipients,
as indicated above, in this medical jumble: They get
less good care than they should, especially if poor;
and they are not admitted to the sanctified halls of
medical practice if they, themselves, wish to be
physicians (Walsh, 1977; Savage & Wilson, 1977).

Women, as physicians, have not always fared so
poorly in medicine. In 1893-94, the percentage of
women enrolled in a number of American medical colleges
ranged from under 12 percent (Univ. of California,
and U. of Buffalo, N.Y.) to over 25 percent (Denver
Medical College, Gross Medical College, Colorado,
Council Bluffs (Iowa) Medical College and Tufts
University) (Walsh, 1977, p. 193). More recently the
number of women physicians in the United States was
8.6% in 1976 (out of a total of 357,762 physicians);
this figure had not changed materially for women who
were physicians since 1950 (Walsh, 1977, p. 186), when
the percentage was 6.1, in a total of nearly 200,000
physicians nationwide. Historians of the women's
movement in the U.S.A. and of medicine as well have
tended to ignore problems related to the decline in
the number of women in medicine in the first decades
of the 20th century. Two sets of explanations have
been suggested for the 20th century bias against women

in medicine: That with professionalization of medicine, accompanied by licensing reform, laws tightening the practice of medicine in most states. Stemming from the 1910 Flexner report, medicine was in such ferment women had no chance to gain admittance in any significant numbers. Other explanations tend to blame women themselves as not being professional enough, not cutting out and following careers in medicine that rivaled men in devotion and in contribution to medical causes, and the old story of women divided: home and family careers interfering with the practice of medicine even when women were licensed, practicing physicians. This bias persists today in several if not many, schools, even with a general national increase in women enrolled in medical schools--e.g., Albany Medical College, Yale Medical School, Emory University Medical School, and Loyola Medical School, have expressed discriminatory practices toward women admissions in a publication by the Association of American Medical Colleges (Walsh, 1977, p. 243). Attempts to unravel these biases in published literature has for decades met with unsuccess (Williams, 1950; Walsh, 1977). Supporting these biases against women physicians, as physicians, are some of the myths we encountered above: "Women physicians are not emotionally stable..." "Lady doctors talk too much...they're always on the defensive..." "They get pregnant and cannot work regularly..." "If married, the woman doctor is divided by her family's needs and neglects her practice..." or "If she is unmarried or if she is married and childless, she is frustrated..."

The prominence of nursing as a woman's medical-related profession grew markedly over the early decades of the 20th century. In 1890, 30 nursing schools in the whole country graduated about 470 nurses; in 1926 they graduated over 2,000 nurses, all women (Walsh, 1977, p. 246). Women turned to nursing, and were expected to do so, in lieu of acceptance into medicine, or to other paramedical opportunities. Not many women persist in the expectation that they can enter medicine; from among a group of National Merit scholars many women in high school were nurturing thoughts of a career in medicine only to drop these notions in college. Three years later, only 8 percent of the applicants to medical school consisted of women.

Impressions of how women are discouraged in their motivation toward medical careers is not only supported by anecdotal information but by research as well. Horne

224

and Walsh (1974) and Horner (1972) used projective tests to study achievement motivation in women. A hypothetical test situation was presented the subjects, all women, in regard to a woman, "Anne" who finds herself at the top of her medical class after the end of one term. The women responding to the projective test situation attributed to the hypothetical "Anne" a number of negative consequences, seeing "Anne" as losing femininity and suffering from social rejection and isolation. Additional characteristics assigned to "Anne" were that she was unhappy, aggressive, manipulative of others in order to get ahead, and--in terms of the stereotype even women hold to--unmarried.

Like most myths, the ones about women, achievement, women in medicine, and so on, are unsubstantiated. Most women physicians do marry today (Walsh, 1977, p. 251), with 71 percent doing so before finishing postdoctoral medical training. The further myth that women who do become physicians practice only in small numbers appears, also, to be incorrect. A Carnegie Commission report indicated in 1970 that 91 percent of women physicians were in active medical work; Walsh marshalls evidence to show that between 84 and 91 percent of women physicians are actively working full or part-time in medicine (Walsh, 1977, p. 253). Women achieve nearly as well in medical school as men (Weinberg & Rooney, 1973).

Another myth about women, medicine and a long, active, working life indicates that while women lose an average of about 5 years from medical practice (men lost about 2 years) usually in connection with childbirth, they work longer than men. For example, over 86 percent of the men end their medical careers by age 60, whereas only 50 percent of women physicians retire by age 60 (Walsh, 1977, p. 254).

Stressers

The stresses from the profession of medicine that impinge forcefully upon women are a cumulative lot and they adversely affect women whether they enter medicine and practice, or not. The first stress is whether women can be admitted to medical school. An immediately following stress is whether they will continue, do well, drop out, or accell in ways that stereotypically rob them of their femininity. During medical school, internship, and post-doctoral work, they may want to be married, or even get married, but if child-

225

birth comes along, clinics, hospitals and other facilities are usually reluctant to give them time off for family and related issues. They are under further stress if they pursue part-time careers even for a short period of time. To show that these stresses from the medical profession and environment are considerably biased against women, the results of Kaplan's studies invite attention (Kaplan, 1971; 1972). Kaplan developed a flexible training program in the practice of psychiatry for married women physicians with families. The program in seven years trained sixty-four physician-mothers, no one of whom had to suspend training due to pregnancy or family and child care. Although exemplary in its implications, Kaplan's work has also invited much criticism and misinterpretation.

Women do not earn as well as men in the practice of medicine. In 1972, male physicians earned an average of nearly $48,000.00 yearly, with women physicians earning about $27,000.00 - $28,000.00 annually (Walsh, 1977, p. 258). Studies of medical economics over the years have substantiated the fact that men earn 50 to 60 percent more in medical practice than do women with comparable effort and training. Walsh says in describing women physician's plight as to their economic positions: "It almost appears as if the American medical establishment, steadfast in its opposition to socialized medicine, had decided that women could supply a voluntary form of low-cost medical care (Walsh, 1977, p. 260).

Although the plight of women in medicine is doubtlessly improving, the changes are not necessarily coming first from medicine, but from extant social pressures arising out of governmental financial support, pressures from the woman's movement and the gradual recognition in society that women can perform as well as men in all occupations and professions, save possibly those requiring high levels of enduring physical strength. Women are now making up about 25% of the admissions to American medical colleges (Weinberg & Rooney, 1973). Medical schools get easily one-half of their funds from the federal coffers, thus governmental influence weights heavily on medicine and on the treatment women receive. Women are also helping themselves, thus minimizing the stresses that have been inherent in medical training for women. The American Medical Women's Association is assiting young women in a variety of ways: helping them with family and career conflicts, helping women understand academic

226

medicine (the "male-buddy" system), providing role models for women in various branches of medicine, and assisting women in times of crisis (Hilberman, 1975). Despite all these and other "good signs," skepticism about the role of women in medicine and the stability of recent gains leads Walsh to say: "The medical establishment, while retreating in the face of feminist and federal pressure, has yet to acknowledge any fundamental committment to the medical education of women. There has never been, in fact, a willingness on the part of more than a handful of male medical leaders to recognize the fact that women as physicians can make a positive contribution to medicine" (Walsh, 1977, p. 273). If the plight of women in medicine continues to improve, or if they merely hold-their-own over the next decade, against the onslaughts of inflation, higher technology, and other problems, it will be because women have seen the problems clearly and have taken up their own cause with continuing vigor.

For anyone noting that women have suffered discrimination at the hands of physicians when women themselves became physicians (or tried to), the record of discrimination and stress related problems among nurses is even more telling. Nursing has often been the repository for the dashed hopes of expectant women, physicians. Articles in the daily press as well as some in professional journals further testify to the stresses placed on nurses (the profession is almost entirely composed of women, although the number of men entering nursing in recent years has increased). They suffer from long, hard-working hours (nursing is an occupation that tests physical strength and endurance almost as much as construction work), from irregular schedules, from relatively low pay, and from other strained relations with physicians and hospital administration (Hodges, 1980). The nurse is a lackey, and in so being in many situations, the nurse suffers from all the inhumanities that servants tolerate but do not like. These stresses act to drive women out of nursing, into non-medical jobs, into combination medical and office jobs (receptionist-nurse in a physician's office), and other occupations. Hodges reports that the State of Virginia, for example has 40,000 registered nurses, and 17,000 licensed practicing nurses, but of these an estimated 30,000 nurses (both RNs and licensed practicing nurses) are non-practicing (are unemployed or work in other occupations). Thus over three-fifths (over 60%) of licensed nurses in

Virginia have left their posts, not a good figure to recommend nursing to young women (or men--although their plight seems somewhat better economically than women nurses, and they characteristically stand up better to physicians, hospital administration and other organizational pressures). McCarthy (1980), also writing in the Washington POST about the problems of nurses, observed that we do not have enough nurses, meaning, of course, that nurses who are trained and licensed are not practicing nursing. McCarthy (1980) quotes the American Nursing Association to the point that of one-million-four-hundred-thousand registered nurses, 420,000 are inactive; that is about one-third of trained nurses declining to nurse. Various states in the U.S.A. experience particular shortage of nurses, often in hospitals in slightly populated areas, and in rural areas.

Watching what a nurse does all day would soon acquaint the observer with the stresses and strains visited upon nursing practice. Night shifts are particularly undesirable, especially when the nurse has a family and/or when the shifts change every two or three weeks. Nursing is 98 percent female, and these are beholden to male physicians and administrators, not a circumstance exactly flattering to female nurses or to "getting ahead" in the nursing profession. Some nurses have taken to private duty to escape the administrative pressures and hospital and office routines, but the chances of employment in private duty nursing are not numerous, sometimes round-the-clock pressures are great, and employment is chancy. Despite these disadvantages, more nurses in the last few years have gotten into diagnostic, treatment and prescribing activities, sometimes felt to be treading unsafely on physicians' grounds. Women nurses moving into these more sacred territories are also inclined to do less scut work--changing diapers, moping up after incontinence on the part of patients, cleaning up spilled food and drinks, etc.--leaving these menial jobs to laboring help in the hospital wards. Using nurses for more professional and technical work is gaining ground (McCarthy, 1980), and some physicians recognize that nurses can carry out--as can physician's assistants--a very high percent of the work of physicians, especially if the physician uses his supervisory skills and technical knowledge without a heavy hand and sufficiently reinforces the nurse's efforts. After all, if the physician is worth his fee it is not vested alone in highly skilled services to patients,

228

but in his knowledge and judgement; nurses can draw blood, repair minor surgical wounds, and thousands of other things as well as any physician. Physicians are highly trained professionals doing technician's work most of the time, and getting professional pay for it! Nurses and properly trained assistants can do most of the physician's job; and as this is recognized more clearly and openly, physicians will include nurses more in professional level work and compensate them accordingly (in status, money, responsibility, and more). Failing these more constructive measures, nurses continue to be "held down" far more than is humane, necessary or productive of good patient care. In the long run, inequalities not only hurt nurses, they also demean physicians and certainly cost the public, the consumer more money for lesser care, with preventive measures taking a back seat and emergency care less able than it might be.

With physicians as busy as they are, running from one patient or appointment to another, nurses could fill in many gaps. We know from the chapter on nursing that nurses get their greatest benefits from personal contact with patients and that patients revere nurses more than physicians in this personal touch matter. Even physicians who treat each other (Lear, 1979) are often careless in treatment and more so in interpersonal matters. Lear observed that her husband's heart disease was worsened by medical inattention, indicating how often physicians ignore patient complaints (consider them hypochondriacal, which is no excuse or basis for relegating them to 'the mind' as if this made the complaints unimportant - it may make them more important) and treat physical problems superficially or with a technology that is not relevant to the particular patient's life situation. Nurses could make vast contributions in this area of practice as they have more time than physicians, are more caring (usually) and know more about the individual patient as a person.

In this connection, nurses may be considered to offer skills that would cut health care costs. There is much clamor today regarding rapidly escalating and highly costly health care (Rich, 1980), much of which arise from expensive and often not-needed medical technology which becomes a basis for high physician service costs, perhaps in many cases costs which could be replaced by better and more humane nursing care. The way hospitals are run and the exhorbitant costs of

medical technology--without any proof that thes measures
are worth the effort--give credence to the thesis that
organizations (professions) run away with selfish
interests and end up costing the consumer more money
without any gains in service or care. Better nursing
care, based on more respect for nurses, might greatly
reduce medical costs and give the patient more consideration. We have already seen in the chapter on
medicine that the illnesses of today are stress-related,
not the older, infectious diseases (Galton, 1973; Glass
& Singer, 1972; Kiev, 1974; Klausner, 1968), and that
less needed is high-faluting technology but better
personal care. As many have observed and as death
statistics confirm, the real killers today are guns,
cars, cigarettes and alcohol; better health education
would help in curbing these killers, and nurses could
go a long way toward providing information, counsel
and care in this regard. Physicians have made few or
no contributions to these great "killers," but nurses
could make contributions if an emphasis on their work
shifted from menial care and always supplementing the
physician's role toward more independent counseling
and general health care. Society in time will demand
these skills of the health occupations; physicians and
conventional medicine can hold back nursing from these
roles only for short--but costly--periods of time.

     Nursing is figuring larger in the care of the
handicapped and in rehabilitating these folks and
caring for the elderly (Gliedman & Roth, 1979; Bowe,
1979). There is very little a surgeon can do after he
has repaired the leg or arm of a post-polio victim;
the athetoid movement of people with spastic conditions
do not submit well to surgery or other medical care
(including drugs), so the matter of continuing care and
counsel are bound to be more important. Drugs can
often be used by the physician to quiet concern, but it
may be the very concern we wish to meet on more
substantive grounds; the environmental stress, resultant care and other services being more important than
medical technology. Nurses, along with rehabilitation
counselors and others trained in these health related
matters, can offer services long after and for more
substantial reasons than can physicians. Physicians
do not need to "look over" the care, education and
rehabilitation of the handicapped, the elderly (except
in cases where they have treatable diseases); the
physicians get in the way and superimpose their heavy-
handed technology and medical arrogance when counsel
and care are indicated. Nurses are ideally trained

for these roles but they need to assert themselves
more vigorously than they have done in the past.
Medicine will not yield gracefully to people with
skills more appropriate to the handicapped, the
elderly.

Women And Economic Stress

One can regale the professions until the end of
time--unless they change substantially--and not
improve the plight of women unless economic means are
found to bring on more equality between men and women.
Rich (1980) reports that women workers in general earn
three-fifths (60 percent) as much as men do. This has
evidently been true for at least two decades, since
1960, or longer. In 1939 the median income for full-
time, year-around female workers, all occupations, was
58 percent of the medial for men (Rich, 1980). This
includes, however, the fact that women were almost
entirely occupied in teaching, nursing, household/
domestic duties, with very few being employed in other
professions, especially the more lucrative ones such
as executive roles in business, medicine, and high level
sales and enterpreneurship. Women in the more lucrative
occupations would help raise these median income figures
somewhat, but we have already seen above that women
physicians earn about 60 percent of what men physicians
earn. Perhaps the three-fifth to two-thirds figure, as
an economic proportion between women and men, is a
general statistic with considerable validity. It would
be a target figure to aim to raise among those seeking
to improve the plight of women on the economic front.
These studies indicate that women are paid less for
equal work, and after equal preparation, than men; this
matter was "corrected" in principle in 1963 with the
Equal Pay for Women Act, but as yet the equalitites are
still wanting in most professions and occupations.
Aiding women's improved economic status--although one
has to admit readily that they have a ways to go--is
the fact that more women are working full-time, more
are returning sooner to work after child-bearing, and
more are not having children as they are devoting their
time wholly to careers. More women, too, are gaining
admission to medicine, dentistry, other professions,
albeit not in resounding numbers, but some gains are
being made toward economic betterment. It may nonetheless take a long time before women are fully equal
with men on the economic front. If the economic
matter could be resolved, probably many of the other
unfairnesses and abrasive differences between men and

231

women in professions and occupations would be
diminished; at bottom--or, as the economists and
accountants say, "the bottom line"--the matter is
economics. Psychological, social, occupational and
related differences and unfairnesses between men and
women cannot be alleviated unless the economic issues
are faced first and foremost. As things stand now,
economics is "bad psychology"; correspondingly "good
psychology" between the sexes) would be "better
economics." It may be futile in offices to hope for
sexual equality, employment equality, non-sexist social
equality, unless people are being paid the same for
the same work.

Placing these matters of equality between the
sexes on economic, social and psychological grounds
(noting the interrelationships) is more heuristic
than trying to say that men are father-wounded and
womb-less (Chesler, 1978), or that women have penis-
envy, and these are the basis of misunderstanding,
jealous, competitiveness and prejudice between the
sexes. One cannot do much about women not having
penises, or men not having wombs and giving birth to
babies, these structural/biological matters are rooted
in the phylogeny of the race of mankind and while they
are important for some differences between men and
women, they can hardly account for the myriad of
current, social problems that ramify into economic,
professional and fairness issues. We have to treat
the latter on their own grounds; it is difficult enough
to find salient variables in the extant social network
of sexual differences and relationships without
borrowing from a biology that is only hopelessly distorted when pushed to explain other matters in our
complex social/occupational/professional lives.

Women In Culture Conflict

Not only are women not equal to men in the treatment they receive professionally, economically and
socially, they have probably never been accorded the
place they deserve in western history and culture.
The fact that we are so urgently trying to catch up
in our responsibilities to women is attested to in the
recent plethora of writings on the subject, and on the
place of women in history (Degler, 1979; Norton, 1979).
Women, and the study of families, which is to recognize
how pivotal women are, are now belatedly coming in for
proper scrutiny. Most of the previous studies of
women and of family history have centered on demographi

232

factors, on outstanding women in history, with very little in either case being devoted to the place (i.e., the dynamic interrelationships) of each in cultural and economic life. Since the revolutionary days, men have been concerned with the "outside world", with work and careers, whereas women have been wedded to domesticity, child-rearing and family concerns. The nearly two-hundred year precedent in these respects go a long way toward providing an understanding of how new are some recent trends to liberalize and equalize the roles of women, and how the biases of the past yield only stubbornly. Although women, both white and black were given the vote in the state of New Jersey between 1790 and 1806, this freedom pertained to unmarried women (spinsters and widows) only, since married women were to "obey" their husbands, hence were not "free." These curious twists of logic and socio/political/economic practice have plagued men-women relationships in all spheres of life for generations. The "clean-up" campaign now going on for women's rights may rectify these inconsistencies and ills.

More of the up's and down's of women's rights economically and professionally come not only from the past but from where we might not expect it, from the active present in science. Roark (1980) reviews some of the problems of women in science in universities, in large research centers and in industry and government. Family members and marriage partners are split owing to the man's and women's independent allegiance to job/career over marriage/family. These are known as "commuting marriages." Men and women in the Roark article are depicted as having different motivations: women more concerned with problems related to success, men more fearsome of failure. This simplistic explanation may not take us far. More complex but more penetrating might be that both men and women want success as defined by each of them, as individuals or as members of the sex, and these are exemplified in sometimes vastly different ways, even to the point of pulling them apart insofar as marriage and the family are concerned. It is almost as if both men and women said, "I can get another spouse but I cannot get as good a career opportunity." Women are also depicted in the cited article as being timid before men critics when the women have to present ideas and are unable to hold steadfastly to their values. Withall, women scientists seem to appear better off than women

233

professionals in other fields, but unemployment among women scientists is two to five times higher than it is for men (Roark, 1980, p. 4).

When women are in positions of authority and administrative power, they often decline to employ other women, or see misfortune in the wake of such hirings. Roark quotes women science/administrators as saying they found women "unpleasant and bitchy... (feeling as if) "...they had to prove something" (Roark, 1980, pp. 3-4). Thus the rocky road to freedom and equality in professional work is not just a matter of women getting fairness in comparison to men; they have, also, to learn how to "wear the new mantle." In a popular article, Shearer (1980) reports that women prefer to work for men bosses over women bosses, even though men in superior administrative positions may cause sexual harrassment and embarrassment for women. Men are preferred because of natural sexual attraction between the sexes, because men are considered to be more interesting and stimulating, because men are more comfortable and experienced with power, and because men appear less jealous and insecure. These men-over-women features, may, of course, grow out of the greater opportunities they have had and the milieus in which they work.

Women In Business

Do women fare better in business? Is the vastness and the looseness of the business world more open to women, their skills and talents and more responsive to their needs? Traditionally, no. But the matter, like many others with women, is changing (Vandervelde, 1979). How much change, how penetrating it is into the corporate structure, and how much men-in-business are changing in attitudes toward women remains moot. Vandervelde says, "It is an indisputable fact that women's roles are changing and that attitudes about women are being shaken up" (Vandervelde, 1979, p.21). Then she relates the changes to having been more prompted by recent affirmative action legislation: "No sudden attacks of conscience have occurred to enlighten male executives about equality for women" (p.21). In fact, an equally significant movement or trend seems to be that women are split between those moving into executive-like roles, aspirant as men, and imitative of men, vs. those women who retain the older roles and feel threatened by the "new role women."

234

We will see in Chapter X how women in the clergy have been "yoken-in" traditionally to the husband-ministerial role. It is also apparent that women who were the wives of corporate executives also fitted, silently, compliantly, into the man's highly articulate and demanding role as an executive. The young women coming up in the business world are more likely to see the possibilities of changed roles and to pursue them than are women already yoken-in to their corporate roles. Vandervelde describes the subordinate corporate wife role as: Women were "...expected in that corporation to look right, say the right thing and entertain properly at small dinner parties; there was concern expressed by both executives and wives about any wife who did not fit the mold" (Vandervelde, 1979, p.33).

Examples of stress on women prompted by the corporate wife role are legion. To begin with, about 70 percent of all psychiatric (and psychological) patients are women. Corporate wives figure highly in this group. Vandervelde says, "If corporate wives did not break down so often, many of the fancier private psychiatric hospitals like Menninger's in Kansas, Austin Riggs in Massachusetts, and Silver Hill in Connecticut would have to close their doors" (Vandervelde, 1979, p.49). Female admissions to all manner of out-patient and in-patient psychiatric/psychological services gives women an edge over men from twenty to forty percent, based on figures as recent as 1975 (Vandervelde, 1979, pp.51-52). Torrey (1976) reports similarly on men/women mental-emotional disorders: Alcohol (men 2 1/2 times as common as among women); drug disorders (1/3 more often found among women); depressive disorders (twice as common among women); and transitional situational disturbances ("crises") (about 50 percent more common among women). While these figures do not spring forth wholly in relation to women-in-business, the problems of women in society generally impinge on their public image, on the stresses they experience in business, and the possible areas of exacerbation when women do attempt to compete successfully with men in the business world, especially in high executive posts.

Vandervelde studies corporate executive attitudes and their wives' attitudes as to how the corporate world sees the corporate wives's roles, among the 500 largest industrial companies listed in Fortune magazine, May, 1975. Between 20 and 25 percent of the

235

questionnaires were returned, not a convincingly representative number (Vandervelde, 1979, p.67). Emerging from this study is a profile, briefly reported, of how the executiv corporate wife is to look: Have a sense of humor, be gracious, intelligent, adaptable and friendly; avoid too much gregariousness (especially with the lower eschelon persons), avoid too much independence or creative thinking. In short, one could say the corporate wife should be submissive, seen but not particularly heard, and always loyal to the husband's role and the corporate cause. Here is a personality profile patched up by the corporation, giving little or no credence to the individual women, herself, and possibly causing, in time, a good deal of stress on the corporate wife to comply with the model. It is no surprise to learn that this model of a wife in the corporate sense does not meet 100 percent approval. According to Vandervelde's figures derived from her report, 28.5 percent of the corporate wives admit engaging in extramarital sex, from among the families of chief executive officers who earned more than $50,000.00 per year, in 1974. Other data on the fidelity issue among executive populations indicate that as the men grow older and earn more money, their tendency toward extramarital affairs increases; perhaps more income not only provides more cover for illicit affairs, but goes along with the wife's ageing as well and her less likely access, in contrast to her executive husband's access, to extramarital opportunities.

Adding to family instability and possibly to stress on the wives are moves from one locale to another as the executive moves up from a minor post to a vice presidential level. Over a 20 year span, from the executive's age 30 to 50, the executive's family can be expected to move three to five times, or to move on the average of every five years. This may not be an oppressive figure in a country that has as mobile a population as the U.S., and must certainly compare favorably with high level officer moves in the military, foreign service, and other governmental agencies dealing with international commerce, politics and business.

As part of the relative conservatism of the chief executive officers and their wives, despite the presence of considerable extramarital affairs, is the extent to which the executives and their wives are in their first marriage: 92 percent. This stability

236

bodes well for the effectiveness of the corporate model of how a wife (and executive-husband) should behave: No behavior that would reflect unfavorably on the corporate image is allowable.

Vandervelde tries to pull out of the corporate wife's plight something good (Vandervelde, 1979, pp. 127-183). This effort includes the sharing of seminars and talk sessions between corporate executives, their wives, and professional therapists, usually in some clinical setting or under the sponsorship of some clinical person (psychologist, psychiatrist, social worker). Remedial efforts for the corporate wife and her role may also include: appreciating the benefits of travel and meeting other interesting people with equal economic, social and financial advantage; developing one's own career in non-obtrusive ways; engaging in psychotherapy if one's personal problems require it instead of being lonely, depressed, resentful, and taking to alcohol, illicit sex and various forms of irresponsible behavior; being selfish in the sense of self-development; see the benefits in moving and acquiring different friends, seeing the world, and learning to adapt; and more. One interesting observation on Vandervelde's recommendations on how the corporate wife can gain more from her corporate life and cut the losses, is that the emphasis is put almost entirely on the wife. Not much is said about the husband's role (except by implication where husband and wife share group therapy, discussion seminars, and the like), and little or no responsibility is put on the corporation to become self-conscious about how it influences people, what its values are, and the cost in places on its executives and their families to conform. No social awareness is needed on the part of the corporation; the wives and the husbands must still adapt, see the benefits of the corporation by gingerly asserting themselves a bit more (not too much, though!), and letting the ole' corporation have its way and keep up its customary pace.

Kanter' study (1977) also emphasizes the role of women in the corporate structure, one that is tacitly important--even profoundly necessary--but seldom recognized for its full value, and certainly not by giving full credit to women as unseen members of the corporation. Kanter observes, "Young wives anticipated increasing sacrifices for the company as their husbands' careers progressed, pointing to effects on their marriages of the men's daily fatigue, travel,

and evenings away..." and "Some wives considered
themselves unpaid workers for the corporation, in the
sense both of direct services and of opportunity costs
for options in their own lives they had foregone"
(Kanter, 1977, pp. 105-106).

Kanter dwells rather more on the corporate
wives' problems of a personal/family nature than
Vandervelde. She points out, quoting both the
literature and her own study of "Indsco" (a fictious
name for a real corporation) how the corporation
prevails in the life of the corporate wife. The
corporation closely monitors the wife and her role
in the case of men the corporation was considering
for employment at executive levels. A kind of
"groupmindedness", to use the phrase suggested by
Whyte (1956) prevails here; a mindless regard for
people, determined only by the corporate need. The
literature describes "...the corporate wife as a
helpless casualty, even when a willing one. Moving
from place to place frequently, subject to rules and
constraints, excluded from the office world, stuck
with almost exclusively household responsibilities,
and lacking their husbands' opportunities for learning
and adventure... the "...victims of a too demanding
system" (Kanter, 1977, p. 109). Kanter, in a hard-
hitting phrase also says, "Corporate wives, in short,
have been seen as outsiders, swallowed up by a greedy
organization that tries to absorb totally the lives
of its managerial employees" (Kanter, 1977, p.111).
With these extant pressures on the corporate wife the
meaning of "choice" on the part of the executive
and/or his wife is lost; nearly everything--enter-
taining, vacations, friendships, privacy in the social
community of the corporation, promotions, gossip,
casual remarks, purchases, materialistic values,
everything--comes somehow under the watchful eye of
the corporation. One would think that corporations,
busy and competitive as they are, would have better
things to do than monitor so closely the lives of its
high-level employees. DeLorian, in his scathing
description of General Motors' upper echelon reports
similarly on that garguantian corporation, putting
much more flesh on the corporate skeleton than either
Vandervelde or Kanter (Wright, 1979).

Whereas many schools of thought concerning the
stresses of corporate and organizational life put the
emphasis on the individual, his/her past and the
pathology persons bring to their jobs, as well as

job-incentive and reward characteristics, Kanter and others tend to think more fully in <u>social</u> terms. In the latter case the problems developed by the individual, or by collections of persons (those who divorce, those who have emotional "breakdowns," those suffering from alcoholism or other drug abuse, etc.) reflect more the social structure in which people work, their interpersonal positions with peers, subordinates, superiors, and the way the organization is managed (the limits and controls it sets), which, in a broad sense, accumulate stress over stretches of time, and result in a myriad of problems. Part of the confusion that arises from these different theories of how stress, health and psychological problems arise among women, among minority groups, among the executives in corporations and among other professional members, arises from the fact that distressed individuals arrive at some point where they need treatment or attention, hence are individually defined as "sick," "alcoholic," "disturbed," or the like. They are spotlighted as individuals, and people ask, "What's wrong with John (or Mary) that they have to behave that way?" The broader and more enlightening question, but one sometimes hard to answer, should be "What kinds of living/working situations are John and Mary part of that results in such stress/tension/anxiety for them?" We learn how to view organizations and professions, and the various roles they impose on members and participants much the same way we learn how to look at the behavior of children. We no longer ask, if we are enlightened, about child/family interrelationships, "What's wrong with the child?" We ask, rather, "What is wrong with the context (family, school, etc.) in which the child is a member that leads the child to act in a given way?" We can address both health and ill-health questions this way: "What styles of living make for longer life, which for early death?" "What styles of living are related to more healthful and robust living, which ones related to the opposite?" "Which styles of child rearing are related to children's behavior problems --Which not?" And so on.

Depression

Brown and Harris (1978) studied depression in women. Although finding individual patterns in the background of some women, the social context was judged to be of vast importance in setting the stage for, and in bringing about, depression among British working women. They state, "There is a long and highly

239

complex series of links between economic, cultural, and political systems and their eventual impact on particular individuals. We have concentrated on demonstrating that there is a link between clinical depression and a woman's daily experiences, in the belief that once this is done we will be in a stronger position to sort out the intricate links with wider structures" (Brown & Harris, 1978, p.4). Not only might these social conditions be the forerunner of emotional disorders in the sense of the Brown and Harris observation, specific economic cycles may be correlated with the specific health problems, not in women only, but in the general population (Brenner, 1971, 1975; Eyer, 1977). These authors have observed trends in death rates for heart disease and alcohol-related disorders where an average two-to-three year delay between peaks of unemployment coincide with the raised death rates. Possibly, also, since the business cycle itself tends to run in four-year long cycles on the average, it is possible to observe the peak of death from heart disease and from cirrhosis in relation to the economic cycle. People in the executive world may be victims of some such cycles, although the specifics of these cycles have not been recorded for wives of executives, or for executives, probably because they constitute a too small and too select population for this kind of relationship to show clearly. Eyer (1977) suggests that prosperity may be a 'cause' of death. Perhaps wide swings in cycle of economic growth and prosperity, alternative to depressive periods may set the stage for emotional instability among people highly dependent upon the business cycle for their own personal integrity and self esteem. If so, we would expect an effect to be felt among corporate members, their wives and families (Brenner, 1971).

While all diseases and causes of death among women are of course not attributable to psycholsocial factors--stress, tension and anxiety--some of the more flagrant causes of death (suicide) are related to gender among some professional groups (not including executives). For example, we saw that women physicians are more prone to suicide than men physicians (Steppacher & Mausner, 1974); whereas male physicians have a suicide rate only about 1.5 greater than men in general, female physician suicides are over three time as likely as female suicides in the general population Women in male-dominated occupations such as medicine may be more stress-prone and even more suicide prone.

240

Mausner and Steppacher (1973) also found suicide more common among female psychologists than among male psychologists; and Li (1969) reports female suicides more common than male suicides among chemists. On the other hand, nurses (women, not men) do not appear to have suicide rates different from women in general (Stone, Cohen & Adler, 1979, p. 426). Suicide appears not to be a differential problem among women schoolteachers, social workers or clergy (Stone, Cohen & Adler, 1979). Suicide is, of course, only one-- albeit it an important one--example of stress among women, or among men (husbands) in specific professions. Many other signs of stress are also in evidence among the wives of various professional men. Among a number of signs, or results, of stress the following may be considered important and impinge on women if not directly, at least as one-half the population: In the U.S.A. today, nearly one-half the marriages end in divorce; up to forty percent of children born in the present decade will be reared during part of their childhood in one-parent homes (mostly by mothers); the number of single women heading households has nearly doubled in the last decade; approximately one-third of young women with children under age three work out- side the home, either full or part of the time; fewer people in the 20-34 year group are getting married (a 10-20 percent decrease) and are either living alone or with a partner to whom they are not married, as the number of unmarried couples living together has doubled since 1960 (Goldberg, 1978, p.11). In all these family changes, womens' roles are perhaps changing the most, although, of couse, mens' roles are affected. One cannot have a change in the role of either men or women without considerable influence being felt on the other. Women are increasingly more at work outside the home: At the beginning of the 1980's, about one- half of all women over 16 years of age were in the labor market, including up to one-half of all mothers with school age children (ages 5 or 6 to 16). With all these job-oriented women actually working the economy will reflect these changes in a variety of ways, one of which puts more stress on women to manage jobs, home and child-rearing, and the other is to receive equal pay for equal work in jobs, not the least of which is in the various professional fields.

A study of women and their relationship to the economy (working women, professional women, and others) --the apparently great precursor to stress, tension and anxiety--shows that while gains have been made,

241

especially among younger women (now under age 40), older women are in far less advantaged situations. For example, older women are seldom employable except on a very low economic level; one in three over age 65 lives alone; about 75 percent of all nursing home residents are women; only a small percentage of widows get their husbands' pension benefits; a significant percentage of working women today (about 25 percent) can expect to be poor in old age; and women over 65 are the fastest growing segment of the population (Ferrell & Slade, 1980). These portends must be reckoned with along side our efforts to give women better shakes in all the professions and simultaneously to avoid sex-stereotyping occupational classification and employment. Society needs to look more fully at the entire age range of women--especially including older ones that make up the statistics cited above--as well as forage new opportunities for the young, bright, professional woman. Gains made at the younger age levels may or may not ramify into the older age groups; special effort must be made in the latter case.

The study of major life changes, reported elsewhere in this volume, also impinge directly on women. Since men die earlier than women on the average, the death of a spouse can be considered one of the major stresses of life. Most married women are victims of this circumstance since coronary disease has increased 500 percent over the last 50 years, leading to a condition where over 30 million Americans have some type of major cardiac or blood-vessel disease, in turn bringing about over one million heart attack victims each year, with 65 percent of these dying, most of whom are men between ages 45 and 65 (Goldberg, 1978, pp. 19-20). If we are to believe much of the research on how women fare in pressure-laden jobs (the professions, executive work, etc.) the characteristics of stress-related occupations now affecting men so adversely will come to affect women perhaps as adversely. If women want and acquire more status, equal pay for equal work and other non-prejudicial handling, they will perforce take on the same stresses that men now experience (Whitfield, 1978; Selye, 1974). Perhaps women can acquire equality without equal risk, only time will tell, but if women foresee this possibility their quest for parity can be better guided and better evaluated.

242

Or, women may see the rapidly expanding conflicts with society and the correlated health problems ever-present in the professions and elect to change the professions in ways ranging far beyond their increasing presence in the major professions. Instead of just being accepted into extant professions more fully, and being satisfied with this change of status, women may see the handwriting on the wall and seek fundamental changes in the professions, especially those professions, like medicine and dentistry and executive work, that have so long kept women at bay. A doubly significant change could be in the offing--one based on quantitative changes in the increasing number of women in some professions, and a qualitative change moving the professions toward greater social sensitivity and responsibility.

CHAPTER IX

BIBLIOGRAPHY

Baer, H.R., & Sherif, C.W. A Topical Bibliography
    (Selectively Annotated) On Psychology Of Women.
    University Park, Pennsylvania: Pennsylvania State
    University, 1974.

Biles, G.E. & Pryate, H.A. Myths, Management and
    Women, Personnel Journal, 1978, 57, 572-577.

Bowe, F. Rehabilitating America: Toward Independence
    for Disabled and Elderly People. N.Y.: Harper
    & Row, 1979.

Brenner, M.H. Economic changes and heart disease
    mortality, Amer. J. of Public Health, 1971, 61,
    606-619.

Brenner, M.H. Trends in alcohol consumption and
    associated illnesses, some effects of economic
    changes, Amer. J. of Public Health, 1975, 65,
    1279-1292.

Brown, G.W. & Harris, T. Social Origins of Depression:
    A study of Psychiatric Disorders In Women. N.Y.:
    The Free Press, 1978.

Burlin, F.D. Locus of control and female occupational
    aspirations, J.of Counsel. Psychol., 1976, 23,
    126-129.

Cherler, P. About Men. N.Y.: Simon & Schuster, 1978.

Cole, J.R. Women In The Scientific Community. N.Y.:
    Free Press, 1979.

Degler, C.N. Women and Family In America From the
    Revolution To The Present. N.Y.: Oxford U. Press,
    1979.

Ehrenreich, B. & English, D. Witches, Midwives and
    Nurses: A History Of Women Healers. Old Westbury
    N.Y.: Feminist Press, 1973.

Eyer, J. Prosperity as a cause of death, Intern. J. of
    Health Services, 1977, 7, 125-151.

Firestone, S. The Dialectic of Sex: The Case For
    Feminist Revolution. N.Y.: Bantam Books, 1971.

Friedan, N. The Feminine Mystique. N.Y.: Dell, 1963.

Fee, E. Women and health care, in Navarro, V. (Ed.)
    Health and Medical Care In the U.S. N.Y.:
    Baywood, 1975.

Ferrell, T. & Slade, M. The rage of older women, N.Y.
    TIMES, 1980, Oct. 19, p. 8E

Galton, L. The Silent Disease: Hypertension. N.Y.:
    New American Libr., 1973.

Glass, D.C. & Singer, J.E. Urban Stress: Experiements
    on Noise and Social Stressors. N.Y.: Academic
    Press, 1972.

Gliedman, J. & Roth, W. The Unexpected Minority:
    Handicapped Children In America. N.Y.: Harcourt,
    Brace and Jovanovich, 1979.

Goldberg, P. Executive Health. N.Y.: Business Week,
    1978.

Hilberman, E. Support groups for women in medical
    school: a first-year program, J. Med. Educ.,
    1975, 50, 867-875.

Hodges, P. Nurses: Turning in their caps, Washington
    POST, May 1, 1980.

Horner, M.S. Toward an understanding of achievement-
    related conflicts in women, J. of Soc. Issues,
    1972, 28, 157-176.

Horner, M.S. & Walsh, M. R. Psychological barriers to
    success in women, in Kundsin, R.B. (Ed.) Women
    and Success: The Anatomy of Achievement. N.Y.:
    1974.

Kanter, R.M. Men & Women of the Corporation. N.Y.:
    Basic Books, 1977.

Kaplan, H. Women physicians, New Physician, 1971,
    20, 11-19.

Kaplan, H. Part-time residency training: An approach to the graduate training of some women physicians, J. of Amer. Med. Womens' Assn., 1972, 27, 648.

Kiev, A. A Strategy for Handling Executive Stress. N.Y.: Nelson-Hall, 1974.

Klausner, S.Z. Why Men Take Chances: Studies In Stress-Seeking. N.Y.: Doubleday, 1968.

Lear, M.W. Heartsounds. N.Y.: Simon & Schuster,1979.

Li, F.P. Suicide among chemists, Archives of Environmental Health , 1969, 19, 518-520.

Mason, K.O. Sex and status in Science. A review of Cole, J.R., Women In The Scientific Community. N.Y.: Free Press, 1979. Science, 1980, 208, 277-278.

Masters, W.H. & Johnson, V.E. Human Sexual Response. N.Y.: Little, Brown & Co., 1966.

Mausner, J.S. & Steppacher, R.C. Suicide in professionals: A study of male and female psychologists, Amer. J. of Epidemiology, 1973, 98, 436-445.

McLaughlin, G.W., Hunt, W.K., & Montgomery, J.R. Socioeconomic status of women seniors in high school, Vocat. Guid. Quarterly, 1976, 25,155-162.

McCarthy, C. Why we don't have enough nurses, Washington POST, Mar. 2, 1980.

Millett, K. Sexual Politics. N.Y.: Doubleday, 1970.

Nieva, V.F. & Gutek, B.A. Women And Work: A Bibliography of Psychological Research. Ann Arbor, Michigan: Institute for Social Research, Univ. of Michigan, 1976.

Norton, M.B. The Revolutionary Experience of American Women. Boston: Little, Brown & Co., 1979.

Peters, J.H., Terborg, J.R., & Taynor, J. Women As Managers Scale (WAMS): A Measure Of Attitudes Toward Women In Management Positions. West Lafayette, Indiana: Purdue University, 1974.

Quaranta, B.M.A. Androgynons, sex-typed and undifferentiated college freshmen and seniors; their professional college chaise and related characteristics, Dissertation Abstr. International. Ann Arbor, Mich.: Univ. of Mich. M-Films No. 76-24669, 1976.

Rich, S. Panel presses HEW on ways to cut waste in health care, Washington POST, Mar. 22, 1980.

Rich, S. Women workers earn three-fifths as much as men, Washington POST, Apr. 5, 1980.

Roark, Anne C. Women in Science: Unequal pay, unsold ideas, and sometimes, unhappy marriages, The Chronicle of Higher Educ., Apr. 21, 1980, pp.3-4.

Rohfeld, R.W. High school womens' assessment of career planning resources, Vocat. Guid. Quarterly, 1977, 26, 79-84.

Ruby, M., et al. Women at work, Newsweek, Dec. 6, 1976, pp. 69-70.

Savage, R.C. & Wilson, A. Doctors' attitudes to women in medicine, J. Royal Cal. of Gen'l Pract., 1977, 27, 363-365.

Selye, H. Stress Without Distress. Phila.: Lippincott, 1974.

Shearer, L. Intelligence Report: Boss preference, Parade Magazine, Apr. 27, 1980, p. 13.

Steppacher, R.C. & Mausner, J.S. Suicide in male and female physicians, J.A.M.A., 1974, 228, 323-328.

Stone, G.C., Cohen, F., & Adler, N.E. Health Psychology. San Francisco: Jossey-Bass, 1979.

Torry, J.W. A psychologist looks at women, in Suttermeister, R.A. (Ed.) People and Productivity. N.Y.: McGraw-Hill, 1976.

Vandervelde, M. The Changing Life of the Corporate Wife. N.Y.: Mecox Publ. Co., 1979.

Vriend, T.J. The case for women, Vocat. Guid. Quart., 1977, 25, 329-331.

Walsh, M.R. Doctors Wanted: Women Need Not Apply.
New Haven: Yal Univ. Press, 1977.

Weinberg, E. & Rooney, J.F. The academic performance
of women students in medical school, J. Med. Educ.,
1973, 48, 240-247.

Westbrook, B.W. The relationship between career choice
attitudes and career choice competencies of
ninth-grade pupils, J. of Vocat. Beh., 1976, 9,
119-125.

Whitfield, M.D. Stresses associated with career
success for women, Psychia. Assn. J., 1978, 23,
9-14.

Williams, J.J. The woman physician's dilemma, J.
Soc. Issues, 1950, 6, 43.

Whyte, W.H., Jr. The Organization Man. N.Y.: Simon
& Schuster, 1956.

Wurter, D.G., Stewart, A.J., & McClelland, D.C.
Husband's motives and wife's career level,
J. of Personality & Soc. Psychol., 1977, 35,
159-166.

Wright, J.P. On A Clear Day You Can See General
Motors. Grosse Point, Michigan: Wright
Enterprises, 1979.

CHAPTER X

CLERGY

For centuries the church has been the dominant institution in our society. The clergy has been the major ideological influence as a result of the church's power. The view of the clergy by the populace has been so sacrosant that only recently have people begun to look objectively at ministers, their conduct and their strengths and weaknesses. The influence of the church and the influence of clergymen have, however, undergone change in recent decades; some would say that the power of the church and the role of the clergy have both diminished and are continuing a down-grade path. Nonetheless, at the level of the community and the parish, both the church and the clergy retain power and influence. Any characteristics that can be used to describe the clergy, their health and their functioning would, perforce, be of importance to understanding the profession of being a clergyman. The clergyman, or minister, remains one of the most important persons in the lives of everyday people in everyday walks of life.

Ministers, like teachers, are motivated to offer services to others. The minister has a more other-worldly orientation than the teacher (or the physician, dentist, or nurse), but the idea of service remains predominant. Ministers or clergymen are also more passive and acquiesing persons than are other professional groups, such as businessmen, physicians, dentists, executives, political leaders, and the like. Ministers "belong to God." They share beliefs and practices not always fully shared by other members of the community, although others may be religious in the usual sense of the term (believe in God, believe in a life-after-death, go to church, and more). The minister is more denotive than clergyman, and speaks more to the religious activities of this profession and less to the administrative, church-related, and executive roles associated with the term clergy. The idea of service to others, to God, and to others in God's interest, are dominant themes in the lives of the minister.

Strong Motivation For The Clergy

Traditionally, men (and more recently, women) have gone into the ministry as a result of a "call" to duty to serve God. Ministers often speak of the occasion

249

when they "received the call" to serve God via the
ministry. But this tradition, too, is changing. More
recently, ministers have been moved to serve their
religious motives in more professional ways, akin to
other professions that offer primarily services to
others (students, clients, patients) such as teachers,
nurses, and lawyers. Placing the ministers in a more
professional framework and rendering less important the
"call to duty" (although this still remains a consideration in studying the motivations of ministers)
allows us to look at the activities of the minister
along with other professions, to assess their emotional
health, and to study the pressures arising from their
ministerial activities; and the impact these factors
have on their personal and family lives. Despite their
"calling" and the often sacrosant nature of their work,
ministers are subject to pressures, to the vagaries of
life, and to unfulfilled expectations as readily as
others. In short, they experience stress, tension and
anxiety.

Ministers, like other professionals, are capable
of being described in terms of social, psychological
and attitudinal characteristics that seem to help
identify the forces leading to their selection of the
ministry. They have interests and preferences that
propel them into the ministry, just as other professional groups are self-selected and derived their
profession from interests, abilities and preferences.

Daniels and Hunter (1949) studied the personalities of various occupations on the Minnesots Multiphasic Personality Inventory. They regarded various
occupations as presenting rather fixed "personality
demands" which, when matched with the characteristics
of the professional members (and the profession itself)
make up the characteristics of people participating in
various professions. Further, people with fairly
definite personality patterns may tend to gravitate
toward certain occupations in that these occupations,
more than others, will satisfy the individual's
personality needs and characteristics. Thus all
occupations, especially professions with high demand
ratios, tend to act like magnets in drawing people into
their fold. Thus, department store saleswomen are
different in their personality demands from (say)
ministers and, in turn, each occupation adjusts to
different requirements of the occupation or profession.
The complex of personal attributes meld with the job
demands and form a constellation which then can be said

to characterize ministers, sales persons, machinists, physicians, and all other occupations and professions. However, some professions have more crystallized characteristics and less variation than others. How, then, do ministers stack up? Daniels and Hunter (1949) studied nearly 900 male veterans coming through a Veterans Administration Guidance Center, in Arizona, following the close of World War II. They looked primarily at the Masculinity-Femininity, the Psychopathic, Schizophrenic and Hypomania scales of the MMPI. Ministers scoring high on the M-F Scale (Masculinity-Femininity) are interested in understanding the problems of other persons, a kind of "bedside manner" in the religious setting, with readiness to counsel and offer help to those in need. The ministry and other occupations of a high cultural content show these and other M-F traits which add up to sensitivity toward others, their problems, attitudes and general outlook on life. By the same token, ministers tend to be low on the Psychopathic Deviate personality scale of the MMPI. People scoring high on this scale are anti-authority oriented, may present aggressive and asocial profiles in other ways, characteristics opposite to those of ministers who submit to the authority of God and try to invest others in this same attitude. Likewise the Schizophrenic scale on the MMPI signals asocial attitudes in the sense of distance from people, a withdrawal from and dislike for intense social contact, characteristics unbefitting the ministers (most ministers are the opposite to these schizoid characteristics); and more likely characterizing attitudes on the MMPI associated with (say) draftsmen or accountants or others who work in more "lonely" ways on their jobs. The Manic pattern on the MMPI (Hypomania scale) is seen as related to people with much overt activity, warmth toward others, gravitating toward social contacts of both a passing and more intense nature. Ministers have to function in these ways in order to be successful with their parishioners: now and again offering counsel in close, intimate, therapy-related ways to some in need and showing more of a "glad hand" to the congregation as it files in and out of the church for religious services, social meetings, funerals, weddings, and the like. The minister's versatility here, always attuned to the needs of others (in the interest of the religious doctrines subscribed to, however), is constantly manifest; and one going into the ministry can ill afford to show little of these characteristics and personality inclinations.

251

In his study of the relationship of personality maladjustment and occupational interests among 503 university (Michigan) students, Feather (1950) avers that there is a positive relationship between occupational interest and emotional adjustment. He states the probability is high that individuals with certain styles of maladjustment will tend to move toward certain occupations (talent, experience and expertise aside), and that professional schools should acknowledge this tendency and be "on guard" lest it create problems for the various professions such as law, medicine, teaching, the ministry, the arts, and so on. Used in the study by Feather were the familiar Kuder Preference Record and the Minnesota Multiphasic Personality Inventory. The 503 individuals studied were divided into "normal" and "maladjusted" on their MMPI scores (those scoring over a critical standard score of 70 were arbitrarily considered "maladjusted" without reference to their actual daily life behavior). The more "normal" scoring individuals on the MMPI tended, in turn, to score relatively higher on the Mechanical and Scientific interest scales of the Kuder, and those classified as "maladjusted" on the MMPI, according to the criteria used, scored higher on the Kuder on such scales as Music, Literary, Artistic. While these empirical results are sound for the time and conditions under which they were obtained, with the growth in the fine arts, the performing arts, and other cultural areas in the universities (and, generally, in society) over the past several decades, it is unlikely that these decisive results would be duplicated today. When occupations relegated to "lower" status are considered, especially if they require much training as do Music, Art, and Literature, the basis for entering these professions is bound to shift and to draw more "normal" individuals in today's world. Ministers tend to be "soft" in their outlook and to gravitate toward the softer areas of discipline such as literature, the arts, music, and other cultural subjects. While ministers are not as artistically, musically, or literally inclined as persons specializing in these professional fields, they do overlap noticeably in their interests with experts in these respective fields and are more characterized by a less "hard-nosed," scientific outlook on mankind, society and human problems than are engineers and physical scientists. Ministers have changed more over the past three or four decades in regard to interest and outlook--maintaining, however, the core of interest in people, philosophical, religious and welfare

considerations--and can be less accurately characterized as initially drawn to the religious area
because of maladjustment in the sense used in the
Feather study. Ministers, as we shall see below, do
have their social, emotional and personality problems,
as do all other professions, but these appear to stem
from the nature of the "calling" than from initially
maladjusted individuals being drawn into the ministry
en masse.

Selection And Mental Health

Some data bearing on the question of the selection
of men into ministerial training was addressed by
Christensen (1961, pp. 226-228). He reports on
screening of ministerial candidates by psychologists,
psychiatrists and already ordained ministers, over
several years. In one group a total of 364 candicates
were examined with 21 percent rejected due to
"neurotic difficulties" and others were rejected for
the ministry owing to lacking motivation, temperamental
unsuitability, poor physical health and other reasons.
In a second population of 73 candidates for missionary
work, 23 percent were rejected outright because of
"serious mental illness". In yet another report by
Christensen, of 70 consecutively studied people already
in the profession of religion, 36 percent were judged
by psychological tests and psychiatric interviews to
be ill enough to be referred for intensive therapy.
These investigations indicate that the ministerial
profession has been self-conscious about its candidates for training and has made a valiant effort to
screen out those judged potentially incapable of
meeting the rigors of the clergyman's life. Perhaps
these screening processes go some distance in building
the kind of stamina that ministers characteristically
possess, their longevity, and the absence of suicide
among them, compared to people in general and compared
to other professions.

Kildahl notes in the same publication citing
Christensen's work (Kildahl, 1961, pp. 201-208) that
there are many hazards built into the "high calling"
of the ministry and cites such feelings as the
minister's sense of responsibility, their feeling of
urgency in their work, singleness of purpose and the
dangers inherent in a too unilateral philosophy, a
tendency to use the church to satisfy personal needs,
some tendency to shun non-professional satisfactions,
and their occasional ignoring of the "five elemental

emotional needs" (self-esteem, coping with one's environment, good interpersonal relationships, physical health and vitality including sexual satisfactions, and a unifying view of life).

Southard, in the same publication (1961) contends with the notion that ministers might be breaking down more frequently than before, and in relation to other professionals. Southard sees the main problem the minister faces as a conflict between his religious role as a minister and the kind of life he wants to engage in as a human being, apart from his ministerial role. Southard's conclusions are that ministers are, indeed, not more prone to breakdowns than others--but are even less prone--and that proper handling of the conflicts cited above tends to insure good religious service and a satisfying life.

When ministers were hospitalized (Meiburg & Young, 1961, pp. 237-257) they tended to diseases of the circulatory system, to Genito-Urinary System diseases, but also a number of psychoneurotic reasons for hospitalization were noted. These figures match those reported by King (1970) elsewhere in this chapter. On the whole, then, whether we look at the mental health of ministers in terms of early diagnosis and screening, during the course of their ministry, and in terms of reasons for hospitalization, we find they came off well--and generally superior to most other professions-- as early as the 1930 - 1960 decades of this century. The overall emotional stability of ministers has been noted for a long enough time to consider their mental health status well-established, at least until very, very recently.

Change In Status

Ministers do not today have the prestige they once had. This change in the social status of their occupation may have an effect on who goes into the ministry, who stays in this religious calling, and who fares best over the years. In the first study ever done of the prestige and social status of occupations, Counts (1925) found that ministers ranked number one in status by high school seniors and school teachers, and ranked an overall fourth in status by a composite of 450 persons sampled who were students in public schools, in trade schools, freshman in college and school teachers In this same sample by Counts, bankers ranked first, overall, in prestige, while college professors ranked

254

second, physicians ranked third, and lawyers ranked
fifth. One might argue that high school students knew
best, in 1925, the local ministers (especially the one
in their own church) as did the local school teachers
and college students. More contact was probably had
with the minister than with other leading professionals
such as physicians and lawyers. The prestige of money,
handling money, having it available, seen in the
banker's role was also of high status in 1925.

But these matters began to change shortly and some
of the prestige positions of professions reflect these
changes. In 1947, Deeg and Patterson repeated the 1925
Counts study, using the same type of questionnaire and
ranking procedures. In the Deeg and Patterson (1947)
study based on 25 of the original 45 rated occupations
and professions, they sampled opinions from 475 high
school and college students, and found banker had
shifted to position number 2.5 (meaning this position
was tied in third place with lawyer which shifted
upward from 5th in status), and minister was not even
included in the Deeg and Patterson study; physician
was up to the 2nd position in prestige and elementary
school teacher moved to 8th rank from an original 13th
position. Social changes associated with World War II,
the coming into focus of new occupations and professions
due to the spread of new technological knowledge and
the loosening of social and family bonds during and
after the war--although the overall ranking of professions and occupations in the Counts and Deeg and
Patterson studies correlated +0.97--may account for
some of these changes in the prestige and status of
particular occupations and professions.

A few years later, Welch (1949) studied the
rankings of occupations on a status/prestige scale,
using the procedures previously recorded by Counts and
by Deeg and Patterson, and substantiated the latter's
findings among 500 teacher's college undergraduate
and graduate students. The overall rank order of the
first few ranks in the Welch study went as follows:
#1, physician; #2, banker; #3, lawyer, #4, superinten-
dent of schools; #5, civil engineer; #6, high school
teacher; #7, foreign missionary; numbers 8, 9 and 10,
respectively, elementary school teacher, army captain
and insurance agent. Again, the clergy was not ranked
in this abbreviated scale, but it is doubtful if it
would have been in the first few had it been included
in the study. Teachers rank as well as they do in high
school and college populations, especially among

students of teacher-training institutions, owing to the prevalence of contact with teachers and with the ubiquitousness of this role in the lives of young people.

One can account for some of the changes in the status of the ministry over the past two or three decades in terms of general social factors related to education and to economic (or socioeconomic) factors. Anderson (1970) studied the problem of rich and poor protestants, their ministers and church/religious beliefs. Anderson found that various American religious groups differed widely in median family income, in years of education, and in the percentage of white-collar employment associated with membership in varous religious denominations. The Episcopalian Protestant membership scored higher in income, education and white-collar employment than any other Protestant denominations; scoring lowest in all three attributes were Roman Catholics and Baptist. Since these religious denominations--Catholics and Baptist-- make up a large percentage of the general population assigning themselves to a given religious denomination, prestige factors which rank the minister (or priest) are not going to be high and the role of the minister is not going to be seen as high in status compared to people-in-general.

Further changes in the role of the minister, other than prestige factors and ratings, relate to actual changes in the functions of ministers. More and more ministers look like psychologists, psychiatrists and social workers, at least in terms of some important aspects of their career activities and career lines. Associated with this trend is a greater psychological emphasis on the problems of theological students who are studying for various ministerial roles, and the emphasis on self development found in this literature (Pattison, 1965, 1977; Anderson, 1970; Leslie, 1960; McCarthy, 1942).

Studies such as those of Schuldt and Stahmann (1971) indicate that vocational choice is a product of personality in the broad sense of the term. These authors found one population of ministers (United Methodist clergymen serving Iowa churches for less than 15 years, N = 55) being interested primarily in social, artistic, intellectual and enterprising activities, on the Holland Vocational Preference Inventory. These are expected results compared to employed men-in-genera who tend to score higher in realistic and conventional areas of interest, meaning they are more concerned with everyday problems in the executive of their businesses and jobs, and general circumstances of living. Schuldt and Stahmann (1971) summarize the interest pattern of clergymen as follows: "Pastors may be described as most sensitive to personal, humanitarian, social and emotional influences. They are least sensitive to materialistic...roles which require structured and conforming behavior" (p.1027).

Stress And Personality

In a study somewhat related to the Schuldt and Stahmann report, Schuldt (1970) studied the social and psychological characteristics of United Methodist ministers leaving the ministry (Bustanoy, 1977). Why did they abandon the ministerial role?

The execution of the ministerial roles involve close communication by the minister with people who, in turn, are often experiencing various forms of stress (grief from someone dying, concern over the welfare of a family and friends, distress from job loss and other vicissitudes of daily living). Thus not only do ministers experience stress, tension and anxiety in their own lives, they take on and are often pressured by similar issues--as are physicians, nurses, therapists, social workers--in the lives of their parishioners. One could say that ministers get a double dose of stress from their environments, resulting in tension personalized in their own lives but somehow with less anxiety-ridden aftermath than many other professionals who serve people in anguished and perplexing situations.

One important difference between ministers and (say) physicians--although they share similar stress--is that the former have more religious and humanitarian interests, values and goals, and correspondingly less competitive, materialistic and ambitious motives than physicians (McCarthy, 1942). Similar to the findings in the Schuldt and Stahmann (1971) study, relating vocational choice to personality, McCarthy found that 229 Catholic seminarians had high religious values, some neurotic tendencies, above average intelligence, and a high degree of self-consciousness. Seminarians also tended to be submissive, but to be above average in sociability and introversion. Compared to protestant seminarians or ministerial students, Catholic seminarians have more social structure

provided for them in their later priesthoods and may
not need to put as much emphasis on social motives,
sociability, and interpersonal relationships as
Protestant clergy who have often to work hard to
remain the minister in a church, "sell" themselves
to new parishioners, and the like. The McCarthy
study used a variety of standardized personality and
ability tests, common during the 1940's and 1950's as
measures of personality--the Bernreuter Personality
Inventory, the Bell Adjustment Inventory, the Allport-
Vernon Study of Values, the Otis Intelligence Test and
the American Council Psychological Examination; in
addition, faculty members who knew the seminarians
rated them on especially prepared scales constructed by
McCarthy which looked, in part, to the staying power of
the seminarians in the priesthood.

Changes in the ministry are proceeding apace as
are changes in other professions. The minister at the
turn of the present century experienced a "calling"
and either got his training on-the-job (among
religious groups less concerned with the Minister's
theological and academic preparation) or they went to
a seminary serving the particular denomination.
Ministers were a lot like their wives in that there
was essentially a repudiation of material and worldly
matters in favor of religious, other-worldly and
spiritual values and concerns. As the selection and
training and employment of ministers became more
"professional" the simpler routes to the ministry
began to be more complicated. The role of minister
extended gradually beyond the spiritual confines out
to more social concerns in terms of the mental health
of the parishioners, the offering of counseling and/or
psychotherapy by ministers to church members, an
emphasis on the social and economic forces that brought
stress to peoples' lives, leading to a generally less
other-worldly outlook (Fairlie, 1979; Time Magazine,
1979; Christianity Today, 1979).

The Wife

Physician's and executive's wives are not the only
spouses that experience pressures occasioned--and exa-
cerbated--by their husband's profession. Issues
concerning minister's wives and their emotional and
social plights have been written about for decades--
even longer (Douglas, 1965; Beecher, 1859; Anonymous,
1832; Weaver, 1928; Johnson, 1939). The minister and

his wife and their interpersonal relationships have also been fictionalized over the years (Davis, 1948; Ritchie, 1867; Young, 1928). The vicissitudes of the minister's wife in dozens of ways--factual, fictional, religious, anti-religious, secular and what-not--have come under the microscope countless times. In ordinary, daily affairs, also, the minister's wife is under a looking glass. Her sincerity, religiousity, faith, devotion and energy--applied to the church, to God, to the ministerial calling of her husband and to her marriage to a minister--are all criteria by which she is judged and misjudged. One vivid way in which the minister's wife is tied to the minister's profession or calling is illustrated in the frequent reference to the wife as a "yoke fellow" to the minister (Anonymous, 1832, Douglas, 1965).

Early on the minister's wife was expected to renounce the world and the material things of the world. The wife gave up her own pursuits and interests "in pursuit of God's work," and followed suit with her husband-minister in any effort, trial or response that might be required (Douglas, 1965, p. 4). The minister's wife has been held in conspicuous light by the church members. She was to be a model for other church member women (and mothers), and to exemplify at every hand the proper regard for charity, love, Christian fellowship (a similar role may be required by the Jewish Rabbi's wife) (Tennenbaum, 1978), sacrifice, piety, and endurance in the face of hardship. The endurance in regard to worldly matters--remember, worldly things were to be tolerated, suffered, endured, but in the long haul they counted for naught unless they paved the way for the salvation of the individual-- might traditionally have included such trying conditions as poor housing, poor schools for the minister's children, frequent moves, low pay, no health or sickness insurance, and much peer pressure, gossip and criticism. In the face of all these stresses and strains, the minister's wife was expected to be stalwart, fair-minded and utterly devoted to advancing the faith no matter how flagrantly the parishioners contested and violated these hoary objectives in their own limited and selfish lives.

The minister's wife does have wordly responsibili-ties nonetheless--and has had them from antiquity-- such as support of her husband in her church and religious responsibilities, to be a good wife as wives go, to be a ready hostess to visitors to the parsonage whether their reasons for dropping in were idealistic, inquisitive or demeaning, and showing and feeling the call to religious duty in the church (in the familiar yoke-role with her husband) at all times. As Douglas put it,

> What a minister's wife is as a person is at least as important as what she does as a homemaker and church worker. In general, this "uncrowned queen of the parish" is urged to follow the golden mean. She is to be attractive but not over-dressed, poised but not oversophisticated. She is to be educated and well-informed, but not lacking in common sense or the common touch; sympathetic and concerned, but not overly sentimental; radiating peace and serenity, but brimming with contagious energy and enthusiasm (Douglas, 1965, p.9).

In addition--as if these measures of virtue were not enough--the minister's wife exemplified the church getting "two workers for the price of one." When the church engaged the minister--and the minister responded to the call--this co-worker, this yoke-partner, this wife (the measure of all great and beautiful things) came free. How much more could the "system" ask for? The church, that is, as a religious (and social) system? The executive's wife also has come free, as an equally identified yoke-partner. But even among physician's wives, and executive's wives, the belongingness of the wife to the system has never been as great as has been the minister's wife to the religious system and its professionalization (Douglas, 1965, p.10; Weber, 1958). The likeness here of the roles of capitalism and religiosity are striking: activism, aesceticism, compulsive working and equally compulsive repudiation of pleasure-seeking, all found in both the religious role and the executive (capitalistic) role. Maybe the fostering of capitalism by and through standard religious practices, and vice versa, come "naturally" in our society. The Protestant work-ethic is equally an ascetic work ethic and a capitalistic work ethic. Which shoes the participant wears may be indidental to the basic role definition (Douglas, 1965, pp.10-11 and pp. 209-210).

Multiple responsibilities characterize the minister's wife. These are not limited to piety and religious practices, but to supporting the minister-husband in times of strife and conflict, for the pressures on the minister are multiple and profound. The wives are admonished to help the husband "get ahead," avoid nervous collapse; the wife should avoid being a "wife problem". If executives and professional men found separating business and family/home life difficult and soul-searching, the minister's dilemma and confusion in this department is profound. There is no difference in the religious objectives and the home/family life for many ministers (the Catholic church requires the repudiation of family/home life)--the minister belongs to, and is immersed in, the church; and the wife is there, too. The very definition of a minister is in terms of this role--no such thing as a nine-to-five job, no weekends off (that's when the most important work is done), or even vacations away from God/church/religion. All these responsibilities the wife shares with the minister-husband, and more too.

How involved are minister's wives in point of fact? Tradition, expectations, and role definitions have them yoken-in, as the expression has it; and the essentially idealistic views of minister's wive's roles as cited above have been the reported norm. But are all minister's wives so thoroughly and narrowly characterized? Hardly. Yet the ideal remains. Douglas' study yields some facts in regard to the actual practices and beliefs held by minister's wives. Douglas studied a five percent sample (8,000 wives of ministers) of over 160,000 protestant parish ministers (Douglas, 1965, p.22), by means of a questionnaire. Over forty Protestant religious groups were included in the study. Of the 8,000 sampled, nearly 5,000 (over 60 percent) responded with usable data. Results indicate about twenty percent conform pretty closely to the ideal minister's wife characterizations; fulfilling a "very involved...teamwork" role, where the husband and wife are yoked together in the full range of ministerial and religious duties and functions.

The Douglas study further revealed that about sixty percent of the minister's wives are less involved, less yoked, and play a more "supportive" role. This latter role, while religous and supportive, is also one allowing less participation by the wife and allowing her a broader range of religious activities and

261

interests. These minister's wives, in Douglas' phrase "...tend to have more interpersonal sensitivity and less available energy and competence than teamworkers" (Douglas, 1965, p. 43).

The final twenty percent--the tailend of the distribution of attitudes found in the Douglas study-- of the minister's wives are shown to have no more involvement in the minister's role than if the wife were with a husband in any other occupation or profession. These wives are the "bottom" in attitude strength and committment vis a vis the minister- husband's role.

This distribution--20 percent truely faithful, 60 percent supportive and 20 percent detached--represents as well a change in minister's wives' orientation toward religion, toward the wifely role, toward devotion to the church, and toward yoke-ism with their husband's roles. The minister's wife's role is changing. This change is having two consequences for the ministers: A change of pressure (stress) on the husband-minister himself, and a broadening of the wife's role vis a vis her husband-minister, the church, and the "call to religious duty."

Whereas in the past, ministers and their wives shared the pressures together now more and more the minister is carrying the stress and feeling the tensions and anxieties in his own right. Yoke-ism is diminishing in religion as it is in the corporation (Stylites, 1955; Denton, 1962; O'Neall, 1963; Gordon, 1978; Peale, 1971; Terkel, 1974; Sarason, 1977; Krantz, 1978). Perhaps the men--professional, religious, as well as sectarian--are experiencing more stress in their professional roles, less yoken-in support by their wives, and consequently more tension in their own right. Ministers have lived longer and had lower suicide rates than many other professional groups (King, 1970), but more recently the literature is beginning to reflect a greater incidence of divorce, alcoholism, and other problems among ministers. Also, the popularity of various professions among high school students (juniors and seniors) shows only 11.0 percent of the males and 11.6 percent of the females saying "they would like" the occupation of minister, priest or rabbi (Slocum, 1974, pp. 246-247). In earlier times ministers ranked higher than lawyers and physicians and other professions (Douglas, 1965, p.210).

Ministers have generally been a healthy group of professionals if we are to follow the statistics gathered by students of the professions (King, 1970; King & Bailar, 1969; Russek, 1965). King's study (1970) covers various professions, ages 20 - 64, in the U.S.A., England and Wales, Scotland, New Zealand, and South Africa, covering a period of nearly 100 years, 1860 - 1953, in regard to longevity, and various causes of death. Clergymen have the lowest death rate per 1,000 persons, ages 25-65 (whereas physicians had the highest) in King's findings which include data from countries cited above. Further, clergymen had the lowest death rate from suicide among professional groups in the United States and England, whereas British and American physicians had the highest suicide rates among professional groups (King, 1970, p.264). People eventually die of something and, although death certificates may be unreliable as to the major cause of death, clergymen reportedly tend to die from hyperplasia of the prostrate, ulcer of the duodenum, intestinal obstruction, and diabetes. Opinions arising from research among the professions as to their morbidity and mortality rates often includes the observation that clergymen are less beset with illnesses and seem, historically, to have suffered less from stress and tension owing to their non-materialistic and non-competitive orientations and to their belief systems which puts an emphasis less on ephemeral and more on abiding concerns. Clergymen (and, secondarily, teachers) are almost the opposite to physicians and dentists in their value systems. This difference is probably an important consideration in studying the health of professions, and in indoctrinating and educating fledging professionals as to what the world of professions holds for them as they survey career options. Common interests initially among such apparently different occupations as medicine and dentistry on the one hand, and ministerial work, and teaching, on the other hand show concern for human life, for serving people, and in dealing with human problems, actually diverge markedly in training, in values, and in the actual execution of their professions. The more materialistic and power and money-oriented health professions of medicine and dentistry accumulate stress and tension patterns, acquire a variety of stress-induced illnesses, live shorter lives, are more prone to suicide, and family problems. None of these is characteristic of the ministry, and they are relatively less characteristic of nurses, teachers, and college professors than of medicine and dentistry (King, 1970; Dublin, et al, 1949). The old saying that power and money corrupt are evidently borne out to some degree among the rather pervasive and deep-going features of several leading professional groups.

Despite the generally superior health status and longevity patterns of all clergymen in several countries, over a number of decades, the picture of health in this professional group is not entirely glawless and it may be changing for the worse. A study by King and Bailor (1969) showed Catholic priests to be hospitalized for emotional problems more frequently than would be expected from comparable men-in-general. In Britain, mission workers and itinerate preachers died sooner (from vascular lesions of the nervous system) and were more often suicide victims than their breatheran among the Anglican clergy (King, 1970, p.267). Kurz (1952) and Madigan (1962) found Roman Catholic priests to have a lower longevity record than members of some protestant ministerial groups. The "lower" record of longevity and greater stress among ministers and priests who move about often, or who get transplanted from one parish or church community to another, may indicate greater personal tensions and anxieties. The adverse results appear to grow out of the uncertainty associated with their more fleeting social contacts and frequently changed religious calling; hence they harbour more physical and psychological distress and lesser longevity. These findings, if they turn out over still greater periods of time to be reliable, may signal, again, the importance of the professional milieu in determining the health status of various professional groups.

King (1970) concludes his very comprehensive review of health problems of various professions by referring to the problems of the clergy thusly:

>...there is a high degree of occupational
>stability among the clergy, thereby
>increasing the validity of the basic data
>and mortality rates. While clergymen have
>a relatively low total mortality, death
>rates for coronary heart disease and
>strokes seem to be disproportionately
>high among both Protestant and Catholic
>clergymen...there has been an increasing

264

concern over the mental health of clergy-
men--Protestant, Catholic and Jewish
alike--implicating such factors as role
stress and mobility anxiety...(p.273).

King notes, then, what other research and clinical
reports observe: The role of the clergy is changing
and succumbing to some noticeable extent to the various
stresses in the occupation itself and to the tensions
provoked by these environmental stresses in the daily
lives of clergymen. As local tensions accumulate for
the clergy, anxieties lest they succumb to illnesses
and other problems will likely grow and, in time, the
clergy may be beset with the same degree of stress,
tension and anxiety as other more materialistic and
power-oriented professions. Needed for study are more
detailed accounts of the actual health habits of
various professional men and women. Then, problems in
environmental stress and tension can be better correlated with individual background factors, thus placing
longevity data, causes of death, occurrence of suicide,
the presence of family distress, emotional problems,
"burnouts" and breakdowns, in a more substantial
context.

King's 1970 report was anticipated somewhat by
Madigan's study (1962) almost a decade earlier when
the latter studied 1,247 Catholic priests between
1953-58 as to longevity, causes of death, stress and
other factors in what he called a "closed population"
of professional men in religious service. Madigan
observed qualitative aspects of the priests' lives and
noted they seldom took their allotted two-week annual
vacations, that they were too strenuously involved
with retreats, workshops, special parish activities
and the like. This researcher observed further that
priests tend to have high cholesterol diets, exercise
less, lead more sedentary lives generally, hence
should be expected to succumb to cardio-vascular-renal
diseases more often than men-in-general of the same
age. However, the more Madigan studied the "closed
population" of priests, the more impressed he became
with their health stamina, saying "The central death
rates and life-table mortality rates of the priests
were consistently much more favorable than corresponding rates for white males of the American general
population" (Madigan, 1962, p.646). Compared to white
males in general, per 100,000, years 1953-1957, he

found priests living 28 percent longer lives than males in general, and 21 percent longer lives than married men in general, age range 20-74, years 1949-1951, for both priests and the control population. After delineating the stress factors in the lives of priests, and showing similarities in their lives to physicians (who live much less long than priests and also less long than non-Catholic clergy), Madigan concludes that priests have more favorable longevity patterns owing to the "...typically high degree of role satisfactions experienced by priests...[which] ...more than offset the curtailing effects upon length of life caused by the excessive life stresses they undergo" (Madigan, 1962, p.647). In spite of these excessive life strains presumably characteristic of the lives of priests, they also experience many career benefits usually not available to people-in-general: The regularity of life in the religious order begets stability and personal satisfaction; the lack of competition for positions and income and security in the order contrasts with people-in-general who experience far more job insecurity and turnover; and the religious order screens out unhealthy persons--both physically and psychologically--thereby reducing the likelihood of early deaths among the clergy and increasing the probability of longer life spans. The seemingly important factor of "role satisfaction" may account for the prevailing differences between the general health status and longevity of priests over most other professional groups (especially among the health professions)(Madigan, 1962, p.649).

Just what additional and more detailed factors contribute to the global "role satisfactions" motifs are not clear and need to be studied more fully among all professional groups. Surely the rigors employed in selecting priests at the seminarian level, the constant scrutiny of their lives and development in the religious order all contribute to a more and more select group by the time these candidates actually enter the religious order as fully-trained priests. Role satisfactions may be more extant in religious training, based as it may be on a strong philosophy of life, a high regard for humanistic and personal interests toward people, and schooling in carrying out these concerns; compared to other professions which purport to hold fast to service and to humanistic interests but who are also under more uncompensated-for-personal-strain and who hold more to materialistic gain as self-reinforcing conditions. Supporting the role

266

satisfaction notion for clergymen--perhaps of all denominations, although in the Madigan study only Catholic priests were studied--is the extent to which the clergy believe in poverty (a matter of vowing in the Catholic clergy), in chastity (also a prerequisite among Catholic priests)and obedience (probably applies to clergy of all denominations). These vows, or beliefs, and perhaps other, similar beliefs, depending upon how much they may be subscribed to, may constitute large philosophical positions which insure the clergy against the onslaughts of materialism, social stress, competitiveness and economic gain. They constitute alternative life styles, compared to the life styles of executives, physicians, dentists, and others who subscribe to a general "get ahead" motif in their lives (Jencks, 1979). It is as if the factor of stress and tension were presumably equal, or near-equal, among clergy, physicians, dentists and executives--as shown in the stem of the "Y" figure on page 268 but the off-shots from the base of the "Y" carry the clergy in the direction of non-materialistic concerns, typified by longer life and fewer illnesses arising from stress; whereas the other, more materialistic professions, veer off to the left displaying a divergent interest or life-motif from the clergy (less role-satisfaction, less of a non-materialistic belief system) and consequently an association with shorter life span, more psychological and social problems, in short more ill-health. There is not implied here a cause-and-effect relationship, but an associational tendency.

Physicians and dentists, and perhaps executives in high corporate positions do not all fail to experience some role satisfactions, but the actual satisfactions, although these have not been fully research, in the case of the clergy may be more under their own control, may be more equally and reliably associated with effort, and may derive value less from competition and more from good service to others. A corporate executive may "pull off a good deal" and thus derive satisfactions, but in so doing he (possibly she), in the competitive milieu, has cost another competitor a substantial loss. Only one can win. Somebody else (or several somebody-elses) have to lose. The physician or dentist may accomplish an important operation or extraction and receive plaudits from others and much self-satisfaction, but the domination of technology, the interpersonal psychological distance between physician or dentist and patient and the monetary gains from these

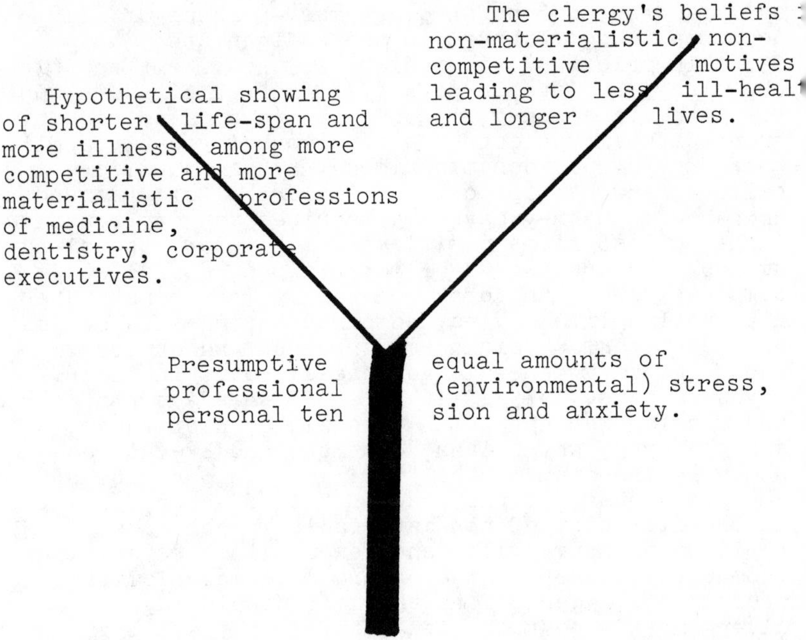

Hypothetical showing
of shorter life-span and
more illness among more
competitive and more
materialistic professions
of medicine,
dentistry, corporate
executives.

The clergy's beliefs :
non-materialistic non-
competitive motives
leading to less ill-heal
and longer lives.

Presumptive
professional
personal ten

equal amounts of
(environmental) stress,
sion and anxiety.

Figure 1. Hypothetical illustration of how
the clergy may share occupational and
professional stress with other professions
(physicians, dentists, executives) but veer
off into compensatory relief arising from
their role satisfactions and belief system,
and showing greater longevity and fewer
signs of ill-health associated therewith.

successful events may loom larger for the physician or dentist than the personal satisfactions and the benefit to the patient. Surgeons, for example, are often characterized as being impersonal, not later recognizing the patient they operated on, and have little or no follow-up from the results of the operation (this is more likely left to the patient's "regular" physician, placing the surgeon in the role of a temporary "fix-it technician"). The clergyman, however, gains much personal contact with those whom he "saves" or benefits, and these contacts may lead to life-long warm, personal and even intimate associations. The bases, then, for various types and orders of role satisfactions among various professionals remain somewhat unclear. It is now only possible to speculate about how deep and wide role satisfactions are in various professions, how much they pivot on material gain (as contrasted with personal gain for the benefactor and the recipient), on competitiveness, and how much technology interposes its role in the execution of the benefaction.

Role satisfactions may, in turn, be easier for clergymen to maintain than it is for executives, lawyers, physicians, dentists and other busy and divided professionals. Catholic clergy do not marry, hence cannot be accused of being "bigamists"--i.e., "Married" to their jobs as well as to their wives, an approbation sometimes applied to corporate executives (they're called "corporate bigamists" (Vandervelde, 1979, p. 279)) and to physicians, lawyers, dentists, and other professionally preoccupied men (more lately, wives, too) (Vandervelde, 1979, p.284). If divided and conflicting roles add stress to the practice of a profession--which seems amply to be the case--then role satisfactions would appear to eminate from mono- lithic roles rather more freely than from diverse roles, the former being more characterized among ministers or clergymen. Also, traditionally, the minister's wife, as earlier pages have documented, has been "married" to the church and to the religious calling, as she has supported her minister-husband, as much as the minister-husband has. It is only among the less committed minister's wives, as we have seen, that they tend to go their own way, fail to share fully the minister's devotion to religion and the church and his "calling." It would be interesting to know if, among Protestant clergy, those with "yoken-in" wives live longer and have fewer stress- related health problems than similarly trained and

269

devoted clergy who have more independent wives. The many and important and interesting comparisons between role satisfactions among clergy with and without wives, with and without yoked-in wives, and other considerations, are all research questions yet to be studied. Since the health of professions is a general field of knowledge of burgeoning importance, more and more research questions will be asked and pursued by members of the various professions as well as by psychologists, sociologists, and other social scientists.

Other Considerations

Role satisfaction, however, may not guarantee priests against untoward stress in other ways. Emotional illness among the clergy (Catholic and Anglican priests) was studied by a'Brook et al (1969), among 51 hospitalized and out-patient clergy in various British hospitals, over a ten-year span, 1954-1964. These authors observe that the clergy tend to live a life that separates them from laymen in an intimate sense and that the public often fails to know the extent of psychological problems among the clergy. This all-male population with an average age of 53 years (range 25 - 85 years), half being married and half single or widowed, were found to be diagnosed mostly as depressed or involutional melancholy cases, although other diagnostic categories such as alcoholism, neurosis, personality disorders and non-alcoholic drug abuse were noted. As a group they felt themselves to be overworked, moved too often from one post to another without considering their preferences, to be overly concerned with impossibly high standards, to be low on money, and sometimes reportedly found themselves placed in declining parishes or churches. Pressure comes from clergy occupying privileged positions in the community but also being expected to show exemplary behavior and unrelenting devotion to their work and other extraordinary qualities. Given some lacks in social skills from childhood and adolescents (many were judged to be too dependent upon their mothers, to have been somewhat socially isolated as adolescents, highly serious about self and life) they tended to succumb to adult and professional pressures. These clergymen broke down later in life than did physicians showing similar psychological problems and the Catholic clergy, along with the clergymen in general, tended to live longer than physicians. The clergy were cooperative in their psychological

270

treatment and discharged themselves from the hospital against medical orders less frequently than physicians. There were no suicides among the clergy in the a'Brook et al study, a very favorable finding compared to many other professions. Findings similar to a'Brook et al are reported by Booth (1961), Christensen (1960), and Lake (1966).

Appearing in studies over the past two decades or so--such as reports and research by a'Brook (1960), Booth (1961), Christensen (1960) and Lake (1966)--are indications of the importance of alcoholism among priests and other clergy. Volume 26 of the proceedings of the National Clergy Conference on Alcoholism refers to some facts of importance in understanding the emotional and related problems of the clergy: About 10% (6,000) priests in the U.S.A. are victims of alcoholism and/or drug dependency. Few of these are in programs intended to help them recover from this problem. Brothers of the various religious orders number about 10,000 among 100,000 total) who have serious problems with drinking and/or drug dependence. Sisters, too, may show serious problems with alcoholism to the extent of about 5% (8,000) of the total number (150,000). These alcoholism problems are serious enough that The Blue Book (1974, p.xiv) indicates that alcoholism among priests contributes heavily to failures in priesthood and religious life, to chronic inability to discharge their priestly responsibilities, to death or permanent disability, to a jaundiced view of the church and its teaching held by religiously abiding persons. The annual National Clergy Conference on Alcoholism and the publications eminating therefrom are serious attempts to draw in priests with drinking problems, and others who purport to help them too. Meetings that surface the problem of alcoholism and attempt to develop corrective measures are planned. These annual conferences also try to promote among religious leaders some compassion for the alcoholic priest and the circumstances leading to such a problem. The publication (called The Blue Book) reports on the convention proceedings, giving those concerned reference sources for help, and highlights the extent and nature of the alcoholism problem.

The longevity factor among clergymen, cited above, is further substantiated in a study by King, Zafros and Hass (1975).   These authors studied the length of life among Presbyterian and Lutheran clergy,

271

in comparison to men-in-general and white males in the U.S.A. These authors and others (Dublin, et al, 1949) observe that one's work influences to a considerable degree one's life style, one's health and, ultimately, one's longevity. Among the clergy their work is their life style, as many researchers have stated; therefore we expect the lifestyle to be reflected in matters of health and longevity. The King et al study (1975) covered 9,160 Presbyterian and 4,689 Lutheran (Missouri-Synod) clergy, over the decade 1950-1960. In this study population, 28% of the Presbyterian clergy and 13% of the Lutheran clergy were already over age 65. At all ages up to 85 the expected and observed standard mortality rate for men-in-general exceeded the mortality rates for both Presbyterian and Lutheran clergy. These authors state: "All these [data] seem to indicate strongly an association between the clergy profession and a definite pattern of mortality" (King et al, 1975, p. 252). They also conclude that the characteristics of the clergy lifestyle is important in the longevity and health status findings. In regard to the latter, the clergy rate of suicide is very low compared to the general population, being from one-third to one-tenth of the expected rate in general, whereas some other professions (e.g., medicine and dentistry) have suicide rates in excess of the standard population rates. Despite the fact that both Presbyterian and Lutheran clergy die (65% of deaths) from cardiovascular-renal diseases, these diseases still occur less frequently than among the general population as is also true for malignant neoplasms, lung cancer (despite these clergy having no strong inhibition against smoking) and prostrate cancer. In summary, it was noted that the King et al study (1975) was similar in findings to an earlier study by King and Bailar (1968) on mortality among 3,914 Lutheran clergymen as of the September 1, 1950 to August 31, 1960 decade; producing evidence that clergymen have a lower mortality rate than males-in-general and lower than males from medical and legal professions. Only college presidents/professors/instructors had an overall mortality rate below that of Lutheran ministers (King & Bailar, 1968, p. 541). The general consensus from these data is that the less robust in health may originally not themselves select, (or otherwise be eliminated from the rigors of) ministerial training. Also, once in the ministry the lifestyle is supportive of health, modest living and the handling of health risks, stress, and tension, in ways that do not wear

and tear on the ministers as much as similar socio-
psychological factors weigh on other professions
(such as law, medicine, dentistry).

Without any concern for mortality or any of a
myriad specific health problems, Gleason (1977) studied
general stress among clergy and their wives on a 43
item questionnaire. Each item was rated on a 5-point
scale by 21 parish clergy and 11 wives. How representative these clergy and wives were of clergy in general
was not attended. Each, clergyman and wife, had his/
her predominant stressors (defined as "a problem: or
"provocative stimulus," or a problem "posed to the
minister for solution") (Gleason, 1977, p.248). The
commonest stressors for the clergymen were as follows:
proliferation of activities, being perfectionistic
about work, lack of time for study, role conflicts,
surprises, conflicts in the church, organizational
difficulties, living a "goldfish bowl" existence,
effort to show self as a hard worker, lack of tangible
results from work, illness among parishioners, previous
unresolved stress, and inferiority feelings. Absent
in this list but present in many other clergy-related
stress were: moving often, assignment to unwelcome
parishes, financial burdens, and conflict with
superiors in the church hierarchy. In the Gleason
study the wives rated the following stressors as most
oppressive: unwelcome surprise, anger, intangible
results from work, perfectionism, proliferation of
activities, self-image, inability to relocate, low
salary, feeling inferior, role conflicts, family
problems, "Goldfish bowl" existence, loneliness and
the illnesses of parishioners. Among the many items
checked by both clergymen and wives, separately, eight
were found to co-exist in their ratings. That clergy
and their wives experience a number of stresses is
beyond doubt. As modern living becomes more stressful
and as organizational activities in the church increase,
there will be expected a continuing proliferation of
stress among the clergy and their wives and families.

An American study, comparable to the a'Brook et al
(1969) study among hospitalized clergy in England, was
done on 140 Protestant ministers admitted to the
Menninger Foundation for Treatment for psychological
problems over a 8-year period, May, 1964 to January,
1972 (Bradshaw, 1977). These clergy ranged in age from
27 to 68 with an average age of 41 years. Nearly all
were married (90%). While Bradshaw and his associates

273

seemed somewhat preoccupied with diagnostic classification rather than identifying specific or collective stress in the ministers' lives, suffice it to say that they fell into psychotic, character pathology, and neurotic diagnoses. Bradshaw was perplexed to find that these men had functioned so long in daily life before evidencing a breakdown. The literature answers Bradshaw in pointing out that the lives of clergy, despite stresses they experience, are healthful lives and that much psychological support comes from the nature of the profession and the beliefs of clergymen. Evidently not enough attention was given to these matters by Bradshaw. Studies of this sort need to focus more on the actual daily circumstances--role conflicts, overburdened committments, uncertainty in parish assignment, and the like--of the minister if we are to advance our understanding of stress, tension and anxiety among the various professions.

Related to the lack of concern for the actual lives of the clergy in the Bradshaw study (where only diagnostic classification was given), is an article by Smith (1953) showing thirty years ago that migration, structure of the clergy's setting, and cleric ideology, all figure prominently in why men enter the clergy and how much they value the success of their religious undertaking in these lights. Twenty-four clergymen (12 each from Congressional and Episcopal clergy) were assessed by interview; reasons for their entering the religious life were based on having had relatives or close family friends in the clergy, with receiving a "call" as the second most prominent reason. The men interviewed had up to 35 years of service in the ministry. Moves were a source of stress although often accepted owing to the promise of "wide religious service," or acquiring a larger church. Success-- and also sources of stress for these ministers--was seen in their ability to improve the economic condition of the parish, aiding community welfare, engaging in pastoral counseling, developing the loyalty and identification of parishioners to the church. Economic security and income ranked low in the values of these clergymen, perhaps partly because these items just do not generally rank high among any clergymen, plus the fact that clergy from these denominations ten to be supported by well-education and upper middle class parishioners, hence marginal security is usually not a problem.

Emotional Problems

The emotional problems of the clergy are evidently increasing. Not only do surveys and descriptive articles indicate this increase, there is growing literature pointing to remedial efforts being activated by religious bodies (The Blue Book, 1974; Mehl, 1977). One difficulty in the remedial and therapeutic literature on handling breakdowns and other family/vocational/emotional problems of ministers is that the remedial emphasis has been put too much on psychiatric bases, neglecting the career, and sometimes the minor emotional and professional problems. Mehl's article testifies to this possible mis-emphasis on psychiatric help. While clergy breakdown is proportionally less than among men in general (about 15-20 per 10,000 clergy vs. 231 patients in mental hospitals among 100,000 population in the U.S.A.) (Mehl, 1977, p.243), the treatment given these people may be suspect on grounds that very few of the clergy returned to their professional calling after an 8-12 month hospitalization period (the clergy were from the Lutheran Missouri Synod). Mehl's article reports that only two of seven completing a psychiatric program returned to the ministry; and among eight in the program current with Mehl's report, only one was judged ready for return to his parish responsibilities. If only two or three among 15 candidates for psychiatric rehabilitation are returned to their original professional calling, and alternative careers are largely ignored as possibilities, then the remedial program is too narrowly based, or is proceeding on the basis of faulty diagnosis of the ministers' problems. What with the accent today on career change, and with enlarged possibility everywhere of alternative careers, it is possibly a too narrow version of ministers' problems--even though they be emotional in kind--to view them exclusively in psychiatric terms and hospitalize these persons away from their homes for periods up to a year. This disruption alone would make career--hence emotional/social/personality problems-- for anyone and obfuscate issues relating to rehabilitation. Mehl observes that the essentials of occupational counseling are largely ignored in the psychiatric program for these ministers, leaving out objective assessment of abilities, aptitudes and interests, or giving them short shrift (Mehl, 1977, p.246). Additionally, when the ministers are employed, as part of their rehabilitation, they are given jobs in hospital maintenance, in rental equipment agencies, in

rug cleaning and sales businesses; more appropriate
would be positions in libraries, in schools, colleges
or universities assisting professors of religion,
history or related disciplines, or in other kinds of
educational work. To take a man away from home, put
him in a hospital for up to one year, and employ him in
a highly disparate occupation, are all inimical to
psychological rehabilitation. The occupationa/
vocational/professional dislocation alone would disturb
anybody! Those programs that try to keep the minister
in his natural orbit and in his prepared-for role
(except in cases of genuine need for career change
which should be approached on grounds assessing abilities, interests, etc.) are more likely to reap beneficial rehabilitative results. The same generalization
would appear to other professionals who run into severe
role conflicts and emotional problems in their chosen
careers. Radical career change is altogether possible
(Sarason, 1977; Krantz, 1977), and even likely in a
small percentage of cases, but these changes need to be
brought about not by suspending life and occupation
but by working out viable alternatives based on proper
assessment of needs, and on the strengths and weaknesses of the persons involved.

Organizational Change

Sometimes organizations, professions and corporations change in unusual ways. Whereas corporations
tend to get more powerful in our economy, and, most
professions are becoming more "professionalized"
(especially medicine, dentistry, nursing and possibly
public school teaching), churches, preaching and the
ministry generally are undergoing a different kind of
change. The organization of religion in terms of the
well known sects are commanding the attention and
support of fewer people and the evangelical movement,
so called, is gaining more adherents, at least more
followers and listeners. Listeners there are.

The publication, Christianity Today, reported
recently (December 21, 1979 issue) on a Gallop Poll
sponsored by the publication, an inquiry into the
pervasiveness of evangelicism today. In a question-
and-answer format, Gallop is reported as saying 20%
of all adults today are evangelical in their religious
leaning. Moreover, teenagers are embracing evangelical
movements more than the adults. The evangelical
followers give more to their respective churches than
do non-evangelicals and they also seem to prefer the

ministers to speak out frankly on social and political issues. These trends take the church, the minister (who may be a radio or TV "Personality") and the congregation away from traditional churches and its problems and concerns. Anti-evangelical sentiments consider the evangelicals as coming on too hard, as too simplistic in approach to problems, and as pitching their message more to mass appeal (perhaps more to conservative views of political and policy issues) than to traditional religious concerns. The evangelicals appear to concentrate more on obvious problems-- alcoholism, drug abuse, divorce--than on more subtle health, welfare and basic economic issues. The evangelicals tend toward accepting the Bible as complete, literal and uncontestable authority, whereas many denominations are inclined to treat the Bible as a historical--but important--document and as a general guide to living. Gallop reports 50% of Protestants questions favored a literal interpretation of the Bible (Christianity Today, 1979, p.11). The orthodox evangelical group is reported to have 5 basic tenets: Jesus Christ is the Divine Son of God; hope for Heaven comes only through personal faith in Jesus Christ; the Bible is the Word of God, unmistaken and incontestable; evangelicals should read the Bible at least once per month and attend religious service at least once a month.

What do the evangelical trends mean for the clergy, their health and psychological well-being? Direct answers are not forthcoming at this time, but indirect or general consequences seem likely. Also, trends other than those reflected in the evangelical movement are also influencing today's clergy. As a result, the clergy may be changing fairly rapidly from the highly devoted, pristine, servant-of-God-and-the-parish flock model to one that is "looser" in its ties to parishioners, more devoted to the emotional and personal welfare of the devotees, and less assuming of a role of God's representative through the Church and on earth.

Many religious leaders, pastors included, have for years assumed a more liberal religious posture. They have espoused less the doctrine cited above characteristic of evangelicals in their beliefs about the Bible, Jesus Christ, and the church. The publication Christianity Today notes this trend in the Gallop Poll article, saying "American educational philosophy has rigorously tried to exclude any notion of God...

[from Education]...and for over 50 years has given our children a steady diet of secular education" (Christianity Today, 1979, p.15). This philosophy, embraced in part in a separatist viewpoint regarding church and state, has also influenced many clergy (often more likely to be noted privately in talks with clergymen than espoused from the pulpit), and has been the "official" American stand on important church-state religious issues. The Christianity Today article is noting, it avers, a trend away from this liberal viewpoint, one toward a more orthodox and conservative view.

While all the evangelical movement is going on-- more or less outside the boundaries of the traditional religious denominations--clergy within these denominations are less inclined toward traditional pastoral religious activities and duties and more toward pastoral counseling and other social concerns. The yoked-in wife is less visible in these new pastoral roles (Hartley, 1978; Hartley & Taylor, 1977; Glass, 1976). Furthermore, the minister's direct role to his church and parishioners is changing in the direction of a less idealized, symbolic model. Pattison (1965, 1977, 1978) and Ragsdale (1978) have written in this connection about the pastor and his parish in terms of a "systems approach". The former says,

It is a mistake to assume that in the symbolic role the pastor must attempt to be a paragon of virtue...The point of symbolic reference is not oneself but the Lord...the Head of the whole body. The pastor is not a model but a symbol. This understanding of the symbolizing function enables the being function. It frees the pastor to be a person (Pattison, 1977, p.64).

Leslie (1960) anticipated some of Pattison's remarks in his article on helping the theological student "dare to be himself". Pattison (1965) also wrote similarly in discussing the minister's role in a community mental health center. The bibliography in these just-cited articles reads like those from purely psychological journals (with a humanistic emphasis) in that a mental health posture, and not a religious one, is uppermost. References to Maslow, Rogers, Rollo May, Kohlberg, Roheach, as well as to subjects relating to moral development, to personality integration and to the impact of social forces on the adjustment of persons abound (Hoffman, 1960).

278

The specific emphasis among many current ministers' writing includes books on crisis counseling (Stone, 1978); on counseling in regard to specific emotional and social problems (Oates, 1978); on grief and separation (Irwin, 1975); on youth (Colston, 1978); on handicapped persons and on psychotherapy (Clinebell, 1977 & 1975); on mid-life problems and on marriage enrichment, respectively (Clements, 1976 & 1979); on counseling for liberation and counseling for the aging.

The major changes going on _within_ the ministry are those directed toward a more man-centered, society-centered, mental health and public welfare centered religion and less toward the model role of God's representative in the church (Browning, 1966). Whether this role change portends an improvement in the mental health of the clergy is moot. The stress traditionally associated with the minister caught-in-the-middle between man and God, trying to serve each in exemplary and sometimes conflicting ways, may be yielding to a more modest, more human emphasis with less role conflict and more personal satisfactions (Coburn, 1963; Turnbull, 1964; Hadden, 1969; Shrader, 1970). These apparent changes are both welcome and unwelcome--parishioners are _still_ hard to please, wanting both traditional men-of-God and more earthy counselors and therapists, exemplary models and friendly peers. These new roles, then, are not without stress (Stewart, 1965).

Whether the role changes going on in the ministry are passing or profound, only time will tell. What we extract from the history of the clergy and their health and emotional status over the last several decades is that their fortunes are apparently related to their non-competitive and humane lives, their concern for others' welfare, and their compassion for the human situation. As they become more "worldly" these personality characteristics may change, and they may become more like other professions, especially if evangelistic motives take precedent over other religious motivations and purposes. With societal changes of a profound and intensive nature going on all about us (The Global 2000 Report, 1980), religion and the clergy may change markedly in the direction of most other professions, and hasten the day when the social networks that relate man-to-man will become even more shredded and torn.

CHAPTER X

BIBLIOGRAPHY

Andersen, C.H. White Protestant Americans - From National Origins to Religious Groups. Englewood Cliffs, N.J.: Prentice-Hall, 1970.

Anonymous. Hints for a clergyman's wife. London: Haldworth & Ball, 1832.

Beecher, E.W. (Mrs. Henry Ward). From Dawn to Daylight. N.Y.: Derby & Jackson, 1959.

The Blue Book. Barry College, Miami Fla., Vol.26,1974.

Booth, G. Unconscious motivation in the choice of the ministry as a vocation, in Wayne, E. Oats (ed.), The Minister's Own Mental Health. Great Neck, N.Y.: Channel Press, 1961.

Bradshaw, S.L. Ministers in trouble: a study of 140 cases evaluated at the Menninger Foundation, J. of Pastoral Care, 1977, 31, 230-242.

Brook, M.F., Hailstone, J.D. & McLaughlin, I.E. Psychiatric illness in the clergy, Brit. J. of Psychiatry, 1969, 115, 457-463.

Browning, D.S. Atonement and Psychotherapy. Phila.: Westminster Press, 1966.

Bustanoy, A. Why pastors drop out, Christianity Today, 1977, 21, 14-16.

Christensen, C.W. The occurrence of mental illness in the ministry: family origins, J. Pastoral Care, 1960, 14, 16.

Christensen, C.W. A psychiatrist and seminary consultant replies, in Oates, W.E. (Ed.) The Minister's Own Mental Health. Great Neck, N.Y.: Channel Press, 1961.

Christianity Today. Interview with George Gallop re: religious attitudes and practices, Christianity Today, pp. 10-19, Dec. 21, 1979.

Clements, W.M. Counseling for Liberation. Phila.: Fortress Press, 1976.

Clements, W.M. *Care and Counseling of the Aging.* Phila: Fortress Press, 1979.

Clinebell, H.J., Jr. *Growth Counseling for Marriage Enrichment.* Phila.: Fortress Press, 1975.

Clinebell, H.J., Jr. *Growth Counseling for Mid-Life Couples.* Phila.: Fortress Press, 1977.

Coburn, J.B. *Minister - Man in-the-Middle.* N.Y.: MacMillan, 1963.

Colston, L.G. *Pastoral Care with Handicapped Persons.* Phila.: Fortress Press, 1978.

Counts, G. The social status of occupations, *School Review*, 1925, 33, 16-27.

Daniels, E.E. & Hunter, W.A. MMPI personality patterns for various occupations, *J. Appl. Psychology*, 1949, 33, 559-565.

Davis, K.S. *The Years of the Pilgrimage.* N.Y.: Doubleday & Co., 1948.

Deeg, M.E. & Patterson, D.G. Changes in social status of occupations, *Occupations*, 1947, 205-208.

Denton, W. *The Role of the Minister's Wife.* Phila.: Westminster Press, 1962.

Douglas, W. *Ministers' Wives.* N.Y.: Harper & Row, 1965.

Dublin, L.I., Lotka, A.J. & Spiegelman, M. *The Length of Life.* N.Y.: Ronald Press, 1949.

Fairlie, H. *The Seven Deadly Sins.* Washington, D.C., New Republic, 1979.

Feather, D.B. The relation of personal maladjustment of 503 University of Michigan students to their main occupational interests, *J.Soc. Psychol.*, 1950, 32, 71-78.

Glass, J.C. Ministerial job satisfaction scale, *Rev. of Relig. Research*, 1976, 17, 153-157.

Global 2000 Report to the President. Superintendent of Documents, GPO, Washington,D.C., 1980.

Gleason, J.J. Perception of stress among clergy and their spouses, J. of Pastoral Care, 1977, 31, 248-251.

Gordon, H. The Minister's Wife. London: Routledge & Kegan Paul, 1978.

Hadden, J.K. The Gathering Storm in the Church. Garden City, N.J.: Doubleday, 1969.

Hartley, S.F. & Taylor, M.G. Religious beliefs of clergy wives, Rev. of Relig. Research, 1977, 19, 63-73.

Hoffman,H. (Ed.) The Ministry and Mental Health. N.Y.: Association Press, 1960.

Irwin, P.B. The Care and Counseling of Youth in the Church. Phila.: Fortress Press, 1975.

Jencks, C. Who Gets Ahead? The Determinants of Economic Success in America. N.Y.: Basic Books, 1977.

Johnson, A.F. The Making of a Minister's Wife. N.Y.: Appleton-Century, 1939.

Kildah., J.P. The hazards of high callings, in Oates, W.E. (Ed.) The Minister's Own Mental Health. Great Neck, N.Y.: Channel Press, 1961.

King, H. & Bailor, J.C. The health of the clergy: A review of demographic literature, Demography, 1969, 5, 257-281.

King, H., Zafros, G. & Hass, R. Further inquiry into protestant clerical mortality patterns, J. of Biosocial Sci., 1975, 7, 243-254.

Krantz, D.L. Radical Career Change. N.Y.: The Free Press, 1978.

Kurz, J.T. Length of life of religious males: Society of Mary, 1820-1941. Dept. of Sociology, unpubl. M.A. Thesis. St. Louis, Mo.: St. Louis Univ., 1952.

Lake, F. Clinical Theology. London: Dorton, Longman and Todd, 1966

Leslie, R.C. Helping the theological student dare to be himself, in Hoffman, H. (Ed.) The Ministry and Mental Health. N.Y.: Association Press, 1960.

Madigan, F.C. Role satisfactions - length of life in a closed population, Amer. J. of Sociology, 1962, 67, 640-649.

McCarthy, T.J. Personality Traits of Seminarians. Wash., D.C.: Cath. U. of America Studies in Psychology and Psychia., 1942.

Mehl, L. G. Occupational-rehabilitation of psychiatric hospital clergyment, J. Past. Care, 1977, 31, 243-247.

Meiburg, A.J. & Young, R.K. The hospitalized minister: A preliminary study, in Oates, W.E. (Ed.) The Minister's Own Mental Health. Great Neck, N.Y.: Channel Press, 1961.

Oates, W.E. Pastoral Care and Counseling in Grief and Separation. Phila.: Fortress Press, 1977.

O'Neall, F.S. The Better Half of the Ministry. Boston: Christopher Publ. House, 1963.

Pattison, E.M. Functions of the clergy in community mental health centers, Pastoral Psychology, 1965, 16, 21-26.

Pattison, E.M. Pastor and Parish - A Systems Approach. Phila.: Fortress Press, 1977.

Peale, Mrs. Norman Vincent. The Adventure of Being a Minister's Wife. Englewood Cliffs, N.J.: Prentice-Hall, 1971.

Ragsdale, R.W. Mid-Life Crisis of a Minister. World Books, 1978.

Ritcher, A.C. The Clergyman's Wife and Other Sketches. N.Y.: Charleton & Co., 1867.

Russek, H.I. Stress, tobacco and coronary disease in North American professional groups, J.A.M.A., 1965, 192, 89-94.

283

Sarason, S. <u>Work, Aging, and Social Change</u>. N.Y.:
      The Free Press, 1977.

Schuldt, D. L. Men leaving the pastorate - Social
      and psychological factors involved in career change
      of United Methodist ministers. Unpubl. M.A.
      Thesis, U. of Iowa, Iowa City, Iowa, 1970.

Schuldt, D.L. & Stahmann, R.F. Interest profiles of
      clergymen as indicated by the Vocational Preference
      Inventory, <u>Educ. & Psychological Meas</u>., 1971, <u>31</u>,
      1025-1028.

Shrader, W. <u>Anguished Men of God</u>. N.Y.: Harpers, 1970.

Slocum, W.L. <u>Occupational Careers</u>. 2d Edit., Chicago:
      Aldine, 1974.

Smith, L.M. The Clergy: Authority,structure, ideology,
      migration, <u>Amer. Social Rev</u>., 1953, <u>8</u>, 242.

Southard, S. An overview of research on the mental
      illness of the minister, in Oates, W.E. (Ed.)
      <u>The Minister's Own Mental Health</u>. Great Neck,
      N.Y.: Channel Press, 1961.

Stewart, J.T. <u>The Deacon Wore Spats: Profiles of
      America's Changing Religious Scene</u>. N.Y.: Holt,
      Rinehart & Winston, 1965.

Stone, H. W. <u>Crisis Counseling</u>. Phila.: Fortress
      Press, 1978.

Stylites, S. New look in preachers' wives,
      <u>Christian Century</u>, 1955, <u>72</u>, 1489.

Tennenbaum, S. <u>Rachel: The Rabbi's Wife</u>. N.Y.:
      Wm. Morrow & Co., 1978.

Terkel, S. <u>Working</u>. N.Y.: Avon, 1974.

TIME Magazine. American Preaching: A Dying Art? Time
      Mag., pp. 64-67, December 31, 1979.

Turnbull, R.G. <u>A Minister's Obstacles</u>. Westwood, N.J.
      F.H. Revell Co., 1964.

Vandervelde, M. <u>The Changing Life of the Corporate
      Wife</u>. N.Y.: Mecox Publ. Co., 1979.

Weaver, G.C. The Minister's Wife. Cincinnati: Powell
   & White, 1928.

Weber, M. The Protestant Ethic and The Spirit of
   Capitalism. N.Y.: Chas. Scribner's Sons, 1958
   (Trans. by Talcott Parsons)

Welch, M.K. The ranking of occupations on the basis of
   social status, Occupations, 1949, 27, 237-241.

Young, E.H. The Vicar's Daughter. N.Y.: Harcourt,
   Brace & Co., 1928.

CHAPTER XI

UNIVERSITY PROFESSORS (AND STUDENTS)

One of the most interesting, elusive and misunderstood of the professions is that of university or college professor. It is the only profession that has "professor" or one who professes to know in its very title. It is, of course, traditionally one of the so-called learned professions along with law, the ministry and medicine. Despite its status it has received very little study. Lynn says "Only medicine and the ministry have received anything like the scholarly attention appropriate to their important" (Lynn, 1965, p.x). Even when studied, most professions have been written about in terms of philosophical and technical issues, not in terms of their functioning, how well they serve the public, he health of the members and the intracacies of the lives of the practitioners.

University professors have another significance: They stand at the crossroads in the training of all other professionals. Medicine, law, the clergy, all of the sciences, people trained in all of the arts, almost invariably are taught by unversity professors, if not entirely then at crucial junctures in their careers. It is university professors who influence the great minds and achievers of each generation. There is no profession more accustomed to or more devoted to the acquisition of knowledge, to the intellectual life, to the advancement and criticism of culture. Except for the pulp magazine and book markets and strictly commerical publishing, most books, articles, learned treatises, are written by university professors. The filling of the chief appointments in the government--in the arts, in science, in politics--mostly come from university faculty members, or those who have held important faculty posts in the past. Universities rever achievers in all departments of knowledge and make places for them if they have heretofore not been part of a university faculty. The great "think tanks" in the nation are made up of present and past university professors for the most part. The advancement of knowledge has stemmed in recent years from some commerical enterprises, especially in the rapidly burgeoning areas related to computers, but all of these people have been university trained and often hold teaching posts jointly with the other scientific work.

Growth of Universities

The demand on universities for more people trained in needed manpower (person power) fields has been in evidence since the decade after World War II. Not enough persons were trained in the 1960's in basic science, mathematics, economics, and foreign language fields, and universities had to somewhat lower their selection and training standards to meet public demands. These demands required more university professors to train and educate the others. This pattern of almost endless growth has gone on and on, until recently.

With all this growth and importance there has also emerged a rigidity of purpose and procedure. Educationists have steadfastly said that only people taking education courses could become teachers - in the public schools, that is - denying the fact that most of their college and university colleagues have never set foot in an education course; nor have many private school teachers. Curricula have multiplied and courses have been spawned as fast as they could be printed in the college or university catalogues. With all the growth, except for a few fields, women have been denied the opportunities afforded men. In contrast to the U.S., in the mid-1960's, Russia had nearly 400,000 women engineers and over 330,000 women physicians and surgeons, compared to very few women engineers in the U.S. and about 14,000 women physicians. We have seen in the chapter on women that the prejudice against their entering medicine is slowly and grudgingly changing for the better, but there is much yet to be done to close the gap. The gateway to greater acceptance of women into the professions, especially medicine, law and engineering, will depend upon how liberal the universities become in their admission policies toward women and how much they value knowledge service and public responsibility over the maintenance of their own narrow image of their elitist selves.

The growth of the economy in the past three decades has placed an enoumous burden on the university. It has resulted in lower standards, in proliferation of courses and fields of work. Economic growt has put universities in financial crunches (the cost of physical plants, the escalation of professorial and administrative salaries, not to mention rising costs of supplies, laboratores, libraries, and other necessar accrutements of the university), and has made them

vulnerable to the money marketplace and to the wiles
of commercial interests which are basically inimical to
the purposes and proper functioning of the university.
The university has, in short, been corrupted in the
past several decades, and the professors (and administrative staff) are right in the middle of the seeming
decadence. The question now remains whether the
university has strayed so far from its intellectual
and scholarly courses that it might never retrieve its
former self, and might along with the industrial/
military complex, and medical/industrial complex, now
make up the educational/industrial complex. That is,
the university may become so engrossed in the profit
and continued growth motives of the industrial world
(which, not incidentally, along with the federal
government feeds billions of dollars of funds to the
universities each year (Ridgeway, 1968; Lynn, 1965))
that the acquisition and preservation of knowledge
will take a tertiary place and the university will no
longer be its own person. The reason the university
has been so important is because of its harbouring of
special knowledge, delivering an esoteric service, and
possessing capabilities found nowhere else (Lynn, 1965,
p.1). All of this presumably made available under non-
prejudicial and objective auspices. If the university
falls under the demands of the business and industrial
world, because of its need for money, then it will lose
its professed status (News Service, 1980). It may have
lost much of this status already!

Not only would the university be weakened and its
professors corrupted if they are both to follow the
dictates of the industrial and business world, the
larger issues at the university would be lost or
placed in jeopardy (Roark, 1980). Not only do lawyers,
trained in universities, dispense law, develop techniques for analyzing cases and ponder the meaning of the
law, they also develop a social philosophy. That is,
for better or for worse, they steer society through
law into ways of thinking about society, its philosophy,
its values, and other ramifying issues. Not only do
physicians learn to cut, sew up, heal and prescribe,
they come up with larger notions of illness, individual
and public health, longevity and how society can learn
from the physicians and be benefited by their knowledge
and service. Every profession, in addition to its
particular expertise, has a hunk of society in its
hands, so to speak. Architecture, social work,
clinical psychology, dentistry, the clergy, various

289

physical and biological scientists--all of them expound
on and about society and help steer its course. If
these lofty, but sometimes flawed, purposes are
corrupted by the university which may no longer be
capable of instructing tyro lawyers, clinical psychologists, physicians, architects and other professionals--
owing to its bowing to the dictates of the marketplace--
then the university will have not only demeaned itself,
it will have pulled the pillars out from under society.
Freedom of inquiry and the objective pursuit of knowledge, wherever it may lead--the greatest purpose of
the university and its faculty--will have been ditched,
plowed under, in the quest for growth, power, and money.
For shame!

The Industrial/Educational Complex

Where the university is now in terms of its hoary
history and presumptive public image may be farther
from the ideal than most of us recognize. Ridgeway
(1968), in The Closed Corporation: American Universities In Crisis, provided us with more than a glimpse
of how America's leading universities, and some not-so-
leading-ones, have been brought under the control of
big business and the federal government (mostly under
the auspices of the department of defense). His is a
shocking account of how much we now have the industrial/
educational complex at hand and how far the universities
have been pushed off their course.

Ridgeway asserts that the university of today (he
was writing in the mid-1960s, but there is no substantial reason to think that conditions have changed since
then other than for the worse) appears to be more like
a center for industrial activity than a place where
knowledge and scholarship are uppermost. The changes
in the university appear to pivot on the leading
schools, the ones most respected for research, scholarship, high standards of teaching, and for superior
equipment (laboratories, libraries, etc.) He
indicates that a 1964 congressional study of 2100
American universities showed that ten universities
received 38 percent of federal funds for research and
development: University of California, MIT, Cornell,
Columbia, University of Michigan, Harvard, Illinois,
Stanford, Chicago and Minnesota. Much of the
university budget comes from federal grant monies,
hence the university is not only beholden to the
government for the money to pay professors, do
research, keep the plant running, the very topics for

research, the values placed on research, the selection
of war/industrial/commercial-dictated research vs.
following the leads of the professors themselves--all
of these matters are called into question. In the
federal support of universities for their research,
there develops an unusually complex intertwining of
university professors, government liaison people,
contract research centers, and the industries or
businesses involved. Money changes hands not unlike
in a poker game. All this complexity resembles big
business at its worst.[1] Ridgeway says, "...the modern
university more nearly resembles a conglomerate

_____

[1]The Gomberg and Atalsek (1977) study of the
composition of College and university governing boards
indicates that most trustees are male (85 percent),
minority group board members are small (7 percent), two-
thirds of all board members are age 50 or older, and
nearly 40 percent are from executive positions (mining,
manufacturing and banking firms) with only about 10
percent counted among faculty or officers from higher
education. Other professionals--clergy, medicine, law,
dentistry--number about 15 percent. There is, then,
considerable weight to the proposition that college and
university governing boards are composed of, and run
by monied interests, interests that may not be
compatible with the avowed purposes of colleges and
universities. In a recent article on trusteeship at
the George Washington University, Washington, D.C.,
it was revealed that of eight new trustees, four were
from business or banking, three were members of large
law firms (serving mainly corporations and businesses?)
and one was from the government. None was from
education, the sciences, the arts, the clergy, or the
humanities (G.W. TIMES, 1980, p.2).

corporation on its own" (1965, p.9). Corrupted, or at
least changed in this process, is the professor, the
pivotal role-maker in the university/industrial
complex, viewed thusly by Ridgeway: "Professors once
sneered at businessmen and the profit motive, but
since they have been so successful in taking up the
game themselves, the profit motive is now approvingly
referred to as the 'reward structure' " (Ridgeway,
1965, p.11).

Not only do the universities have their hands in
the financial pockets of large corporations, the defense
industry and various other governmental agencies, there
is equally alarming intermingling of officials from
each quarter on the boards of the other. It is well-
known that most university boards of regents or trustees
are largely made up of prominent businessmen and
politicians--most of whom know nothing about education,
about any particular field of sciences, the humanities,
or the arts--and care less. But the serving of
university officials on the boards of directors of
large corporations is going one step further. Among
the ten largest life insurance and utility companies,
six have university representatives on their boards,
likewise for four of the largest merchandising
companies, and four of the biggest transport companies
(Ridgeway, 1965, p.23). This intermingling is not
promoted to educate the industrial/business complex in
the scholarly ways of the university; it is promoted
to make more money for the corporations (picking the
brains of the university professors and rewarding them,
in turn, with money, research opportunities directed to
business interests, and other essentially non-scholarly
pursuits). One observation Ridgeway makes is particularly searching in regard to the intermingling of
university professors and businessmen: "One survey
indicates that of the 350 insurance professors in the
country, over half either consult or teach part time
for the industry. Which may well help to explain why
there is so little interest in correcting abuses in
the insurance industry" (Ridgeway, 1965, pp.23-24).

Among other university/business comingling too
numerous and too detailed for our scrutiny here, yet
that leaves us with a profound feeling that the
universities and the professors are "being had"
(albeit at their own willingness - for money and
power) are the following: The university as a type of
investment trust itself, where it buys and develops
real estate, bonds, stocks, etc., runs businesses, and

292

so forth, all leading to a vastly different set of
interests from scholarship, individually determined
research, and the following out of ideas for their own
worth, not for market value. The proprietorships
started by university professors is another example of
the university extending itself into the business
community at the expense of its alleged investment in
knowledge and scholarship. Here the centers for "
"social problem solving" and related matters hinge on
communication theory, techniques of system analysis,
and the like, funded by war-related questions and
financial support, but allegedly able to apply to
human behavioral systems, social systems, poverty,
education, the handicapped, and the like. Not many
crums from the enterpreneurial and proprietorship
efforts fall to the "needy," however. I have had many
graduate students in engineering and the hard sciences,
sometimes from law, consulting about personal and
career problems, while also (along with their schooling)
being employed in war-related industries, who left
these lucrative jobs as soon as they could and after
they provided alternatives for themselves in more
interesting and non-war-related or non-industrial/
educational complex positions. The young men and
women at a relatively early age had more thoughtful-
ness about their values, the career directions and
the social implications of their technical work,
present, past and future, than did their professorial
mentors. This idealism, we hope, will hold up and
influence these professors-to-be to work for science,
knowledge and scholarship and not sell out to money and
power interests. Their plight is reminiscent of the
plight of fledging physicians, dentists and other
professionals who begin with idealism and end with
economic considerations being uppermost (see the
chapters on medicine and dentistry in this connection).

Still another example of possible conflict of
interest among university professors and their roles
in business, industry and government are those presidential and other governmental appointees from the
university community needed to solve extant social and
commercial problems whose presence also raise ethical
and moral issues. An example is President Johnson's
appointment of Dean George Baker, the Dean of the
Harvard Business School to study the Post Office and
hopefully to put it on better operational and
financial basis. What was overlooked--and reported by
Ridgeway--was that Dean Baker's suggestion that the
parcel post system might better be under private

corporate control, had also to be viewed in the
context of Baker's chairmanship of the Transportation
Association of America which had, among its expressed
purposes: "[Reducing]...government competition with,
and threats of socialization to, one or more segments
of the transport industry" (Ridgeway, 1965, p.73).
Baker is reported to have had board-of-director positions with important business interests that, in turn,
financed portions of the trucking business. It is very
easy to move from such positions of influence to outright favoritism for given business and industrial
interests (for money) and to convert scholarly writing
to serve exactly the same purposes (Ridgeway, 1965,
p.77).

Another stroke against scholarship and knowledge
comes through the support of classified (military
related) research on college and university campuses.
Here the gigantic war machine funds research on germ
warfare, extrapowerful explosives designed to kill
people without damaging the land (or vice-versa) and
many, many other generally destructive weapons of war
using sophisticated techniques developed usually in
an applied, war-related context (although sometimes
"spin-offs" to civilian, humanitarian and social uses
may be extracted). The problem raised here for
professors and universities is not only that they
are spending time in research with destructive ends,
in lieu of more gainful research and writing, but that
the research--inimical to science--is conducted in
secret. There have been many "exposures" on college
and university campuses in relation to post World War
II exploitative and concealed research and much of
this secret research has been brought into the open
with full disclosure of university complicity. The
exposures have at least issued public warnings against
both such complicity and against the secretive manner
in which the research has been carried on.

The multiversity, like multinational corporations,
is an outgrowth of the tremendous proliferation of
university power, its hook-up with the military/
industrial and medical/industrial complex, most all of
which purposes have not been to serve traditional
scholarly and research interests. Ridgeway documents
ways in which the multiversity has aided and abetted
private propietary interests in various parts of the
country and ways in which the multiversity has worsened
social problems among for example Mexican itinerate
workers rather than try to lighten the enormity of

294

their living and financial loads. Universities grow to support the interests of the monied and power centers which undergird them, and the common man is not thereby benefitted (Ridgeway, 1965, pp.137-192). Many universities in their geographic development have bulldozed their way through neighborhoods, displacing people from their home and causing other local disruptions (see, for example, Ridgeway's discussion of Columbia University, pp.171-192). Other urban universities have chalked up as unadmirable a record.

Economic Stress

What can universities and their professors do that will change the crassness of their recent record? It is not an easy question to answer, since university professors' welfare, financially speaking, is tied up with their consulting and other extra-classroom activities (Magarrel, 1980). Most colleges and universities do not pay well, hence many professors are obliged to consult, do private practice and supplement their incomes outside. This makes them vulnerable and the university vulnerable to money from industry, business and the government; some of which research and consulting is thoroughly honest, relevant, scientifically and socially useful. One cannot condemn all outside activities of universities and their professors. But the idea of a university being a community of scholars, thinkers, and researchers is growing dimmer and dimmer. Something will have to be done to set aside time for more scholarly work, for more community and social welfare work, and other non-profit activities. Universities know best their own needs, their own strengths and limitations; they can decide how best, if given the incentive or if they develop it themselves, to serve the community at large and not just selfish interests. Up and down the university hierarchy some restructuring should be accomplished. Trustees (at the administrative top) should not be only businessmen and businesswomen; they should be chosen because of their accomplishments in the educational world, and because of their social sensitivity. Ridgeway declares that all meetings of university governning boards should be public matters, with thorough financial reports published periodically (Ridgeway, 1965, pp.194-196).

Students should be given a much greater "say" in the running of the university and be on hand to select the boards of trustees and other governing personnel,

295

along with periodic ratings of professors and their teaching and classroom effectiveness. Making the university more democratic would bring about a better intellectual, social and emotional climate for all: professors, students, and the public. But unfortunately the university system in its connections with government even "does in" students in some instances.

Together the universities and the government conspire not to help needy and able students but to keep the system of preferential choice going. Harris (1973) documents how this works. Federal subsidies for higher education are channeled through universities not through students; further the most prestigious colleges and universities, those usually attracting the most upper-income families, are the ones receiving the governmental subsidies. Harris says, "Students from low-income families receive the benefit of subsidies averaging less than two-thirds of the money given students from families with incomes of more than $30,000.00 a year. In every instance, the federal higher education subsidy increases as family income increases" (Harris, 1973, p.18). If this preferential system exists on a very widespread basis, which Harris implies is true, then it is no wonder that Jencks' study of Who Gets Ahead? (Jencks, 1979) turns up the results it does (Morgan, 1980).

Health Problems

Given the pressures developing in universities in recent years, it is a bit surprising that more health problems have not emerged in the university professor (and student) populations. Perhaps there are several reasons why university professors have escaped health problems as much as they have. Traditionally they have been long-lived (Dublin et al, 1936, p.6). These authors computed the average age at death of various leading professional groups, mostly eminent persons, and found inventors, historians, college presidents, geologists, educational theorists, chemists, economists and political scientists, botanists, philosophers, mathematicians, and authors (mostly counted among university faculties) to be long lived as of data colleged in the 1930s and 1940s. Traditionally the scholar has led a quiet and non-tense life, a factor likely contributing to longevity given reasonable health otherwise. Another reason college and university professors may fare well is that they can make changes in their schedules almost a will, at

296

least each year and often each semester. A change of
pace in courses taught may be more stimulating than
pressureful. Although university teachers, as well as
public school teachers, have long hours, the college
teacher can control time more effectively and is not
under the pressure from disobedient students, excess
papers to grade (except for English professors), and
extracurricular activities are usually minimal among
university teachers. The long hours of the physician
and dentist are gruelling schedules compared to what
the university professor experiences even if he
accumulates long days and late nights for work. Much
of the university professor's work is at his/her
behest: writing, research, reading, preparing new
courses, and so on, far less gruelling than the
consulting the professor might do or the relentless
seeing of patients characterizing the physicians,
dentists and nurses' routines.

In the past college and university professors
have had far fewer health problems than most other
professionals (except the clergy). Despite their
generally good health and longevity, recent work
suggests that they are increasingly subject to stress
and that they can do something themselves about this
problem (Arnold, 1974; King, 1973). A recent study
reported by Fields (1980) suggests that faculty stress
is relatively greater among female married faculty
and single men faculty but, overall anxiety and
depression are less common among university professors
than among people in general.

Those university professors who keep up exercise
routines appear to be less depressed and to show some
attitude and personality differences in a favorable
direction not evidence by inactive colleagues (Reid,
1976). Nor have college and university professors
left their calling in any great numbers. In recent
years, however, there has been more evidence of
professors looking to other job areas, to administration, and to other work somewhat similar to university
teaching (consulting, for example). While the idea of
normal mid-life (or later) career change is gaining
ground (Sarason, 1973, 1975;Krantz, 1979) there exists
not very good basis for guiding people into alternative
careers at mid-life. The number of older prople is
increasing yearly; in two or three decades the number
of elderly will be considerable; help with career
change, or props to career stability will grow in
importance. These changes will affect career choices

297

in younger people, the bases over time for job satisfaction, and various educational policies pertaining
to mid-life and older people. Normal physiological
changes, technological changes and changes in one's
interests may relate to mid-life career changes among
professors and other professionally trained (Heald,
1977). With problems of academic freedom, retirement
policies of universities and colleges, and pressure
from younger scholars on older ones to "move over,"
there is additional impetus, other than the individual's
inclinations, to seek mid-career change or to leave
college teaching (Middleton, 1980). Some of the
pressures university members experience that prompts
career change--or digging in their heels, if that be
the case--relate to personal differences between
colleagues, the denial of tenure, and restrictions on
salaries. These issues loom larger than traditional
issues related to publishing or the nature of the
professor's scholarly works, and constitute specific
persistent stresses visited on the college professor.

Although the university professor experiences
stress and although mid-career changes among this
population are increasing, it is not to be assumed
that all mid-career change is perforce pressureful.
Sinick (1976) avers that as the population of expertly
trained people increases, there will be increased need
for counselors to prepare for the problems of this
population and to view these career changes as being
just as normal and interesting as initial career
decisions. Mid-career changes are viewed by Heddesheimer (1976) as natural steps in maturing and changing
as an adult and not necessarily radical in their
departure from one's previous career; they don't
necessarily signal maladjustment or any other special
problem with previous career intentions and patterns.
While Heddesheimer's point is often a valid one, there
are data to show that some mid-career changes among
university professors functions as a valve to let off
steam and to cope with previously high aspirations and
concurrent disappointments (Gosnell, 1977). The issue
has become specific in the case of vocational agriculture teachers where a study of 150 such teachers was
made. Five factors accounted for these teachers
leaving their posts: developing new and different
long-range goals, feeling students were not properly
selected, poor advancement opportunities, long hours
and poor salaries (Dillon, 1978; Knight, 1978).
Managers and other professionals than college/universit

professors also engage in mid-career changes for similar reasons (Thomas, 1979); thus suggesting that the pressures experienced by university teachers are not unlike those experienced in other high-status professions and occupations. The stress of work is apparently pretty general, across many professions, culminating in similar ways, and bringing about mid-life career changes for similar reasons (not disallowing the fact that some mid-career changes do not necessarily eminate from undue pressure).

Snyder et al (1978) explored reasons why professors leave teaching and research posts to engage in new careers in administration. A number of factors have disturbed the tranquility of the professorial life. Whereas medicine, dentistry and nursing, and also the allied health professions are changing due in part to technological innovations, the college professor's life is changing owing partly to the change in his clientel (students). Remarkable changes in student life have come about in the last 10-15 years owing in turn, to social changes, to the war, to economic stresses and to the proliferation of new job and work areas. The university, hence the university professor, is now serving, teaching and trying to influence a population of youth (and many older than youth) quite deviant from the 1965 and earlier period. Eurich (1968) predicted what the 1980s at the university would be like, a risky prediction. Some of the areas in which Eurich and his co-writers missed the boat on the future nature of the student body was to overlook the need for remediation, not advanced placement among college students. High schools have also proliferated "life style" courses, overly practical vocational courses, and have, of course, tried to educate a larger number of the masses. In turn, with the American ideal of upward mobility through education almost rampant, many students have been admitted to college who had not really achieved beyond the eighth grade in arithmetic, in writing, in study skills, and in various uses of the English language. The college professor has become discouraged at meeting classfulls of students who cannot read or write properly. This, in turn, has discouraged many from teaching and has accounted for some of the professorial dropouts cited above.

The economic pressures extant the last few years have cut back peoples' extra funds and so fewer

299

students are going to college (the population downturn has also accounted for lower potential enrollments); now colleges are actually recruiting--almost taking what they can get--and confronting the professor further with material somewhat short of his expectations for well-trained, thoughtful, scholarly types.

The political activism of the last decade and a half--considerably slowed down in the last few years-- has also changed the university, the professors, and the student body and its relationship to the university. The hoary traditions of scholarship took a beating in the late 1960s and early 1970s. How could we fix on traditional studies when the world was on fire? students ask. How could the standards of the past apply when they were born in a socio-cultural milieu so different from the Viet Nam war years? The university became a staging ground for activism. Professor's viewpoints, the assumptions on which courses were built, the curricula in all of the social sciences and some of the hard sciences changed considerably. One would almost not recognize the university of the early 1970s had he slept, like Rip Van Winkle, since the 1930s. All of this has changed again, after readjusting to the radical departures from the recent past.

Student Inclinations And Characteristics

Today students are more materialistic, looking more to vocational matters and less to scholarly pursuits. Although there is great competition for grades, students are not as thoughtful, intellectually inclined or curious about the world as they were. They want the courses that make the money today. Many of the social sciences, education, languages, and basic science courses are generally suffering from decreased enrollment in the university curriculum. More populated are courses leading to law, to accounting to engineering, and especially to business. Magarrell (1980, pp.3-5) observes that today's standards move students toward economic gain; economic pressures are so great that students and their families, putting out tens of thousands of dollars for higher education cannot afford to then let the student languish economically because the field of specialization has no jobs. Education-for-job, not education to become a learned person (or education for life), is the motto. Where is the university professor left in this melee?

300

She/he is now a dispenser of goods, marketplace commodities, information that can be quickly traded-in for funds; the university professor is wasting time, in the student's eyes, if she/he is theoretical, speculative, historically oriented, or critical of presentday values and practices. Let's get on with the grades, the courses, the money, the students say. Magarrell's report backs up some of these assertions: Being well off was ranked as important by 27 percent more men and 77 (yes 77) percent more women in 1979, compared to 1969; business careers were planned by four times as many women in 1979 as in 1969 (4 percent vs. 15 percent); whereas the men barely changed in the percentage going into business between the two decades. Likewise, women are planning more careers in law, engineering and medicine and fewer in education and domestic sciences and arts. These were nationwide findings based on the larger study: The American Freshman: National Norms for Fall 1979 (1980), and were based on over 190,000 students questionnaires obtained in over 350 colleges and universities. The increase in female interests is predictable given the social and economic changes of the last decade.

Some other changes are less anticipated. In spite of this materialism, so called, students still revered scientific accomplishments, being an authority in some field, and being recognized. However, these could be shibboleths - we can honor lofty goals and ambitions but pursue them not at all. One wonders, also, what the next trend in student attitudes will be. We've seen three major movements in the past two decades, perhaps more. Beginning with post World War II, older students returned to colleges and universities, serious, bent on self-development, making up for lost time, and scholarship was high. This was also a time of exploding knowledge in many science and technology fields, some of them calling in new ways on mathematics, physics, biology and psychology as basic science areas that formed the foundation for innovation. Then came the war decade and activism, seeming to throw out all older values and try to remake society; there was danger of throwing out the baby with the bathwater at this time. Calming down, the students now want material gain, ignore the need for social reform, and cast most values in economic terms. They are impatient with thoughtful education although they stop momentarily to admire someone who is creative, innovative or who commands respect due

to high level skills or achievement. There are so many
changes afoot it is no wonder that career changes,
dropping out, burning out, and so forth are becoming
increasingly common. The initial career preparation
is too hastily put together, may often be a submission
to economic and time-bound pressures (do the 4 years
of work in 3 or even 2 1/2 years), and looks very little
to the future. Given this expenditure in college and
universities and on the professors to keep up with an
educational whirley-gig, keeping up, often for unsub-
stantial reasons, becomes a confusing chore, and the
leisurely, thoughtful, savoring of experience,
knowledge and stimulation are passed by because they
do not have the familiar and ubiquitous dollar mark
attached. Education is selling out to ephemeral
concerns and interests.

Students, too, suffer from this kaleidiscope of
educational activities (Farber, 1970). Farber calls
his experiences in the English Department of a
Western College "...an authoritarian and dehumanized
school system" (p.13). Farber's work brought back
explosive censorship and condemnation that only served
to highlight his message, to confirm it indirectly and
inadvertently. The clamor for new blood in the 1960s
led Farber to some of the following comments: "School
is where you let the dying society put its trip on
you," noting that schools are not really run by the
people who purport to do so, nor by the students, but
by "...the most entrenched and rigidly conservative
elements in society...from those solid Chamber-of-
Commerce types--those Colleges and universities are no
better, it is said. A second generalization: "It's
not what you're taught that does the harm but how
you're taught" (Farber, 1970, pp.19-26). Herein
education is seen as a handcuffing matter, too standardized, impersonal and coercive, teaching people not to
learn and not to want to learn. The changes in school
routine and the rigidities of the system reflect an
industrial/educational compex at work, doing the same
job on education that has been done on medicine and
other professions, indeed, on society as a whole.
Perhaps the rebels of the '60s and '70s challenged
the system for a while, under the impetus of fighting
the Viet Nam war and its philosophy, but have now
sunk back into an even greater and more rigid
orthodoxy. The industrial machine grinds so relent-
lessly it catches up and sucks in all matter and
leaves only its own mark in its wake. Everything
becomes part of the corporation; it directs everything

This is inimical to a good school, Farber asserts:
"...one characteristic of a good school is the
freedom to establish its own direction"(Farber, 1970,
p.39, italics original).

Taken from a different vantage point than that of
Farber, but heeling to the lessons of the 1960s in
recognizing student power and student dissent, Keniston (1965;1968) has also written searchingly on the
lessons of that period for education, for social understanding, and for the power of youth to assert themselves. Although Keniston's studies were on Harvard
undergraduates, thus not typical of youth throughout
the nation, many aspects of the alienation of these
youth could lead to better understanding of youthful
rebellion in general. But it was not simply rebellion
that was observed that had impact, it was a full rejection of the values of adult society, values that
allowed the society to neglect many problems and to
concentrate on the war in Viet Nam. Youth showed more
humility than did the government, youth saw other
values than those promulgated by adults, and youth
displayed a wisdom that was sadly lacking in society
at large. Since young people were not powerful
enough to actually change the government through the
electoral process, they took to demonstrations, to
stand-ins, to teach-ins, to writing and in time they
influenced the press, the media, education, and many
other facets of our society. The action came from
those both powerful enough to act, and to act
persistently and consistently; and they impressed the
whole of society in this effort. More university
professors supported the youth than will ever be
counted or told. Curricula changed, purposes related
to education changed, and values changed. The university has not been the same since, and it may never go
back to what it was before the 1960s. Even though a
new conservatism seems to have replaced the radicalism
of a decade or so ago, and even though the university
appears to be in the grips of the industrial/educational
complex, the university is still very different from
what it was earlier. Student rights, freedom of speech
about university values and offerings, and many other
facets of university life, giving way all the time to
new individual values and to more respect for those
who are different, are all now under way and if
challenged there is enough reserve strength and know-
how to expect students to reassert themselves again,
if and when necessary.

303

Some of the observations of Keniston that are
salient in our discussion may be noted here. He
speaks of alienation in the past as having been imposed
on people from the outside. In the 1960's alienation
period, if we can call it that, people chose
alienation as their basic view toward society. Today,
with inflation and economic pressures what they are,
choosing alienation is less easily done than when a
visible target--the injustices of the Viet Name war--
were available. Some new form of alienation may be
called for today. Some of that is seen in Farber's
book where education is brought to task, including the
university. It would be hard to argue today that
Keniston's words in 1965 are not true now: "The
prevailing images of our culture are images of disintegration, decay, and despair...Judged by the values of
past generations, our culture seems obsessed with
breaking down, splintering, disintegration, and
destruction" (Keniston, 1965, p.4).

Keniston feels that new forces are at large in
society that promote alienation, and that alienation
appears to lack purpose: "...I mean to suggest (by
the term 'new alienation') that the origins and forms
of our modern alienations are new: first, that the
roots...lie in a new kind of society, and, second,
that in such a society alienation characteristically
takes the new form of rebellion without a cause, of
rejection without a program, of refusal of what is
without a vision of what should be" (Keniston, 1965,
p.6). Perhaps Keniston is too negative himself here,
because the alienation period, at least in a sloganese
way, did suggest alternatives to the horrows of the
war and to the upturning of society that came in its
wake. Even today the rebellion against nuclear energy
and power centers is both against such centers (as the
alienation period was against the war and what it
stood for) and for other forms of energy production and
cultivation. The alienation period slogan, "Make love,
not war" may have seemed trite to some, and it had to
be succinct and easily understood, but it also containe
a powerful message.

In trying to understand alienation and its affect
on society, on the university, and on those teaching
in the university, we need to see clearly, as does
Keniston, that alienation does not have only a
"personal" aspect, implying causes that lie only in
the individual's maladjustment and pathology. We
note in this book that the pathology seen in the

professions in the form of stress, tension and anxiety
--and their many consequences in terms of health,
broadly viewed--that the roots of the problem are
broad-based and ramifying throughout society. The
roots of alienation then, as now, lie in the highly
generalized "complexes" in society and their impinge-
ment on men and women in corporations, in the medical
and health sciences, in teaching, in the clergy, in
the university...everywhere. More specifically, this
means that the "machines" in society that make war,
that destroy health, that alienate teachers, clergy,
physicians, and others cannot be understood only as
prompting individual rebellion, only promoted by
individual pathology (although some of this is
doubtlessly always present) but are so widespread as
to affect nearly everyone, especially the professions
which are--or have been--the backbone of society.
Alienation in one form or another is not just for the
1960-1970 period; it is for now, clearly and
unmistakably.

Student Stress

The university registers alienation more readily
than other segments of society. Students are free in
a sense that no one else is in society. They are
largely supported economically by their parents; they
are beholden neither to the parents nor to the
university (except to meet broad requirements), and
they are free to think and act largely as they please.
They, the students, and the professors who support
them and feel as they do, are the lightening rods of
society. Students sneeze and the rest of society
catches a cold. Students and the university are
closely interwoven. One outcome from research on
the university community is that people have begun to
realize ever more clearly that students have a
transactional relationship with the university
environment. Understanding student stress and general
intellectual and social development is improved if
the transactional notion is uppermost: What affects
students in the university environment also feeds back
an influence on the university; students impact the
university and affect its course; the reciprocity is
everpresent (Bloom, 1975). The university environment,
then, has to be looked at searchingly if we are to
understand dropouts from school, the students' needs
for counseling and psychotherapy and career help, and
general attitudes toward college and university life
and what it offers.

305

Studies of college dropouts are not easy to carry out with methodological accuracy and relevance. Although dropouts can be differentiated from those who stay to finish, the intrusion of transfer and non-transfer status students must be taken into consideration (some students intend to transfer to another school after one or two years, hence are not dropouts in the usual sense). One question that seemed to differentiate potential dropouts from "stayers," done on college freshmen by Beahan (1966) was: "Do you have alternating moods of undue gloom and cheerfulness?" Just why any one question might be pivotal (although both "yes" and "no" answers contained many "false positives/negatives") is hard to answer; however, searching for initial attitudes among entering freshmen may reveal important predictors of future college behavior and thus allow the university to take remedial or preventive measures. Altogether, American colleges and universities lose about one-half the admissions within a four-year span; only 40% of entering classes graduate on schedule and another 20 percent graduate later, somewhere (Bloom, 1975, p.102). Also, the higher the college aptitude scores, based on high school rank, the fewer the dropouts from college. Although dropout information such as cited here goes some distance in understanding college and university life, what is missing are better studies on the institutions themselves and on the actual and potential characteristics of students who do drop out (brought on, presumably, by an interaction process between the institution and the students). When more of these facts are known, university administration leaders can move to change some characteristics of the university in ways that will make life and learning more hospitable and encouraging to students. This kind of move on the part of colleges and universities--taking, as it will, a toll on professors' comforts and stereo-types about students--will be increasingly necessary as college enrollments drop (due to the birth rate declines in the recent past) and with the presence of more part-time, older, more mature, and more self-directing students. Students will not remain as much puddy in the hands of the university as has been the stereotype in the past; the university will increasingly have to concern itself with its impact on the students in terms of mental health, career and other issues, as well as issues centered more on academic learning and preparation.

How much are students themselves affected by the
continuing alienation that is extant in society.
Some answers to that question are available.

More studies of a psychological nature are done on
college students than on almost any other population.
There are usually many researchers in colleges and
universities and the ubiquitous college students
gets called on to cooperate with research several times
a semester if not more often. While much research on
college students does not meet the criteria on which
this book is based, many studies of students, particularly those eminating from mental health settings, are
of value to our purpose. The growth of the college
level student body (112 percent from 1960 to 1970, an
increase from 3.58 million to 7.6 million) and an
increase in the number of public colleges (a 281
percent increase over the same decade) give rise to
many problems of a mental health nature as well as
opportunities for other kinds of research (on social
behaviors, for example, Bolton & Kammeyer, 1967).
Affecting the mental health picture of college
students has been the increase in women students--
from 37 percent in 1960 to 43 percent in 1975
(Glasscote & Fishman, 1973, pp.7-9). Reifler (1971)
studied mental health problems among students on a
number of American campuses and found from 6 percent
to over 16 percent were "disturbed" according to
various criteria used such as questionnaires, interviews, medical history questions and combinations of
these. The rates at which students on various campuses
use mental health facilities varied from 2 percent to
over 10 percent. Drug usage among college students
also varied, some studies in Florida indicating that
up to half of the student body has tried marajuana at
one time but far fewer used it consistently (Glasscote
and Fishman, 1973, pp.47-48). Among the various
universities studied in the Glasscote and Fishman
report, college freshman and sophomores, among both
men and women, tend to use mental health services
more than do upperclassmen; and in one school, graduate
women used mental health services at twice the rate
of men. Most students were seen only a few times for
counseling or therapy, but a few were seen as many as
25-30 sessions. The commonest diagnostic category
was "stress and adjustment reactions" in one school
(52 percent), with categories such as neuroticism,
psychotic behavior, schizophrenia, holding down a
very low percentage figure. The largeness of the
"stress" category points to the changes that have

apparently been accumulating in colleges and universities over the past several decades: more stress on grades, more social pressures to perform, sexual freedoms that also carry with them pressures, and more emphasis on future vocational and money-earning potential (Glasscote & Fishman, 1973, pp.57-58; Hanfmann, 1978, pp.43-50 and 51-72).

Commensurate with more women being on campuses in the last two decades, more also go to graduate school (and professional schools), and more of them seek out mental health help; in some schools the number of women applying to mental health services are found to be higher at all educational levels than men, sometimes in a ratio of two-to-one. Overall, student complaints of stress, unhappiness, depression and lack of goals appear to be on the increase, especially in the larger schools (where facilities are more readily available to detect students needing help and to offer mental health help to them); and more particularly among women. The problems revolve around various daily problems in living that result in stress/tension/anxiety rather than the more traditional diagnostic categories, although depression is very common (Fang & Howell, 1977).

Hendin (1975) is of the opinion that more college students are suicidal now than previously; the trend having increased in the past 20-25 years, despite the emotional climates on campuses having changed from the "quiet 50s" through the political activism of the 60s and early 70s, and on to the drug culture and the recent return to more conservativism. Hendin sees these suicidal youth as never having freed themselves from their parents and consequently failing to gain pleasure from new relationships and from trying out their skills and knowledge. Mishara, et al (1976) looked at suicide attempts among college students over the last decade, noting that both suicides and suicide attempts may be underestimates of the realities concerning suicide. They found via questionnaire and interview that among 293 college students who reported having attempted suicide one time, fifteen percent had made earlier attempts. Females attempted suicide by overdoses of pills and slashed wrists; males preferred overdoes and strangulation or a combination; sometimes drowning and being hit by a car served as suicide attempts (Mishara, et al, 1976, p.843). They conclude that "...suicide behavior is

308

a serious problem among college students and underlies the need for further retrospective studies of the prevalence of suicide attempters" (Mishara, et al, 1976, p.841). Wexler, et al (1978) presents data showing suicide to be on the increase in the general population, and find it more common among younger people (under 30) and among women. The college student increase in suicide apparently fits with larger, general population trends. Parrish (1956) produced one of the early studies of suicide and other causes of death at Yale University, 1920-1955. The most frequent cause of death in 209 deaths studied was from automobile accidents (23.6 percent) and secondly from other accidents (20.2 percent). Active youth take risks and sometimes the risks kill. Suicide (12.0 percent) was the next most frequent category of causes of death, far outnumbering all physical and medical illnesses. In comparisons with other college students, and from a very early study by Diehl and Shepard (1939), again, the most frequent cause of death from non-accidental causes was suicide (8.0 percent). It is also possible, as is often the case with suicide statistics, that "accidents" mask suicidal efforts and results. The Diehl and Shepard study surveyed 9 universities, covering deaths of 327 students during the decade, 1925-1935. Statistics comparing deaths among Yale students in the Parrish study showed that only suicides were greater than expected in the general population, but about 40 percent, in the college age group. Thus suicide is a potent cause of death in the university population and, along with accidents, a cause for concern.

As everyone knows, the use of drugs has been rampant among youth over the past two decades, and college and university campuses have had their share of such usage, if not more than their share. One way in which youth has rejected the adults standards they see around them has been to alienate themselves from society, to drop-out and to refuse to become part of the social fabric. Lesser repudiation is seen in resort to drug use on a mild but habitual basis. Corder et al (1974) studied trends in drug use at five widely scattered universities in the U.S., surveying a population of 792 students which represented one percent of the total university population in these five schools (nearly 80,000 total). An earlier study, 1970-71 had also been conducted. Between the 1970-71 and 1973-74 periods, students in all five universities

evidence more than a doubling of the use of marijuana.
The use of LSD also doubled; and Mescaline usage was
up substantially. These trends were consistent from
school to school. Students utilized in the study in
all universities were from liberal arts, education,
business, fine arts, and general studies (no engineering students were studied). These trends, the authors
said--surprisingly--referred to daily use of marijuana,
indicating [at] "...all five universities...marijuana
continues to be a social drug second only to alcohol"
(Corder et al, 1974, p.387). Moreover, the use of
marijuana among the athletic population was somewhat
greater than its use among students in general.
Despite the widespread use of marijuana, the 1973-74
report also found discontinued use of the drug,
especially by previous one-time users. Alcohol usage
was higher than marijuana, running as high as 92
percent usage by the student body in one university,
and reflecting some increase in usage between the 1970-
71 and 1973-74 study years. The authors conclude that
drug usage is pretty much in evidence on college and
university campuses and that "...ongoing surveillance
programs are an urgent necessity if we are to understand and cope with this issue" (Corder et al, 1974,
p.389).

Sinnett and Wampler (1972) carried out a more
intensive study of the pattern of drug use among 33
college students who had had a variety of experiences
with different drugs. The number of different drugs
(substances) used ranged from 3 to 17 among this
population of students with an average of 11 different
substances tried. They looked at the pattern of drug
use in terms of the availability of the drugs, the
safety of its use, and the frequency with which a
substance was used. Alcohol was judged most frequently
used, most available but considered less safe than
marijuana; speed and barbituates, although readily
available, were used less than alcohol, marijuana and
psychedelics; and so on. Among several colleges from
which samples of drug and alcohol usage data were
collected by Sinnett and Wampler, it was noted that
the use of alcohol in different schools ranged from a
low of about 70 percent to a high approaching 100
percent (1974, p.144). Widespread drug usage and
consistent patterns of usage, are, then, in evidence
widely among colleges in the U.S.

Schools As Stress Promoters

In Campus Shock (Lamont, 1979), the author documents many of the ways in which the university has an adverse affect on students, not in the mass aliena- tion sense of the late 1960s and early 1970s, but in more specific ways. His opening gambit is illustrative: "As a reporter returning home after five years abroad, I caught unmistakable signals from friends with college- age children that all was not right, that something was poisoning the life of undergraduates at the most prestigious universities, that many students were unhappy, beset by tension, trapped insecurity and frustration (Lamont, 1979, pp.1-2). And to tie in the 1960s and 1970s, Lamont says, "...if the 1960s had resembled in some respects a media-orchestrated protest revel, the 1970s were a decade of quiet but no less real revolution among students--a revolution of new social experiences, aspirations and responses to pressure (Lamont, 1979, p.2). Thus the mass demon- stration of a decade ago are missing, but a more under- ground, insidious sense of displeasure and alienation on the part of students is present. These observations find their reality in the number of students applying for psychological help at university clinics and coun- seling centers, the rise of "hot line" services (Berman, Davis & Phillips, 1973), an increase in "crisis centers" in communities and on campuses (Ewing, 1978), the increase in campus suicides, student drop-out increases, the alarm with which cheating is increasing, the "drug abuse" increase, and other signs of distress, even despair (Hendin, 1975; Hoffer, 1972; Lamb, 1977; Munter, 1975; Alpert, 1962; Sherrill et al, 1971; Bonzaft et al, 1973; Shelton & Hill, 1969). The problems are almost too numerous to mention and far too pervasive to summarize in one small volume. And the outcome of this stress, even if students did graduate and reach higher levels of achievement, might give "...rise to doubts about whether the brightest of these young people would mature into anything more than ultrasmart lawyers and overpaid medical whizzes" (Lamong, 1979, p.3).

Some of the complaints underlying the student rush toward psychological help are documented in Lamont: About one-third of the undergraduates at Cornell in the mid-1970s complained of loneliness; administrators reported difficulty keeping track of where students were living at another Ivy League school; students complaining that administration didn't

care about the students' quality of life; a Harvard
undergraduate survey in 1974 indicating that less than
one third of the students who had expected to sit with
great teachers ever considered they had that experience;
college presidents unknown to and unrecognized by the
student body, the presidents themselves almost
alienated from college life, relegated to fund-raising,
promotional work and financial crisis intervention;
a widening gulf between student and teachers owing in
part to some of the same troubles experienced by
professors and their off-campus committments making
them unavailable to students; seeing professors as
"opportunists" who used teaching more as a jumping-off
place for other glories and stimulation; and so on
through one interminable set of complaints after
another. Increasingly college premises and dormitories
became the victims of vandalism, fires, petty thievery,
and other signs of lack of respect (Lamont, 1979,
pp.8-13). Nearly all campuses are now "policed" day
and night; rapes are not uncommon; assaults on women,
older people on campuses, and even professors are noted
more frequently, purses are stolen from desk tops with
abandon, files pried open for their contents (often
examination copies); homicides; robbery; general crime
rates increasing by hundreds of percentage points;
students coming to class, or even to counseling
sessions, drunk or "high" on drugs; and many, many more
problems making university life vastly different from a
decade ago, and almost a completely different world
from two decades ago. Add to these current individual
problems and malcontentments, racial distrust and
conflict, and sexual problems among the committed, the
alienated, the married, and the just-living-together
couples (Lamont, 1979, pp.22-44; Bowers, 1964;
Yankelovitch, 1974). Doubtlessly people are more
concerned today about the quality of life, hence
problems long tolerated surface now as more urgent, as
intolerable, or as blights on one's life and on society.
All change between the past and now in college life is
not due to rottenness or deterioration, but some is.
The more serious problems--e.g., suicide among college
students--appears to have been on the increase;
whether this will continue is, of course, problematic.
We shall look into this problem more below.

"Careerism"

A topic of considerable importance in this book is
related to careers and what happens to peoples' professional life. "Careerism," so called, has permeated the

university, according to Lamont (1979, pp.45-56). This is where students stress careers at the expense of learning, a tendency already noted above; an excessively limited professional motivation among undergraduates, most of whom are entering business, law, medicine or dentistry. Competition in connection with professional school admission is great: Sometimes the ratio of applicants to those selected can run as high as 100 to 1 in some programs in some schools. Among those trained but not accepted, statistics show that many are over-trained: hundreds of thousands are trained to levels not commensurate with available jobs, and the number of degrees--B.A., M.A., and Ph.D.s-- awarded in 1977 were double those of a decade ago. With all this competition and no clear sights at the end of the road as to likely employment or career opportunities, college students experience a lot of stress and even more discouragement upon graduation. Lamont says, "The ripple effect of university graduates wasting in jobs that called for employees of a lower caliber threatened to produce a whole new class of malcontents, along with a highly combustible economic situation" (Lamont, 1979, p.49). This is what is meant by saying that morale problems today, alienation or whatever one wishes to call it, stems more from self-fulfillment frustrations, from economic and career goal blockage than from external causes of a highly visible and specific nature such as making war. This uncertainty, prompts, in turn, fashions in courses and major fields. During the Viet Nam war years, engineer- ing, physics, electronics and chemistry were anethema, owing to these areas being associated with war making prowess. Now, a decade later, these subjects, along with business are beginning to boom on college and university campuses, especially engineering, and business. It is a topsy-turvy world, the university... The university is more a collection of professional programs and schools, less a center for educating people. It is becoming more and more a center for drawing students (clientel) from any and all walks of life to prepare for any kind of degree program that happens to have currency. It is a center for the proliferation of courses, often in aimless and mindless fashion. It is an institution in which presidents and department heads are more valued for their money- drawing and gift-prompting skills than for scholarship. It is a setting in which students are less valued as individuals and more for their numbers; more for alumnae membership which can swell the university

313

coffers than can point to scholarly and abiding contributions to society. The university has submitted to the industrial/educational complex and it may not recover its hoary past. In this wild melee for commercial and business success the university has lost most of its attraction to scholars, and university professors (and students) are more stressed to stay on than benefitted.

CHAPTER XI

BIBLIOGRAPHY

Alpert, R., & Haber, R.N. Anxiety in academic achievement situations, J. of Abn. & Soc. Psychol., 1962,
65, 427-428.

American Freshman National Norms for Fall, 1979. Los
Angeles, California: American Council on
Eucation, 1980.

Arnold, L.E. What teaching does to teachers: a set
of rules for insightful redirection of teachers'
reactions to pressure. J.Sch. Health, 1974, 44,
561-563.

Article (unnamed) Six new trustees elected, GW TIMES,
1980, 9, #4, p.2.

Beahan, L.T. Initial psychiatric interviews and the
drop-out rate of college students, J. of the
Amer. College Health Assn., 1966, 14, 305-308.

Berman, P.J., Davis, A.W., & Phillips, E.L. George
Washington University volunteer hotline, a
descriptive study, Psychol. Reports, 1973, 33,
364-366.

Bloom, B.L. Psychological Stress In The Campus
Community. N.Y.: Behavioral Publications, 1975.

Bolton, C.D. & Stammeyer, K.C.W. The University
Student. New Haven: College and Univ. Publ.,
1967.

Bowers, W.J. Student Dishonesty and Its Control
In College. N.Y.: Col. Univ. Bur. of Appl. Soc.
Res., 1964.

Bronzaft, A.L., Stuart, I.R., & Blum, B. Text
anxiety and cheating on college examinations,
Psychol. Reports, 1973, 32, 149-150.

Corder, B.W., Dezelsky, T.L., Toohey, J.V., & Tow, P.K.
An analysis of trends in drug use behavior at
five American Universities, J. of School Health,
1974, 44, 386-389.

Diehl, H.S. & Shepperd, C.E. The Health of College Students. Wash., D.C., Amer. Council on Educ., 1939.

Dillor, R.D. Identification of factors influencing vocational agricultural teachers to leave teaching, J. of Amer. Assn. of Teacher Educators in Agric., 1978, 19, 34-39.

Dublin, L.I., Lotka, A.J. & Spiegelman, M. Length of Life. N.Y.: Ronald Press, 1936 (rev. edition 1949).

Eurich, A.C. Campus 1980: The Shape of the Future In Amer. Higher Educ.

Ewing, C.P. Crisis Intervention As Psychotherpy. N.Y.: Oxford Univ. Press, 1978.

Fang, B. & Howell, K.A. Death anxiety among graduate students, J. Amer. Coll. Health Assn., 1977, 25, 310-313.

Farber, J. The Student As Nigger. N.Y.: Pocket ooks, 1970.

Fields, C.M. Faculty stress is found to be highest among married women, single men, The Chronicle Of Higher Education, 1980, 21, #3, p.1

Glasscott, R. & Fishman, M.E. Mental Health On The Campus: A Field Study. Washington,D.C.: Amer. Psychiatric Assn., 1973.

Gomberg, I.L. & Alelseh, F.J. Composition of College and University Governing Boards. Washington, D.C.: Amer. Council on Education, 1977.

Gosnell, J.W. The relationship between work experience and occupational aspirations and attrition from teaching, Clearing House, 1977, 51, 176-179.

Hanfmann, E. Effective Therapy For College Students. San Francisco: Jossey-Bass, 1978.

Harris, F.R. The New Populism. N.Y.: Saturday Review Press, 1973.

Heald, J.E. Mid-life career influence, Vocat. Guid. Quart., 1977, 25, 309-312.

Heddesheimer, J. Multiple motivations for mid-career change, Pers. and Guid. J., 1976, 55, 109-111.

Hendin, H. Student suicide: Death as a life style, J. of Nervous and Mental Disease, 1975.

Hoffer, W. What's being done about campus suicide, College Management, 1972, 7, 8-11.

Jencks, C. Who Gets Ahead? N.Y.: Basic Books, 1979.

Keniston, K. The Uncommitted: Alienated Youth In American Society. N.Y.: Harcourt, Brace and World, 1965.

Keniston, K. Young Radicals: Notes on Committed Youth. N.Y.: Harcourt, Brace and World, 1968.

King, M. The anxieties of university teachers. Universities Quart., 1973, 28, 69-83.

Knight, J.A. Why vocational agricultural teachers in Ohio leave teaching. J. of Amer. Assn. of Teacher Educators in Agric., 1978, 19, 11-17.

Krautz, D.L. Radical Career Change. N.Y.: The Free Press, 1978.

Lamb, R. Professional school: Cram courses in tension and trauma, N.Y. Times Mag., 1977, No. 20.

Lynn, K.S. & The Editors of Daedalus. The Professions in America. Boston: Beacon Press, 1965.

Lamont, L. Campus Shock, N.Y.: E.P. Dutton, 1979.

Magarrell, J. Pay of professors at 68 universities increases 5.3 percent, Chronicle of Higher Educ., 1980, Vol. 20, Apr. 14, p.9.

Middleton, L. Mean little cases' give new dimensions to controversies over academic freedom, Chronicle of Higher Educ., Vol.20, April 28, p.1.

Mishara, B.L., Baker, H., & Mishara, T.T. The frequency
of suicide attempts: A retrospective approach
applied to college students, Amer. J. Psychiatry,
1976, 133, 841-844.

Morgan, D. Scaling those ivied walls is easier starting
near the top, Washington POST, 1980, August 30,
p.2.

Murrter, P.K. Depression and Suicide In College Students.
Boston: Harvard U. Health Serv., 1975.

News Services, Schools warned against 'scientific
illiteracy,' Washington POST, 1980, Oct. 23, p.7.

Parrish, H.M. Epidemiology of suicide among college
students, Yale J. Biol. Med., 1957, 29, 285-295.

Reid, R.M. Attitude and personality differences in
physically active and inactive university teachers,
Percept. Motor Skills, 1976, 42, 523-526.

Ridgeway, J. The Closed Corporation: American University in Crisis. N.Y.: Ballantine Books, 1968.

Reiffer, C.B. Epidemiologic aspects of college mental
health, J. of the Amer. College Health Assn., 1971,
19, 159-163.

Roark, A.C. Academic researchers protest rules
requiring strict accounting of time, The Chronicle
Of Higher Education, 1980, 21, #9, p.1.

Sarason, S.B. Jobs, Aging and Social Change. N.Y.: The
Free Press, 1977.

Sarason, S.B. Aging and the nature of work, Amer.
Psychol., 1975, 30, 584-592.

Shelton, J. & Hill, J.P. Effects on cheating of
achievement anxiety and knowledge of peer performance, Developmental Psychol., 1969, 1, 449-455.

Sherrill, D., Salisbury, J.L., Horowitz, B., & Friedman
S.T. Classroom cheating, consistent attitude,
perceptions and behavior, Amer. Educ. Research J.,
1971, 8, 503-510.

Sincle, D. Counseling older persons: Career change an
retirement, Vocat. Guid.Quart., 1976, 25, 18-24.

Sinnett, E.R. & Wampler, K.S. Consistency of patterns of drug use, Psychol. Reports, 1972, 31, 143-152.

Snyder, R.A. Mid-career change in academia: The decision to become an administrator, J. of Vocat. Beh., 1978, 13, 229-241

Thomas, L.E. Causes of mid-life change from high-status careers, Vocat. Guid. Quart., 1979, 27, 202-208.

Wexler, L., Weissman, M.M., & Kasl, S.V. Suicide attempts 1970-75: Updating a United States study and comparisons with international trends, Brit. J. Psychia., 1978, 132-180,185.

Yandelovitch, D. The New Morality: A Profile of American Youth in the 70's. N.Y.: McGraw-Hill, 1974.

CHAPTER XII

LAW

One of the fastest growing and most influential professions today is law. Lawyers are being graduated at an accelerated pace, a trend that has been apparent for several years (Freund, 1965; Lynn, 1965; Gallagher, 1979). And next to medicine, law is one of the most expensive professions in which to be educated. Law is also one of the traditional learned professions, along with the clergy, teaching and medicine. Law is a venerated profession.

Law has grown, lawyers have become more common, and legal practice more important as society has grown in complexity. Law provides some of the links between the tenuous interconnections in our social fabric. Toffer (1970), in discussing social complexity, says that the super-industrial revolution accounts for the impression that our society is cracking at the seams...[The industrial revolution] "...is why everything grows increasingly complex. Where once there stood 1000 organization entities, there now stand 10,000--interconnected by increasingly transient links" (Toffer, 1970, p.265). Law has played and increasingly plays a central role in this growing complexity, trying at once to patch up the inconsistencies and to adjudicate natural differences and proprietary interests. An example of what the law and lawyers are faced with, under a discussion of the diversity of life styles, is cited by Toffer: "In San Francisco, executives lunch at restaurants where they are served by bare-breasted waitresses. In New York...a kooky girl cellist is arrested for performing avant garde music in a topless costume. In St. Louis, scientists hire prostitutes and others to copulate under a camera as part of a study of the physiology of the orgasm...civic controversy erupts over the sale of ...dolls...equipped with male genitals" and so on (Toffer, 1970, p.268). How can the law and lawyers function in such a multiplicity and contradictory set of standards and values? The answer is, probably, that they don't. The law is confused and contradictory in its sexual values, and so are lawyers. I have appeared in court in support of young men arrested for "exposing" themselves in public when not more than a block away topless girls (sometime bottomless ones, too) expose themselves not only regularly but for approval, money, attention and under the <u>protection</u>

321

of the law (as part of the business of a bar and/or restaurant). Perhaps no other profession faces so many contradictory values as law and the practice of law. Lawyers know, if they observe and think at all, that they cannot serve all values and masters; they often compromise in the practice of law, wink at inconsistencies, or rigidly hold to their interpretation of the law as a function of their own personal, social and religious values. Lawyers are, then, as much in a quandry as anyone else in society; perhaps all the more so because they purport to settle disputes, adjudicate fairly, and protect the rights of individuals and society. What an order! This stance alone could make lawyers a perplexing collection of people and law a confusing profession.

In a more formal sense, law appears integrated, lawyers appear to be trained in the practice of law and hold their services up to society as important, necessary and fair (Freund, 1965). But even scholars of the law will admit that there are important cleavages between the actual practice of law, the rules that guide the judiciary, and the academic study and preparation for the law. Law experiences more theoretical splits than medicine, teaching, the ministry or perhaps any other profession. There is presumably more disparity between the law and practicing law on the one hand than there is between practicing medicine and the state of health of the patient, between teaching, and the state of knowledge of the pupil and between ministerial work and the spiritual condition of the parishioner. Law is a schizophrenic profession and every young law student who reflects on his/her experiences in law school will testify to that observation - I have discussed it with innumerable law students, and find that they are particularly sensitive to this point.

Traditionally lawyers have practiced alone or in small groups. In 1965, about 70 percent of the lawyers in the U.S. practiced alone, but the trend soon after that time began in the direction of large firms, especially those dealing with corporate law, real estate, business and commerce. Some large law firms have dozens, even hundreds, of lawyers from the lowest clerk level up to major partner status. Young lawyers now graduating can be more assured of income by joining established firms, especially if they are interested in some area of expertise and concentration akin to business. If they are interested in public

322

service law, domestic cases, or consumer law, they are more likely to go with small firms or practice alone. The American system has proliferated lawyers to the extent that they are about three times as common in the U.S. population as they are in Great Britain (one in 700-800 population in the U.S. compare to one in 2000 - 2200 in Britain).

Although law, like medicine, is a learned profession--traditionally--lawyers are often described as parochial: "Lawyers, when put beside national or social scientists, are parochial; their expertness ceases at the water's edge" (Freund, 1965, p.37). Also, by the very nature of the subject matter involved, scientists, physicians, economists, etc. are at home within range, in any country in the world; blood does not run differently in Pakistan than in Canada, economics do not differ materially in Argentina from Ireland, but the law is very different in different parts of the world. Law is beholden to cultural complexes, but not as many lawyers realize this as would be desirable. The provisional nature of knowledge escapes the lawyer, as she/he is expected to construct matters in black vs. white, not in terms of contingencies, conditions, or gradations; and this orthodoxy serves the lawyer well in the courtroom but is a knowledge and a skill that sometimes goes against the grain of the culture or fails to see the larger cultural context; this attitude may also injure the client's interests.

Lawyers in their practice are also beholden to the culture in another way, in terms of economics (Cohen, 1976). In medicine, poor people get the same diseases (with but a few exceptions) as more well-to-do, but the problems of the poor vs. those of the corporation, or the problems of the consumer vs. those of the businessman may differ widely as faced by the lawyer. Consumer law and/or workman's compensation law are as far from estate planning and corporate law as the north and south polls. Moreover, clinics for the poor may instruct the physician--if she/he has a social perspective--about some aspects of medicine that are highly salient to knowledge and to practice, but the skills of a public clinic lawyer are pretty much confined to the content of the clinic's legal problems. Limitations and a rigid structure everywhere confront the lawyer. While all professions can err markedly and professional teachers, physicians. architects, etc. have to defer opinions and conclusions

to the judgement of others, judges pretty much rule in
authority that is unquestioned (except where appeals,
usually very expensive and time-consuming, are
concerned). Since antiquity, judges and legal scholars
have been reminding each other, as did Justice Holmes,
that judges are not God; to merit so many reminders,
there must be a great tendency to violate this
admonotion.

Standards

How well the legal profession measures up to its
standards, like any other profession, is moot. Freund
(1965, p.41) says any profession must be measured by
three standards: its independence, its availability,
and its learning. Lawyers owe loyalty to clients,
independent of other considerations, a matter of
important ethics. In this day and age, and with so
many law suits levelled against professionals--
including lawyers--the veracity of this proposition is
being constantly tested if not found wanting. Bar
associations, too, have a responsibility to see that
its members adhere to this ethic. With so many
lawyers in training, so many demands placed upon
lawyers, and so many, even yet, not trained in
accredited law schools, the validity of this ethic
may frequently be placed in question. Availability
is, too, a questionable matter among lawyers; often
for the poor, the uneducated and the socially marginal.
On a limited scale the legal profession has attempted
to provide legal assistance where there are needy
clients: lawyers appointed by the court to serve
without compensation, some who serve through charitable
funds, some out of social consciousness (usually
young lawyers still with high ideals but without
demanding economic aspirations), and public defender
offices supported by publicly paid lawyers. These
services are comparable to those provided by medical
clinics for the indigent, although medical professionals
fare better than lawyers in this connection since
insurance provides some medical services and support
for almost everyone.

The learning of the legal profession is a
complicated matter with cases proliferating at an
enormous rate; in 50 years, from 1880 to 1930 there
was three times the accumulation of cases as occurred
in the previous 200 years, and between 1931 to 1961,
the previous 50 year accumulation of cases was matched
and then some. Since then, the rate has increased.

The number of recorded cases is so intimidating that it boggles the mind; computer assistance is now absolutely mandatory to keep track of cases and decisions, even in small areas of jurisprudence. All this complexity causes again and again the surfacing of the admonition that society is not only interested in producing lawyers but in producing minds trained in and for the law--a formidable task.

Power And Politics

Another complication--although some would view it as an asset--affecting lawyers is the extent to which they seek political offices, seek to start or colla- borate in business ventures, and the like. As lawyers have increased in number, many of these have aspired to "higher offices" and to more power, money and prestige associated with business and political ventures. Seldom do medical men aspire to political positions (but very often do engage in business ventures), evidently because they consider medicine sufficiently prestigious, powerful and financially rewarding. Not so with lawyers who are dispositiion- ally given to politics (that's where much of the law eminates from) and temperamentally suited to it. Also, the practice of law, with very few exceptions is a more or less "closed system," whereas medicine and some other professions (those dealing with the sciences, the arts and the humanities) are more "growth" professions, gaining new empirical knowledge all the time and reincorporating it at will into their various practices. To change the law--to pass new laws, to modify or rescind existing ones--may take a prodigious amount of effort; changes in other professions come more easily and are actually more indiginous and integral to the more empirically based professions. Whereas most professions are empirical or data-based, law is precedent-based, but with the accumulation of prohibitively large case files, summarizing the findings now takes computer assistance, thereby providing a natural transition to data-based decisions. Also, many technical areas of law, involving the sciences--psychology, medicine, engineering, etc.-- have to be decided upon empirical grounds as legal precedences are weak, obscure or too easily found conflicting with knowledge from the sciences.

The versatility of law, providing the opportunity for lawyers to practice law but also to engage in politics and business, sometimes strains the ethical

325

boundaries usually provided by law. Many popular articles (Diehl, 1980) and some scholarly ones indicate how lawyers use their legal knowledge and legislative positions for self gain. While there is always a thin line between getting ahead personally and service the public unselfishly, too many in political positions who are also lawyers seem to combine the two roles for personal, rather than social benefits. The record of politicized lawyers in many states attests to this tendency and to the advantage-taking inherent in such ambiguous situations. A more articulated set of ethics for business and politics would help remedy these profiteering situations. These politicized lawyers would seem to violate the four cardinal attributes of professions (especially law): generalized and systematic knowledge, primary orientation to the community interest in contrast to self-interest (a principle apparently often violated), a self-control of behavior through codes of ethics practiced by individuals and reinforced by professional associates (also violated) and a system of rewards, both financial and prestigious (taken more in financial terms by the politicized lawyer, as these lawyers seldom ever achieve awards). Although lawyers qua lawyers do have and follow ethics, as they step into the political and business areas, their role definitions become more "politician" and "businessman" and consequently come less under ethical control. The sociologist, Durkheim, said long ago that since there were professional ethics for priests, lawyers, and magistrates, there should also be ethics for businessmen. But since our society, as Tawney observed long ago (1920), is an "acquisitive society" individual gain supervenes at the cost of social welfare or considerations and so the role of "businessman" can "enjoy" financial gain above all else (called profit). When questioned about their fees, lawyers sometimes respond wholly in profit-motivated terms, according to a newspaper report by Robinson (1980), thus showing little regard for ethical considerations or the socially conscious role presumably adhered to by lawyers. The profit motive was uppermost in the mind of the lawyer in the Robinson report who was quoted as saying, upon receiving a complaint regarding a fee charged a client, "I frankly don't give a damn about what you think about my charge..." and so on.

The unilaterality of lawyers (and judges) is also recorded frequently in the popular press, in magazines, and even among people speaking out against injustices

326

who are also members of the bar association. Meyer (1980) records an instance of a judge who hinged his decision involving the fate of a defendant upon whether he, the judge, could land a paper clip in a nearby styrofoam cup. Here is a case sorely in need of correction in terms of defendant rights, and a chance for liberal and activist lawyers to influence court decisions.

Fees And Ethics

Since one of the ethical problems emerging more and more often for lawyers revolves around fees, the press is asking that there be a forum for clients to question legal fees. While other professional fees are often exhorbitantly high, there are rules and precedents regulating medical and related fees, partly by third party insurers and partly by the competition governing medical services. Also, the relative specific nature of many medical services and the tendency to set the charge in advance (e.g., so much for childbirth) vary from the nature of legal services where time is billed without a clear specification or backup of the actual time involved. Kiernan (1979) says, "there is no shortage of disgruntled clients who want to hash out disputes with their lawyers over the fees for divorce, real estate deals, automobile accidents and other issues." While lawyers are human like the rest of us and will certainly err or even be unfair at times, the plethora of such complaints about fees against lawyers suggests something else is afoot. The fee conciliation service run by the District of Columbia Bar (there may be similar services in other cities) has been obliged to return $25,000.00 in fees over the past year and testifies to the considerable size of the problem.

Supporting the rigidities of fees is the adamant position taken by the legal profession concerning clients applying for (say) a divorce without the benefit of a lawyer. When two people agree on a divorce and terms, why should a lawyer be necessary? Who is being served by this practice? The clients? No. The lawyers? Yes. Where is the obligation to professional service vis a vis society? Pursuing legal action on one's behalf, pro se, is a socially responsible act; why not encourage it instead of contesting it? Resources exist in many communities where couples who (say) want a divorce and have agreed upon terms, can find exemplary guides to previous

327

upon terms, can find exemplary guides to previous actions and can study copies to this end.

Complicity also is not uncommon in the legal profession (Weisskopf, 1979), where banks ready to settle with home purchasers disallow the purchasers choosing his/her law lawyer; but, instead, require that the purchaser use the bank's law firm, often resulting in much higher settlement fees. It turns out in some such cases that a member of the law firm receiving the settlement benefits has a member sitting on the backboard, surely a conflict of interest if one tries to draw a line between being a lawyer and following the ethical standards ascribed to by the profession, and carrying on business deals that inherently do not overlap with the practice of law. Even if there is a legitimate overlap between law practice and business, certainly legal and ethical, the requirement of referral to the law firm acting in complicity with the bank touches firmly on ethical grounds. But where money is to be made in an acquisitive society, "Why bother about ethics?" the businessman says (or the lawyer says who is wearing the hat of a businessman). Such traps perpetrated on unsuspecting home buyers, to name one area of legal practice, is certainly an ethical problem not well attended to by lawyers or the profession.

Heeding these ethical precautions is difficult for the legal profession when young lawyers fresh out of law school are able to comman $25,000.00 - $30,000.00 per year as beginning salaries. Money talks, sings, and dances. Why bother about these ethical matters? Why bother about social responsibility? Perhaps those starting at lower salary levels--$15,000.00 to $20,000.00 per year--will give more credence to ethical and social responsibilities as they are less monopolized by financial considerations.

Women And Law

The legal profession has recently been admitting more women to law school. But in the case of higher positions, judgeships, and similar appointments, women still lag far behind men. Recently women judges have been pressuring the government--at least indirectly--to appoint a woman to fill the next vacancy on the U.S. Supreme Court (Kaye, 1979) which has occurred. The National Association of Women Judges reported that there are only about 300 women judges in

328

the nation, and 15 of the 50 states have no women judges; of 605 active federal judges, only 28 (4.6 percent) are women. This association reports the same prejudices here--in terms of the "old boy network" that has been commonly reported to suppress womens' opportunities in medicine. Instead of professions leading the way to social reform, they are often the worst foot-draggers. Law, which might be expected to be exemplary in the fairness matters, scores very low, along with medicine.

Lawyers sometimes become judges, and judges rule. A TIME magazine feature article (1979) calls judges a "secular priesthood." The trappings of judging are imposing, perhaps intimidating to the average person who has to go to court. Judges are, however, just like the rest of the lawyers, seldom distinguished, appointed by politicians for the most part, but once in the robe and on the court bench they are expected to be honored and revered. Judges act to delay the settlement of cases, act highly inconsistently in meeting out fines and sentences, appear arbitrary in declaring mistrials, and often berate and lecture lawyers in the courtroom in ways that are inimical to the presentation of evidence and the support of justice. With the litigation explosion in the United States in the past few decades, judges' patience, wisdom, fairness and knowledge of justice are strained to the breaking point. With all the confusion, respect for the law for courts and for judges is on the decline. One act judges not infrequently perform is to take over governmental boards and agencies when these offices refuse to obey a judge's orders, hence the judge ends up (say) running the school board, the mental hospital, the welfare agency, or the like. They are called on to rule in matters far beyond their province or their knowledge. Do they invite and take on these admonitions becuase of a thirst for power, or is the law so confused that proper avenues are not open to solve most of our social problems, especially those involving services to large numbers of people such as mental hospitals, school boards, welfare agencies, and prisons? Appointing more judges for more of these roles will not help much; some more fundamental change is called for. Yet over against all these adversities and unadmirable judges and their practices are the Judge Siricas who tenaciously push justice forward and get to the truth; more of his calibre are sorely needed.

329

The Highest Court

The hoary tradition in which the U.S. Supreme Court is clothed appears to be at least open to question, if not actually demeaned. The penetrating study of the Supreme Court by authors Woodward and Armstrong (1979) reveals a good deal of injustice. Just the simple act of these authors gaining access to former law clerks was, itself, a breach of court secrecy; and a further breach in that the former law clerks talked! Revealed are many bickerings, internal brokering and trading-off and politicking by the judges, as well as occasional feuds that hampered the court's work and efficiency. Law professors and judges around the country were quoted in the TIME article as being upset by the breach of secrecy more than the details of court emotionalism, bickering and inefficiency. Preserving the image, to some, was more important than the truth or seeking ways to improve the court. Do these facts not speak critically of how our judicial system, from top to bottom, from local justices of the peace to the U.S. Supreme Court, is run? Differences and disputes are probably normal in a court, especially when the members are so closely intertwined and often come from different legal and political backgrounds and persuasions. But the absence of leadership, charged in the Woodward and Armstrong volume is more nearly inexcusable. All manner of human enterprises--science, business, the legal system, the church hierarchy--have their disputes and dissentions and these must be taken in stride by all of us, but when the leadership faulters, there is occasion for concern. These difficulties, in turn, reflect adversely on the court in the public eye, and damage our legal system from the lower levels upward.

When asked later if his (and Armstrong's book) "rang true," Woodward said that earlier criticism of their book, The Brethren (Woodward and Armstrong, 1979) had died down and people, including lawyers, had begun to realize that there was a good deal of truth in their exposure (Zahradnik, 1979). Woodward is reported to have said further that the system of explaining the law (in the U.S.A.) is not very honest, that the Supreme Court made many decisions affecting the lives of people while the reasons behind the decisions were made public only in the publication of The Brethren, and that Chief Justice Warren E. Burger took away the rights of people in prison by refusing to review petitions from those incarcerated.

Stern (1980) severly chastizes lawyers, legal
practice, and the profession, as shown in the title of
his book--Lawyers On Trial--and the terse blurb that
goes with it: "A Book For People Who Are Fed Up With
Lawyers And For Lawyers Who Are Troubled About Their
Profession." Items of criticism levelled against
lawyers include indictment of legal education,
lawyers plying their skill only among the rich,
problems with the probate system, high fees and the
failure of lawyers to police their own professional
behavior. Since lawyers are in the driver's seat
when it comes to legislation, it is hardly likely that
they will turn a searchlight on their own activities.
More lay people, and more persons from other professions acting to check legal opinions, and more openness
in the whole legal profession (especially the courts)
might be antidotes to the abuses attributed to
lawyers. The Woodward and Armstrong book has already
gone a long way toward giving voice to peoples
suspicions about the legal profession and the activities of lawyers; but much more is needed.

Internal Criticism

When criticism of the legal system comes from
inside rather than by journalists and external critics,
people are even more prone to listen carefully and pay
attention. This is so for the second autobiolgraphi-
cal book by William O. Douglas (Douglas, 1980).
Douglas reveals, among other things, some of the
working prejudices of high court members--Justice James
McReynolds called blacks, "niggers," and regarded
President Franklin D. Roosevelt as "insane"--and
expressed opinions of court members as being mediocre
lawyers (Justices are appointed by the President and
confirmed by Congress, although potential appointees
may be suggested by the bar and by competent lawyers,
usually politically selected). And how much opinions
of the high court members may be emotionalized
versions of their own life experiences (e.g., Justice
Hugo Black's unsympathetic view of picketing in
relation to his own home having been picketed during
the pre-court time when he was a member of the Ku
Klux Klan!). Douglas avers that ninety percent of any
decision--especially at the constitutional law level--
is emotional. Since anyone can supply the emotionalism
for his/her decisions about most anything, it is
superfluous to vest Supreme Court Justices with
credibility when they may be acting in many cases no
wiser than the common man. As law and the practice

of reaching legal decisions become more data-based,
perhaps biases and emotionalism will be reduced.

Obviously criticism of lawyers has increased
considerably in recent years, leading to articles
and books on the general topic of how to choose a
lawyer. The problem of alleged overcharging for fees,
plus the confusion arising from the presence of so
many different kinds of lawyers, and the absence of
good, consultative advice about lawyers has led to
this information explosion. Consumer Reports
published an information article, "How To Choose A
Lawyer" in their May, 1977 issue. They point out
that in some states the restriction on advertising by
lawyers and the consequent publishing of fees for
various services (wills, divorces trusts, etc.) has
given the consumer a break. They emphasize the
consumer taking the steps needed to choose a lawyer,
not take potluck from the yellow pages. Certain
procedures can help in this choice of a lawyer: talk
with someone you know who has recently used a lawyer;
consult the phone book and/or the bar association in
a given area for a lawyer-referral service; call the
dean's office in a law school; determine if your area
bar association has published a directory of information on lawyers, including fees, areas of speciality,
and the like. Sometimes legal clinics are available
which tend to have smaller fees than lawyers in private
practice (see Consumer Reports, 1977, May, p.287).
Generally speaking, if lawyers and other professionals
are not willing to discuss fees or give some
preliminary information to a consumer, there is something amis in their public service attitudes and the
consumer would do well to seek advice elsewhere.

Consumer Regulation

Since much of the consumer movement to determine
more about lawyer's fees and services has resulted in
modifications in legal practice, the government, too,
has surfaced complaints regarding lawyer fees.
Babcock (1979) in an article on fees quotes then
attorney Griffin B. Bell as saying, "We (the government) aren't here to make lawyers rich." One case
of sex discrimination against a government department
resulted in a legal fee of $160,000.00 which was five
times larger than the court's award to the offended
party, the victim of job discrimination. Such irregu-
larities bode poorly for the public image of lawyers
and raise consumer ire, as well as the government's

ire. Should a psychologist or psychiatrist charge
more than their hourly rate to a client who, by
virtue of the treatment received, has been kept out of
a mental hospital that might have cost the client
$3,000.00 to $4,000.00 for a month's stay? Lawyer
fees sometimes are excessive on grounds that they
"save" the client other monies, hence their services
are worth more than their hourly rate. The consumer
never knows what she/he is facing in such a case; the
lawyer is calling all the shots and for his/her own
selfish purposes.

Consumer reactions to lawyers' practices has also
resulted in the recent development of legal insurance.
Pre-paid legal service plans, sometimes sponsored by
union and employee associations, are arrangements
where members pay a small monthly fee that affords
them access to legal help with routine legal problems,
much the way medical insurance works. Going beyond
the union and employee association legal insurance
arrangements one finds some insurance companies that
are promoting legal insurance policies to the general
public, just as they would promote any insurance
policy. The advent of such plans, if widely acquired
by the public, would go far to help standardize legal
fees for various services and to help preclude the
all-too-common practice of overcharging.

Lawyers Criticize Law

Lawyers themselves attack legal practices
(i.e., lawyers' activities) as do governmental representatives (see ref. to Attorney General Bell, above).
No less noted lawyer than F. Lee Bailey wrote "The
trouble with lawyers..." for Parade Magazine (1978)
in which he said that lawyers--unlike physicians and
other professionals--attack people. In writing letters
for their clients, lawyers attack the alleged offender
and set peoples nerves on edge and increase resentment
and uncooperativeness. Bailey seems to consider the
lawyer trained in "ugliness," saying that wives of law
school students have been the subject of warnings
about their husband's alleged change-in-personality as
he moves through law school, owing to training in
aggressiveness. After law school experiences may
further aggravate the lawyer's disposition since there
are too many lawyers and competition is rife: There
are said to be over 450,000 lawyers in the U.S., one
for every 500 persons, and the ratio is even more
severe in New York City, one for every 200 persons.

This rush to get clients can lead to poor quality of service, leading President Carter to say that 90 percent of the nation's large collection of lawyers serves only 10 percent of the people, a ratio even worse than that practiced by physicians. Bailey feels that many lawyers are poorly trained in courtroom procedures, hence do not represent their clients well. Bailey says that legal training does not provide instruction on such techniques as speaking to jurors, cross-examining witnesses, or doncuting investigations with depth (Bailey, 1978, p.4). Supporting these criticism which come from individuals in high places is a more disturbing trend, viz., the number of mal-practice claims against lawyers and legal firms. These claims have doubled in the last 15 years, leading to over 15,000 such cases in 1977 alone. The report further claims that awards against lawyers has risen as much as 200 percent recently. Lawyers must be psychologists, too, since clients often want to use a lawyer as a "fall guy" to make up for their own guilt or to substitute for the client's own aggressive feelings and intentions.

President Carter was very outspoken in some of his criticisms of lawyers (Carter, 1978 in the New York TIMES). He said that expensive talent is often arrayed on each side of a issue and that as inter-minable delays accumulate, this costs the client (and the government, who may be the client) excessively and delay may actually tilt the victory to one side unrelated to the delivery of justice. He noted also that our prisons are full of the poor and disadvan-taged who could not afford lawyers to defend themselves; that plea-bargaining serves the convenience of judges, not the ends of justice. He observed as did Bailey that we have an abundance of lawyers in the U.S., three times as many as England, four times as many as Germany, and 21 times as many as Japan. More litiga-tion does not mean more justice! Lawyers trade on adversity, President Carter averred: Divorces that may be uncostly become costly; title searches are repeated over and over as the same property is resold; minor car accidents clog the court's docket while no-fault auto insurance is opposed by lawyers; malpractice suits against lawyers and physicians skyrocket; and so on in testimony to the low social consciousness of lawyers. Carter's most stinging remark is seen in the following summary: "In may own region of the country, lawyers of great influence and prestige led the fight

against civil rights and economic justice. They were
paid lavish fees by their states and heaped with honors
for their efforts. They knew all the maneuvers, and
for too long they kept the promises of the Constitution
from coming true. The basic right to vote, to hold a
job, to buy a home, to be informed of one's rights when
arrested, to have legal counsel if an indigent--these
rights have been denied for generations and are being
recently won only after intense struggle" (Carter, 1978,
p.11). Goldstein (1978) summarized and elaborated on
President Carter's article, cited above. He said the
President's speech was viewable as an attack on the
legal profession. Goldstein reemphasized President
Carter's attack on court delays, on plea bargaining,
on delayed and drawn-out litigation, on "legal
featherbedding," on laxity in pursuing "big-shot"
crooks, and in so doing went to the heart of our
economic, political and social system. Some critical
rejoinders said that President Carter, himself, might
act to remedy some of the injustices of our legal
system and the way lawyers appropriate for themselves.

    In a disturbing article, Berentson (1980), in the
Washington POST indicated that it is easy to find a
dishonest lawyer. Berentson quotes a Gallop Poll in
1977 inquiring of people their notions of the
integrity of various professions. Only 26 percent
felt lawyers had "high" or "very high" standards of
honesty, a rating well below most other professions
and one on par with undertakers. Berentson's
Washington POST article is taken from a lengthier
article and study in The American Lawyer, in which
this publication posed an "accident victim" case to
thirteen negligence lawyers in New York, a potential
"case" in which the lawyers might receive a large
contingency fee if the lawyers would aid the "victim"
in perjuring herself. Berentson says: "The results
will disappoint those members of the bar who assume
that because they are honest, their colleagues are,
too. Five of the 13 lawyers offered to set up the
fraud for me--to engage in the felony of aiding and
abetting perjury. In fact, under the New York State
penal code, even by having the conversations with me
that they did, the five appear to have commited the
Class A misdemeanor of criminal solicitation"
(Berentson, 1980, p.1). What might be equally
astonishing is that few lawyers or the bar have acted
to rectify the presence of such a willingness on these
parts of the lawyers reported on the article and the
public seems to have a "ho-hum--so-what-else-is-new"

attitude. There is so much blatent misuse and violation of public confidence that it takes a catastrophe to shake most people these days. Even the shocking Woodward and Armstrong report on the U.S. Supreme Court merited only some temporary jogging of the Americal consciousness and a few yells from the lawyers and the bar association itself. Are we so innured to ethical violations that we no longer register even the most elemental complaints and look not at all for change?

The Teaching Of Law

Lawyers have however reflected encouragingly on the teaching of law, on law schools as instructional institutions for the practice of law, and related problems (Seligman, 1978; Turow, 1977, Auerbakc, 1976; Greenhouse, 1978; Hazel, 1978). Complimentary books on Nader by Gorey (1975) and by Buckhorn (1972) have used Nader's socially conscious work to comment on law school training and the contrasts between training lawyers to do the biddings of business vs. serving the public's interest. All of these authors have said that law school teaching has not kept up with social and professional demands, that the curriculum has been rigid and narrow and more self-serving than serving the public (Seligman, 1978). Greenhouse (1978) observes that the President of the United States estimates that 90 percent of American lawyers are devoted to protecting the "comfortable isolation of privilege," and that the Chief Justice of the Supreme Court is of the opinion that half of our lawyers lack the skill to try a serious case. Quoting a Bar Association poll the indications are that 41 percent of American lawyers agree with the Chief Justice. Greenhouse draws the conclusion that "Nobody seems to like lawyers much these days, so it is scarcely surprising that the country's 168 law schools, which turn out 30,000 lawyers a year, have themselves become objects of scrutiny (Greenhouse, 1978, p.22). Some writers, especially Seligman, have suggested establishing "schools of public law" to train lawyers for public service, that is, to represent the poor, the elderly, minorities, and others, including social agencies and the government. How well such reform would work, especially if opposed by the Bar and existing prestigious schools is, of course, debatable, but it does suggest that some members of the legal profession are thinking about their social responsibilities. One reason that such reform is sorely needed is that the

336

law profession has taken a bad ethical and moral beating in the past two decades. starting even before Watergate. Auerback's words apply here: "Nothing in the modern history of the bar presaged the sustained crisis of professionalism that began during the 1960's and culminated in Watergate...amid the most severe national crisis since the Civil War, faith in legal authority disintegrated; and once it did, the revealed role of lawyers in preserving a discriminatory rule of law, followed by evidence of the complicity of lawyers in lawlessness, demolished claims of professional neutrality. The elaborate structure of ethics and values which had defined professional responsibility for nearly a century collapsed in a shambles" (Auerback, 1977, p.263). This passage, if it is a true criticism of the legal profession, suggests that a profession cannot practice in ways inimical to its ethics and then have the strength to withstand adversity and challenge; the emphasis law has placed on serving selfish business interests has come home to haunt the lawyers. The conflict between public interest and profit (or self interest or business) is a continuing challenge. Seligman says, "Ever since the beginning of the urban industrial era the bar had adopted a series of compromises to reconcile public responsibility with professional self-interest--and to conceal the distance between them. These compromises unraveled once the Cold War thawed and public attention shifted to neglected domestic concerns" (Seligman, 1977, p.263). And further, "The civil rights struggle, followed by the brief war against poverty, exposed standards of professional behavior which preserved the glaring inadequacy of legal services for citizens who were black, poor, or both" (Seligman, 1977, p.263). A serious chain of indictments against the legal profession, those of Seligman!

The Bar Association

Helping to maintain the practices of the legal profession is the American Bar Association. It recently celebrated its 100th anniversary and some reflection on its services is naturally in order. Early on the Bar Association was reputed to be full of prejudice: anti-black, anti-Catholic and anti-Semetic, probably laying the groundwork for the need for legal practice reform the past few decades but also erecting a bulwark against such change. Today 230,000 lawyers belong to the American Bar Association (Goldstein, 1978, p.24). but this includes only about one-half the total number

of practicing lawyers; there are, also, 1,700 other
bar associations but with less power than the ABA. The
ABA has had a very conservative history and that may
be why no more of America's lawyers belong: For
example the ABA criticized the Sherman Antitrust Act
as "unsound" and opposed the introduction of the income
tax as an "encroachment on private wealth" (Goldstein,
1978, p.24). With this kind of professionalism and
officialdome behind lawyers, it is little wonder that
they have served primarily selfish interests and opposed
innovation in the direction of social justice.

The history of the American Bar Association (ABA)
and of the operations of the legal profession in the
U.S. indicate that the profession is prejudiced. How
has it fared since the advent of the civil rights
movement? According to Kiernan (1979) the National
Law Journal found only 12 blacks among more than 3,700
partners in the nation's 50 largest law firms; of whom
6 work in Washington,D.C. Among the associates in the
leading law firms, there are 14 blacks among 341 total,
a bare 4 percent. There are about 11,000 black
lawyers admitted to the bar in the U.S. Although
prejudice may be rampant here, other issues may
account for the disparity of black lawyers in leading
firms: too few blacks to choose from among the
leading law school graduates (Harvard, Yale, Columbia,
Stanford, Chicago, Michigan and Berkeley); greater
appeal from governmental and industrial jobs; general
lack of "paper credentials." Also most clients for
the major law firms found among business and management
and the leading corporations, most executives and
managers from which are white; they may look to
dealing with white lawyers only as part of their
prejudice. Black lawyers may be discouraged at the
thought of applying for jobs in the leading law firms,
given the latter's histories and apparent biases.
Moreover, it takes an aggressive stance on the part of
the law firms to solicit the interests of black
lawyers; a passive posture will not solve the problem.
Given their inherent conservatism, the law firms are
not likely to move very aggressively toward equal
opportunity practices. As reform builds up in the
legal profession over fees, lawyer's attitudes and
social consciousness, there may develop in time a move
toward assertively finding and hiring black lawyers.

Public Reactions

A cover story in TIME magazine, April 10, 1978 reviews in a popular yet salient way the many, many criticisms extant against lawyers and the law (and courts). They point first to the enormous power vested in lawyers and the legal profession: as many as 100,000 laws are passed annually in the U.S.; more than one-half the members of Congress and one-fifth of state legislators are attorneys; federal agencies pass over 35,000 new regulations yearly; and the profession turns out 30,000 - 35,000 new lawyers each year, adding to their numerical unpopularity. Public polls are likewise critical of lawyers, one poll placing law firms at the bottom in ratings of confidence among 16 agencies. The Watergate scandal deprecated lawyers further, especially the culpable ones, despite the remedial effect of some "good" lawyers such as Sam Ervin, Archibald Cox, Leon Jaworski, and John Sirica. Despite qualitative changes in law school admissions, the competition is great, the pace unrelenting, and the drop out rate is something to be concerned about. Some who do graduate choose not to practice law, using their knowledge in business, teaching or perhaps in other professions (psychologists and psychiatrists are increasingly interested in law for their own professional reasons). More and more women are entering the legal profession and this may be a good thing (up from 6 percent in 1960 to 25 percent recently). The law and lawyers maintain their intimidating standby and through the use of what is to the layman obscure and highly technical language; perhaps along with medicine, language is a great armour worn by these professionals that seems to glitter and to make them impervious to ordinary discourse and understanding. One pays heavily for this bit of esoteria, in both law and medicine. Since our legal system is based on adversary proceedings, lawyers can easily keep issues alive and inhibit solutions or reconciliations. One gets the impression that most divorce prodeedings are unnecessarily adverse owing to legal action (or inaction), ultimately costly to the clients, as are accident cases and many other, even minor, disputes.

Perhaps this condition and similar ones has led people such as Gallagher (1979) to write a consumer manual on how to judge a lawyer and what to do when employing one. It is a good thing when lawyers take it in hand to instruct the lay person about the law and lawyers and the pitfalls associated in dealing with

both. He begins his instructive manual by saying:
"The public's criticism of lawyers in particular, and
the legal profession in general, is increasing at a
rate which can only be construed as alarming by
responsible members of the profession" (1979, p.9).
He considers the following traits desirable in
lawyers: competence, integrity, judgement, dedication,
maturity, and compassion. Gallagher regards lawyers
more as businessmen, less as professionals, and goes
very thoroughly into the matter of fees, billing
procedures that underlies fees, referrals to other
lawyers, keeping the client informed, and clarity of
language. Advice to consumers using any and all
professionals should be written in the practical and
high-calibre way Gallagher has written about the legal
profession.

One problem with the legal profession that
demeans its professional responsibility is that it
does too little to police itself (except for books
like Gallagher's). The 1969 Code of Professional
Responsibility is said to be too vague, merely well-
meaning, but not salient to present issues. The ethics
tend to view lawyering more as a business than a social
responsibility. One interesting book that notes the
business/professional split was written many decades
ago (Cohen, 1916), and seems to have been a portend
of what was to follow the next half-century or more.
Activities of lawyers that feed their business
interests and not their professional concerns are:
unnecessary delays arising from crowded dockets,
lawyer's schedules, and the desire to avoid having
the client come to terms with the law; the endless
demands arising from allegedly "newly discovered"
information that wears-down the opposition; the old
saw of "ambulance chasing"; contingency fee arrangements often leading the lawyer to complicate the
client's case to get a higher fee; basing fees on the
apparent or alleged "saving" to the client, as in tax
cases and real estate cases; and the ubiquitous
divorce case where high fees are charged for a small
amount of routine paper work and minimal court
appearances.

Working to improve ethics among lawyers are broad
social movements such as the civil rights movement,
spontaneous groups of law people moving to get legal
consultation on an organizational or group basis,
group legal insurance, the advertising of fees which

340

allows the potential client to compare and select
among lawyers, the growing number of suits against
lawyers, and an increase in the number of small claims
courts that resolve small differences readily. As the
law becomes less concerned with "victimless offenses"
such as smoking marijuana, gambling, private sexual
arrangements among consenting adults; and with no-fault
insurance laws and the use of paralegals to do much of
the minor clerical and decision-making work, legal
costs may be expected to continue to come down in many
quarters. However, high priced lawyers are still
plentiful and, as we know, serve only a small percent
of the population.

Special Pressure

Some of the education of lawyers and judges may,
however, serve non-professional purposes. Guzzardi
discusses how judges are ushered into the world of
economics in seminars sponsored by large corporations
and geared to indoctrinating the judges with the
problems and viewpoints of corporate giants
(Guzzardi, 1979, pp. 58-61). Matters relating to
complex business problems, to mergers, to anti-trust
actions are not well within the judges' legal reper-
toires; they were considered to be "...tourists in an
alien land" in regard to complex business matters.
One could also train judges further in the social
sciences, in domestic and marital matters, in the
care and nurturing of the handicapped: Who will put
on seminars for judges in these pressing social areas?
Business? Not likely.

Rebellion within the ranks of lawyers, those
pushing for reform and a more liberal and less
"professionalized" stance are seen among the avant
garde publications from Washington,D.C. and New York:
Legal Times of Washington; The American Lawyer; and
The National Law Journal. Sometimes less scholarly
than the traditional technical law journals, these
publications (in the form of "newspapers") grapple
with current issues, with reform, with data on the
profession that are of social value, and with matters
of news and opinion. The National Law Journal under
the byline of Frank M. Tuerkheimer(1980) makes the
observation with supporting evidence that top corporate
officers have ways of insulating themselves and can
get by without penalty in the face of offenses of a
criminal nature. This author says that corporate

341

violence is not hard to detect, the discharge of highly toxic chemicals into Love Canal being a flagrant example, and the high rate of lung cancer in industrial areas being another example. In the case cited, trucks were kept on the highway performing hauling duties for a large corporation when the braking system was known to be faulty; as a result the brakes failed in a critical traffic situation and two people were killed and two others seriously injured when the truck with faulty brakes hit a passenger car carrying four family members. The corporation's notion of such a situation is that of an unfortunate mishap, or accident, but it occurred under a working situation in which the trucks were to be kept on the road "making money." A contrasting safety position might be held to represent the regular highway user's rights and privileges, particularly that of the family involved in the accident. Tuerkheimer says "...the untempered desire for profit led to violence and death. It is hard to imagine more socially-offensive conduct. Yet within the panoply of applicable federal penal statutes this conduct is less than a misdemeanor; it is called a petty offense--with penalties ranging from $200 to a $400 fine" (Tuerkheimer, 1980, p.22).

Malpractice

Lawyers as we know have long been involved in malpractice suits but, of course, against other professionals, especially physicians (Mallen & Levit, 1977; American Bar Assn., 1979). Recently, however, there has been a noticeable growth of suits against lawyers for malpractice, as reflected in articles in the three news journals of the legal profession--Legal Times of D.C., The National Law Journal, and The American Lawyer--cited above. These publications report news items and trend analyses of malpractice concerns against lawyers as well as against other professionals. Malpractice costs have risen so high for lawyers that they have begun to start their own malpractice insurance agencies. One such effort is called "ALAS" (Attorneys' Liability Assurance Society, Ltd.). The reasons such compensatory efforts have been developed are, of course, the mounting suits against lawyers through commercial insurance companies, as well as costs. Studies of malpractice suits against lawyers tend to be explosive in one state or area, while quiescent or declining in others; the situation is so volatile, clear trends cannot be easily predicted

(Couric, 1980). As one might guess, most malpractice
suits against lawyers revolve around fees (Marcus,
1979; Mallen & Levit, 1977) but often, also, interpersonal and professional relationships between
lawyer and client surface.

Mallen and Levit (1977), recognizing how well
physicians and dentists have prepared themselves
against malpractice suits, and have recommended to
lawyers greater care in their client relationships.
They discuss the large and ranging topic of preventing
malpractice (1977, pp. 12-27), by referring to more
carefully constructed office procedures, fees and
how they are set, files that back up agreements and
progress on cases, index systems, docket control,
referring some clients to more properly qualified and
specialized lawyers (as medical practitioners do), and
better client relations. Given more care in their
legal procedures and in their client relationships,
lawyers might forestall or greatly reduce the recent
increase in malpractice suits against them. The newer
attitude will put people, not profits, first, and fees
will not be "all the market can stand," but more
reasonably arrived at agreements.

Social Irresponsibility

The departments of life in which lawyers seem to
have the most problems are those, as we have seen,
dealing with fairness, justice, reasonable fees,
having a pro-social stance, and suffering increasingly
from malpractice law suits. One could say by
stretching the terms some, that the greatest problems
of lawyers is that they are "sociopathic."[1] A sociopath
is one who is unreliable, does not uphold his/her
social responsibility, carries self-interest to the
extreme, and deceitfully pursues his own interest when
purporing to help others or follow their interest.
Sociopaths in life do not harbour many anxieties; they
are not usually depressed; and they do not "look" like
neurotics, or stressed persons in the usual sense of

---

[1]The term "Sociopath" is used advisedly; it is
not meant to denote a clinical (psychological or
psychiatric) category, but rather to point to a class
of behaviors, somewhat characteristic of lawyers,
which closely resemble some features of anti-social
behavior.

the terms. Perhaps lawyers are in just this position vis a vis society and in contrast to physicians, the clergy, executives, teachers, and others. There is little or no literature on lawyers from a clinical/psychological/psychiatric standpoint. They are hardly mentioned in the large and comprehensive work by Stone, Cohen and Adler on Health Psychology (1979). Printouts on the professions and their problems of a psychological nature seldom include studies on lawyers. Perhaps lawyers, unlike college professors and students, the clergy, physicians, dentists, teachers and nurses, are seldom captured for psychological studies because they are not interesting in this respect, or because no one has considered them subject to stress in the manner described for most professions in this book. It may be, also, that there is actually less day-to-day and hour-to-hour stress in the legal profession than in other professions, hence they do not build up the tension and anxiety states so characteristic of most professions.

Somewhat close to the problem of psychological distress among lawyers (or law students) is a study by Brown (1977) on 2,718 law students from three law schools in Sydney, New South Wales, Australia. Of interest in the study was the question of law students' attitudes toward the use of drugs, particularly marijuana, thinking that perhaps these attitudes would eventually influence how the law would view drug offenses, especially minor ones. Thirty-eight percent of the over 2,700 law students returned the questionnaire. Over half of the population studied felt that drug involvement should not be punished, that its use should not be punished and that its use should not even require compulsory psychological or medical treatment. In conclusion, Brown says "It is apparent that law students are overwhelmingly in favor of not just reducing penalties for marijuana use, but of removing them entirely, and a majority favor this approach to the use of all drugs, including opiates" (1977, p.453). Further the law students studied failed to see the illegality of drugs as a deterrent to their own use, over half of whom had used marijuana, with the most lenient attitudes and practices falling in the 26-30 year age group. Whether these attitudes would find correspondence in the U.S. is unknown. But the very occurrence of these more liberal attitudes among law students may signal changes in some ways in which the law is interpreted and enforced.

Not only are these attitudes concerning drugs among law students significant, vast changes of a similar nature are observed among high school students. An Editorial (1980) in the Washington POST indicates that the fraction of 12 - 17 year olds who have ever used "pot" has increased more than four-fold since 1967 (7 percent to 31 percent 1967, 1980 respectively, national figures). Moreover about 40 percent of the current high school graduating class are alleged to be marijuana users. The long-range consequences to the health of these youngsters over the next few decades testifies to the seriousness of the drug use problem, the health of the populous and the seeming impotence of medicine, law and teaching to grapple successfully with the drug usage problem.

A study of the personality characteristics of 130 German lawyers was done by Weyrauch (1964), using interview and questionnaire techniques. His population was spread over a wide age range (under 40 to over 70), but he made no effort to sample appropriately the totality of German lawyers, so the representativeness of his findings can be questioned. Among the characteristics noted were those who appeared as malcontent, as disgruntled individuals; others were seen as working themselves to death, many were uncomfortable socially, and some given to spurious ethical practices, Weyrauch notes, but fails to say what percentage fall into these categories or how seri were the characteristics. One could interview any population of people and come up with similar descriptive categories. More clinical categories were used to identify some as hypochondriacs, and some as sexually maladjusted. The author says in this connection: "...lawyers seem to engage in any conceivable activity that promises release from inner tensions. Observed activities include heavy smoking, alcoholism, and addiction to medicaments and drugs. It may be assumed that lawyers are especially susceptible to so-called psychosomatic illnesses" (Weyrauch, 1964, p.272-273). What is lacking in the mental health field concerning lawyers are studies on how budding lawyers look when first entering law school, how they appear in comparison upon graduation, and how these features change--if they do--over time as the young men and women accumulate years of legal practice.

In an important way law stands at the crossroads between society and other professions, allegedly protecting society without doing damage to the professions or their members. However, in this gate-keeper position, law and lawyers can be seriously faulted, for they are not only protecting society, they are taking advantage of the "system" of correction and protection for their own purposes. The trust placed in lawyers and in the law is rapidly changing to distrust, and lawyers are behaving somewhat like a different category of patients--sociopaths--in contrast to the neurotic, depressive and sometimes near psychotic behavior of other professions and profes-sionals. The profession of law appears to be struggling less with society for a place in the sun--as are nursing, teaching, the clergy and allied health professionss--they are struggling more against society while at the same time purporting to be society's gatekeeper and counselor. Rebellion against law and lawyers is mounting and what has been their strength as counselors to society now turns to be their weakness arising from their sometimes betrayal documented of society.

CHAPTER XII

BIBLIOGRAPHY

American Bar Assn. Professional liability of trial alwyers: The malpractice question. Proceedgins of a Nat'l Institute, Oct. 27-28, 1977. Hotel Mark Hopkins, San Francisco, Calif., Amer. Bar Assn., 1979.

Averbach, J.S. Unequal Justice. N.Y.: Oxford U. Press, 1976.

Babcock, C.R. U.S. fees to lawyers draw challenges, Washington POST, May 6, 1979.

Bailey, F.L. The trouble with lawyers..., Parade Magazine, 1978, Dec. 17, p.4.

Berentson, J. It's easy to find a dishonest lawyer, Washington POST, June 15, 1980, p.1.

Brown, R.A. Preliminary survey of drug use among law students in New South Wales, J.Drug Issues, 1977, 7, 439-455.

Buckhorn, R.F. Nader: The People's Lawyers. Englewood Cliffs, N.J.: Prentice-Hall, 1972.

Cohen, J.H. The Law: Business or Profession? N.Y.: The Banks Law Publ. Co., 1976.

Carter, J. Excerpts from Carter's speech to the bar association, N.Y. TIMES, May 6, 1978, p.11.

Consumer Reports. "How to choose a lawyer", May, pp. 284-290, 1977.

Couric, E. Big firms form own malpractice insurance group, Legal Times of Washington, 1980, April 14.

Diehl, J. How lawyer-legislators prosper, Washington POST, Mar. 2, 1980.

Doublad, W.O. The Court Years, 1939-1975. N.Y.: Random House, 1980.

Editorial, Getting High/Getting Hurt, Washington POST, July 3, 1980.

347

Freund, P.A. The legal profession, in Lynn, K.S. and
     the Editors of Daedalus, The Professions In
     America. Boston: Beacon Press, 1965.

Gallagher, B.M. How To Hire A Lawyer. N.Y.: Delta/
     Seymour Lawrence, 1979.

Goldstein, T. A.B.A. marks century as voice for
     lawyers, New York TIMES, June 10, 1978.

Gorey, H. Nader and The Power of Everyman. N.Y.:
     Grossett & Dunlap, 1975.

Greenhouse, L. Teaching of the law is far below grade
     level, New York TIMES, July 23, 1978.

Guzzardi, W., Jr. Judges discover the world of
     economics, Fortune, 1979, 99, 58-61.

Hazel, R. The Bar On Trial. London: Quartet Books,
     1978.

Kaye, J. Women judges urge naming one of their own as
     justice, Washington POST, Oct. 28, 1979.

Kierman, L.A. Survey finds only 12 blacks as partners
     in nation's 50 biggest law firms, Washington POST,
     1979.

Kierman, L.A. What forum for clients to dispute law
     fees? Washington POST, December 10, 1979.

Lynn, K.S. (Ed.) The Professions In America. Boston:
     Beacon Press, 1965.

Mallen, R. & Levit, V.B. Legal Malpractice. St. Paul:
     West Publ. Co., 1977.

Marcus, S. One-million dollar malpractice suit filed,
     The American Lawyer, 1979, 1, 11.

Meyer, E.L. Southern Maryland justice: Judges do
     much as they please in rural counties, Washington
     POST, April 24, 1980, p.1.

Robinson, T.S. Bar unit slow to act in case of D.C.
     lawyer, Washington POST, April 12, 1980.

Seligman, J. The High Cididel: The Influence of Harvard Law School. Boston: Houghton-Mufflin, 1978.

Stern, P.M. Lawyers On Trial. New York: Times Books, 1980.

Tawney, R.H. The Acquisitive Society. N.Y.: Harvest Books, 1920.

TIME Magazine, Those # * X Z !!! Lawyers, April 10, 1978.

TIME Magazine, Judging the judges, TIME, August 20, 1979.

Toffer, A. Future Shock. N.Y.: Random House, 1970.

Tuerkheimer, F.M. Top corporation lawyers can insulate themselves from criminal liability, The Nat'l Law J., 1980, 2, 21-22.

Turow, S. One L. N.Y.: Putnam, 1977.

Woodward, R. & Armstrong, S. The Breathren, 1979.

Weyrauch, W.O. The Personality of Lawyers. New Haven: Yale U. Press, 1964.

Weisskopf, M. Many home buyers sent to lawyers with-whom lenders have business ties, Washington POST, Nov. 19, 1979.

Zahradnik, R. Woodward says book rings true, The Hatchet, 1969, Oct. 16, p.3.

349

CHAPTER XIII

EXECUTIVES

More than with any other profession, the chief
executive officer (CEO) in large corporations, is under
the most intense and prolonged stress imaginable.
This stress (or the specific stressors, as they are
called, making up the broad-based stress) gives rise
to many somatic, psychological and health-related
tensions, and to anxieties seen in many forms.
Further evidence of this statement, together with the
impact such stress has on the lives and families of
executives will be marshalled in this chapter.

More than a few books testify to the stresses
that impinge on the chief executive officer in large
corporations and, although not studied as much, the
same stresses beset the lives of executives in
smaller businesses and corporations. Some signs of
this concern with executives (going back a number of
years) is seen in such titles as Management Self-
Inflicted Wounds (Austin, 1966; The Executive Life
(Editors of Fortune magazine, 1956); Personality And
Organization (Agryris, 1957); Walking The Executive
Plank (Burger, 1972); The Frustrated Titan (Uris,
1972); Executive Success (Jennings, 1967); and more.
What are these clinical, observational and administrative reports which deal with the stresses
encountered by executives? The answers are numerous
and far-reaching. Many volumes could be written on
the impact stress has on the executive; herein a few
examples of some of the major kinds of stress and their
consequences will be discussed.

Success is often seen as an unmitigated good.
Jennings (1967) points out, however, that the very
success the executive seeks and relishes may itself
turn out to be precarious. Success is based partly
on luck, partly on opportunities and seizing them
propitiously, and partly upon the continuing good
reports, compassion and support from others more
powerful than one's self. Especially where others
are concerned, their whims, shifting emphasis, and
corporate goals themselves that change from time to
time may further test the delicate balance maintained
by executives in large corporations. Jennings (1967,
p.19) says: "The executive knows that successful
achievement of the goals and values of the corporation
as represented in his job situation may spell failure

351

without the blessings and support of superiors." Thus
an executive can be faithful to the corporate goals,
even highly achieving with respect to these goals,
and still be diminished by those who judge the executive
severely. In discussing the motivations of the chief
executive officer in large corporations, Jennings
states a succinct proposition that affects many
executives: "Arriving is departing." Arriving at a
new step upward embraces two consumate sets of conditions: involving one's self emotionally with the
corporation and its goals and the activities associated
therewith in the upward mobile steps, and detaching
one's self from previous managerial and executive roles,
a not uneasy task, one filled with conflict and
divided interests, unfulfilled ambitions, and mixed
identifications. Further refinement of this point
derives from Jennings' (1967, pp. 21-22) discussion of
the three basic points where stress may be encountered:
First, upon entrance to the corporation. Here the
executive candidate is sized up scrupously by his
superiors and he, in turn, surveys his prospects carefully. Each prospective step is met with conflict
between the values and benefits of the present job
versus the undertainties and new demands offered with
advancement, plus the risks associated with each
advancing step. Second, the aspirant executive officer
takes on managerial duties as he moves to the middle
executive ranks, thereby dropping some, or many,
technical competencies; this adds some conflict to his
functioning due to an inherent opposition between
upcoming job duties and past competencies and reasons
for advancement. There is a considerable inconsis-
tency in this set of requirements thereby producing
stress on the rising executive. A third source of
concern termed "anxiety" by Jennings arises when the
conflict between previous and upcoming roles is inten-
sified to the point where the executive does not know
which skills are required in given instances and what
will be the consequence of his miscalculations and
inappropriate actions. The reference to anxiety in
Jennings book matches the descriptions of anxiety in
relation to stress, tension and anxiety proffered in
this writing. Stress comes from the environment--the
roles specified by the job and how one meets them;
tensions result and impinge on the individual when
one is unsure of his efforts vis a vis the organization
and judgements received; and anxiety is a natural
consequence of the stresses and tensions as they
become part of the person, interiorized so to say, and

no longer part of the job tasks and roles but now part of the makeup of the person taken with him wherever he goes and whatever he does.

The Making of Executives

What makes executives? Surely a number of factors are involved, as with any complex task. But achievement motivation is uppermost--some call it a need to achieve (Jennings, 1967, p.23). Affiliation is another important trait found in executives; they identify strongly with the corporation and its goals. Needless to say this is a precarious state of affairs if their efforts are not judged to be successful or appropriate by those above them. Strong identification, while an essential prerequisite of executive status, is still not enough to sustain progress. Ardour, affiliation, identification, and so on, with corporate goals are not enough to guarantee success in climbing up the corporate ladder.

Given this somewhat precarious state of uncertainty as to advancing through the executive ranks, what is the prospective executive to do about it? He can put more trust and confidence in himself irrespective of his advancements. He can use himself as the center of his ambitiousness, defining the latter as contingent upon positive self-esteem and not wholly a matter of selling one's self short just for corporate goals and advancement. The all encompassing abdication of one's own selfhood in favor of gains spelled out by and through corporate goals and avenues of advancement can leave the executive both selfless and powerless, if he does not become successful through total alignment with corporate ideals and prospects.

Reliance on one's self in the corporate uptrend is further referred to by Jennings (1967, pp.28-29) as constituting autonomy and integrity. Autonomy implies a measure of independence from the corporation, avoiding a wholesale immersion in corporate aims; and integrity implies the ability to keep one's self whole and functioning with respect to whatever one's goals are. Priorities are involved in both of these trials-- integrity and autonomy--as one sets up the "firsts" and "seconds" and so on among his options in the executive climb. One may set up advancement as a high priority, but not at the cost of one's personal anxieties and family responsibilities. One may be proud of one's achievement but skeptical of it if it costs too much in terms of personal anxiety, marital and family estrangement, and health problems.

Executives can take these matters of advice proposed by Jennings or they can rebel against the corporate demands. However, they make a choice with risk; there are no risk-free avenues open to the executive. In fact, the opposite is the case: all options are full of risks by the very nature of the corporate setting, its aims, and the motivations of the participants. This high-risk environment has three broad characteristics, according to Jennings (1967, p.79): pressures from superiors who control rewards and punishments; pressures that arise in relation to the goals and aims of the organization or corporation itself; and, thirdly, pressures arising from the personality makeup of the executive himself. In the latter instance, the individual characteristics of the executive are such as to sensitize and motivate him to accept and pursue the first two sets of corporate pressures. These three sets of stresses and tensions make up what Jennings calls the "corporate tri-angle" (p.79).

Power From Above

Stresses the executive experiences stem firstly from the power others have over one, especially the rising executive. The brutality of punitive measures applied to executives--sudden dismissal being one of the most inhumane (Terkel, 1974)--are beginning to give way to more considerate measures, according to Jennings (1967, pp.110-114); such as ample warning of the need to change, try-outs on alternative positions, being by-passed for promotion momentarily with some instructions on how to improve, being "kicked upstairs" into less active or relevant posts, given problems that do not need (or allow) solution, and so on. Even though the self-esteem of the corporate executive may be damaged in many of these alternative measures, the devastation arising from summary dismissal is disallowed and time may permit rehabilitation or at least adjustment to a new business life and prospect.

There is a tendency to place much of the responsibility for corporate casualties on the personal lives and histories of executives (Jennings, 1967, pp.78-205). Jennings devotes more space to the individual personality topics--varied as they are,

inherently--in relation to executive stress and corporate characteristics than he does to the corporations
themselves. While it is doubtlessly difficult to
separate the two, especially when allowing for early
selection of "types" who enter corporatedome, and who
shape their behaviors to meet the exigencies of
corporate pressures, it is equally important to recognize that if executives are made (not born), they are
also made casulaties (not born casualties). Much
"psychology" of the executive's perils are not really
"inside" the individual but represent the individual
bending to the extant stresses. The pattern of stress,
the resulting tensions and abiding anxieties are all
too common in the major professions for us to seriously
think that all potential professionals are flawed from
the outset. If the executive orients himself to the
corporate demands as Jennings often states is the
case (e.g., he says, p.141: "Counseling business
executives shows that success in the administrative
role is a central, if not the central value around
which pivots their whole life style"), how can this set
of shaping pressures be held other than largely
accountable for the ensuing tensions and anxieties so
characteristic of executives and their relationships?
An imbalance in attributing and studying the results
of stress will not only place an onerous load on the
executive's own personality characteristics and
perhaps constitute a self-fulfilling prophesy, but
it will allow corporations and organizations to
escape responsibility for more objective and responsible investigation of their motives, actions and
their consequences.

Uris (1972) addresses the problem of executives
by pointing to the stress, tensions, and anxiety
patterns evidenced among them. He says, "There are
factors at work in most business organizations that
thwart their executives, and the most capable are
often the most hurt. Accordingly, the average
company is a cesspool of resentment, frustration,
anguish, and hate. And these destructive emotions
still further cut down on the availability of executive
talent" (Uris,1972, p.17).

One could say, as Uris does, "Why don't the
executives quit?" if they find their jobs and roles so
distasteful. Quitting is not easy; maybe it is even
harder than putting up with barely tolerable situations.
They don't quit because of salary (can't match the
executive's salry elsewhere); they feel quitting would

be tantamount to failure and they do not see their distress as resulting from or leading to failure; they do not usually relate health, social and family distress to elements on the job or stress in the corporation (or they dismiss such results as passing at best). And they feel that tomorrow will bring relief and better opportunities to achieve the goals unhampered, those toward which they originally aspired.

One aspect of the shaping of executive behavior comes from several characteristics of corporations and large organizations. They have their myths. The fledging executive is admonished to get ahead, to compete, to put forth his best foot, to be hardworking but patient, and so on. Uris calls these and other myths "rocks in the road" (P.67); and refers to several myths that have a particularly adverse effect in that they, in practice, conflict with the idealized version of things. One myth is to excel in your present job as preparation for advancement. The trouble here is that referred to above, viz., that changing skills concommitant with new tasks will not only often create tensions and anxieties for the executive, but may lead to disclaimers on the corporation's part (by higher executives still) that the old skills are so well-practiced they should not be abandoned through a promotion, and that the new (promoted) job may weaken the person's skills that have been developed and proven useful to date. And a second myth is that of preparing one's assistant to take over. The assistant may be jumped over the to-be-promoted executive and/or the pressures from underneath the prospective promotee may not be clear enough to warrant the promotion of the aspirant person; more time is needed and postponements supercede so that in time the prospect of promotion looms dimmer and dimmer, despite apparently ready and available skills and interest.

Prejudice may also act to still individual's chances for promotion. While racial or ethical prejudice among professions has diminished in recent decades (Uris, 1972, pp.68-78), there is still ample evidence of prejudice at the executive level in corporations. Some old prejudices against Jews, the Irish and other national/ethnic groups have given way to prejudices against blacks (especially since more of them are being educated, hence knocking on the executive doors), women (similar to blacks in many respects), those with altered life styles, and homosexuals. The liberation movements have counted some gains but not as much as the liberators would like to see. For example, women accounted for four percent of the executives in the U.S.A. in 1940, 6 percent in 1971 (Uris, 1972, pp.69-79); hardly a significant rise in three decades. Corporations hire and promote blacks and women, partly under legal pressures, social pressures, and the willingness to "look good" to the public by not being obviously prejudiced. But within ranks the minorities do not fare as well as they might and promotions to higher executive posts are jealously guarded in favor of the "company man," the "old boys, old cronies" syndrome and a general unwillingness to experiment with the new executive blood.

The problem of the contribution of individual characteristics versus corporate or organizational characteristics to the problems of executives looms large in Uris' work as well as in Jennings' book. Uris discusses "distractors" such as sex, drugs, alcohol and family disorganization (Uris, 1972, pp.136-163). Again, it is difficult to tell which comes first, the executive's predispositions derived from his past, or the stresses of daily corporate life, according to Uris. However, whether these distractors are symptoms of corporate or organizational stress or personal tensions (derived mainly from one's history), they are still subject to study and to remediation at the level of both the corporation and the individual. Remedial work at the individual level may include psychotherapy for the executive (and his wife and family), and at the corporate level it may include group therapy (among highly placed executives), pointed attempts to reduce stress in the organization, and other means. All working together should produce less stress; however, more stress is added if there is an on-going battle as to who is to blame, the corporation or the individual, for individual suffering and professional and vocational confusion.

Burger (1972) brings his criticism of executive and corporate stress right down to the corporate level. He says, "The free-and-easy firing of corporate executives is primarily but not exclusively a pheno-menon of the United States industrial scene. Nowhere else in the western world are executive dismissals so quickly considered, so smoothly executed, and performed so frequently" (Burger, 1972, p.vii). One method set to cope with ameliorating this practice, according to Burger, is to pay more attention to hiring the "right man" in the first case. The

357

unrelenting moving up year by year into higher salary and responsibility levels may be paced too rapid for both individuals and corporate structures to absorb. Some slowing down of this ratio of increase may be indicated without de-motivating individuals. Also, lesser posts for non-successful executives may be considered; one does not have to drop from $50,000.00/ $70,000.00 per year to zero, as there are many intermediate jobs, functions, and levels of skill that may be utilized to preserve both the integrity of the individual executive and the functioning of the organization (Burger, 1972, pp.22-27). One might also help the executive who is unsuccessful and a "misfit" for a given job to transfer to another company, to undergo some retraining in some skill area he has even a modicum of interest in, or otherwise reshape his outlook through very pointed refurbishing of his talents and interests. A viable alternative to the summary dismissals of executives lamented by Burger is the "hired for life" theme found in Japanese industry. If Japan is America's chief competitor in the industrial world markets, how come they can adapt such humanitarian practices and not experience deterioration in the effectiveness and efficiency of organization, one may ask. Only if an executive commits a felony, Burger notes, is he dismissed from his job in Japanese organizations. The risk involved in such highly humane practices pivots on hiring people more thoughtfully in the first place. There is a track system operating, with the best executive jobs going to university graduates; and the practice of entering governmental, high executive or middle management jobs--based presumably on one's capabilities--is a "fix" for life as well, in the Japanese system. Less mobility may give way to more security and less competitive organization-vs-individual stress in the Japanese system. In turn, according to Burger (1972, pp.36-37) morale among executives and workers alike in Japanese industrial organizations is high, pride is extant, and identification with corporate goals is clear. Burger observes, "They take a different attitude toward work than our American managers do. They think nothing of working extra hours. The spirit of joining together and working together toward a common objective dominates the corporate picture" (p.36). Corresponding to this apparently higher state of morale among Japanese workers and managers in contrast to Americans in the same positions is that the Japanese executive is given another assignment if he faults in his first one. The

358

emphasis on remediation is placed on the corporation to find alternatives rather than simply dismissing the failing executive. What a difference in values! The price we pay for individual freedom, so called, at the individual level in America has hidden costs attached to it: Equal freedom to act unilaterally on the part of corporations with temporizing dismissals of individuals that reflects adversely on both the corporation and the individual. Enormous stress is born with this practice.

Above we discussed some myths about executive opportunities and prospects. Another myth may be added here, according to Burger's discussion (1972, pp.48-51), that being the folly of expecting "warnings" to the faulting executive to effectively induce him to "get his act together," to use the common phrase. Actually, most warnings are vague hints of dissatisfaction with one's performance, not specifics about how to remediate the situation. More specifics are needed, but even then it is doubtful if one can be expected to increase his efficiency more than a few percentage points. It is expecting the impossible to think otherwise, Burger feels, and further creates a spurious tendency to place blame on the executive and the expectation of change wholly on the individual when it is the whole system--from hiring through promotions--that is the stressor in such cases.

As implied in Burger's comments and in the contrasting characteristics separating American and Japanese industrial/corporate organizational systems, the failures of the American executive may be laid almost entirely at his doorstep (Austin, 1966). The very title of Austin's book--Management's Self-Inflicted Wounds--tells us where he places the emphasis. While all authors credit managers and executives with a share in their plights--the organization cannot be held 100% responsible for ills, just as it cannot be credited with 100% of the successes--Austin seems to go further in placing responsibility for improvement on the executive. Numerous unsavory characteristics of bosses are adumbrated (he cites 76 self-inflicted wounds, p.310) without relating these characteristics to the chief executives own stresses and tensions derived from the system (the organization) he so aptly follows, identifies with, and lives and breathes. Correcting these 76 self-inflicted wounds can hardly

--realistically--pivot entirely on the chief executive
officer himself, although no one would discourage the
boss trying to improve upon his stance, his values and
his practices.

The Fortune Magazine report on The Executive Life
(1956) demures in the face of defining who executives
are. Today the editors of this magazine would still
not agree on what executives are and what they do in
their entirity. However, the results of their studies
indicate that the younger the executive the more likely
he has had college training, all the more so if his
field is business/economics or science and engineering
(Fortune Editors, 1956, p.34). Most of the executives
these editors studied came from families with business
backgrounds, hence there has likely been a profit
motive and a "get ahead" motive in the executives'
families, (more than a technical or science related
motive). This kind of self-selection is matched with
the more explicit selection practices going on in
organizations. With all the emphasis on personality
characteristics and background found in the literature
on the executive, it is important to note what the
Fortune report observes about executives in various
fields and their salaries: "The specialized character
of the electric-power industry makes it understandable
...that top utility executives have had more education
than the executives in any other industry. Yet these
utility executives are paid less than any others. By
contrast, the miscellaneous purveyors of articles that
affect most closely the mores of the coutry--tobacco,
publications, liquor, radiobroadcasts, cosmetics,
movies--are as a group at once the best paid and the
least educated of all" (1956, p.38). These comments
are further substantiated by lists of high salaried
executives from recent polls (Saunders, 1978). Sales,
profit, competition, and unrelenting stress are probably
more likely to be found in the lives of executives
working for the industries that play on our morals,
values and entertainment (radio/TV, movies, tobacco,
liquor, etc.), the volatile areas of our common
existence.

Marketing Executives

Pursuant to the interests in executives selling
themselves (along with the products they represent in
their organizations), there has grown up in recent
years a kind of "marketing" of executives that gives
them a face value, so to say, that is appealing to

prospective employers, organizations, industries, and the like (Thomas et al, 1976). This marketing approach to getting executives hired appears on our discussion above regarding careful initial selection of executives as well as bearing on the stresses and strains they subsequently experience throughout their careers. With more emphasis on their "personality profiles" there is added stress on them as persons to measure up, to meet the needed criteria and to appear as paragons of excellence for their intended posts. They are prepared in ways suggestive of the politicians who get marketers, advertising and image-making experts to "present them to the public" in ways that will attract votes (White, 1968, 1973; Spero, 1980). The executive is looking for a job, of course, and not votes, but the methods are strikingly similar. This may be an unfortunate practice for executives (as it is for politicians) because it may actually stress superficial characteristics rather than the substantial ones that make for enduring accomplishment. And, of course, it circumvents acknowledgement of the role of the organization and its stress-producing attributes, rather than seeing the mesh between executive and organization. Perhaps this interest in "selling themselves" grows out of observations made a number of years ago by the Fortune editors, viz., "Top executives are... 'just as stupid about selling themselves as a youngster trying for his first job' " (Fortune editors, 1956, p.45). How else can one see this image-making and marketing of executives other than a total play for the market-place, adding risks to their selection and subsequent progress, and putting them forth as commodities to be manipulated for the good of the organization. When executives are thus selected and groomed, how can they, then, in positions of judgement exercise the human, considerate and person-centered attitudes and practices that organizations so sorely need? They are, with such image-making/marketing practices succumbing wholly to the purposes of the organization and possibly contributing to their own long range stress.

Executives do "crack up," as the Fortune magazine editors observed many years ago. How do these disabilities come about? Partly due to long, stressful hours of work. The Fortune editors observe: "Putting all the commitments together we get a work week something like this: forty-five to forty-eight hours of daytime work; one night working late at the office; two nights working at home, one night entertaining--all

in all, some fifty-seven to sixty hours. And this
evidently is a minimum; come convention time, a trip,
a company emergency, and the week can easily go to
seventy or eighty hours" (Fortune editors, 1956, p.
65). For how long has such stress been put on the
executive? Perhaps as long as organizations have
existed in the modern, industrial world, but surely
more and more since the beginning of business/indus-
trial/commercial expansion following World War II.

Although one observer's list of why executives
submit to such intense work is probably no better than
another's, the Fortune editors think the compelling
reasons are as follows: Self-expression; sense of
contribution; responsibility, prestige; fear. Perhaps
self-aggrandizement, money, conspiciousness and ostentation should be added. Given these attributes as
approximately correct and applicable, it is difficult
to see how some psychiatrists in industry could say
that a healthy executive should not breakdown, but
should adjust to mounting pressures by transferring
work, unshouldering part of his load, and the like.
The intoxication with power, money and prestige are
the very motives that belie the psychiatrist and that
explain why the executives don't shoulder their enormous loads. The medical model of stress and breakdown
posits an "internal weakness" in the individual--which
may, of course, be true as none of us is thoroughly
integrated and impervious to stress--which comes in
contact with special stress, resulting in a breakdown.
The Fortune editors state it thus: "The true
influence of work in the crack-up of an executive comes
down to this: a neurotic individual encounters in his
work a special stress (or a series of stresses) that
at some point unbearably intensifies the conflicts
in his own personality; then he goes to pieces"
(Fortune editors, 1956, p.81). This passage puts the
onus squarely on the executive. One should be so
integrated one can take any stress, this passage says.
This is a bit like saying that if a swimmer drowns it
is because his training has not been sufficient to
prevent it, giving no value to the circumstances which
can override any of our skills, attitudes or endurance.

Stress History

Recent interest in stress on the job for all
manner of professions and callings is not as new as one
might think. Over twenty-five years ago, and for
decades even prior to the mid-1950's, stress has been

362

regarded as lethal for both physical and emotional health. The cardiac syndrome was known decades ago, as were syndromes resulting in ulcer and other personality problems. Ostensibly the executive is in tune with authority, but he may also not be in tune with himself--he may be oversubmissive to authority, harbouring tacit resentment, or he may openly rebel, thus bringing on more stresses for not being a "good corporation team member." Adequacy may be superficially evident in one's work and demeanor but tacitly one may have many suspicions about one's skill; this conflict may keep one in a state of tension and be easily exacerbated by pressureful circumstances. The two-sided nature of crack-ups is evident in executives lives--a matter of both what the individual brings to the situation in terms of previous learning and adjustment and the present exigencies--and must be taken into account for a whole cloth version of executive stress, tension and anxiety.

Besides the list of virtues-turned-vices in the makeup of the executive cited above, there are also contingencies in the job setting that add stress. Redlich and Hollingshead (1958) found that mobility can be a disturbing factor in one's mental health. The faster an executive moves upward, the more likely a move is to accompany the "getting ahead" syndrome: moving to a new job in a different community; taking on a more expensive home in a more prestigious neighborhood consonant with his new status; more expensive acquisitive practices in regard to cars, boats, vacations, schools for the children, and the like. The list is endless. Moreover, promotions exact more time, more devotion to job and to economic prospects for one's company and for one's self; these selective activities often diminish the importance of one's health, one's family, and other personal matters. A vicious circle of more work, more prestige and money necessitating abdicating roles relating to family, health and personal life, leading, in turn, to more opportunities and promotions and more time away from the non-work setting. No one is impervious to this spiral leading to personal impoverishment, undue risk, poor health, and family disintegration. That's how executives crack-up.

The Fortune editors deal with the most abrasive of interpersonal relations at the executive level: firings. They discuss firing with impunity, thus indicating how integral a duty it is among executives, yet

363

allowing that it is a tough problem. The difficulty
resides not only at the individual levels--the
executive vs. the one he's firing--but at the corporate
level for allowing such inhumane practices (as we've
seen above). These editors observe that abrupt firings
occur more than infrequently, to wit: "Abrupt firing
tactics are still practiced...One executive tells of
watching a woman who heads a cosmetic firm to to work
on a colleague who had come into her office to resign.
She walked over to him and said, 'Don't you know that
no one ever resigns from this firm? You're fired!"
She then slapped his face, shoved him out into the
hall and into the elevator, and tossed after him the
hat and coat he had dropped during the onslaught
(Fortune editors, 1956, p.181). What a brilliant
testimony to the integrity, the humane and business-
like motives of American executives!

Nor is the picture of large American corporations
much different today (25 years later than the Fortune
document) if De Lorean's book (Wright, 1979, p.5) on
why he quite a high executive post in General Motors
is typical: "Soon I found myself questioning a much
bigger picture, the morality of the whole GM system.
It seemed to me that there was (and is) a cancerous
amorality about this system. The undue emphasis on
profits and cost control without a wider concern for
the effects of GM's business on its many publics seemed
too often capable of bringing together, in the corporation, men of sound, personal morality and responsibility
who as a group reached business decisions which were
irresponsible and of questionable morality." The
immorality about which De Lorean spoke resulted, in
part, in GM producing the Corvair which was highly
faulted by Ralph Nader the consumer advocate.
De Lorean observes GM's corporation attitude stressing
profits only when he said, "Charley Chayne, vice-
president of Engineering, along with his staff, took
a very strong stand against the Corvair as an unsafe
car long before it went on sale in 1959. He was not
listened to but instead told in effect, "You're not
a member of the team. Shut up or go looking for
another job! The car was approved even though serious
questions were raised about its engineering" (Wright,
1979, p.5). This passage not only speaks loudly about
the immorality of large corporations when human safety
is at stake, but equally loudly about the strong
pressures corporations as entities place on their
employees. Either the executive goes along with the
company or he is humiliated, relegated, or perhaps

fired. Maybe justice prevailed in the long run in the GM Corvair vs. Nader case. Wright observes through De Lorean's comments on the Corvair, "When the safety of the car was called into question by Ralph Nader in his book Unsafe At Any Speed (1972), the corporation reaction was just as irrational as was the approval of the car. Nader was tailed and spied upon, and attempts were made to destroy his reputation by raising questions about his morality of his personal life. They failed and so did the Corvair" (Wright, 1979,p.6).

Psychologists have looked at many of the problems created by large organizations and have been doing so for a number of years (Argyris, 1957). In his book on organizations and their impact on individuals, where inevitable conflict ensues, Argyris suggests some interesting propositions that might help us to define problem areas between individual and organizations and to better understand why organizations and corporations are so "difficult" to tolerate in our society, even though they seem to be integral to society. Some propositions (liberally interpreted) are:

> Overspecialized and overstandardized jobs tend to produce worker apathy.
> Alienating work is boring and unsatisfying, leading to tension and resentment on the part of the employee.
> If the number and strength of need satisfaction is decreased in a work situation, workers will tend to feel less positive toward the work group and toward management.
> Individuals need group support and sanctions in order to feel positively about their work.

One implication deriving from these propositions is that the way the work situation is constituted--including executive level work as well as more routine manual jobs--goes a long way toward determining individual involvement, motivation, satisfaction and perseverence. Individuals--even those as highly placed as De Lorean--do not have ultimate control over the organization and cannot redirect or reintegrate group pressures. Organizational behavior then, is often paramount and needs to be carefully studied if we are to understand how corporations work, how they impact the individual and how they tend to grow insular and often inimical to societal objectives. Argyris

365

concludes on this point by saying, "...the analysis of organizations begins with a discussion of the basic properties of the human personality and of the formal organization. Once these properties are described and their probably impact analyzed, we conclude that the needs of healthy individuals (in our culture) tend to be incongruent with the maximum expression of the demands of the formal organization" (Argyris, 1957, p.229). If true to the extent stated by Argyris, this is a serious indictment of organizations and corporations and seems to pose them irrevocably against the individual. How understandable, then, is the high level of conflict between individuals (executives, others) and corporations, how intense the effort to "program" the individual to corporate structure and goals, and how severe the resulting impact on the individual's health, social integrity, family, motivation, and perseverence. It is no wonder that dropouts, burn-outs, numerous career changes, health and psychological and social and family problems, breakdowns, crack-ups and alienations occur! Perhaps the system that characterizes large corporations manages as well as it does owing to many vitiating influences on the organization, influences that protect the individual from the unrelenting pressure and tension from the organization. Argyris says, in this connection that "...the informal organization helps to decresase the basic causes of conflict, frustration, and failure ..." in the exchange between individuals and organizations (Argyris, 1957, p.230).

The Corporate Wife

Given even the smallest likelihood that the strictures about corporations and their impact on individuals (especially executives) is correct, there is no way the corporate wife could escape untoward consequences in her life (Vandervelde, 1979; Kanter, 1977). We have seen how physician's wives and minister's wives are impacted by both the husband's role vis a vis the profession, and the pressures and tensions eminating from the organization qua organization; comparable pressures exist in many ways in the lives of corporation executive wives. Kanter (1977, p.xii) and some supporting work by Merton(Merton, 1961 Merton, 1968) indicates that the social structure of the organization has a compelling effect on the "personality" factors associated with individual behavior; and might even go as far as subsuming the individual behavior under the social ribrics.

366

Kanter (1977) studied a large company she ficti-
tiously called INDSCO (Industrial Supply Corporation)
and, among other considerations, paid a great deal of
attention to the role of wives of corporate managers
and executives. A number of generalizations from her
study may be extracted.

1. Although they were important role-players,
   wives were almost never seen on company
   premises. They were never paid, officially
   recognized, never included in any formal
   way in the organization.

2. Having a wife and a family was a good sign
   of stability on the part of a male
   executive.

3. Some corporate issues generated an interest
   in wives' opinion because of their impact
   on the husbands (executives). Pre-retire-
   ment career planning, moves and transfers
   were examples of topics wives were
   consulted about.

4. Wives knew the company's impact on the
   husband's time and energies was important
   to them; wives, too, are married to the
   company.

5. Wives felt the need to sacrifice personal
   goals for company goals (and husband's
   matched goals) as the husband went up the
   corporate ladder.

6. Career women in the corporation contrasted
   boldly with executives' wives in their
   attitudes and motivations, leading some
   executives to be uncomfortable with career
   women in the corporation and to try to
   see them in subordinate roles comparable
   to their wives' roles.

7. Corporations got two persons for the price
   of one, i.e., the wife "came along with" the
   husband, and her characteristics might
   weigh heavily in selecting men for important
   posts. Among women in the corporation,
   there was no comparable "corporation
   husband" role equivalent to the "corporate
   wife."

367

8. Corporate wives might be jealous of women working with their husband in the corporation. Rivalry between these two sets of women was common.

9. Wives were often as conflicted in their motivations to participate (or not) in their husband's corporate roles as the companies were in sponsoring (or not) such roles. Wives complained about limited, peripheral roles (be good hostesses, socially active, supportive of husband's work) yet avoided opportunities to be more involved with husbands' work. Company attitudes were similarly divided.

10. The wife's role has been described, in part, as a product of "groupmindedness" observed by Whyte in several articles (1951a; 1951b; 1952; 1956). This predeliction, again, emphasized women taking traditional female roles, being subordinate and supportive, going and coming under husband's and the organization's commands, being the victim of a highly demanding system, with few instigations to develop herself on her own terms. The wife, then, becomes a "...high class assistant, bound by marriage rather than salary but otherwise facilitating the work goals with the same sense of efficiency the husband would expect of his secretary and other office personnel" (Kanter, 1977, p.110). Kanter observes further that corporate wives have been engulfed in a greedy company tending to absorb both the husband's and the wife's lives, both submitting to the organization's goals.

11. Women in corporations experience a kind of "career progression" according to Kanter (1977, pp.112-113); in that three phases are identified: A technical phase which finds the wife engaged in supporting the husband's pre-management technical work, qualifying him in time for executive or managerial posts. A managerial phase follows where managerial duties are available through promotion for the husband, and the wife takes on social tasks and fits more visibly into the social network of the

368

corporation. A final--third--phase, called the institutional phase, pivots for the wife around the husband's top-of-the-organization assignment. Trust, loyalty, fitting-in all give meaning to the wife's role and also to the husband's role at this level; further, the wife becomes an official hostess, a public relations professional, a link to the outside world, and one sensitive to the social network within the corporation. This progression results in an intricate web of responsibility that captures the wife and holds her hostage, so to say, to the husband's role and to corporate aims.

12. A sort of "social professionalism" sets in for the wife when the husband hits middle management jobs; that is, friendships and socializing are no longer based on the wife's personal inclinations, but, again, subserve the corporation. "Appropriateness" of friendships and socializing loom large.

13. Many social rules are to be followed by wives as soon as the husband advances in rank: Wait for "superiors" in the corporation to invite you first for a social gathering; do not discuss jobs or the corporation with other wives; never get drunk at a party, nor show up at the office unexpectedly; blend in, be inconspicuous; avoid association with wives of other managers who could be by-passed by your spouse; and so on.

14. With all, the wife is an informal clue to the personality and character of the husband. Being liked, projecting the right image, yet demuring are all important traits for the wife to exhibit. Ability and technical competence become subordinate to social considerations (see, also, Wright's book on De Lorean's experience with General Motors to get more details of this point: Wright, 1979).

15. Not only do women fare less well than men, both men and women in Kanter's study (1977, pp. 197-198) prefer men supervisors, feel women should not be competitive, and feel

feminism precludes women taking a supervisory role. An earlier study by Bowman, et al (Bowman, Worthy & Greyser, 1965) found that among 1,000 men and 900 female executives, two-thirds of the men and about one-fifth of the women registered discomfort with having a female boss. This disparity in viewing men and women in executive roles by both sexes who are already executives further hardens the differences between women in subordinate corporate roles (as wives) and those in career roles in corporations.

The Changing Roles of Women

Vandervelde (1979) looked at the changing role of women in corporations. She finds, as have other students of the corporation, that women have been shaped unmistakably by the forces in her family life (deriving from the husband's job) and from the highly rigid structure of the corporation. Vandervelde surveyed the Fortune 500 CEO (Chief Executive Officer) and their wives and found, among other things, the following: The woman's identity was the least important characteristic of the corporate wife, being at the bottom of a suggested list of 22 "ideal" traits for the corporate wife to show. This finding is, of course, expected as only recently has any concern emerged among corporate wives attesting to their identity. Lacking identity, too, makes one more vulnerable to emotional problems, is often associated with excessive drinking, and with other behaviors that disallow one being poised socially and personally secure and confident (Bowman et al, 1965).

Interestingly enough, a sense of humor was judged by the Fortune population of CEOs and their wives to be the most important quality of the wife. Humor seems to depend upon composure, confidence, the capacity to see things differently, and thus would be predicated on self-assurance and maturity. Adaptability and graciousness (to be expected) were also valued highly as corporate wife traits. Although in the Vandervelde study intelligence was important, independence was ranked low; again, such traits as identity, separateness, doing one's own thing, and independence (meaning not subordinate to the corporate goals) are inimical to the "good corporate wife."

370

Vandervelde found that attitudes toward corporate wives have not changed in recent years to any great extent. How can this be juxtaposed along side of changes in womens' roles generally? Does it mean that the corporate world is still a world apart insofar as human equality is concerned? Perhaps so. Yet, among the younger corporate wives (Vandervelde, 1979, pp. 18-24) things are changing to the extent that the wife is developing her own career in spite of the fact that men executives have not done an about-face regarding their attitudes toward women, in or out of the corporation. Corporations having to accept the overwhelming fact of increased divorce rates (especially among those married 20 years or longer), some increase in women with careers, and women generally proving themselves as competent as men, all impinge on the corporate eye.

Vandervelde stresses the "one-down" position of wives in the corporate structure and rightly observes how important this position has been to the husbands and to the corporation. However, she overlooks the fact that the regimentation in the corporate world regarding wives' roles has been matched among the clergy. She observes, perhaps wrongly, then: "In no occupation except the corporate world is the wife's involvement so imperative, so prescribed, so regimented, and so demanded" (Vandervelde, 1979, p.25). One could argue persuasively that the nurse in the hospital or in the physician's office--while not in a marital role--is also imperatively in a one-down position vis a vis the physician, and even in relation to hospital management (see Chapter III). Being a "team member" has not implied any professional equality of status; there always have to be the "side-kicks," the subordinates, even the slaves, who carry out in a taken-for-granted way the more mundane, supportive and less cherished roles required by the "chief" (Whyte, 1951a, 1951b, 1952, 1956).

The expectation of upper mobility in corporations also sets up problems. As in society at large, mobility implies change, moving to new locales, stress from knowing (or not knowing) that something more will be expected of one, stress from expecting too much from mobility followed by disappointment and depression. Change breeds problems despite the fact that it may also prompt self-development and the greater exercise of talents. If movement is stressed, competition increases; a condition opposite to stability, peer

acceptance and group solidarity develops. It is from
this state of tension that psychological, health,
family and social problems are found to be rampant
in the lives of executives.

Reactions To Stress

Characteristics of stress and the resultant
tensions and anxieties found among executives are
similar to other professions. Given stress and
resultant tensions and long-range anxieties, there are
but few reactions people may show: Type A behavior,
hypertension, job dissatisfaction, family problems,
various health problems, attitudes that separate the
executive from others, and often depression and social
isolation. Hershey (1974) suggests ways of identifying
early the functioning, but disturbed, executive. And
Ginsburg (1974) has considered the many problems of
the "burned out" executive. Both of these authors are
seeking means of reducing the vulnerabilities of
executives, looking not only at the behavior of the
executive himself but the setting in which the disturbances appear. Hershey says that executives are so
preoccupied with their functioning and their own
efficiency, they overlook the human reasons why
programs fail, why they fail at various efforts. Some
general reasons why executives fail to function well
spring from a variety of sources: problem employees
(alcoholic employees, poorly placed employees, and
those emotionally disturbed) that harrass the
executive; inadequate work place for subordinates
giving rise to complaining, irritaability and disgrun-
tlement, mostly directed at the chief executive
officer; mental health problems among employees leading
to exaggerated role conflicts and supervisory problems.
In turn, the executive's behavior worsens--or perhaps
lessens--the above-cited problems, but whatever the
outcome, the stress is on the executive to produce
results. Since most executives are not as strongly
humanely oriented as they might be, they are more
irritated at interpersonal problems and wish to concentrate only on executive roles that have little to
do with human behavior (except that which is ordered
well and progressing according to plan). They are
impatient with and give short shrift to programs such
as testing and assessment of employees, training,
safety, human relations, and can, due to their own
disturbances and disinterest, distort, misinterpret,
or unwittingly sabotage efforts to make the organization more humane. Antidotes to the remedies for the

372

influences of disturbed executive officers are not easy
to come by. Peer ratings are often distorted will-
fully by executives who obligingly trade-off favorable
ratings of each other; subordinates can usually be
relied upon to give more objective ratings of executives' functioning, but their perspective is often
narrow and fragmentary. Outside consultants can often
do the best job, but, of course, they cost money and
take time.

Those malfunctioning executives who are not
identified early and given remedial help may drone on
and on, only to become the "burned-out" executive in
time (Ginsburg, 1974). As Ginsburg says, "It's a long,
hard climb to the top for most executives and once
there, although it may seem as though they have it
made, the tensions and the pressures to prove themselves can dull the will to excel and stifle ambition
--results: Burned Out executives to whom the job is
no longer a challenge" (Ginsburg, 1974, p.598). It is
the high achiever who is most vulnerable to burn out--
stepping over or rolling over others as he does
(Freudenberger, 1980). Competition and unrelenting
effort "pay off" in time and result in the exhiliration
of power and high office glories. But the vulnerabilities are still there; if the executives don't burn
out they may be overcome by equally talented and
ambitious competitors. "The climb to the top has been
so tough, tension filled and debilitating, that the
base has been firmly laid for a good case of being
Burned Out" (Ginsburg, 1974, p.599). Executives are
admonished to develop antidotes to burn-out: Non-
working vacations, development of hobbies and other
outisde interests, community involvement, changing the
pace of work, having regular medical check-ups,
providing for moments of solitude, and trying new
areas of endeavor. Organizations can help the cause
of preventing executive burn-out by providing for a
change-of-pace for executives, allowing more short
vacations, hiring organizational psychologists who
conduct seminars and group discussions appropriate to
executive needs, and allowing for extra time off,
special leave periods, travel, and the like. The
burned-out executive is not the product solely of his
own psychology; the organizational setting is highly
responsible for the antecedent conditions leading to
burn-out and equally responsible for remedial measures.
If the organization fails to take a positive, problem-
solving attitude toward executive burn-out, it worsens

373

the problem and hastens the day when it--the organiza-
tion--will, itself, suffer ill effects from executive
burn-out.

Positive Stress

Although stress may often be oppressive, milder
amounts of stress and crisis from stress may be a
boon to some leaders (Burke, 1976). This author
studied the relationship between 14 stressors on the
job and 12 sources of satisfaction, among 228 male
executives who were professional engineers or
accountants in large business settings. Burke found
that more stress produced lesser job satisfaction.
Stresses that tended to produce satisfaction instead
of dissatisfaction were those connected with enlarged
job demands and challenges. One possible implication
of this study, although possibly limited to accountants
and engineers, who have very specific technological
skills to employ on the job, is that stress might be
increased in small steps, monitored carefully, and be
related to enrichment of the job rather than simply
added-on administrative duties.

Stewart (1976) found the manager's job to be
characterized by three dimensions: demands,
constraints, and choices. These might, of course,
apply to non-executive positions as well. Stewart
studied 450 jobs at management levels in business and
industry, through interviews and questionnaires. Jobs
that required innovations, sustained application,
adjustment to intermittent schedules, and so forth
were found to produce different patterns of demands,
constraints and choices. Managers might do well to
investigate their jobs on the basis of these criteria
to see if the tasks could be broken down so as to
reduce stress, and to see if the tasks would yield to
better regulation over time. Many managers act as if
each problem or even temporary stress were a crisis
and thus mount unnecessary tensions and anxieties in
the coping process.

Following from Stewart's findings, Rogers' (1977)
study of 113 upper-middle, male, Canadian managers
showed that work load was the main precursor of tension
Organizational structure and design of the organization
also precipated stress in that these factors could be
inhibitors to work, to completing jobs, and to effective interpersonal relations. Stress was a general

and pervasive factor in mid-management, unrelated to age, level of education of the manager or the type of industry in which he worked.

One possibly significant negative outcome of excessive work load is that the person tends to lose his identity and sense of well-being and order when stressed. As we pay more and more attention to the psychological nature of work (as distinct from making money or performing skills, although these will always be of some importance), we focus attention on the worker as much as on the job (Yankelovich, 1978). One problem that executives experience is that the more they progress on the job, the more they regress psychologically. That is, the negative psychological aspects (stress, tension and anxiety) supercede the importance of skills, absorption in the job, ability to find meaning in the work, and good social relationships in the job context (Royles, 1980; Tyler, 1980). We know more about what handicaps and kills executives than we do about how to actually prevent these monsters from creeping up on the executive.

Not only is stress found in specific managerial and executive settings in business and industry in the current lives of men (and women) in these positions, the problem has generally loomed so large in recent years that vocational counselors are looking back on data from adolescent studies as predictors of satisfactory reactions to subsequent positions involving stress. Heath (1976) used a vocational adaptation scale (VAS) based on 28 occupational demands, and related ratings of these demands to the personality needs of the managerial participants. Items most importantly related to personal needs were the following: doing the type of work for which one is most suited; having the job able to satisfy one's strongest personal needs; fitting the job to one's life style outside the job setting; the availability of personal involvement in the work; availability for personal growth; fulfilling self in one's work; and work being central to one's self-concept. While these items overlap a good deal, and are also derived from one's own need-fulfillment efforts (not exclusive properties of the job), they signal the personal values and satisfactions as being uppermost in job satisfactions. Although technical skills are central in professional executive level work, many of the skills are readily learned and have then to be practiced in a context that offers personal and social satisfaction;

otherwise the job tensions will loom larger and eventually discourage the executive in one or more of several ways. The tie-in between adolescence and late adult level vocational functioning came into focus through an emphasis on maturity; emotional maturity at adolescence or a decade later consistently predicted vocational adaptation and adjustment among sixty-eight professional and managerial males in the study. One difficulty with such pencil-and-paper studies where people answer questionnaires and rate characteristics is that the items themselves are abstractions, not welded into the tensions of everyday functioning. Direct observations on executives in their daily exchange with others and with problems of the corporations may sometimes yield data different from studies based on generalities. The social context can create tensions of considerable magnitude, as this whole review indicates; thus if the social setting is so important in eventual tension provocation, it must be equally important in influencing how job characteristics intermingle with the personal characteristics of executives. Similar findings came from a study of 25 bank managers in India (Sen., 1976), where the personality characteristics of managers were found to be related to occupational characteristics. High in the motivational hierarchy of these managers were such traits as dominance, orderliness, achievement, deference, intraception and abasement. This study is consonant with numerous other findings, viz., that power (dominance) and achievement figure prominantly in the activities and motivations of executives and, indirectly, form the basis of much of the stress they experience as these attributes are pushed to the breaking point.

Pushing these attributes of power and achievement to the straining--or breaking--point among 10 executives was studied by Thomas, et al (1976) in an investigation of "corporate dropouts." This study was admittedly based on a non-random sample of executives who left their jobs mid-stream, but who did not return to school for retooling and/or redirection. All were mid-management or higher, ages 37 to 51. The authors were searching for ideas and hypotheses on the phenomena of drop-outs rather than testing hypotheses rigorously. While there have always been career changes extant, the phenomena of "drop-out" and "burn-out" appear to be related to the increase in stress in modern life and in corporations (and in other professions, as well, as we have demonstrated) of more

recent origin. The more we can find about the phenomena of drop-out the more we can move to counteract or
ameliorate it, as it appears to be on the increase.
The Thomas et al study found 5 of the 10 drop-outs to
be "their own drummer." They were more tender-minded
(as opposed to tough-minded or hard-nosed), more
humanitarian, and failed to fit the corporate executive
model close enough to give them the satisfactions they
needed. Several of the "own drummer" group gave as
reasons for dropping out: boredom with work, objecting
to the plethora of meetings and memos they had visited
upon them, and reporting they were tired of meeting
others' deadlines. Overall, the drop-out executives
stemmed from different backgrounds, had somewhat
different trajectories in their managerial progress,
and left their posts for a variety of reasons. The
drop-outs seemed not to have rejected societal values
or institutions, however. With studies of larger and
more representative numbers of cases of executive
drop-out, more secure generalizations may be arrived
at, the authors aver. Such information will prepare
executives for mid-life change and also provide for
improved selection of those who enter executive positions at the beginning of their careers (Thomas, 1975;
Heistad, 1971).

Sisson, et al (1977) studied the ratings of
various success factors in the lives and occupations
of executives from the top 100 industrial corporations
in America, executives from the 25 largest banks, 100
military officers ranked captain or higher, 100
academic deans from outstanding universities in all
50 states, and about 500 people from the general
professional population, nationally (physicians,
lawyers, dentists, teachers, college professors),
totalling 1,000, from which mailing they received a
30% return (300 questionnaires). Again, questionnaire
approaches to complex problems may net stereotyped or
pat responses, but interviews with hundreds of persons
so widely sampled over the U.S.A. are not possible.
Results, limited by the method and sampling used,
included: Intelligence and education were not rated
high as contributing to "success." One should remember,
however, that intelligence and education are prerequi-
sities for entry into all of the sampled populations,
and it would be difficult to assess such essential
variables among these highly homogeneous and selected
populations. Once the members are in the professions,
ambition was ranked highest among executives and
bankers (66% gave this the highest rating), persistence

377

ranked highest as a personal trait by college deans;
and military leaders also ranked ambition high (50%
gave it the priority rating), while the general population of teachers, lawyers, physicians, dentists, etc.
divided their composite ratings about equally among
ambition, concern for ethics, family concerns, and
persistence, as reasons for success in their respective
professions. Looming large by implication in this
study is the finding clinically reported by De Lorean
and other critics of the executive world and its
stress-producing characteristics--viz., that ability,
per se, is not a decisive factor in corporate (or
professional organization) success, but persistence,
doggedness, being at the right place at the right time
in the organization, currying favor with superiors,
being a "yes" man (this group of reasons together
representing a composite of "ambition"), being a
"team man", and hanging-in-there and not-rocking-the-
boat, all add up to greater importance in determining
success. The obvious stress-producing characteristics in high-level jobs, found in this rather general
study, and others, are that the higher reaches of the
executive ladder depend upon personal characteristics,
highly selected and finely chosen. These high positions
favor non-technical knowledge, fail to place intelligence at a premium (except as an initial selection
factor), and show that success "up there" ultimately
hinges on personal-social relationships that make a
person subservient to the corporate aims. This is
not a flattering picture of the use of human talents
and abilities. It is a depressing picture of the use
of superficial social and personality characteristics
(although sometimes substantial and important
personality characteristics are valued) that teach
one to subordinate higher goals and abilities to the
shaping and modeling examples offered by the corporation. Thomas (1975) made the latter observation when
one of his interviewees in a study of mid-life career
change said, "Look, everyone from the elevator operator
to the president of the company thinks about quitting
and going off on his own" (Thomas, 1975, p.37). If it
is truly common that executives in highly stressed
circumstances are continually thinking about dropping
out and covertly visualizing a better life, yet at
the same time kow-towing to corporate demands that put
a premium only on being a "team man" in the sense
discussed by Thomas, De Lorean and many others, how
superficial their lives must be! They silently believe
one thing yet daily live another set of values; this
is an ideal arrangement for producing stress.

Possibly potentially adding to the tensions besetting the corporate executive is the theme found in some vocational and career education that says indoctrination for the higher levels of business and corporate life have to prepare individuals more for the pressure-to-succeed. Sisson, et al (1977, p.197) observe that "In today's world there is an ever-increasing pressure for young people to succeed and to be highly achievement oriented." With this kind of motivational impact on youth, the selection for managerial jobs and the ultimate arrival at high level executive jobs cannot help but be based on an accumulation of ambition, stress, and anxiety. We're getting what we ask for!

Singer (1976) studied beliefs and human value systems among 100 executives over a ten-year span. An early report on the study indicates that the most successful leaders exhibited more social consciousness and followed values earlier incorporated in their careers. Less successful executives showed motivational ambivalence and expressed occupational dissatisfaction; they looked back on their careers differently from the successful executives. The most successful leaders valued power and economics over other considerations (intellectual, social, aesthetic and spiritual values). The most successful executives earned, in the 1960's, 3-4 times as much per year as the unsuccessful executives, thus measuring "success" in this study largely in terms of power and economic considerations. There is no doubt but what successful executives--rated in terms of climbing high on the corporate ladder, earning large sums of money and exerting power over many people--are distinct in their motivation, sometimes in their histories, and in attitudes toward their jobs. We have seen that abundantly in this review. What is not as often documented and what is sorely in need of much more research by the people who select, nurture, and reinforce executive talent is the price executives pay for their success in terms of health, family and personal stability, and the cost to the broad range of human values not highly visible in the corporate world (Miller, 1976; Kaagen, 1978; Rumme & Rader, 1978).

Health patterns in relationship to Type A behavior in a managerial population was studied by Howard, et al (1976). Characteristic of Type A behavior are a number of stress related tendencies: an attitude of struggling chronically and excessively, being

379

competitive, being highly ambitious, and displaying
impatience. These characteristics are often assayed
in interview situations where the interviewee answers
a large number of questions about him/her self from
which are abstracted these tendencies making up Type
A behavior. People displaying this behavior are prone
to coronary heart disease (Rosenman & Friedman, 1971).
Among 236 managers, studied over a three-year span,
Howard et al found 61 percent classifiable as Type A
persons. Students of Type A behavior have suspected
that this syndrome has increased over the past two
decades and shows no sign of letting up. In this
managerial population, the authors found Type A
behavior clearly related to cardiovascular symptoms,
to emotional distress, to insomnia, to Gastrointestinal
distress and to diabetes. Among Type A executives in
the study, Systolic and Diastolic blood pressure
ratings were higher than for non-Type A persons, as
were cholesteral and triglyceride readings. A higher
percentage of Type A managers smoked a larger number
of cigarettes daily; Type A managers also exercised
less than non-Type As. Perhaps people with these
behavioral tendencies, given a certain educational and
intellectual background, gravitate toward executive
and managerial positions; in turn these Type A
behavioral tendencies push the fledging executive ahead
and also tend to exacerbate the stress-related
behaviors, resulting in time, in persons who fit the
findings revealed in the Howard et al study. Summing
up all the findings in this study the authors found:
"...our Type A's to have about a 50 percent greater
risk" (than non-Type A persons for developing coronary
heart disease) (Howard et al, 1976, p.31).

Combating Stress

Recognizing industry's involvement in the health
of its executives, Cathcart (1977) studied 22 high
level executives over a period of four years. The men
studied were given annual health examinations and
"risk hazard appraisal" which were based on an assessment of their life-style habits. Cathcart saw his
executive population as mostly Type A persons, people
with intense ambition, competitive drive, a sense of
urgency and a tendency to face deadlines, real or
imagined. The executives enjoyed the "good life" owing
to their favored economic position; fourteen were
moderately to excessively overweight, the leanest being
the physically most active. Hypertension and cigarette
smoking combined to create the greatest health hazards

among this group, slanting them toward cardiovascular
disease. The most illness prone members had hypertension, were obese, exercised very little, smoked,
and presented a family history of heart disease. In
the industrial setting, these executives were encouraged
to engage in health and fitness programs to which both
the individuals and the industry responded.

The chief executive officer of the United States
is, of course, the President. If executive positions
in business and industry are consumed with stress,
how about the presidency? It is common knowledge
that presidents leave office looking much older than
their years or, by implication, older than they would
have looked had they been employed under less stressful conditions. Moses and Cross (1980) discussed
this problem in Presidential Courage and think that
our presidents may not have had the best medical care
(not consulting the "best" medical advisors of their
times), have developed "unique" diseases associated
with the stresses of the presidency, and have shown
as a group such illnesses and ailments as cancer,
heart disease, liver disease, depression, nervous
breakdowns, and alcoholism. Part of the common lot,
the presidents! One important distinction between
presidents and CEOs from corporations is that the
president has no further climbing to do--no place to
go, except to succeed one's self in office--whereas
CEOs do have other options. The president usually
falls into relative oblivioun upon completing office
(if still living and healthy), and this sudden change
in life-style and ways of coping may be a jolt as
devastating as upwardly mobile changes among CEOs.

Studies such as those by Cathcart and Howard et
al and Moses and Cross raise, again, the question of
how much the individual characteristics of the
executives lead them to select a way of life, to an
intense involvement in work, and toward motivation to
move ever-upward in the organizational hierarchy; or
how much the system, qua system, selects, nurtures
and exacerbates these tendencies among individuals,
which tendencies may be minor at the start of an
executive's career. Likely both sets of tendencies
exist and one or the other may be stronger for given
individuals. But however the tendency toward
psychophysiological reactions to stress occur there
is not much difficulty in exacerbating these
tendencies; by the age of 50, sometimes sooner, we see

381

the pattern discussed by Howard et al and by Cathcart
emerging with some clarity. What research has not
told us to date is how many persons in executive roles
do not succumb to Type A behaviors, how many meet
stress with equanimity, how many do not suffer
psychosocial or psychophysiological untoward consequences. Further, we do not yet know how many lower
level managers, single enterprenures, minor executives
suffer from the same stress/tension/anxiety syndromes
characterizing top executives; perhaps the workings of
continually faced stress are about the same regardless
of whether the executive works for General Motors as
a top manager, has his own small business or engages
in a daily "rat-race" for economic survival as a minor
governmental employee. Kanter (1977, pp. 250-253)
argues persuasively for the influence of the organization on the individual in matter relating to interrelationships between the two. She adumbrates five
underlying assumptions in regard to this point: First,
"Jobs and the relations of people to them cannot be
understood without reference to the organized systems
in which the contemporary division of labor operates."
Second, behavior in organizations is an adaptive
process: "What people do, how they come to feel and
behave, reflects what they can make of their situation,
limited though it might be..." This second assumption
may pivot more on observable tasks and attitudes
extant in organizations, less on health histories or
stress that results in excessive eating, drinking,
smoking, and inactivity. Kanter's third assumption
regarding person-organization relationships notes the
flexibility between person-organization interrelationships, holding them not to be inevitable, but
recognizing that "...the person still has a degree
of latitude in deciding how to combine latent possibilities into action." Fourth in Kanter's list is the
observation that jobs have formal tasks and obligations
formal ties to other aspects of the organizational
structure, and that these ties and tasks determine to
a considerable degree--despite formal structures
existing under or parallel to the formal ones--the
clearest prediction of what people will do, how they
will behave, in the organization. Fifth, and last,
among Kanter's assumptions regarding the person-
organizational interface is the observation that
ability to do the job is of utmost importance, calling
it "...an emphasis on competence..." and that psychosocial analyses of organizational behavior fail to
sufficiently note this importance. However, Wright's
account of De Lorean's experience with General Motors

382

(Wright, 1979, p.40) seems to contradict Kanter in this respect: "A system which puts emphasis on form, style and unwavering support for the decisions of the boss; almost always loses its perspective about an executive's business competence...executives are graded not on how they perform as businessmen but on how they perform as system-men." De Lorean's account of his experiences at General Motors (Wright, 1979) may or may not be typical of other large businesses, but De Lorean finds the person-organization relationship so important that he devotes a whole chapter to it. In the following chapter, Wright has De Lorean writing on "How Moral Men Make Immoral Decisions", a chapter right to the point of person-organization interrelationships; in this espousal, the individual comes off looking badly, succumbing at every turn to ridiculous, costly, innane pressures from the corporate structure to behave in short-sighted ways, ways that eventually hurt the corporation itself (Wright, 1979, pp.49-72).

Getting Ahead

Young men and women join large organizations probably because they feel they can "get ahead" in the corporate structure more easily and faster than if they go-it-alone. Also seed money is extremely important in one starting his/her own business; better to latch onto an extant structure, many would say. If no promotions were possible, or if they were extremely long in coming, perhaps many fledging executives would not develop the psychosocial and psychophysiological problems so common among them. If corporations played up the humane aspects of their corporate life and functioning, then money and profit would not loom so large, and competition would abate, together with the stresses and strains it tends to create. If the Japanese system cited above, could be shown to produce fewer health problems, less social/family/personal disorganization, and less personal anomie among corporate executives then, perhaps, Americans should begin to modify their corporate purposes toward the Japanese model. Cross-cultural comparisons are always tenuous and drawing strong inferences from them may be unwarranted; however, the evidence in the Japanese system of corporate functioning is somewhat in the direction of more humane treatment of persons. We could use a little more of this in the United States, even if we modified it considerably to meet our own preferences and life styles.

The essence of this chapter or indeed the whole book points to the need for change in the professions if they are not to deteriorate more, disaffect further the health of their members and discredit their important roles in society. We can treat society as a total fabric or try to remove the spots here and there that represent the thread bare or tarnished appearance of the total social fabric. Or we can look upon society and the professions in bipolar terms, where it is apparent we cannot now live comfortably with or without the professions in society. Have we no alternatives to the professions and their problems with themselves and with society? We may want to add a third leg to the problem, converting the apparently limited bi-polar alternatives to another option wherein professions are explicitly required to serve society better, else their own roles and rewards are placed in jeopardy.

Meeting Societies Demands

Beginning with corporate power and the executive position, these entities may be required in the third-leg-of-the-stool model to meet society's demands before the entities themselves can gain their financial and other rewards. Their continued functioning would be made contingent on society's satisfaction as determined by representative bodies of ordinary citizens (as well as corporate members and chief executive officers) judging corporate performance. Levels of profit, use of the environment, contributions to various social problems and their responsible solution would be the subject matter of citizen-peer reviews of this type. Such a review process will replace the unilateral and arrogant ways now characteristic of corporate (ir)responsibility (Macrae, 1976). As these measures take hold, corporations will mature in time into good citizens and as a result receive their reinforcement therefrom and not from arrogant control of others for their own purposes.

Universities, too, could play a forceful role in socializing corporations. Most of the business executives in large corporations receive their degrees in business from a dozen leading undergraduate and a dozen graduate degree programs (Coughlin, 1980). It would not be difficult to introduce into the curriculum of business degree students (especially those heading for executive roles) topics that assign greater

384

importance to health, social responsibility, the impact on the community, and other issues salient in the lives of corporations and their chief executive officers and families. Touching the student's future home base in this way, bolstered by reviews of the literature, citing applications to various corporations in specific ways, would begin to influence the up-coming generation of CEOs into the why's and how's of health and social responsibility in the corporate world. Universities could be funded as research centers continuing to examine corporations not simply as money-making machines but as integral social forces playing constructive roles in the lives of individuals and communities. What a world of difference such attitudes, properly reinforced and realistically executed, could make! This kind of education-for-business-leadership would not only blunt the sharp edge of corporate knifing of society, but it would allow the university to stand more firmly on its own legs and reduce the likelihood that higher education and education for the professions would be taken over by big business (Biemiller, 1980; White, 1980; Biemiller and Coughlin, 1980).

As corporations mature in social responsibility, the health of the members will improve--it is asserted--since their values will have changed to accommodate broadly shared social objectives. In caring about and for others, one--including corporations (and the professions)--will gain in personal-social integrity and feel much better about themselves. Do we not already have evidence of the good effect on self and profession (at least until recently) in the professions of teaching and the clergy, and possibly with nursing? Doing well for one's self at a cost to others can only continue to promote a poor "self-concept" and poor health on the part of erring professions. What is true in individual lives--that selfishness breeds personal malcontentment and ethical impasses--applies to larger social aggregates as well.

In more scientifically defensible terms, we can say that the kinds of environments we permit and build greatly influence individual health and behavior. That is what this whole book is about. Models of society based on power, authority and rule-subservence breed a particular kind of society, one avaracious, money and profit oriented and one abrogating the rights of individuals at every turn (Katz & Kahn, 1978).

385

Wholly economic models of society.."economic man models"--also breed an avaraciousness. The two--power authority and unilateral role on the one hand, and economic and external rewards on the other hand--are twins, hardly separable. In such societies--name most of the Western world among them--professionalism is rife and individuals not part of the power elite, and the rest of society, suffer. What has not been fully recognized is that the professionals themselves are suffering, too, as this book amply illustrates. Societies valuing humanistic ends and self-integration and satisfaction take a broader view of mankind--this is what the professions started out to do and from which path they have lost their way (Shoup, 1979). The various industrial-medical, industrial-educational and other complexes (all dominated by the "industrial" viewpoint) are the apparent culprits in not only their own (coming?) demise (and that of the professions) but in their own present ill-health and social disorganization. If professions live a selfish and avaracious life they will not only visit attendant ills on others, they will--often subtly--visit the same untowardness on themselves. What kills or injures others will kill or injure them. Likewise, living more wholesomely-- socially and healthfully--will improve the lives of all professions and their members, as well as society at large.

CHAPTER XIII

BIBLIOGRAPHY

Argyris, C. Personality and Organization: The
    Conflict Between System And The Individual. N.Y.:
    Harper & Row, 1957.

Austin, C.F. Management's Self-Inflicted Wounds: A
    Formula For Managerial And Executive Self-Anaylsis.
    N.Y.: Holt, Rinehart & Winston, 1966.

Biemiller, L. The continuing scandal of college
    athletics; Business's dangerous presence on
    campuses, The Chronicle Of Higher Education,
    1980, 21, #6, p.23.

Biemiller, L. & Coughlin, E.K. The pains of teaching
    doctors how to teach: a'meanness mania' among
    the middle class, The Chronicle of Higher Educa-
    tion, 1980, 21, #7, p.25.

Bowman, G.W., Worthy, N.B., & Breyser, S.A. Are
    women executives people? Harvard Business Review,
    1965, 43, 14-30.

Burger, C. Walking The Executive Plank: Why Manage-
    ment Firgins Happen--and How To Reduce Them.
    N.Y.: Van Hostrand Reinhold Co., 1972.

Burke, R.J. Occupational stress and job satisfaction,
    J. of Soc. Psychol., 1976, 100,235-244.

Cathcart, L.M. A four year study of executive health
    risk, J. of Occup. Medicine, 1977, 19, 354-357.

Coughlin, E.K. I.R.S. ruling is seen threatening
    supplies of many scholarly and professional books,
    The Chronicle Of Higher Education, 1980, 21, #6,
    p.1.

Crittenden, A. The new critics of big farming, N.Y.
    TIMES, 1980, Oct. 19, p.1.

Editors of FORTUNE Magazine, The Executive Life. Garden
    City, N.Y.: Doubleday, 1956.

Freudenberger, H.J. Burn-Out. New York: Anchor Press,
    1980.

Ginsburg, S.G. The problem of the burned-out executive, Personnel Journal, 1974, 54, 598-600.

Hage, J. Communication and Organizational Control: Cybernetics In Health And Welfare Settings. N.Y.: Wiley, 1974.

Heath, D.H. Adolescent and adult predictors of vocational adaptation, J. of Vocational Behavior, 1976, 9, 1-19.

Heistad, D.E. Changing Careers at Thirty-Five. N.Y.: Columbia Univ. Press, 1971.

Hershey, R. Identifying the functioning disturbed executive, Personnel Journal, 1974, 53, 349-352.

Howard, J.J., Cunningham, D.A., & Rechnitzer, P.A. Health patterns associated with Type A behavior: A Managerial Population, J. of Human Stress, 1976, Mar. 1976.

Jennings, E.E. Executive Success: Stresses, Problems, and Adjustment. N.Y.: Appleton-Century-Crofts, 1967.

Kaagen, S.S. Terminating people from key positions: Philosophical, ethical and humane considerations, Personnel J., 1978, 58, 96-98.

Kanter, R.M. Men And Women Of The Corporation. N.Y.: Basic Books, 1977.

Katz, D. & Kahn, R.L. The Social Psychology of Organizations. N.Y.: Wiley, 1966.

Katz, D. & Kahn, R.L. The Social Psychology of Organizations. 2nd Edit. N.Y.: Wiley, 1978.

Merton, R.K. Bureaucratic structure and personality, in Etzioni, A., Complex Organizations: A Sociological Reader. N.Y.: Holt, Rinehart, 1961.

Merton, R.K. Social Theory And Social Structure. N.Y.: Free Press, 1968.

Miller, N. Career choice, job satisfaction, and the truth behind the Peter Principle, Personnel, 1976, 53, 58-65.

Moses, J.B. & Cross, W. Presidential Courage. N.Y.: Norton, 1980.

Nader, R. Unsafe At Any Speed. N.Y.: Grossman, 1972.

Redlich, F.C. & Hollingshead, A.B. Social Class and Mental Illness. N.Y.: Wiley, 1958.

Rogers, R.E. Components of organizational stress among Canadian managers, J. of Psychol., 1977, 95, 265-273.

Roseman, R.H. & Friedman, M. Observation on the pathogenesis of coronary heart disease, Nutr. News, 1971, 34, 9-14.

Rummel, R.M. & Rader, J. W. Coping with executive stress, Personnel J., 1978, 57, 305-307.

Saunders, D. The Boss' Paycheck: Who Gets The Biggest? Forbes, 1978, 86-111.

Sen, A. A study on the personality make-up and off-the-job activities in a group of executives, Indian J. of Appl. Psychol., 1976, 13, 42-46.

Shoup, L.H. Power and Politics In The 1980's. Palo Alto, California: Ramparts Press, 1979.

Singer, J.A. Human values and leadership: A ten-year study of administrators in large organizations, Human Organiz., 1976, 35, 83-86.

Sisson, P.J., Arthur, G.L., Fierro, S.V., & Gazda, G. Success variables in outstanding business and industrial leaders in America: A national survey, Vocat. Guid. Quart., 1977, 26, 197-205.

Spero, R. The Duping of the American Voter: Dishonesty and Deception In Presidential Television Advertising. N.Y.: Lippincott & Crowell, 1980.

Stewart, R. To understand the manager's job: Consider demands, constraints, choices, Organizational Dynamics, 1976, 4, 22-32.

Terkel, S. Working. N.Y.: Pantheon, 1974.

Thomas, L.E. Why study mid-life career change? Vocat. Guid. Quart., 1975, 24, 37-40.

389

Thomas, L.E., Mela, R.L., Robbins, P.I., & Harvey, D.W.
    Corporate drop-outs: A preliminary typology,
    Vocat. Guid. Quart., 1976, 24, 220-228.

Tyler, P.E. National Bank of Washington: A financial
    citadel in hot water: Conflicts of interest
    become a way of life, Washington POST, 1980,
    Oct. 12, p.1.

Uris, A. The Frustrated Titan: Emasculation Of The
    Executive. N.Y.: Van Nostrand Reinhold Co., 1972.

Vandervelde, M. The Changing Life Of The Corporate
    Wife. N.Y.: Mecos Publ. Co., 1979.

White, E.M. How (perhaps) to keep students satisfied,
    The Chronicle Of Higher Education, 1980, 21,
    #7, p.29.

White, T.H. The Making Of The Presidency, 1968. N.Y.:
    Athenium, 1979.

White, T.H. The Making Of The Presidency, 1972. N.Y.:
    Athenium, 1973.

Whyte, W.H., Jr. The wives of management, Fortune
    Magazine, Oct. 1951a.

Whyte, W.H., Jr. The Corporation and the Wife, Fortune
    Magazine, N., 1951b.

Whyte, W.H., Jr. The wife problem, Life Magazine,
    Jan. 7, 1952 (pp.32-48).

Whyte, W.H., Jr. How hard to executives work? In The
    Executive Life. Garden City, N.Y.: Doubleday,
    1956.

Wright, J.P. On A Clear Day You Can See General
    Motors: John Z. De Lorean's Look Inside The
    Automotive Giant. Grosse Pointe, Michigan:
    Wright Enterprises, 1979.

Yandelovitch, D. The new psychological contracts at
    work, Psychology Today, 1978, May, 46 - 50.

Yoyko, M. Meet Mr. Davis, but don't speak, Washington
    POST, 1980, Oct. 10, p.2.

WHERE IS IT ALL GOING?

Everywhere there is criticism--resounding, pointed, searching and valid criticism--of our society. Not only are the professions under fire as this book amply demonstrates, but the larger society that makes and shapes professions is often held in contempt. Professions could not present the problems they do--for their members, for the professions as organizations, and in relation to society--if there were not larger issues to consider. The professions reflect the society of which they are part.

Books are appearing at an increasing rate that call our values into serious question. Time magazine, surely a product of the aggressiveness and dominance of big business in American, asks if capitalism is working. The newspapers and magazines of the nation are replete each week, if not more often, with horror stories of how people in power take advantage of those in lesser positions, be they examples from business, from the professions, or from government.

What is going wrong in society that affects us all, but particularly those not in power, is that we are losing our connections to society, to the social fabric. This affects our purchasing of goods and services, especially those goods and services that we need to sustain life: food, clothing, shelter, education, medical care, but also others. The availability and delivery of goods and services are part of what we call a consumer (or consuming) society (Douglas, 1979). But this consumption is not alone a matter of utility, it is also a matter of social processes. It is often this interconnectedness, this social interrelationship that is affected by an aggressive and avaracious society, one that takes consumerism so seriously that it destroys the basis on which consumption might normally exist. The emphasis is put on profit, selfish gain, and neglects the role that social factors play in consumption. The emphasis is so strong that even economists emphasize it out of proportion-- according to Douglas--and thus we have economists talking about rational purchases, making rational appeals, and so on. She says: "To name one more familiar grief with economic theorizing: the idea of the rational individual is an impossible abstraction from social life. It is clearly absurd to aggregate millions of individuals buying and using goods without reckoning with the transformation they affect by sharing consumption together" (Douglas, 1979, p.5). An interesting contrast to the supposed rationality of economists as they punch and probe into the market place, into production and distribution, and into profits, is the fact that advertising is mostly an irrational process. Our society, then, uses an irrational process to bring about changes in which is fundamentally assumed to be (alleged to be) a rational process.

Goods (and services, to an extent) are part of a live information system, according to Douglas' viewpoint. Poverty is hamstringing not alone by lack of possessions but due to estrangement within the social network. People are powerless not only because they have no money, but they have no (social) influence and/or involvement. Is this why we need lawyers so desperately?

People want goods because of their social value. A person buys a hoe because he needs it for his garden and the garden, in turn, is a socially approved of, economical and need-satisfying matter ("John grows the best tomaties in the countryside:). Savings, similarly, are referrable to the social context, not just a matter of how much one earns, or a function of increase in income producing a proportional increase in savings; provident use of money in one context may be improvident in another.

How economics has taken over morals and social values--or vice versa--is seen in Weber's study of the Protestant Ethic and Capitalism (Weber, 1958) in which he pointed out that an early Catholic morality disapproved of private accumulation followed by a later Protestant one that approved of the accumulation of possessions. The point here is not which moralist is correct or which religion is, but how social values determine other matters and how the economics changes as the social values are altered. There is, of course, an intertwining and the exact origin of change via economics, per se, or moral/social values per se, is moot; but the social context, of which economics is part, is compelling. Once a system is set in motion, economic considerations become powerful determiners of behavior, but behind the economics are the social values which the economic factors exhibit, reinforce,

392

or magnify. If in corporate structures, living in a given part of the city or driving certain makes of cars are socially approved of--not to mention stripped suits, ties and shirts--then the social context is saying a lot about economic behavior, and economics, in turn, is saying to the observer that such-and-such a person lives under a highly selected set of social circumstances. As Douglas said, "Pick up the thread of economics, social behavior, religious/moral belief' anywhere and follow it around--it will lead back to the same place" (Douglas, 1979,p.28).

Economic Power And Assets

Having economic power implies the accumulation of assets. In the Middle Ages the church was the dominant power, but after the industrial revolution, what we now call corporations began to acquire this power through property ownership and through ownership and control of the means of production. Part of the power of corporations and organizations--and of professions as they acquire the characteristics and ploys of corporations--is not only to acquire these assets but to continue to hold them, as if they were endowed-- unlike the individuals making up the corporations--with eternal life, in perpetuity as the legal expression has it.

Somewhat analogous to the exposition offered by Max Weber regarding the changes in attitudes toward economics (and the acquisition of property) found in Catholicism and Protestantism, we see a possible parallel change now going on in the economic structure with regard to corporations and organizations and with regard to professions. Corporations and professions are social units, related integrally to society by providing for social needs (broadly defined, as well as strictly economic needs), but as the integrity of the corporation (or profession) is more sturdily structured, as it becomes more articulated, it deve- lops its own reasons for being--social, interpersonal, reasons based on skills, on an esoteric language, and on many avenues leading to the acquisition of power-- and increasingly sees its own interests coming first, over the interests of society. Put another way the social interrelationships between members of a profes- sion--choose medicine and the law as prime examples-- take on a greater importance than the social (and professional) relationships between each profession and society in general. In fact the compulsion; if

393

we may call it that, within a profession to dominate
and limit the activities of professional members is
so great that the individual is caught up in the
system before he/she knows it; identification with
the profession having once taken place, mostly without
articulate recognition of same, the individual is so
thoroughly a member of the group (profession, corporation) that one's own thinking, feeling, valuating,
and so on are largely capitulated.

Douglas' discussion of why people save, as part
of her discussion of why economics must be understood
more in social theory terms, comes on to the point of
group pressures on the individual: "The group
imposes group values and so prevents deviant individual
[behavior...defining] what counts..." and "As part
of the process of strengthening its hold on individual
members, the group makes levies on their time and
income" (Douglas, 1979, p.37). These strictures may
apply very well to the behavior of organizations,
corporations, and professions. One difficulty, of
course, is that the acquisitiveness of professions
allows the stricter rules by which professions are
purportedly guided to be relinquished, hence the
individual often has more to say about what is
appropriate ethical and professional behavior (in the
interest of profit) than does the profession. We have
seen in the discussion above--especially in regard to
medicine, dentistry, executives in corporations, and
lawyers--that the individual members often take
liberties that not only defy their own professional
standards (mute as they may often be), but fly directly
in the face of society, social interest and fairness,
and set up a reaction on the part of society against
both the individual members and against the profession.
This is where the matter of ethics enters so glaringly,
about which there is so much concern today in
relation to professions and their responsibilities vis
a vis society. We can truthfully and confidently say
that not only are the major professions unhealthy in
a medical sense, they are equally unhealthy in an
ethical sense. If health is a matter of "living right"
and caring for one's body and one's psychological
make-up, then ethics is a matter of living right and
caring for one's social responsibilities. The individual acting unhealthfully in a medical sense, or
unethically, is making decisions and taking actions
much the same as that suggested by Douglas in her
discussion of consumption and utility theory in

economics. "It seems extraordinary, but it is an outcome of the way that traditional utility theory has been used, that the consuming unit acts as if its decisions to spend on this or that were made in isolation and independently from those of all other consumers" (Douglas, 1979, pp.43-44). Translate this passage from strict economics-utility theory to professional behavior that is advanced in isolation and taken independently of others' considerations. Utility theory in economics may be one bulwark of support the current professional has in mind when he/she takes in hand the decisions to act in unilateral, unhealthful and unethical ways. The obtuseness with which businesses make decisions pursuant to profit are but other examples of utility theory gone wild. These decisions are often taken at the expense of society, but also they boomerang at the expense of the unilaterally acting business (or profession). If this boomeranging effect were not the case, there would not have accumulated over recent decades the enormous health problems facing professionals, and the considerable ethical problems facing professionals and corporate people noted in these pages.

Not only are some of the allegedly basic tenets of economic theory to be held in question, ways in which all of capitalism may be looked askance at are also with us (Peterson, 1979; TIME Magazine, 1980; Wright, 1979). One question that arises repeatedly is whether we have a free and competitive market, or whether the power centers controlling steel, autos, soft drinks, the building trades, and many, many others are simply averaciously hogging the markets in ways that prevent competition and innovation. Spiraling inflation, increasing unemployment, crises in one industry after another all portend poorly for the whole economy, regardless of how these forces have been let loose. Along with these signs of unrest the annual output of goods has decreased, whereas previously the trend was a 2.5-3.0 percent yearly increase. All of these bad signs are not in America alone; the economic sufferings plaguing Europe as well and even the healthier economies of Japan and West Germany. Remedies are a dime a dozen: slower growth, no strikes for wages in one industry that puts a hardship on other industries, less risk-taking, and so on. Remedies also call asking for governmental support; whereas capitalist have long despised governmental support for other aspects of our economy,

they are now asking for help: "The search for a fail-
safe society is also pursued by businessmen. Though
they still extol free enterprise's virtues in after-
dinner speeches, American capitalists can often be the
system's most dangerous opponents. Rather than
embracing the marketplace and competition, many
businessmen look longingly to those societies, notably
Japan, in which the government intervenes to sponsor,
subsidize or otherwise ease the way for business"
(TIME, 1980, p.42). Complicating all these factors is
the increasing disparity between the well-to-do and
the poor, between the "great society" changes of the
1960's (now defunct) and present opportunity, education,
and innovation; with everything--even the drudgeries
of life--more and more dependent upon money. How
much the whole mess is due to the acquisitiveness-
turned-avaraciousness theme is hard to say. Thinking
of all the "forces" in the economy studies by the
economist, then thinking of how much Douglas attributes
economic behavior to peoples' values and to the social
network, one quickly gains the impression that economists treat the economy like rainfall--there is
little or nothing they can do about it and human
involvement is not anywhere to be seen. The traditional Adam Smith economic position--from over 200
years ago--stressing the importance of treating the
individual in an unfettered way belies the point of
view that sees human behavior as socially determined
(whether behavior is seen in terms of economics,
sexual conduct, religious beliefs, or anything else).
Even if the economic theories held to over the past
two hundred years, with minor modifications, were
true, the apparent cumulative effect on the professions seem to be a deleterious one. How can economic
systems that are always in such hot water and that
breed so much malcontent and unhealthiness be valid?
In the face of so many problems, attempts to "improve
management" and to bend the individual more and more
to the organization, to the corporation, to the
profession are not far short of nonsense (Baldridge
& Tierney, 1979; Karman, 1968). Such efforts are
like those inveighed against in the Nader Report,
The Madness Establishment, by Chu and Trotter (1974),
who stress the importance of looking at the living and
working environments of people and the contributions
these conditions make to poor mental health, rather
than adding more psychiatrists, more mental health
facilities, more drugs, and more hospitals to our
armamentarium of "treatment facilities."

396

Mental Health Costs

Despite all these cautions about our economy, the precariousness of it all, and the unending maladies and costs in mental health terms, our press and our educational philosophies continue to stress the rush for the dollar. A good example is seen in the article, "The Fast Track To The Good Life" (Maeroff, 1980) in the Business and Finance section of the New York Times, May 18, 1980. Herein one encounters the glories of the M.B.A. in producing salaries in the high twenties and thirties (thousands of dollars per year), as starters, and the prospects for salaries above $40,000.00 per year in a few years. While these young MBA's do not intend to kow-tow fully to the corporate image (they may not stay a lifetime with their first corporation), they are nonetheless full joiners in the system that is now, and has been, the greatest contributor we can identify to the health, ethical and economic problems of our society.

An earlier chapter of this book documents how precarious is the job of the chief executive officer and the meat-grinder routine that characterizes most such jobs. Accordingly, Hayes (1980), documents the recent histories of the (now) two successors to Harold S. Geneen, former CEO of International Telephone and Telegraph Corporation, calling this job the "biggest meat-grinder job in corporate management." The first successor to Geneen, Lyman C. Hamilton, Jr., was dismissed after eighteen months on the job. The trajectory of I.T.T. under Mr. Geneen was a "success-ful" one, giving profits their due; but even this kind of accountability began to falter, casting some doubt on the value of the methods used and the value of unending growth. Basic to I.T.T.'s growth was a management policy, under Geneen, of agression and contention where conflict was promoted, not only tolerated. While such management tactics and policies belie those commonly associated with "scientific management,: and may be held accountable, in part, for the stress so often encountered in the corporate structure, there appears to be few lessons learned by business and management about these costs to organizations and to the people working in them.

Lauding further the drive-to-the-top, one reads about young men under forty who become chief executive officers of their companies (McDowell, 1980). Although

competition at middle management levels is great, and
the average CEO (among 3,600 senior-level executives
in the nation) is in his mid-fifties, some do ascent
much earlier. Many stand on their father's shoulders,
however, and walk into opportunities others would
struggle to attain. There is little wonder, then, that
motivation-for-profit-and-power is as prominent as it
is. The field of competition is getting larger and
more severe, with 50,000 MBA graduates expected in
1980, compared to about 6,000 in 1964. All of these
facts and trends build toward a psychology of power
and profit; the corporation is off and running and the
references to social consciousness are all but totally
missing.

    Some of the many ways in which large businesses
neglect their social responsibilities and take advan-
take of the consumer/citizen are documented in the
daily press. These are examples of the very power
that is so easily misused for selfish purposes (Zonana,
1980). Dow Chemical with a traditionally good reputation has recently faltered terribly in regard to
promoting and selling a polystyrene roofing insulation
(called "Roofmate"), that has repeatedly over a 12-15
year period developed roof cracks and leaks in houses
and buildings. The company even kept selling the
produce abroad after phasing it out of the U.S.
market. This practice is womewhat like taking safety
risks with products that can easily result in injury
or death to users; in this case, not only were the
ultimate consumers involved but so were builders,
roofers, contractors, and insurance companies. Errors,
or willful disregard for property, safety, and life,
can often ramify and hurt not only the little man
but other big businesses as well. Claims against Dow
Chemical, world wide, range close to 100 million
dollars, it is estimated; these are costs that do not
account for loss of reputation, personal inconvenience,
embarrassment and lack of confidence in American
businesses. The kind of thinking and the exhibit of
values that supports Dow's actions can be none other
than extreme profiteering and selfishness. What is
more important than the dollar?

    An interesting and sometimes even amusing approach
to harnessing and controlling corporate power on the
rampage is seen in attempts by then President Carter
to "jawbone" big business into one or another kind of
restraint. Pine (1980) reports on President Carter
"jawboning chemical executives", in a recent attempt to

convince 30 executives of the nation's largest chemical companies to hold down their price increases, even if lower profits were involved. The last phrase--even if lower profits were involved--underscores the crux of the matter. If being "good guys" just meant holding on to some constraints, that would be one think, but to sacrifice profits, that would be the holiest of denials. The psychology of the marketplace is well captured in the key words, "jawboning," "hold down prices," and "lower profits". There is not better testimony to the selfishness of big business than this simple interaction between the President and several CEOs.

Further testimony to the selfishness of large business is seen in two articles in the Washington POST by Mintz (1980a; 1980b). As giant businesses grow, especially in the direction of "take-overs" or mergers, many smaller people are affected in the wake of such moves. Action to prevent the take-over of one company in the midwest resulted in a review of the losses to the local community that would have accrued had the merger gone through. The local office would have been closed and its payroll stopped, resulting in yearly salary losses in the hundreds of thousands of dollars; monies to the local and state governments from taxable incomes and sales would have been sacrificed; philanthropic and charitable contributions arising from the company and from its employees would have amounted to hundreds of thousands of dollars; and the whole relationship of the business to the community would have been obliterated. Here is where the meaning of Douglas' observation about the role of social factors in economics comes to astonishing light. People losing their jobs from a potential merger would no longer have been "connected" in the same viable way to the community; morale problems would have arisen; family planning and stability would have been affected; schools, other businesses, cultural, religious and other institutions would have been adversely affected. Is that progress? Is profit for the merger-invoking conglomerate the overriding issue here? What about the mental health of the hundreds of people who would have been affected had the merger occurred? The cost to remedy ("patch up") the mournfulness resulting from a merger and the closing of the local business would have been born by the taxpayers paying for a "much needed new mental health facility in the community." Fortunately the take-over did not occur; the article documents other examples

of local resourcefulness in rising to meet the challenge of similar take-overs by large, impersonal and
(locally) destructive corporations. What satisfactions
and feelings of unity and purpose must surface when
local communities rise to protect their economic,
social and personal integrities! The Mintz article
quotes some other research that indicates that conglomerates are the cause of many plant and business
closing, thus producing hardships for local communities
and giving them no say in their own destinies. How
can there be a sense of relatedness when one's
economic and social existence can be summarily snuffed
out by people in remote sections of the country, and
only for their own profit?

Is Larger Better?

     Often large businesses are touted as the bulwarks
of our economy and the maker of jobs that help create
economic stability for all of us. In the Mintz
article cited above, there is a reference to the
number of new jobs in the private sector over a 7-year
period ending in 1976. The 1,000 largest industrial
firms accounted for only 1.3 percent of the new jobs;
small businesses accounted for 98.7 percent of the new
jobs. This figure not only contests the stereotype of
big business being the friend of the working person,
but shows that its impact is exactly the opposite. In
these barebone figures, we are neglecting the cost to
individual and family lives in mental health matters.
The impact of big business actions, the mergers that
destroy local production (hence incentive and well-
being), and the actions of conglomerates, all serve
for the most part to destroy the local community
scene. The chief motivation for these big industrial
and business actions is simple: profit. The cost to
human life is almost incalculable, especially in
mental health matters. The health of a profession
of CEOs that promulgates these costly actions must
also be in question. Can stress for the populous be
more calculably produced than by letting big business
run our lives?

     Correlated well with the Mintz article is the
recent report from the White House Conference on Small
Business, January 13-17, 1980, held in Washington, D.C.
(1980). This report indicates in general how important
is small business to our economy, how many additional
problems women face who enter small business, and the
many barriers to entrepreneurship that exist for men

and women (prejudice arising from the traditional male/
female roles, outright discrimination, lack of educational opportunities for women, and financial
constraints put on women receiving loans and other
support for small business efforts). Extoling the
general virtues of small business, despite the
opportunities for women (they are, of course, no
better-even worse--in large businesses and corporations), the report on the small business conference
indicates that there are some 14 million small and
independent businesses, representing over 100 million
people, and 58 percent of all private sector jobs in
America; they represent 48 percent of America's gross
business product; and--this is highly important--50
percent of all new inventions, innovations and patents
are developed in the small and independent sector of
American business. As these businesses and as opportunity to establish them become snuffed out, everyone
will directly or indirectly come under the auspices of
large corporations, resulting in the styming of
individual initiative of the type now supported by
small businesses and in the exacerbation of the ills
of large corporations.

        Despite the value of small businesses, a recent
report by the National Center for Economic Alternatives (Kramer, 1980) indicates that pressure from
conglomerates and from government regulatory policies
has made small businesses "an endangered species."
Nearly 80 percent of small businesses fold up before
their fifth year, and many others are swallowed by
giant corporations. Small businesses also receive a
disproportionally small share of government procure-
ment and research and development funds (3.5 percent,
yet small businesses account for over half the
scientific and technological development during this
century). The American system of "free enterprise" is
posited on the assumption that there is an adequate
number of competitors; as small businesses fail, as
they get ignored by a government beholden to corporate
power, and as they are unable to draw research and
development support, they dwindle and die and make a
mockery of the free enterprise system. Their loss is
big business' gain. Concentration of economic power
has a sometimes hidden cost in another way: "One
estimate of the cost to consumers where competition is
not allowed to flourish is $175 billion per year...An
active, viable growing small business segment of the
economy is the force needed to bring those costs down"
(Green & Massie, 1980, p.588). Too, small businesses,

important as they are, sometimes ape the manner and
practices of large businesses: They advertise falsely,
they "switch and bait," they pass the buck regarding
faulty products back to the manufacturer (sometimes
correctly, sometimes not), they engage in price-
setting, and they may refuse to make good on their
services and products. Big business has given all
business a bad name, but the bad apples may have
contaminated the whole barrell! Despite these many
local instances of small businesses taking advantage
of the consumer, public opinion still regards small
business as displaying "honesty, dependability, and
integrity" among 25 American basic institutions
(Green & Massie, 1980, p.59). Let us hope this
estimate of small business will grow in fact and in
image and remain a countermeasure to big business.

Another area in which big business casts a long
shadow is in agri-business (Crittenden, 1980). Large
scale agriculture has driven out small farmers,
hastened (if not caused) the decline of communities,
and has shown even more negatively that bigness
cannot be equated with efficiency. Crittenden says,
"...one thing, relatively small farms of a few hundred
acres are often as productive and innovative as giant
farms of thousands of acres and in some cases more
so (1980, p.1).

Health In General

There are both direct and indirect ways of documenting the impact of the environment, peoples' health
habits, and the role of business (big business, the
medical/industrial complex, advertising, etc.) on the
health of people in general. This may sound like a
curious mix of forces, but it is not. A book that
focuses on this collection of problems is that of
McKeown (1979). He writes about the diseases of
civilization--lung cancer, accidents (especially auto),
alcoholism, drug addiction, stress from overwork--and
how the medical profession has contributed little or
naught to the control of these conditions. McKeown
says, "In solving such problems laboratory medicine
has little to offer, and pride of place in biology is
now held by the observational sciences, ecology and
ethology..." (McKeown, 1979, p.180). What is needed
in these instances is better self care, better health
habits, and the avoidance of undue risk. However, if
we follow the ads, we are told repeatedly that one
cannot be healthy, happy or wise, unless he takes...at

402

10, 2 and 4, as a "daily dose", or rubs this or that on the skin, the scalp or the bottom of the feet. Not only has medicine promoted the idea that one has to guard constantly against ill health by taking one or another nostrum, the pharmaceutical/industrial complex tries to teach us to live on such nostrums. The number of remedies for the common cold, if listed alphabetically, might be as numerous as the number of words found in a small dictionary. Medicine has become an institution--a medical/industrial institution--and the physician has benefited by the publicity given health problems in ways that are inimical to good medical practice. Would many medical journals even be published if they did not rely on pharmaceutical advertising? Much public health advice is governed by a Chinese cookie slogan mentality.

All the while that medicine submits to the medical/ industrial complex and its advertising, and makes one think that one has to pour one medicant after another into the body daily, McKeown (1979) says the improvements in medicine yet to come will not eminate from the laboratory but from medicine's influence on people to choose wisely about smoking, exercising, eating, drinking and using drugs. These practices are a matter of common sense, reasonable health standards, and the like, and are hardly representative of medical practice at all. Few if any physicians have contributed materially to "health habits" of people, certainly no more so than psychologists, social workers and teachers. The present, "diseases of civilization," so-called, are hardly within the perview of physicians at all. McKeown says "Doctors have always tended to overestimate the effectiveness of their intervention and to underestimate the risks... (McKeown, 1979, p.177), even where their intervention is valid. Like an inverted pyramid, the skill and knowledge of the physician, where rightly and securely based has been generalized through pharmaceuticals and the medical industrial complex into a thousand remedies for mythical diseases, malaise, and malcontentments that are better controlled by better education of the populous in matters of health.

How medical practice and particularly the mental health realm can come under the control of forces unrelated to the development and management of mental health in the community is seen in the volume by Chu and Trotter (1974). They studied the National

Institute of Mental Health (NIMH) and its impact on community mental health. The point of the book is well-summarized in the introduction by Ralph Nader, the consumer advocate, who remarks: "The community mental health centers became the domain of the psychiatrists, who brought to their newest realm their business acumen, upper-middle-class bias, and professional hubris to burden this massive federal subsidy. They also brought confusion about their role and the kinds of people they are equipped to help" (Chu & Trotter, 1974, p.xii). He observes further, Nader does, that the community mental health centers throughout the nation were not accountable to either NIMH, which founded the community centers, nor to the people in the community they were supposed to serve. The program directives to serve the poor, the aged and the blue-collar worker were changed at the hands of psychiatrists who redirected the community mental health centers to their own purposes. An additional point stressed by Nader refers to the "pathology of institutional structures." He points up rightly that we do not have a science of the pathology of institutions, and asks why there is such a paucity of information on institutional insanity and its victims. This fits well with one of the objectives of this book, viz., that as professions become highly structured, articulate and aggressive, they take on the characteristics of corporations; professions become selfish, self-centered, profit-motivated, and tend to insulate themselves and their services from the community they originally intended to serve. The profit motive hastens this accretion of power and influence, but the profit motive is inimical to professional practice as it is loftily acclaimed by its practitioners. The failure to live up to professional aims sets up ethical problems of considerable proportion. Before we know it the profession becomes more and more like business and is off and running toward profit, power and influence, neglecting the real purposes which fueled the profession's birth and development. The conflict between power/profit/influence on the one hand and professional, ethical and humanitarian influences on the other have come to grip the professions and cause them to suffer--as does the individual caught in similar conflict--from health, mental health and ethical problems.

Returning to NIMH-community mental health center debacle, Chu and Trotter report how the original program got steered into other directions than those originally intended. They state, "Psychiatric domination of the program meant that centers would inevitably regard the problems and needs of clients from the narrow perspective of a sickness requiring medical attention from medical personnel" (Chu & Trotter, 1974, p.21). This viewpoint may have acted as an inhibitor to the development of sufficient numbers of community mental health centers. In 1972, there were 325 such centers throughout the nation, out of a total of 529 funded (as of June, 1972); the overall goal was for 1,500 to 1,600 community mental health centers. After pointing out the enormous number of problems and issues in attempting to fund and establish such a large number of community mental health centers, Chu and Trotter observe that even if a thousand or more such centers were established, the records of their work would still leave doubts about the program, how well it served its original aims, and whether it would (or could) contribute materially to the nation's mental health problems. The intent of such centers to reduce state hospital admissions and retentions was for example not even served well, the state hospital resident population began a decline in 1955/56, years before the community mental health center funding began to operate (Chu & Trotter, 1974, pp.29-49). The whole project gained the epitaph "innovation without change;" thus failing to bring together the professional intentions and social policy of a well-meaning group that yielded to opportunism and power and profit motives.

Institutional Power

The popular press, more than the academic community, continues to revile the medical profession for its economic and professional practices (Lasko, 1979). Here, too, institutional power and politics in the interest of profit seem to prevail. Lasko covers such unprofessional topics as fee-splitting, kickbacks, prescriptions influenced by money and less by medical concern, the performing of unnecessary operations, the overly free use of drugs, the proliferation of cancer cures and treatments, exploitations of foreign physicians, and more. These are examples, even if only partly true, of how the medical marketplace operates and how the incorporation of medical skills and knowledged serves less professional aims and more commercial ones. Here is another example of what Nader called the pathology of institutions (institutions in the sense of a profession taking on

roles that ply mainly commercial interests and not
humanitarian ones), surely a pressing problem for
all professions but more so for medicine and law.

One of the sad but also alarming outcomes of
humanitarian-needs-turned-commercial arises in
connection with serious health problems that develop
on a very wide basis among populations of people.
One such glaring example is the story of DES, the
drug--Diethylstilbestrol--given pregnant women from
about 1941 onward, in spite of reports linking
estrogens with cancer in laboratory animals; the
number of pregnant women believed taking DES was up
to two million. The effect, reported by a physician,
Arthur Herbst, was a rare form of vaginal cancer in
young women, the offsprings of those mothers taking
DES, leading in some cases to surgical removal of the
vagina and other parts of the female reproductive
system. Suits in the hundreds of thousands of dollars
of damage claims have been awarded women affected by
DES. The charge against pharmaceutical companies and
laboratories has been that they marketed the products
without sufficient care and testing, leading in the
case of some victims to emotional and physical scarring
for life. Here, again, the rush to profit, on the
part of the medical/industrial complex and the full-
speed-ahead-despite-cautions on the part of corporations, has resulted in serious health problems for
thousands of victims. When corporations are asked
why they are not more cautious, why they do not take
more responsibility, they often respond as did the
trucking company in the above-cited instance, that
they have to keep the "trucks (products) on the road
(market)" and that it costs too much to exercise
caution.

In this same connection, one of the most glaring
pieces of irresponsibility of corporate behavior is
seen in the Love Canal mishap (Brown, 1980; Molotsky,
1980). Chemical companies have been burying in the
ground for years huge supplies of waste which are now
coming back to "haunt" mankind. Other wastes are
discharged into the air or into streams, rivers and
oceans. These wastes often do not disintegrate or
become dissolved into the environment in harmless
ways. The Love Canal setting is the Niagara Falls,
New York area and has been the site of recent problems
and controversies of a ramifying nature. The Hooker
Chemical Co. discharged waste into the ground in the
area of the company. Now, years later, a number of

406

problems--as well as the chemical poisoning--surfaces:
It will cost about 4 million dollars to relocate over
700 families living in the immediate area of the
pollution; some 11 out of 36 individuals tested were
allegedly shown to have chromosome damage (30%),
whereas ordinarily there would be no chromosome damage
in such a population of people. (The effects of the
Love Canal problem may be moot (Kolata, 1980). There
is currently a see-saw back and forth as to the damage
Love Canal has caused genetically, socially, economically and in terms of community spirit and morale.
No matter how much the damage is disputed, there are
certainly no benefits associated with this catastrophe.
The bottom line is the moral responsibility of the
corporation involved--or other corporations with
other, similar chemical dumps--and what can be done to
correct and prevent similar happenings.) The money
to relocate the affected families would likely be
obtained from the federal and state governments, but
the Justice Department is suing the Hooker Chemical
Co. for 124.5 million dollars to clean up four
chemical dumps in the Niagara Falls area, including
Love Canal (Parisi, 1980; Malatsky, 1980). What an
enormous holocaust to overtake a community and the
lives of individuals possibly affected with chromosome
damage! Where did the problem come from? From
profit-searching efforts by a corporation immune to
human need, to potential suffering, to community
responsibility, to health. When the rush to gain is
so intent that it leaves in its wake this enormous
amount of destruction, something is wrong with our
society, something is wrong with our notions of
community health and welfare, something is amis with
our values and ethics. Until recently, companies
could dispose of waste into the environment with
impunity. It is only when the considerable and
perhaps long-ranging health problems develop of the
sort found at Love Canal (and there are numerous
others: Minamata, Grassy Narrows, Seveso)(Parisi,
1980) that society turns and points a finger at the
offender and asks that something be done about the
hazards and risks perpetrated in the interest of
profit. The institutionalization of power to the
point where it rampages over lives is the culprit we
are dealing with. If there is an ethic for business,
for corporations, for institutionalized professional
practices, there is little evidence of it. What is
abundantly evident is the destruction of health of
many people, the pilloraging of the environment, and
the utter disregard for human life if it interferes

407

with profit. The Love Canal incident, dreadful as it is, may be only one of 1,000 to 2,000 such chemical dumps around the country that might someday begin to erupt, their hazardous wastes being poured in new ways into the environment for years to come, and adversely affecting health for decades.

Remediation?

Unwelcome as these events are, there are mixed signs that remediation is under way in some quarters. The recent "superfund" proposal to have the government underwrite some or much of the chemical dump clean-ups in the country is a case in point (Editorial, 1980; Omang, 1980); with the petro-chemical and related industries carrying "their share" whatever that amount may be. However, in Virginia, a researcher in the pursuit of Kepone infiltration in the environment discovered an alleged five million dollar fund for tracing Kepone's poisonous impact was unavailable for underwriting further research into this problem (Frankel, 1980). The Virginia Kepone fund was activated in 1977 when Allied Chemical Corporation agreed to pay over five million dollars to remedy Kepone infiltration problems in the community of Hopewell, Virginia, where their pesticides and those of other companies had polluted the city's sewage system and the James River as well. The Kepone fund was created in exchange for setting aside a law suit in which the Allied Chemical Corporation and others were charged with some 355 violations of the State of Virginia water pollution laws. The government may sometimes fail to follow-through on the prosecution of flagrant violations of the environment because it, too, lacks conviction about the welfare of its citizens and often submits too willingly to the pressures from business, big and otherwise.

Despite many flagrant social and environmental violations, men (Executives) from big business such as William Agee (Bendix Corporation CEO) may be heard saying positive things about big business and its responsibilities to the citizenry. Agee was, for example, quoted (Pine, 1980) as saying that the new administration of President Reagan should not roll back health, safety and environmental programs entirely (how much meaning revolves around the word "entirely" is moot), and that business must keep up its social conscience by and through affirmative-action programs and environmental clean-up. It is

reassuring to have men like Agee on the side of the
environment and the citizenry, although his influence
in the desired direction is more gentle push than
vigorous shove at this juncture. Vogel (1980) says
that Japan will supercede the U.S. in industrial
development and world trade. One of the reasons for
Japan's predicted potential supremacy in the area of
the U.S. has considered primary is that Japan has
developed better crime control, fairer welfare programs, better governmental and political interrelationships, and an economy in which large corporations
are more responsible and committed to the employee
than to the stockholder, just the opposite to the
U.S. The general program of more corporate responsibility, long a cry in the wilderness by consumer
advocates, may yet come to be realized if the U.S. is
to hold its place in the world.

Over against a general concern for health is the
curious corporate growth of the "health industry" in
the United States. The regional health planning
agencies, some 200 of them in the country, are gaining
power at such a rate that the Justice Department is
now warning them that their methods of planning and
allocating hospital beds and various other medical
services might violate federal antitrust laws
(Frankel, 1980). Inherent in this problem is the
potentially illegal practice among competing hospitals
to limit the number of beds or the kinds of services
offered by the hospitals. These limitations, in
turn, are related to soaring hospital costs, to the
duplication of services and to the absence of appropriate cooperative planning among agencies and
hospitals. Where is the consumer in all this melee?
Is not the corporation, the institutionalization of
power (in the name of health services) overriding all
other considerations? The issues involved may not be
halted until expensive law suits (another avenue where
corporate lawyering gets involved and, again, the
citizen for whom all these services are presumably
designed, gets lost in the confusion) are instituted,
or until--perhaps years later--it becomes evident
that our social-medical-policy making is awry because
so many people needing treatment are not getting it,
or are not able to afford it even if it is available.
When the corporations' purposes takeover as services
become institutionalized in the pejorative sense, all
mankind suffers, especially the poor, the indigent,
the handicaped, the elderly, the ill.

Many other instances of how the public is taken advantage of by large corporations appear in the press frequently (Grubisich, 1980; Mansfield, 1980; Denton, 1980) and in book form periodically (Green & Massie, 1980). These are such items as contaminated pork being shipped to school cafeterias and being eaten by children; pork with dangerously high levels of chlordane and heptachlor (termite and ant-killing pesticides) that may be cancer hazards to humans. A popular drug and variety store is charged by the State of Virginia food inspectors with selling candy and cookies adulterated with "insect filth, insect larvae, moth fragments and rodent hairs" (Grubisich, 1980). An upsurge in the use of and need for psychotherapy throughout the country is related to stress arising from inflation, with much of the content of therapy revolving around economic issues in peoples' lives. In-patient, as well as out-patient care, is reported by Washington, D.C. area hospitals and clinics to be on the rise (Mansfield, 1980). Patients have been paying higher prices for eyeglasses and eye exams than is necessary. Where optometrists advertise, consumer costs drop by about one-third. The word "advertising" here may not be fully correct; what professionals do is make available the fees charged for a variety of services, list their specialties, and any preferences they have for one or another type of patient. This is just consumer-oriented information, not advertising in the usual sense of the term. The public then has a chance to compare and contrast, and can tell more about the nature of the services they are getting, what fees are fair and common, and so forth (Sinclair, 1980).

Mental health problems may not only be on the rise in relation to inflation, but alcohol-related problems may also. A Miami Herald (1978) news report on a Gallop Poll indicates that one person in four feels that personal or family troubles can be related to immoderate use of alcohol; and the report further indicates that the percentage of persons reporting alcohol-related problems has doubled in less than 10 years. These are all signs that the health of the populous is not good and that matters may be getting worse, although long-range trends, covering decades, are not available.

Behind all of these ominous trends lay giant corporations who have so institutionalized their power and control that they can wreck havoc in a community

almost overnight. And their subtle power over economic
and social well-being is so great that health measures
of the ordinary type--the type that school children
are taught daily--can scarcely count for anything.
The growth in "junk food" consumption among youth is
an example. Nader (1980), writing in the introduction
to the Big Business Reader, says that for several
decades businessmen have known and capitalized on the
fact that the corporation has long been the dominant
institution in the American society. Corporate power
extends far beyond the immediate marketplace--it
sways governmental policies and politics, influences
the introduction and passage of many laws in Congress,
influences taxation, largely determines the use of
the environment for a variety of purposes, infiltrates
education, controls most of the media and communication
facilities, dominates charatable and other foundations,
and even manages much of athletics. As world wide
corporate conglomerates grow, they shake themselves
loose from any national control, pit nations against
one another, and avoid responsibilities for taxes and
other obligations everywhere. One of the most
insidious influences arising from corporate influence
is "The calculated penetration of children's minds by
exploitive advertisements on children's television...
[in ways that]...undermine parental authority, as well
as a proper diet" (Nader, 1980, p.1).

Challenges

From time to time the large corporations have been
challenged--by the labor movement, by the rise of the
consumer movement a couple of decades ago, by the
civil rights movement, and more recently by environmental considerations. The more recent environmental
movement, broad and yet penetrating as it is, focuses
more on health problems than have the other movements,
and may yet be the power that breaks the corporate
back, if anything does. We have seen in this review
a small number of instances where environmental
pillorage has had adverse health consequences for large
numbers of people; as more and more people are affected,
the reaction of the masses may bring some far-reaching
and meaningful responsibility to bear on corporations
and their leadership.

One effort to ginger up concern for the influence
of big business came through the occurrence of "Big
Business Day-1980," (April 17th), held in Washington,
D.C. and in dozens of other cities throughout the nation;

and summarized in the publication, The Big Business
Reader (1980). Some of the highly salient topics in
this Reader that bear on the health of professions
issue are the following: How moral men make immoral
decisions; The devastating impact of plant relocations;
Democratizing the workplace; Nutrition and the politics
of food; The corporation and the community; Free
speech within the corporation; The corporate climber
has to find his heart; Another day, another $3,000;
The promise and perils of petrochemicals; A democratic
technology; Babies, bottles, and breast milk; The
dumping of hazardous products on foreign markets; The
uses of an economic system—and of economics; The road
to monopoly; How to investigate your local big
business; On the importance of small business; and
others. Pursuant to the study of the influence of big
business on our lives, especially in regard to health
matters, this Reader documents many of the forces at
work that appear to be causing decay in the fabric
of our social life. As these matters get worse, health
considerations are drawn into bold focus: Love Canal
being a recent and glaring example. The taking advantage of our environment by opportunists can produce
results that are unpredictable as well as ominous;
who knows where the next Love Canal will occur, or
where the next Three Mile Island-like catastrophe will
bombshell its way through the populous? The moral
here is that the health of the professions is also
the health of the populous, and the health of the
latter will put constraints on the actions of the
former—especially those organization men who will
take every profiteering advantage offered them—in
ways that will not only improve the health of the
professions but keep them ethically conscious of
everyone's health.

What is our society like, basically, if it
produces so many problems of a health, ethical, moral
and humane nature? Do other societies, modern industrial ones such as England, the Scandanavian Countries,
Japan, various Western European countries fare as
poorly as does the U.S.? It is hard to say how the
U.S. compares with other countries in the matters
discussed above. We have only meagre intercultural
comparisons, even in regard to health matters.

While we do not know how America compares with
other countries in matters relating to social responsibility on a large and general basis, we do know that
our perspective is limited and selfish. Increasingly

412

in the literature there have been articles about social
responsibility (Kinard, 1974). Kinard says that since
the corporation has long been regarded by the law as
an artificial, legal entity, possessing many rights but
few responsibilities, it--the corporation--has gotten
by with minimal attention to acts that individuals
would long ago have been prosecuted for. It has been
said repeatedly, since Sir Edward Coke, in 1612, that
corporations have no soul. Now that the corporation's
concerns, influence and potential responsibilities are
greater than ever, it is time to realign priorities
and establish ethical guidelines. The corporate
manager is now having to consider the impact socially
of the economic matters the corporation puts forward;
although we have heard this thesis repeated many
times since Karl Marx, Max Weber, Emile Durkheim,
Theodore Veblen and others, today it is becoming ever-
more meaningful. Managers of large firms can no
longer follow their wholly economic and profit-seeking
dictates without regard to the greater social issues--
the social fabric--surrounding the economic ones.
One example of gross social neglect is that in spite
of general prosperity (Saunders, 1978), resounding oil,
auto and other profits, many people live in poverty,
education is poor to almost nonexistent in some parts;
and discrimination, pollution, crime, inadequate
housing, malnutrition and the ever-present bug-a-boo,
unemployment, haunt us daily. In turn, these
neglected environments and the people populating them,
act back in a boomerang fashion to plague corporations
with new problems, such as environmental waste and
pollution. Sooner or later, the corporations have to
be brought to their knees; it may be done by health
problems among their own kind, by health and pollution
problems being rampant in the surrounding society, or
by the populous in the form of the electorate rising
up for reform, but it will come.

The American system--and perhaps that of other
nations--is in crisis. We can no longer afford to
mouth the bromides of the past: We have too many
problems to face to think that all is well with our
"system" (our economy, our education, momentous public
health and private health concerns, treatment of the
handicapped, the aged, the death rate of infants, the
spoilage of the environment, and many, many more
problems, most of which have been in the making for
decades but some of which have prolifitered into
crises in the past decade or two). Now is the time to

413

stop merely extoling our country in 4th of July
speeches and give sober pause to correcting our ills
lest we are no longer around to recognize, let alone
celebrate, the 4th of July (Macrae, 1976; Kiechel,
1979; Meyer, 1979).

Conflictful Solutions

Some recognition of the extent of our social
problems (broadly defined) are addressed in contemporary publications that purport to offer solutions.
While the Duignan and Rabushka volume (1980) seeks a
reaffirmation of the past, and more conservative
economic practices with governmental restraint as a
cardinal issue; the Pechman book (1980) seeks new
paths and declares that "the system" as a whole, as
well as specifics, need revision. It is a debate,
these two books, between private sector determinism
versus social planning that tries to take the whole
of society into account. The plight that we are now
in, considered from the vantage point of health
issues among the professions, would seem to arise in
connection with the rampant practice of the first
alternative, i.e., as lauded in the Duignan &
Rabushka book. They would, apparently, give us more
of the same problems we now have, further emphasizing
the kind of rampant individualism and economic exploi-
tation that has put us in the hole we're in now.
Extrication is difficult, and no one has a solid and
complete answer, but moving in the direction of more
whole cloth planning that takes all facets of the
economy and the society (including sufficient regard
for the health of the populous) into consideration has
greater appeal if we are to address the enormous
health problems we have--just to take one example of
peril in our society--into consideration. If big
business can say "Leave us alone, Mr. Government, to
pursue our ends," the populous can counter with
"Oppress us not, Mr. Big Business, and we'll all be
healthier, including yourselves." We know factually
that the bulk of evidence is on the side of the latter,
on the side of the people, when we consider that big
business has created very few jobs, comparatively, in
the past several decades and has innovated little, in
contrast to small businesses. What justifies big
business blowing on its horn, especially when we add
health problems to the plethora of economic and social
and ethical problems already presented by big
business? The sad outcome of this bifurcation of
purpose and aim would be that we might do nothing in

414

time to avoid crises, but be forced, as we too often
have in the past, to mount remedial measures that are
only temporizing ones and that, consequently, go not
very far in proposing and trying out viable remedies.
If we begin with the question as to what to do to
improve the health of professions--and indirectly the
health of all of us-- we would entertain this question
as the basic one, then ask what economic, social and
other issues would follow. Turning the question
around 180 degrees--from continuing economic growth
at an ever-increasing pact to questions that place
health uppermost--might find us reconstructing our
values, our ethics, and beginning to build a better
social order.

Supporting the more "popular" solution to the
above dichotomously stated problem, is a book by
Barnet (1980). This author says that we need not be,
and cannot afford to be, catapulted from one version
of scarcity to another (real or not), such as oil
depletion, water scarcity, and the like, to form our
policies for the future. While resources are not
abundant forever, policy planning and political changes
that determine the use of natural resources stand
uppermost; and that policy changes rather than hoped-
for technological breakthrough or discoveries will go
far to help our future to avoid catastrophe as well as
preserve resources for all our needs. Too often in
the past (and even now), large corporations have done
the economic and resource planning--sometimes with
government aid--on the basis of our old acquaintance--
PROFIT--and have created emergencies or artificially
scared us into believing in scarcity of a given product
(the oil scarcity of 1979, and earlier being an
example) rather than reflecting real scarcity. Barnet
points out that the corporate power in the manipula-
tion of scarcity cause social problems, even yields
anti-social results. As if not to be outmaneuvered,
the major oil companies are already positioned to take
over the solar energy industry, thus we may have a
further proliferation of the corporation-versus-the
people problem. Barnet calls for a new and democratic
economy planned from the bottom up (rather than from
the top down); suggesting a procedure similar to that
just cited above in regard to making the health of the
people uppermost (planning from the bottom upward)
rather than acquiesing to the powers that be who want
unending economic growth and profit with public health
matters finding a lower place on their scale of values.

Barnet calls the issue of social planning from the bottom upward a necessity although not likely to become an immediate policy or realistic prospect. Putting people to work and keeping them working will not be solved by a corporate policy of scarcity; the human, institutional way in which resources are used to employ people and to give them a viable inter-related, social network, in the manner suggested by Douglas (1979) is commensurate with Barnet's opinions. Always the problems are human ones, not alone resources, scarcity of resources, material gain or economic growth. Further evidence of the relevance of Barnet's thesis is the work of Kuttner (1980) and Wildavsky (1980). In Revolt Of The Haves, Kuttner points out that seeming grass roots reform-- in the cases of reduction of real estate taxes in California, via Proposition 13--can be a mirage, can even backfire to cause more problems than it seeks to remedy, or even benefit those other than the ones seeking benefit or relief. Proposition 13 in Califor-nia resulted in lowering taxes of Pacific Telephone and Telegraph by $130 million, Pacific Gas and Electric saved $91 million on real estate taxes, and Standard Oil of California benefitted by a $13 million tax reduction; with side effects lowering funds to schools, libraries and social and welfare agencies...all in the name of relief to the average real estate tax payer.

Corroborative evidence for the importance of managing corporate growth comes from another important sector of society: The planning of scientific resources (related, of course, to matters of resource scarcity) and the attempt to do what Gus Speth, President Carter's chairperson of the Council on Environmental Quality is assigned to do (Carter, 1980, pp.1009-1012). Speth in his plans for a "conserver society" (one that conserves resources, promotes environmental quality issues, and harnasses economic growth to submit to environmental quality) sees an inherent conflict between the environmentalists and those proponents of economic growth who would roll back environmental regulations in the interest of profit. The environmentalists must develop a broad-based set of political coalitions, develop political strategies, curb the political power of corporations, sponsor at least partial public support for election financing of Senators and House of Representatives candidates, and promote other measures that keep our democracy democratic, Speth contends. Important in

416

this conserver society picture is the practice of recycling, avoidance of pollution, stressing durability over obsolescence, quality over quantity, and greater diversity, and the avoidance of waste. The full-speed-ahead philosophy on the part of corporations in the name of gain, will be contested by Speth. A final note on the Speth article by Carter says, "But Speth thinks the conserver society may be impossible to achieve unless the influence of corporations is checked through reform of political campaign financing. He has called, too, for reform of the way companies are governed" (Carter, 1980, p.1012). Speth points up what many other observers have said, viz., that the people most affected by corporate power and actions are the laborers, the consumers, the communities in general, yet they have the least to say about the corporation's decisions. Speth would have the stockholders of companies elect a number of "public directors" similar to the Nader "Big Business Day-1980" "shadow boards" and would have corporations issue "social reports" periodically, along with economic reports, as is now the case in West Germany and other European Countries. No one is sanguine about all these reform measures involving the corporation taking place--with the obvious benefits to society at social, economic and health levels--but should public sentiment, economic pressures or general social crisis prevail, Speth and others like him woul- be ready for viable programs. Like the manic patients, corporations may sometimes have to run amok before they become open to fundamental change.

Governmental Collusion/Corporation Unreliability

One has only to read the daily papers in metropolitan areas to learn how big business operating through whatever means at its disposal (now comes the government to help corporations) sends its tenacles further and further into the economic and social fabric of society. In a series of articles in the Washington POST beginning on June 22 and continuing for several days, Neumann and Gup (1980) display before the reading public how waste in consulting and researching between large firms and the government are perpetrated. Complicity between government employees, holding contract responsibilities, engage corporations to do consulting and research on a variety of problems that involves some ethical issues: conflict of interest between the governmental awards of multi-million dollar contracts to major oil and chemical

417

companies (as examples), waste in that some research
projects are not finished nor do they satisfy important informational needs, the practice of the
"revolving door" policy (where governmental officials
leave their posts to work at higher salaries for
consulting firms they previously monitored), procure-
ment favors, and more. Some of the large companies
involved in this "litany of frivolity and waste" as
Guy and Neumann called it are: Exxon, the Arthur D.
Little Company, Monsanto, Dow Chemical. All of these
companies denied the charges, denied complicity, sometimes fail to respond at all to querries, and other
tactics that resist the divulging of activities that
pollute the environment, propogate waste in human and
financial resources, and then assume an attitude of
definance about it all. In discussions in seminars
dealing with problems of corporate irresponsibility,
some have suggested widespread dissemination of
knowledge of these and other transgressions, and movements to boycott the products of these industries.
Much public feelings has to be aroused, however,
before boycotts will work; gradually educational
awareness and concern may act to stem the tide of some
of these transgressions on the public treasury and
and confidence. Despite much public lethargy when it
comes to concerted action, slowly and gradually the
public is learning to place less and less confidence
in corporations based on their records of irresponsibility. The Harris Pole has reported a decline in
confidence in the heads of major American corporations
for over two decades: On questions of confidence in
the heads put to the general public, 55% said "yes"
to confidence in 1956, 29% so opined in 1973, and only
15% responded this way in 1975. Others have shown a
similar decline in public feeling that corporations
show a fair balance between profits and public
interest: 70% said "yes" in 1968; only 20% felt this
way in 1974. This erosion of confidence in corporate
behavior will continue a downslide unless something
drastic happens to turn the tide. Part of the problem
of expecting giant corporations to hold steadily to
social and public responsibilities is the change in
the makeup of these corporations. In May of 1980,
Fortune magazine (Hayes, 1980) reported on 25 years
of change in the original (1955) "Fortune 500",
meaning the 500 largest industrial corporations in
America (Fortune, 1980). In 1980, 25 years later,
only 262 (slightly over 50%) of the original Fortune
500 were still on the list of the original Fortune 500;
147 grew too small for the 1980 update, and 30 were no

longer in existence. With the corporate vulnerability being what it is, difficulties in educating the corporations themselves and their CEOs about responsibility seems a long shot. The magazine does not go very much into the problems presented socially and economically by these corporations; the emphasis in such reporting is on whether they still exist and still prosper. Social concern for their status and criticism of same are regarded as mostly "corporation hating" and dealt with very superficially in ways protective of corporate interest (Nickel, 1980).

Following the daily papers and the weekly news reports, one encounters many other ways in which corporations in their hustle and bustle run roughshod over public considerations, the law, and their competition. Mintz (1980) reports on some public chastizement of corporations for their duplicity: Saying to their stockholders that they were prosperous, while alleging to the government and environmentalists that safety and health regulations were about to lead them into bankruptcy. Nader noted that this duplicity was intended to achieve two ends: to delay or wholly block governmental regulations pertaining to safety and health (allowing them to reduce costs or increase profits), and to keep stock prices high thus pleasing shareholders but not tell the latter about possible financial pressures if they did follow regulations. The controversy underlying this duplicity came about due to hearings before the House Commerce Subcommittee which was requiring new rules to compel disclosure to stockholders the same information given to the Environmental Protection Agency. Forty-five corporations were cited as purportedly making inconsistent disclosures. One company, the Mead Corporation (a paper manufacturer), alleged that costs in meeting proposed regulations for the disposal of hazardous waste would cost the company much more than its whole 1978 earnings; a few days later the same corporation filed a so-called 10-K report with the Securities and Exchange Commission saying that over the next five years the Mead Company would spend about one-third the amount they reported to the Environmental Protection Agency, including all federal, state and local air, water and environmental laws and regulations, and including the costs required by the EPA for safety and health. In the testimony concerning various EPA health and safety measures, Nader charged Virginia Electric and Power Company (VEPCO) with the same "crosstown hypocrisy" when the company told its shareholders it could not estimate the cost of proposed hazardous waste regulations but later filed specific cost estimates with the EPA. It is highly unlikely that large corporations run on as tight a financial tether as they could not estimate costs for health and safety or, indeed, for any expenditure, almost down to the last penny. How could VEPCO return repeatedly for rate increases if they did not know costs for various budgetary items rather thoroughly?

In one community in Long Island, a local consumer advocate was reported by Barron (1980) as using "showmanship" to get his points across to governing bodies concerning the need for various health regulations. The consumer advocate, one, Richard M. Kessel, once carried cartons of spoiled milk to a meeting of the Nassau County Board of Supervisors to push for a law requiring dates on perishable foods. One would not have to search long to find other local consumer advocates bringing similar need for reform concerning health, safety and other public matters before governing bodies. Every community probably should have a "consumer ombudsman" in addition to consumer groups to interface between the public and business and between the public and governing boards and committees.

On the topic of delivery of health services to the public, the Federal Trade Commission (FTC) has been having some rough times in its regulatory functions. The FTC has recently been restrained from investigating or regulating legal, medical and other selected professional services under antitrust and consumer protection laws (Dewar & Knight, 1980). The FTC has also recently been pressured by business groups for its investigation of antitrust matters in the auto industry. Similarly, the FTC was investigating and seeking limitations on the control physicians have over Blue Shield health insurance plans. Were the congress to greatly restrict FTC's activities this would have a negative impact on several areas related to the health of professions and on public matters pertaining to ethical issues: e.g., restrictions on investigating the insurance industry, inhibiting FTC's proceedings against television advertising aimed at children, do away with used car warranty requirements, and disallow the need for companies revealing financial data on pricing policies, testing of products for health and safety considerations, and advertising. There is a constant battle going on between government and business to bring business up to ethical standards commensurate

with what allegedly would be a reasonable ethical
position; and the little man is standing in the middle
suffering one health, safety or professional service
violation after another as part of this on-going
conflict. Business wins one round, government another;
government capitulates and then the consumer (the
citizen, all of us) becomes irate and demands recti-
fication, proper disclosure, or the like. It is all
very much like a three-ring circus multiplied many
times. When the health of professions can be
explicitly tied to the health and welfare of the
populous, perhaps the strength and wisdom of professions, inherently present in professional training and
obligations, can surface more readily and aid the
health and safety considerations of the general public.
However, as we have abundantly seen, too often the
professions in their own greed and ambition side not
with the cause of general welfare but with their own
selfish interests and thus become more like the
corporate giants (rather than following their own
professional dictates).

The American Dream

The American dream is that anybody can get ahead,
anyone can become president, anyone can "succeed;"
all of these "goodies" springing from individual will
and incentive. If a person is not as successful, or
whatever, as desired or as considered admirable, well,
"That's his fault--he could if he wanted to badly
enough." This kind of motivation--or, perhaps, one
should say "shared myth,"--is the kind that infuses
corporations and corporate executives with the philosophy that getting ahead by whatever means is the
number one consideration in life. All the stepping
on and over others that it takes is somehow justi-
fiable if it leads to the fulfillment of ambition.
We see this go awry among politicians, industrialists,
professionals, and others. We see the backs and
minds broken among countless numbers of otherwise
normal human beings, in quest of the elusive success
chimera. We see hundreds of people start small
businesses, 80 percent of them to fail within five
years, while at the same time the giants (superficially) thrive but at enormous cost to the health of
the chief executive officers (and middle management
persons, as well) and on the basis of squelching
competition from below or long side.

The Illusive "Success" Motive

Jencks et al (1979) studied the relationship between economic success among American males and their personal characteristics, ages 25 to 64. The four "personal characteristics" were: family background, cognitive skills, personality traits, and years of schooling; studied as the person entered the labor market. The results supplied by Jencks, et al, revolve around these four broad variables. In regard to family background, these authors say, "...we concluded that family background as a whole explained about 48 percent of the variance in occupational status and 15 to 35 percent of the variance in earnings among men aged 25 to 64 in the early 1970s" (Jencks et al, 1979, p.81). That is to say that the variance, or variation in matters of occupational status were clearly related to family background to the extent of exerting about one-half the influence (48 percent). This is a high degree of determination from family background status, and shows that "rising above your status," while it is certainly possible, is not easy. Drake (1978) in discussing medical schools and who gets in made a similar observation: "The chances of getting into medical school steadily increase with the amount of money the applicant's parents make. Applicants from the highest parental income categories are almost 50 percent more likely to be accepted than those from the lowest categories" (Drake, 1978, p.14).

In the Jencks et al study, academic ability (cognitive skills, intelligence, knowledge, etc.) was not as highly related to success as was family background; but the effect of test performance on earnings did increase with age. Non-cognitive or personality characteristics were related to economic success. Personality characteristics measured among high school students' self-assessment, personal behavior, ratings by others, etc., are related to later occupational status and to earnings, even allowing for family background and intellectual skills. Within the realm of "personality characteristics," one must include social skills, ability to influence others, one's motivation, the individuals' view of himself as a leader; all are useful in promoting later achievement. These characteristics may propel the individual into opportunities where better jobs are available, and these characteristics may be the closest to the "American dream" that can be identified. However, they apply, as one might guess, to a very small number of people, not to the whole population.. Moreover, being brought up in a family that prizes achievement, social skills and the like is a good foundation for a young man to start with, provided he has at least above-average intelligence (but not necessarily brillance) and appropriate schooling.

In the matter of education or schooling, the Jencks et al study reveal quite varied results. High school completion is a definite advantage over only elementary school level education, and completing college brings an advantage over simply high school graduation. Clouding the issue of the value of college graduation is the fact that there was a surplus of bachelor degree men in the 1960s thus affecting earning power; but still four years of college are associated with an up-to-about-50-percent earning advantage among people with the same level of experience. One advantage to college completion is higher status, more than higher income.

In summary, Jencks et al state that the answer to "Who gets ahead?" "Who gets the most desirable jobs?" is "...that background exerts a larger influence on economic outcomes than past research had suggested ..." and "If our aim is to reduce the impact of being born to one set of parents rather than another, we still have a long way to go" (Jencks et al, 1979, pp.229-230). The world is a socially structured enterprise, with status, demarcation lines, and both subtle and obvious personality traits (ambition, drive, social skills, etc.) operating not in a vacuum where everyone's chances are as good as another's, but where the starting point has a lot to do with success along the way and with ultimate status and earnings. Society is vertically organized with status piled upon status, and with these levels counting for much in the way of opportunity, background knowledge and skills, and opportunity for advancement. If getting ahead is a primary motivation for many youngsters, following the American dream, it is well to know that one cannot will himself into success or high income. Failure to live up to one's expectations, especially if encouraged out of line with real opportunity, can cause anguish, disappointment, health and psychological problems, and resentment that life has dealt one an unfair blow. And there is also risk among those who do succeed in terms of the standard economic fare: They may have a precarious success, a drive so intense

423

as to hardly ever enjoy life and such as to risk health
and welfare at every turn. Ambition, while it may
help the "get ahead" motive, is also emotionally costly
for many, so costly that life may be placed in jeopardy
and materially shortened.

What is evident here is that our society sets
goals and encourages achievement in mostly economic
terms. Getting ahead more often means being rich,
next being publicly known, and lastly having a good
reputation among one's peers. Status is more a matter
of appearance and more popularly directed than it is
a matter of substantive characteristics. Politicians
get ahead through charisma and social will; scientists,
artists, writers, and thinkers tend to place their
reputations on their contributions and on the opinions
and support of peers, with the public scarcely playing
a role at all (except in unusual cases). Scientists
are seldom moved, anyway, by public images of them
because such an impression is in no way instrumental
in bringing about scientific achievement; in fact,
catering to the public in a publicity sense is almost
wholly inimical to scientific achievement. These
notions may appear biased to some, but one must be
reminded of the recent decision of Harvard University
not to play a role in genetic engineering in its
commercial aspects for fear that it would injure the
educational, research and objectivity roles of this
university (The Chronicle of Higher Education, 1980).
The most viable aspects of society in terms of the substantive contributions that underpin social structure
and social functioning are probably derived from the
intellectual sphere and hardly at all in the ephemeral
economic sphere. The two spheres--intellectual
(including scientific, artistic, and general knowledge
accumulation enterprises such as museums, libraries),
and economic--are at times almost incompatible; society
is still searching for ways for the intellectual
sphere to be fueled by the economic one, and the latter
is beholden to knowledge for progress and the avoidance
of unimaginative stagnation (Magarrell, 1980). Since
the cost of education has risen so dramatically in
the past decade or so, educational institutions every-
where--particularly universities in their research
capacities--are looking for "tie-ins" with the
business and industrial world for support in carrying
out their main functions. How substantial is the
contribution from industry and business to universities
in quest for more knowledge and a better life for all?
The record of business and industry--except where

large bequeaths of money are placed entirely in the
university's hands with few or no strings attached--
is not very impressive in advancing knowledge.
Allegedly, however, if business and industry could
support the functions of universities as we have
honoured them over the centuries, the universities
could advance their cause in the interest of knowledge and social welfare and not be humstrung by
business and industry (Magarrell, 1980; Roark, 1981).
We are already experiencing the coming dearth of
scientific and engineering talent in the U.S.A.
(Ableson, 1980), in comparison to the educational and
scientific forwardness of West Germany, Japan, the
Soviet Union and other countries. These educational
lacks on the part of the U.S.A., according to Abelson
will place us even further behind our competition in
the countries cited above. For example, in Japan one-
fifth of all baccalaureate and close to two-fifths of
all master's degrees are in engineering; whereas in
the United States comparable figures hover around five
percent (Abelson, 1980, p. 965). Moreover, Russian
students encounter mathematics and a scientific curriculum early in their schooling, with algebra and
geometry being taught in the sixth and seventh grades,
with all students required to complete five years of
physics and four years of chemistry (Abelson, 1980,
p.965). Correspondingly we in the U.S.A. are training
too many physicians and will presumably have a considerable oversupply by 1990 if present trends continue
(Hook, 1980, p.3). Our educational and scientific
imbalances must be rectified; the opportunities for
universities collaborating with business and industry
must meet very broad and solid criteria for applicability to knowledge and human welfare, and not serve
only the proprietary interests of business and
industry, regardless of how much "getting ahead" is
lauded in our social framework. Proprietary interests
are seldom if ever acceptable if we wish to fuel
human productivity, knowledge and social welfare; for
even in the arts and humanities we can go awry by
serving selfish and proprietary interests (Mooney,
1980; Scully, 1980), where, under the guise of art,
money and politics play a decisive role.

Some people have reacted to the pressure to
succeed, as we saw in the early chapters of this book,
by "dropping out". Not only is the dropping out
phenomenon apparently on the increase, people are now
writing books about how to do it, how to earn a living

425

without, in effect, working; that is, without
working in the standard, pressure-ridden ways.

Some summary statistics concerning stress in the
environment which has given rise to many of the
problems cited in this book include the following:

Coronary disease has increased about 500
percent over the past 50 years, this
is an increase that doubles the rate
every 10 years.

Well over 10 percent of the U.S. population, all ages considered (30
million Americans) have some form of
heart or blood vessel disease.

One man in five will have had a coronary
attack by age 60.

Cardiovascular disease deaths, not to
mention disablement, occur 50 times
as often as death due to industrial
accidents.

About 25 million Americans have hypertension (high blood pressure) and
most of them do not know they have it.

Death yearly from hypertension equals
about 60,000, not accounting for
those hypertension cases that precipitate heart attacks or strokes.

About 8 million Americans have ulcers;
many more may have ulcers undiagnosed.

Approximately 10,000 Americans die yearly
of hemorrhages or abdominal perfora-
tions that result from peptic ulcers.

About twelve percent (one in every 8
persons) of the general population
suffers from migraine headaches at
some time; regular migraine sufferers
number about 12 million.

At least 12 million Americans are reported
to be alcoholic; many more go undiagnosed,
and many are marginal alcoholics.

Diabetic cases number about 10 million in the U.S.

Americans are drug-happy: They consume 16,000 tons of aspirin yearly, costing the users $500 million. Americans purchase over 230 million prescriptions yearly, including 5 billion doses of tranquilizers, three billion doses of amphetamines, and 5 billion doses of barbituates.

Even though life expectancies are increasing, ten percent of Americans now aged 45 will die before age 55.

Although specific professions have better health records than Americans-in-general (especially the clergy, school teachers, and university professors are long-lived) their health records could be greatly improved with less stress in their lives. Cardiac and circulatory diseases and deaths run high among the medical and dental and executive professions; they harbour tensions and anxieties, arising from environmental stress, that is close to alarming.

The modern world of America promotes tension and anxiety in the individual because the environment is so stress-prone. Here are some ways in which persons can judge the extent to which they are pressured by their environments and the extent to which these stress impinge on the person as tension (felt) and anxiety (real, present and anticipated):

Hurries to get things finished once started; experiences obstructions as great frustrations.

Tends to be early or precisely on time for appointments.

Takes a highly competitive attitude, always comparing self with others' achievement.

Anticipates and overrules others in conversation by constant nodding, hand-waving, interrupting, anticipating, etc.

Always seems in a hurry.

427

Cannot wait easily; restless, pacing, moving, etc.

Tends to move rapidly as if in an emergency, full-speed-ahead.

Tries to do several things at a time; can't wait to start the next.

Generally fast doing whatever person is doing: eating, walking, etc.

Viewed by self and others as "hard-driving."

Keeps feelings to self; afraid that feelings will explode, cause retaliation, dislike, rejection.

Work dominates life; few interests outside of work.

Very amibitious; desires, strives for, quick advancement, pushes for it.

Seeks recognition from others for a job well done; can't rest on own evaluation.

Tends to be governed by deadlines, mostly set by self.

Always feels responsible, cannot delegate responsibility.

Takes work too seriously; works overtime, weekends, nights, extra days, etc.

Overly precise and detailed, "pickey," and miniscule in comments.

Overly critical of self and others; not satisfied with job even though demands acclaim from others.

There are many, many more characteristics that could be delineated, most of which are consistently seen as links between the job and its stress on the one hand, and personal discomfort, ill health, or outright debilitation or death on the other hand.

Other Features

Some people have reacted to the stress of life by dropping out, burning out, changing careers, and so forth, as we have seen in earlier chapters. Recently there has been a surfeit of books on how people can drop out in constructive ways, that is how they can avoid the stress arising from their previous, usual mode of living and adapt themselves to new modes. Articles in the popular press have also noted these new-mode-of-life practices. Some interesting trends and observations are seen in the following accounts of different modes of life and different ways of making a living.

Ronco (1977) suggests stress people create jobs of their own liking, things they may have wanted to do all their lives but "couldn't get around to it." These include engaging in small businesses (often run part-time), crafts, different professional practices than in the past, and odd jobs. One has, of course, to decide on a lower standard of living (usually) in order to reduce the previous stress, but this is an open, acknowledged trade-off, and must be considered from the very beginning. Important in all of these considerations are work tasks that people design for themselves; ownership (however small "it's mine" attitude); reducing paperwork and other formalities; work in a smaller--sometimes a very much smaller-- setting; work with people one likes and enjoys, not simply tolerates; approaching one's work as a craft rather than depersonalization through bureaucratic control; using one's brain and intelligence to solve problems, not just following the dictates of others for the sake of presumed efficiency; being able not only to design one's own work but also one's work-pace and method; expand the work and change the pace and/or proceedings at will, not under some one else's control; view work as wholesome, necessary, rewarding, energizing, not drudgery or lacking in utility (the opposite of the Protestant Work Ethic that views work as a necessary evil, ideally holy and unpleasant, joyless); arranging the work environment to suit one's preferences; and producing to gain as much satisfaction for self as possible, rather than kow-towing to others.

429

Ronco also points out how professionals--archi-
tects, lawyers, businessmen or women--can gain more
independence for themselves, submit to less supervisory regulations, and derive more personal benefit
from their endeavors (Ronco, 1977, pp.95-192).

Three books stress living without a job (Maurer,
1979; Levinson, 1979; Lefkowitz). Some of the ways
people envision their non-working activities follow.
Maurer covers instances where people have been deprive
of work (who, otherwise, want to work), suffer degre-
dation and build strong resentments against their
companies and against society for the treatment they
experience. He states that unemployed people have
been robbed of something important and they know it.
These are people who share the traditional notions
that people ought to work and earn their own keep;
the denial of this ambition is what is devastating fo:
the unemployed, who consequently develop intense ange:
at society and the political system. Work is a
measure of personal worth; men who were former executives not being able to obtain a $3-an-hour job
pumping gas works erosively on their morale and under
cuts any self-confidence they might have had. Then
there are those Maurer documents, who intentionally
did poor work to provoke dismissal so they would not
have to work at all and could live off unemployment
benefits. This group is more anti-social and ulterio:
but "not working" is both an aim and a consequence of
their deliberate behavior on the job. Both groups--
those who want to work and cannot find employment and
those who fein work in order to be dismissed and live
on the dole--are by-products of an economic system
that does a poor job with a large segment of our
population so far as building and rewarding work
incentive is concerned. They are the dregs, sometime
not of their own choosing, of the economic system tha
we have discussed so much in this book as it affects
the health of people. Maurer's work compliments some
what Studs Terkel's Working, fills out some other
aspects of the world-of-work and adds to our understanding of how work, misguided and misfiring, can
lead to the deprecation of the individual through one
or another route; and both books represent how the
system damages individuals in ways that lead to not
working, to not wanting to work, and to getting by
without work.

Levinson's tact is a bit different, yet still
altering the usual notions of working: Earning
Money Without A Job (1979). Levinson's main pitch is
that the economic system is a constricting and controlling entity and that one should seek freedom from
its constraints. In short, one out of a job need not
be out of work; you need no job to earn money, he
asserts and spends his whole book supporting this
thesis. Giving up the formal jobs confronts one with
what she/he wants from life, one's values, the luxuries
one wishes, the basics of living and how expensive and
important they are, and so on. Develop your priorities,
Levinson says, then seek ways to meet these conditions;
earning money without a job is easy--after you get a
good basic start and know what to do! He stresses
versatility in one's approach to earning money: Try
to become extensions of growing businesses, be a module
in a larger aggregate, utilize all kinds of approaches
to producing or selling (goods or services) you create
or engage in, and so forth. A novel idea, and one way
to put it into operation is seen in the following
quotation: "Imagine a service station that picks up
customers' cars after the people are asleep, fills the
cars with gas, changes the oil, checks the battery,
brakes, and transmission fluid, makes any requested
repairs, and returns the cars to the driveway or
garage before the people awaken" (Levinson, 1979,p.9).

Levinson's program is based on a considerable
amount of ingenuity, some capital (or ways to get it),
and enough money, motivation and perspecacity to sustain one's self through the early uncertainties of
enterpreneurship. He is substituting not a new kind,
but a rarer kind, of enterprise for the traditional
one in order to gain what he calls freedom, which
means freedom from the usual hourly and place and
routine structure that most people endure and live by.
This mode of adjusting to our economic, professional
and work world is alternative to dropping out, burning
out, getting sick, living off the dole, being
unemployed, or otherwise refusing to go along wholly
with the system.

Lefkowitz's book (1979) is an amalgam of what work
is like now and what it may be like in a couple of
decades hence. He observes that college students are
less certain today than they were a decade ago that
they can "make it" in the economic world, that they
will be open to non-standard occupations and will be
looking for new vocational worlds since the

431

conventional ones are too hard to enter, too constricting, or lacking in tangible rewards. Too few jobs permit one to express one's self fully, seldom are jobs challenging for a lengthy period of time, and the contributions one can make are moot. Industry will take on more and more ephemeral tasks and will require quick problem-solving skills on the part of professionals, Lefkowitz argues. He says that "Many corporations...have become in Alvin Toffler term 'ad-hocraries.' They respond to changing market demands by restructuring their organizations and by substituting temporary, transient problem-solving teams for a permanent work force" (Lefkowitz, 1979, p.282). This ephemeral nature of many kinds of work, including high-level professional work, will doubt- lessly add to the stress and strain of work, make the work environment less stable and make employment for many professionals less secure. If Lefkowitz is correct in predicting these kinds of industrial and professional changes, it is not unlikely that the issues adumbrated in this book will be on the increase and human suffering will likewise increase. With a kind of patchwork, new professions will arise to ameliorate the stresses encountered by the highly changing work scene. Lefkowitz observes that over four hundred colleges now have majors in "leisure studies," and many colleges and universities offer services termed "leisure counseling." Here, again, is the picture of people not doing or being able to do for themselves what is needed for an integral life, but having to rely on professionals who serve the enormity and complexity of the industrial/medical, industrial/educational and now the industrial/leisure complex.

The most popular book in recent years on jobs and careers, much of it springing from malcontent in one's regular and prepared-for job is the book by Bolles, What Color Is Your Parachute? (1979). It is not a book on how to drop-out or live without work; it is rather, a "seeking and finding" manual on self-develop ment as it applies to the world of work. Most people enter work without enough proper consideration and live to regret it (see Chapter I). Some genuinely want to change occupations. Professionals, as we have seen, number largely in the change-your-career popula- tion. Bolles puts people through a number of paces that will help insure a more thoughtful choice, better preparation for work, and more exacting and telling ways to judge what one has done and, finally, to derive satisfactions not previously experienced in work. The book is a recognition of the maladaptations that exist in the world of work, the stresses people encounter unwillingly or needlessly, and ways to remedy these unwanted states of affair. Many practical guides exist in the book in the form of chapters that discuss the problem area under consideration but, more importantly, tell people (or, better, suggest to them) how they may overcome the previous disadvantages in work and career. Instruction is offered on how to hunt for a job; how to withstand rejection; counsel on how people can ginger-up their motivation; when and where help is needed; how decisions are made, how and where one wants finally to work; and how to enlist the help of people who have the power to employ one and utilize the skills the candidate knows she/he has or can develop. If the job world were not so plagued with stress, tensions, anxiety, uncertainty, this book would never have hit the pulse of people as they view their careers. While Bolles does not tell us how to remedy the ills of the industrial complexes one will face, he does help one prepare one's own initiation, skill, perspacacity and motivation to meet the challenges that are "out there."

Where, then, is it all going? To hell in a basket, as some would say? To such profound changes in the professions that one would scarcely recognize them in a few years? To new professional consciousness and social responsibility such as to insure optimal services to the public? To increasing public control and management of the present power centers in society? Or to other ends? No one can say. The surfacing of the problems of society and the professions as they impact education, health, environmental concerns, and the like are recent enough in their seriousness and urgency to make forecasting with any degree of accuracy almost impossible. What we seem to know from existing research and clinical investigations is that the professions are in a very poor state of affairs; one might say they are "enjoying poor health..." since there is much enjoyment of a superficial (selfish) type coming the professional's way, often masking the poor health of the professionals that one can observe upon looking more carefully into the matter. Needed now are many more studies of the professions that point more specifically to the many health problems they harbour, covering longer periods of time and investigating more searchingly the relationships of professions to society at points where health, ethical and social responsibility concerns meet. Needed, too, are studies of how each profession looks at itself—what it can be proud of and what is anathema to the professions—and how the profession is regarded by society. The present insular attitude of most professions is such that the professions tend to respond poorly to social needs and to neglect their own growth and development at the same time. Perhaps, in time, more self-correction will become each profession. We can also hope that the integrity of individuals will aid the overhauling of each profession as a profession (as an organization) and that combined individual and group efforts will lead to a general improvement of the professions. Change in professions can begin at any point where there is a clearly understood need; as one facet improves that may have an ameliorative effect on other facets. As one or more professions improves in ways salient to itself and to society, that may become an exemplary lead for others.

CHAPTER XIV

BIBLIOGRAPHY

Abelson, P.H. Science and engineering education,
    Science, 1980, 210, 965.

Baldridge, J.V. & Tierney, M.L. New Approaches to
    Management. San Francisco: Jossey-Bass, 1979.

Barnet, R.J. The Lean Years: Politics in the Age of
    Scarcity. N.Y.: Simon & Schuster, 1980.

Barron, J. L.I. consumer advocate thrives on show,
    N.Y.TIMES, April 13, 1980.

Bolles, R.N. What Color Is Your Parachute? Berkeley,
    Calif.: Ten Speed Press, 1979.

Brown, M.H. The Poisoning of America by Toxic
    Chemicals. N.Y.: Pantheon Books, 1980.

Carter, L.J. Gus Speth, Planning the 'consumer society'
    Science, 1980, 208, 1009-1012.

Chu, F.D. & Trotter, S. The Madness Establishment.
    N.Y.: Grossman, 1974.

Denton, H. Contaminated pork shipped to schools,
    Washington POST, May 24, 1980.

Dewar, H. & Knight, J. Senate moves to curb FTC, as
    it reins itself, Washington POST, February 7,1980.

Douglas, M. The World of Goods. N.Y.: Basic Books,
    1979.

Drake, D. Medical School. N.Y.: Rawson Associates
    Publishers, Inc., 1978.

Duignan, P. & Rabushka, A. (Eds.) The United States
    In The 1980's. N.Y.: Hoover Institute, 1980.

Editorial. Calling the chemical industry's bluff,
    Washington POST, 1980, Nov. 18, Editorial Page.

Editorial. Harvard abandons plan for role in genetic-
    engineering company, Chronicle of Higher Education,
    1980, 21, #14, p.1.

Frankel, G. Health plan groups warned against violating antitrust law, Washington POST, May 9, 1980.

Frankel, G. Virginia Kepone researcher finds $5 million cupboard is bare, Washington POST, 1980, Nov. 18, p.1.

Green, M. & Massie, R., Jr. (Eds.) The Big Business Reader. N.Y.: Pilgrim Press, 1980.

Grubisich, T. Virginia charges Dart's food is tainted, Washington POST, May 3, 1980.

Hayes, T.C. New master of the "Geneen Machine," N.Y. TIMES, April 6, 1980.

Hook, J. Psychiatry departments step up efforts to reverse enrollment declines, Chronicle Of Higher Education, 1980, 21, #14, p.3.

Jencks, C. Who Gets Ahead? N.Y.: Basic Books, 1979.

Kiechel, W., III. Playing the rules of the corporate strategy game, Fortune, 1979, 100, 110-118.

Kinard,J.L. About this business of social responsibility, Personnel J., 1974, 53, 825-828.

Kolata, G.B. Love canal: False alarm caused by botched study, Science, 1980, 208, 1239-1242.

Korman, A.K. The preciction of managerial performance: A review, Personnel Psychology, 1968, 21, 295-322.

Kramer, L. Study says U.S. policies imperil small business, Washington POST, January 13, 1980.

Kuttner, R. Revolt Of The Haves. N.Y.: Simon and Schuster, 1980.

Lasko, K.A. The Great Billion Dollar Medical Swindle. Indianapolis: Bobbs-Merrill, 1979.

Lefkowitz, B. Breaktime: Living Without Work In A Nine to Five World. N.Y.: Hawthorne Books, 1979

Levinson, J.C. Earning Money Without A Job. N.Y.: Holt, Rinehart & Winston, 1979.

436

Macrae, N. United States can keep growing and lead - if it wishes. _Smithsonian_, 1976, _7_, 34-41.

Maeroff, G.I. The fast track to the good life. New York _TIMES_, May 18, 1980, p.1

Magarrell, J. College-industry cooperation could strengthen research, _Chronicle Of Higher Education_, 1980, 21, #6, p.7.

Mansfield, S. Mental distress on the rise, Washington _POST_, May 23, 1980.

Maurer, H. _Not Working: An Oral History of the Unemployed_. N.Y.: Holt, Rinehart & Winston, 1979.

Malatsky, I. 710 more families in Love Canal area may be relocated. N.Y. _TIMES_, May 18, 1980.

Miami Herald Newspaper, 1 in 4 report an alcohol-related problem. _Miami Herald_, July 2, 1978.

Mintz, M. Community dislocations: a painful side effect of merger, Washington _POST_, April 20, 1980a, pp.1-2.

Mintz, M. Nader assails Jarvin for 'crosstown hypocrisy', Washington _POST_, May 6, 1980b, p.10.

McDowell, E. Making it: Bosses under 40. N.Y. _TIMES_, March 30, 1980.

McKeown, T. _The Role of Medicine: Dream, Mirage, or Nemesis?_ Princeton: Univ. Press, 1979.

Meyer, H.E. Remodeling the executive for the corporate club, Fortune, 1979, _100_, 82-92.

Mooney, M.M. _The Ministry of Culture: Connections Among Art, Money and Politics_. N.Y.: Wyndham Books, 1980.

Nader, R. Introduction, in Green, M. & Massie, R.J. (Eds.) _Big Business Reader, 1980: Essays on the Corporate America_. N.Y.: Pilgrim Press, 1980.

Nickel, H. The corporation haters, _Fortune_, 1980, _101_, 126-136.

Omang, J. Senate approves fund to clean up hazardous
     waste, Washington POST, 1980, Nov. 25, p.1.

Parisi, A. Who Pays? Cleaning up the Love Canals.
     N.Y. TIMES, June 8, 1980, p.1 Sect. 3.

Peckman, J.A. Setting National Priorities: Agenda
     for the 1980s. Washington, D.C.: Brookings
     Institute, 1980.

Petersen, R. The Philosophy of a Peasant. N.Y.:
     Interaction Books, 1979.

Pine, A. Carter jawbones chemical executives,
     Washington POST, April 12, 1980.

Pine, A. Executive interview: William Agee,
     Washington POST, 1980, Nov. 23, 1F.

Ronco, W.C. Jobs: How People Create Their Own.
     Boston: Beacon Press, 1977.

Saunders, D.A. The boss' paycheck: Who gets the
     biggest? Forbes, 1978, May 29, 86-111.

Scully, M.G. 'Big Brother' At the Endowments:
     Uncovering a cultural conspiracy, The Chronicle
     of Higher Education, 1980, 21, #14, p.13.

Sinclair, M. Prices 32% lower where optometrists
     advertise, FTC finds, Washington POST, May 16,
     1980.

TIME Magazine. Capitalism - Is it working? TIME
     Magazine, 1980, April 21, pp.40-55.

Weber, M. The Rise of the Protestant Ethic and the
     Spirit of Capitalism. N.Y.: Chas. Scribner's
     Sons, 1958.

White House Conference on Small Business: A Prelimi-
     nary Report. Washington, D.C., June 13-17, 1980.

Wildavsky, A. How To Limit Government Spending.
     Berkeley, Calif.: Univ. of California Press,1980

Wright, J.P. On A Clear Day You Can See General Motor:
     Grosse Point, Michigan: Wright Enterprises, 1979

Zonarra, V.F. How Dow Chemical kept selling roof
    parts despite rash of leaks. The Wall Street
    Journal, April 24, 1980, p.1.

CHAPTER XV

ADDENDUM

This chapter seeks to test further the generalizations arrived at in the main text of this book. In so doing, attention is given to very current literature and news releases, popular articles, professional journal articles, moreso than scientific books which are seldom current (often reaching publication one-to-three years after data collection and write-up).

Since our economy and material health and wealth have been in jeopardy for several years, it is unlikely that the professions would have grown in stature or health in the past few years. In fact, the opposite is true: The professions have become even more insular; their estrangement from society and their avowed public purposes have increased as shown in material costs, poorer care or service, more conflict with society, and greater unrest within the major professions. Some ways in which these trends are noted are contained in the remainder of this addendum.

Executives And Their Businesses

Evans and Bartolome have summarized recent business/executive and commercial trends in their book, Must Success Cost So Much? (1980). They surveyed over 500 middle managers, who were in various executive programs at the European Institute of Business Administration, in France. Several countries were represented in this study population. They answered a questionnaire taking over two hours; additionally they were interviewed for about two hours. The investigators saw the work environment of many management people as injurious to healthful living. Jobs, the small work environments, the larger corporations, and their roles, often proved inimical to psychological and physical health.

A spate of books on Japanese business, industry and culture, and their interrelationships has appeared in recent months: Pascale & Anthos, The Art Of Japanese Management (1981); Ouchi's Theory Z: How American Business Can Meet the Japanese Challenge (1981); being two outstanding examples of studies of American business from the standpoint of its internal faults and from viewing its contrasts with Japanese business and management. In Japan, society and

441

business, and government and labor, are more closely intertwined than in America. The welfare and progress of one is seen as beneficial to the accomplishments of the other. In America, divisiveness and competition, stress and anxiety predominate; conflict is so rampant that the pluses from one segment of society do not ramify in positive gainful directions, but often do the opposite: Increased strife. Hence public satisfaction with business, the quality of goods and services, and the satisfactions of workers on the job remain controversial and even negative. Japan seems to have overcome these divisive practices. Ouchi remarks: "When economic and social life are integrated into a single whole, then relationships between individuals become intimate...individuals inter-connect through multiple bonds" (Ouchi, 1981, p.54). This single statement typifies as much as any in the whole book the differences between Japanese and American business and management; and of course, the health, stress and psychological problems attendant thereto.

From studies conducted in America and in Japan by two Harvard Business School Professors (Prof. Hayes and Abernathy), Wayne (1982) reports that their conclusions support much of the recent literature on Japanese management and business as it contrasts with our efforts. More important, American failures in business recently are not attributed to heavy-handed worker relationships, labor unrest, poor work ethic, and the like, but to poor management-worker relationships, as exemplified in the factory, the office and in the field, as well as how the corporation itself is managed. Everywhere there is a new emphasis on better relationships, on more worker inputs into business management, and an increased emphasis on longer-term goals and long-term economic and psychological health of all concerned. A new wave of humanism may yet supplant the old do-or-die, dog-eat-dog, and everyman-for-himself American doctrine.

On the more critical side of the ledger are three recent books re-examining the American "growth philosophy" of the past several decades: Bartlett's Reaganomics (1982); Wolfe's America's Impasse (1982); and O'Toole's Making America Work (1982). In several ways the works of these authors examine American work ethics and work incentive (O'Toole quotes: "My managers--even the top ones--don't seem to care about their work anymore...no real dedication, no committment..."). Companies have failed to cope with

442

worker attitudes and need for community; this ramifies
into poor production schedules, shoddy work, low
profits, decreased morale, and more executive and
management stress and strain. A vicious circle is
set in motion. Bolstered by a new look at "success"
is a book by Maccoby (1982) which says that success
is not always the same as to win; hence competition is
looked at anew, more in terms of cooperation and
integration.

One could argue that idealization of American
business and worker relationships are all well and
good but are they realistic. Can we really function
more harmoniously in America, some would ask, given
our frontier spirit and strident competitiveness, of
over 350 years duration? But not to look in these
new directions is also folly. It is likely not so
much the idealization of change that may lead the
way but the immediacy of the surge in business
failures over the past several years that force a new
look at our practical efforts and may lead the way to
change (Noble, 1981). Business bankruptcy filing
increased over 40 percent in 1981, over 1980. Not
only are these severe economic losses, think of the
anguish, discouragement, personal and family turmoil
that follow in the wake of business failures for
persons concerned; and the mental health problems,
too. The interrelationships between life and work are
so basically integral that failures in one department
are bound to ramify into other aspects of life. The
health of professions depends upon a basic social and
work integrity that we so far sorely lack in America.

Medicine

While some writers are trying to cast medicine in
the older, more idealistic mode (Black, 1982), the
facts speak louder than the fictions. Medicine is
still straying from its intended social and health
ideals and is party to problems in at least three
dimensions: the continuing, stress, tension and
anxiety among its practitioners; the isolation of
medicine from its social goals relative to its avowed
intentions; and a growing criticism from society
concerning the costs of medical services, the shoddi-
ness of its work and the various legal implications
arising from the whole enterprise (Bassey, 1982).

443

Burnham (1982) has recounted what has happened
to American Medicine's "Golden Age". Among the many
problems recently encountered by the medical profession are: Being "deprofessionalized" or robbed of
its professional status by its critics, including
medical people; a growing public mistrust of the
profession; spiraling medical costs; increase in suits
against physicians for alleged malpractice; the
development of more harmful attitudes and practices
toward patients ("Iatrogenic" medicine?) as opposed
to the professed one of doing no harm; and so on.
While Burnham did not attack the actual health/stress/
tension and anxiety problems among physicians themselves, he could well have done so and fit these
observations in with the ones he discussed. Some
supporting literature for these untoward changes in
medicine in recent decades--and also accelerated in
the past decade--include the following: The American
Osteopathic Associations Survey Of Public Attitudes
Toward Medical Care (1981); Berman's The Solid Gold
Stethescope (1976); and Lander's Defective Medicine:
Risk, Anger, And The Malpractice Crisis (1978); to name
a few. Any one of these publications documents the
merits of resounding criticism of the medical
profession, and from many angles. A recent Washington
POST article (1981) continues to record the high
suicide rate among physicians. It is part of the
price we pay for "success," not only in the business
and executive worlds, as seen abundantly herein, but
in the medical and other health professions as well.
(Are the lessons from the "Industrial State" of
Galbraith (1967) now ramifying into all the professions
as well as into the fabric of society generally?)
Similarly, and additionally, there appears to be a
growing problem of alcoholism among university professors of medicine (1982), not alone those suffering
the ravages of private practice. Marriage and family
problems among physicians continue to find their way
to publication and social scrutiny (Smith, 1980).
Mullin's article says that we persist in training
physicians now as we did decades ago, failing to
reflect now the many changes in family life among the
physician's patients, new social needs and responsibilities, and advances in biological and technological
sciences. In part, the rush to technology, rather than
accommodating to changes in the way people live,
tends to misdirect medicine and substitute technology
for care, gadgetry for understanding, and costs
replace responsibility. The latter point--costs-- is
well documented by a brief account of hospital and

444

medical cost increases over the last decade (Barringer, 1981); where they have increased from $133.05 per day, 1970, to over $400.00 per day, 1980, a national average. This rate is, of course, much greater than the rate of inflationary increase over this decade and does not reflect the costs of other medical expenses (nursing care, drugs, X-Rays, etc. (Bergsma & Thomas, 1981).

While positive trends in the practice of medicine from a social standpoint are not convincingly present, some pluses do exist. Veatch (1981) offers some new thoughts on medical ethics. He points out that medical ethics in the past have been "doctor-centered" and perhaps self-serving, reflecting particular times and interests. What is needed, he says, are codes of ethics that accent patient rights, social responsibility and respect, and a "...complex set of understandings among professionals, patients and society in general..." reflecting layers of mutual loyalty, fidelty, responsibility, and support. A large order! We can only hope it will come about.

Education And The University

Stressful problems in the university encompas more than the individual health and psychological problems of the faculty and students. These problems seem not to have abated in the past few years. As the university "goes more commercial," it is expected that more stress will accompany additional health problems.

One facet of change in universities is the issue of how they shall invest themselves--in scholarship and research, or in business, commercial ventures, the commercialization of sports, and the like. It has been pointed out in this book that the industrial/educational complex has taken its toll on the university; the trend unfortunately continues (Coughlin, 1981). She writes that a growing number of scholars serving on corporate boards of directors constitute a "pernicious trend" that challenges the objectivity and scientific credibility of universities. Often the board members also write on public policy, sit on governmental decision-making bodies, or conduct research in fields that promise lucrative monetary rewards rather than the less glamorous road to basic research. Whether university professorships and business/corporate memberships can live compatible

445

together over a span of time remains to be seen. So far, we have indications that these two sets of inclinations are somewhat contradictory (Giamatti, 1982).

Money talks in other ways in universities, in higher education, and in sports in higher education (Britell, 1982; Scully, 1982). In one case, students and faculty are lured away from graduate education and research by extra high salaries, mostly offered by big business and big sports. Students are drawn away from the humanities, also, and into business, accounting, economics and computer technology. Why should an M.A. level computer expert turn down a $25,000.00 - $40,000.00 a year job to finish a Ph.D., only to find academic salaries--post Ph.D.--to be considerably lower? Sometimes students are lured into the higher paying jobs only to sour on them later, missing intellectual stimulation and research challenge thereby. Some have to flirt with wealth first, however.

Not only are the humanities and all basic research areas suffering from the commercialization of the university, science training suffers also (McDonald, 1982). He documents how science departments are asking for more governmental support for basic research, not only because it is legitimately needed, but also in order to offset, in part, the drift of science into commercial ventures that promise fast bucks. Also, information obtained under commercial contract becomes propriatory; knowledge is not shared with other researchers for fear of being "beaten to the draw" on the development of new commercial ventures. Science courses may also be slanted toward commercial interests rather than teaching students to think in terms of basic research problems. Withall, the free exchange of research data and ideas cannot be challenged if science is to prosper; any damper on this process, however commercially successful, is to be avoided.

Perhaps as a part of the commercialization of science in the university, public attitudes toward science show ambivalence and a lack of understanding of what science is about, and the roles universities play in scientific advancement (Miller et al, 1980). Fewer people now than twenty years ago think scientific research benefits have outweighed harmful results; there is some feeling that peoples' ideas of right

446

and wrong have been too strongly challenged by science. If the benefits of science are obscured by improper interpretation and wrongful application ("wrong" in terms of the public good, that is), then adverse reactions are likely to accumulate; in turn, these attitudes may act to undercut support for science in universities and thereby encourage the seeking of commercial support for research and scholarship.

Former and present university presidents have spoken and written about what is happening to universities, and how their direction can be improved upon (Feinberg, 1982; Giamatti, 1982; Bok, 1982). Clark Kerr (Feinberg, 1982) has been working for years to define more clearly the university's role in society (Kerr, 1963), and how to improve upon the university's integrity. In a recent book, Bok (1982), president of Harvard University, has carried on this important discussion, outlining the social obligations of the university. Bok treats such issues as to how the university integrates present commercial opportunities and demands within the university's traditional research and scholarly interests; how the politicizing of the university can be rendered non-detrimental; and how gifts and grants can meet first of all scholarly and human objectives and not give rise to pressure points or force selfish committments on the university.

In spite of many inroads into university functioning and purposes, public respect for learning, at least nominally, tends to remain high. A recent report (Bover & Hechinger, 1981) indicates that the percentage of college freshmen who think national institutions are dishonest or immoral show major corporations as drawing the highest frequency of negative responses (41 percent); whereas only 20 percent of the same group consider colleges and universities similarly dishonest. Churches were ranked as the least immoral (18 percent so opined). With a little bit of help from reality and proper planning perhaps the university can stave off its recent commercial stance and get back to a more substantial role in society. If so, not only will the university and higher education function more productively as a result, these influences may constructively help public education at the elementary and secondary levels, and increase the psychological and health status of both university faculty and students.

447

In a manner of speaking, the law may continue to
be the "Peck's Bad Boy" of the professions. Not so
much because of health and individual stress problems--
although these are present they have not been researched
as well as with medicine, nursing, dentistry and the
clergy--but because of law's position vis a vis
society, in terms of acceptance, criticism, fees and
general social responsibility. Legal grievance committees are overrun with complaints--the lack of justice
in courts, the associations overlooking lawyer's
alleged misconduct, the impression that courts do
not draw out the truth, and so on (Smith, 1982).
Part of the negative public reaction against law and
lawyers stems from the public image that lawyers
promote (Noble, 1981), wherein bloated starting
salaries in the large firms continue to range from
$24,000.00 - $40,000.00 annually, in contrast to
small firms where salaries hover around the $10,000.00
- $20,000.00 annual figure; the passing of many
responsibilities to paralegals; and the general
unavailability of good lawyers to the average client.

Gains have been made by women in law (Epstein,
1982; Dershowitz, 1982), but there is a long way to
go, and the road is still rocky, tortuous, and
circuitous.

Judicial competence is being challenged mostly
vis a vis science and technology (Jasanoff & Nelkin,
1981). The simpler and more traditional issues in
law about right and wrong and factually establishing
whether he "did" or "didn't" do so-and-so are giving
way to complex issues raised by science and technology,
where "...it is widely believed that the traditional
processes of adjudication are no longer capable of
handling many...disputes" (p.1211). Policy and
conceptual issues abound in science and technology
and legal practice may be sorely unprepared for these
ranging issues. Not only is law involved intimately
in such science and technology issues, so is the
whole of society (Mazur, 1981); and the role of law
in technical controversy may be so limiting--as
traditionally practiced--as to harm the public
interest.

Withall, the controversies in the legal profession may be pressing more toward objectivity and
equalization. The Friedman (1981) report is a recent

example of how the legal profession is functioning in some respects in the District of Columbia; it offers some 71 detailed recommendations for improving the legal disciplinary system in that jurisdiction. Some of these recommendations may be put into action to test their salience and applicability. Commensurate with the legal profession moving toward greater self-examination is more responsibility in self-reporting among legal firms (The American Lawyer Guide to Law Firms, 1982). This publication gives the "What's What" as to how law firms function and allows the public to look into the inner life of law firms. One needs this kind of look, also, into how universities function, how hospitals are run, how the professions make their decisions about their own and the public's welfare, and other matters that tend to isolate the professions from their social responsibilities.

The avant-garde publications (Legal Times of Washington, The American Lawyer, and The National Law Journal) continue to publish articles relating to ethics, social problems in the law and among lawyers, and other issues relating the profession more to society. Among such articles include Berreby's "Law Schools On The Brink," (1982) concerning the enormous tuition increases nationwide (about 22.5 percent increase, 1982, over the previous year), the effects these increases may have on who is selected for law school (based on who can afford it), and increasing enrollments despite economic hard-ships. The role of continuing education for lawyers and judges is addressed by McKay (1982), a problem seen in the earlier chapter on Lawyers. It is impor-tant that continuing education does not foster only the economic interests of big business and corporations who can well afford to put on continuing education courses when the poor, the elderly and the handicapped have no such recourse for educating the bench about their needs.

The Clergy

The health of the clergy from a psychological standpoint still exists in a scattered literature; systematic studies are not common, within or across denominations. No current studies appear in one volume to compare with the comprehensive resume offerred by Menges and Dittes (1965). This wide-ranging book requires an update. It dealth with such

449

important topics from a research standpoint as the following: adjustment, health, wives and families, mental illness, personality and psychotherapy, as all of these impacted the clergy generally.

A recent study (Schuller et al, 1980) covers the attitudes of 5,000 clergymen, all denominations, in the U.S. and Canada, primarily with reference to attributes related to "readiness for the ministry." The most important or highly rated factors were: an open style, caring for persons under stress, leadership, theological thought, faith, worship, and denominational collegiality. Negative themes included a tendency to alienate self from congregation, using condemnation as a basis for solving personal problems, undisciplined living, immaturity, and taking personal advantage. It is interesting how much the positively and negatively rated themes among the clergy touch so closely on the ethical and low-social-responsibility themes we have seen connected with medical and legal practice. The latter professions would do well to study these attitudinal characteristics, as the clergy is doing, and openly accent their importance (both positive and negative).

Much has been said about the clergy becoming more interested in counseling and psychotherapy, there being a noticeable tendency in this direction in recent years. Now we have the clergy subject to malpractice in relation to their counseling efforts (Freedman, 1982). One such case occurred, which is far from a trend, but it is nonetheless alarm-sounding, in which a priest-therapist and his church are being sued for "pastoral malpractice" in alleged connection with the suicide death of a teenager who was being given therapy for his personal problems. Arising now in response to this happening are some untoward events, one of which is some interest on the part of insurance companies to claim a new area of insurance coverage: "pastoral professional liability" or "clergyman's errors and omissions" insurance. Are we witnessing the beginnings of a kind of "industrialization" of the clergy and their counseling functions? What this untoward event will bring in ten years is hard to calculate; it may be ominous.

The usual problems in regard to the clergy's relationships with wife and laiety also abound in the recent literature. Oswald et al (1980) have written about the joys and dilemmas of being a clergyman's spouse and the many conflicts faced in such a role. Wives may not be as "Yoked-In" now as they were a few decades ago, but some of this role is still in evidence. One difficulty these authors point out is that there are no support groups for the wives of clergy, and they seem not to spontaneously gravitate toward mutual support. If lessons learned from other professions about the importance of mutual support are reasonably correct, then mutual support among these wives would promise to hold up well for them. Perhaps the seeming reluctance of clergymen's wives to form mutual interest and support groups stems from their reported low or negative self-image. The system that allows (or makes, or encourages?) dependence on the husband also promotes a lower self-image. Resourcefulness does not follow easily from over-dependence.

Harris (1980) and Harris and Hahn (1980) have studied power and stress in relation to the ministry itself; and have developed a 7-week course, based on the Harris book to help guide the ministry members through its many perils, especially in relation to conflicts with lay members and with certain aspects of the ministerial role. Positive reactions to stress are always welcome in a profession; the ministry may be slow in coming to this kind of action, except for meeting the challenge of alcoholism among the clergy. Stress and role conflict may not be as obvious to the ministers--nor ways to overcome the results of such stress as obvious--as is the case with flagrant violations of conduct and propriety, such as is found with alcoholism. However the stress problems are still real.

The stress on jobs that require high levels of executive performance and drive may also occasion untoward results for the clergy. Oswald (1979) has written case reports on clergymen who aspired to, and gained, higher executive jobs, and the early heart-attack-occasioned death (in the 50s) almost immediately ensuing. Or the quick falling into cancerous decline, following within a year or two upon acceptance of a high post. The motivation that propels them to higher executive positions--taking jobs as they do, not unlike those of the chief executive officers of businesses--may at the same time make them more vulnerable to the associated stresses. Retirement, or sudden steps upward can each occasion stress: People are not ready for these changes and

451

being thrust into them at ages between 45 and 60 may
be too much both physically and psychologically. The
problem needs far greater study than it has received;
executive roles at high levels in the ministry are
not common, but as they increase in number, we may
see these particular "religious executives" succumbing
to the same stress ravages that the business world
points up to us so clearly.

Stresses within the job, in the ordinary course
of events, are adumbrated some by Leas (1980a; 1980b).
In both articles, Leas deals with the tensions that
may lead to the clergyman being fired (due to conflicts
with his parishioners, and/or with the executive
branches of the ministry), and offers guides to
conflict management. The role of the clergyman in
many respects is looking more and more like that of
a business executive, and the untoward consequences
of such roles may be shaping up in a similar way.

In a study of the counseling role of the clergy
as part of their ministerial duties, Clark and Thomas
(1979) have divided their population of ministers
into those judged to be religiously liberal versus
conservative, and those with more, or less, amounts
of counselor training. Their findings relate not only
to the religious roles of these people but their
general attitudes. Since the clergy are now--and
becoming more--important in the mental health field,
these findings are arresting. The more conservative
religious clergymen are more religious and more
given to moralizing with clients, in their counseling
roles, than are the more liberal clergy counselors.
The more the clergy counselor has had formal counselor
training (in psychology, in counseling, etc.), the
more s/he emphasizes counseling above religious
considerations. The liberal religious counselor,
then, becomes more like a non-religion-attached
psychologist, and moves away from the role of the
traditional religious spokesperson. This changing
role of the clergy has been noted in the earlier
section of this book, has been in evidence for a
couple of decades. It appears increasingly more
prominent in the attitudes and practices of
religious counselors. What effects this role change
will have on the clergy from a stress and health
standpoint remains to be seen. But that the clergy
roles are influx seems abundantly evident among all
denominations, and these changes have been associated
with increasing stress among all other major profession

452

Psychology

The psychology profession, especially the clinical and counseling branches, manage to stay out of serious trouble, especially from the standpoint of being sued for malpractice. Moving ahead on other fronts, psychology is witnessing an emphasis on studies of business, industry and organizations (Kraus, 1980; Schein, 1980; Brief et al, 1981), much of which fits well with our point of view in this book in that the role of the business is seen more and more in terms of its responsibilities to the employee and to the public. Stress, tension, and anxiety are everpresent in industrial organizations--and others as well--but a more clinical and social emphasis is emerging in this literature which binds the organization in conceptual, practical and social ways to the employee on the one hand and to the public on the other hand. Some other important trends in psychology that affect its social stance are the following: More emphasis on the community and the social setting in clinical work (Bazar, 1982; McNett, 1982); improving state requirements for continuing education of its professionals (Watkins, 1982); and a clearer recognition of the limitations on the role of the psychologist and psychiatrist in crime and punishment issues, especially where insanity concerns are at stake (Gaylin, 1982; Meyer, 1982). And clinical psychology continues to struggle with its research image of itself as data accumulate that show clinicians do (and read) little research (Kelly et al, 1978), a matter that takes clinicians away from the science to more limited (and perhaps monitarily inspired) gains. Where these trends will lead and how they will affect psychology as a profession, especially as a health profession is now moot.

Dentistry

Of late, the same problems have been plaguing dentistry--health, stress and psychological problems-- that have been around for decades (as reviewed earlier on in this book). "New" illnesses, as well, emerge on the scene. Dermatitis is being called an "occupational hazard" for dentists (Caruso, 1981), and evidence is supplied for this set of conditions. Continuing problems relating to ethics, social responsibility, sexism, and the delivery of services to the public as well as the role of women in dentistry are surfacing (Todd et al, 1981). These authors

453

observe the increase of women in dentistry and address
some of the problems for the profession, and for men
and women dentists. We should always keep in mind
that, despite an increase in women of late in all the
major professions, where heretofore they have been
denied access (especially law, medicine and dentistry),
we are way behind some European and Asian countries in
the use of women in dentistry (and other medical
professions). We still have a long way to go and
will doubtlessly encounter many problems in the wake
of these changes. We are only beginning to see the
enormous ramifications of a change in the role of
women in dentistry during the past few years. (See,
also, Waldman, 1981, who discusses similar problems).

Less strictly professional/scientific matters
within the profession of dentistry are seen in the
professions' grappling with "advertising" and its
implications for ethical, professional, service
delivery and public relations issues. Advertising
may be a perjorative term; as long as it is used this
way the profession of dentistry will not be open to
some important advantages associated with candidness
about its services and the development of further
public responsibility to let the consumer know his
rights and his recourses (Gero, 1981).

As with law and medicine, dentistry training is
costing more and more. Here, again, the soaring costs
are likely to bias selection of who gets into dental
school; it may even change some aspects of the nature
of dental training and practice over time. One consequence may be a decrease in the number of dentists
(Stahl et al, 1981) which can easily ramify into many
other issues relating to the profession and its
public and social stance. Dentistry is, then, facing
as many if not more problems now than it has in
recent decades and these problems pertain to stress,
health, psychological matters, and the responsible
delivery to the public of good, economical and usable
services.

Nurses

Nurses continue to be on the forefront of professional ferment and change. One of the main issues in
recent years--as in the past--is the professional
relationship between nurse and physician (Singleton,
1981; Archer, 1981; Devereaux, 1981). While medicine
is "softening" somewhat, there are still major

454

problems in jurisdiction between the professions, shared benefits, costs, and responsibility to patients, and relationships to hospital administration. The older, stronger professions will yield only slowly and grudgingly to the "upstart" professions, and this battle ground is one of the most illuminating in studying the role of professions in society and their interrelationships.

In recent years nursing continues to have its internal problems as we might well expect, given the ferment of the past two or three decades. For example, Hoffman (1981) is looking to more accurate measures of nurse turnover in jobs, an important issue as so many nurses in the past few years have declined to nurse even though they were fully trained and experienced. Lavandero (1981) is studying further the problem of "burnout" among nurses, a phenomenon that has stricken many health care and human services professions and occupations in recent years. This phenomenon ("burnout") may be particularly strong and refractory to change among nurses owing to the overarching administrative problems linking needed changes with medicine and hospital administration. Internal professional changes are thereby rendered more diffi-cult or shorter-lived. Gray-Toft and associates (1981) are looking into the range of stress provocation found among hospital nurses and the causes and effects associated therewith. No great new finds are adum-brated; the familiar tune here has to do with inter-professional relationships and some internal problems of growth and adjustment associated with taking more assertive roles. Among all these changes the "traditional nurse" has been lost (or lost sight of) (Greiner, 1981). An interesting new trend is found in the study of fledging nurses as they function in the large hospital and medical center (Speedling et al, 1981). It is particularly important that tyro nurses be studied--so should the novices be studied in all professions--as they encounter the full profes-sional world of practice. It is only with such studies that we will learn more about how professions train their members (realistically or not); and how further changes are wrought--as we have already abundantly seen--as the fledging professional encounters the full impact of the profession standing firm and resolute (against?) society and for its own purposes.

Pharmacy

More than most people realize, pharmacists have also been striving for a place in the (medical) sun. We saw this earlier manifest around a series of issues relating to clinical skills, clinical opinions and influences, promotions/prestige/professional status, and the like. All these problems continue in recent months. Hardin and associates (Hardin et al, 1981) plow again through the difficulties inherent in how the physician sees the pharmacist and his/her clinical role. This issue will surface and resurface again and again as pharmacists assert their intentions and medical personnel either yield and cooperate or resist such changes. It is not just a matter of "rights" in the pharmacy versus medicine controversy regarding clinical pharmacy but what information the clinical pharmacist can produce and its usefulness (Lipman et al, 1981). More strident comments are found in some of the published literature on this issue (See du Souich and associates, 1981; Lataste and associates, 1981). As all the allied medical professions strive for more independence and equity many changes will be brought in the professions, affecting, likely, medicine most profoundly, but ramifying to the other professions as well. All professions need challenging--indeed, as we as individuals do at times--and they will experience it most personally in their health, stress and psychological makeup, but also in their impact on society as a whole and in society acting back to correct, redirect and reconstitute the role of the professions.

CHAPTER XV

BIBLIOGRAPHY

The American Lawyer. Am. Law Publ. Corp., New York,N.Y.

American Osteopathic Assn. Survey of Public Attitudes
Toward Medical Care and Medical Professionals.
A.O.A., Chicago, 1981.

Archer, S.E. Acquiring political clout. J. Nurs.
Admin., 1981, 11, 49-55.

Barringer, F. Health planning program facing demise,
Washington POST, December 4, 1981, p. 13.

Bartlett, B. Reaganomics: Supply Side Economics in
Action. N.Y.: Arlington House, 1982.

Bassey, L. Space, Time, and Medicine. Boulder,
Colorado: Shambala Press, 1982.

Bazar, J. Families in Need. APA Monitor, 1982,
June, p.14.

Bergsma, J. & Thomas, D.C. Health Care: Its Psychosocial Dimensions. N.Y.: Humanities Press,1981.

Berreby, D. Law schools on the brink. National Law J.,
May 31, 1982, p.1.

Birman, E. The Solid Gold Stethescope. N.Y.: MacMillan,
1976.

Black, D. The making of a doctor, N.Y. TIMES,
Magazine Section, May 23, 1982, p.18.

Bok, D.C. Beyond the Ivy Tower: Social Responsibilities of the Modern University. Cambridge:
Harvard University Press, 1982.

Brief, A.P., Schuler, R.S., & Van Sell, M. Managing
Job Stress. Boston: Little, Brown, 1981.

Britell, J.E. Graduate education: A plague of problems, N.Y. TIMES, Education Sec., January 10, 1982,
p.14.

Burnham, J.C. American medicine's golden age: What happened to it? Science, 1982, 215, 1474-1479.

Caruso, R.J. Dermatitis--a dentist's occupational hazard. N.Y. State Dental Journal, 1981, 9, 543-545.

Chronicle Of Higher Education, 1982, January 13, p.2.

Clark, S.A. & Thomas, A.H. Counseling and the clergy: Perceptions of roles. J. of Psychology and Theology, 1979, 7, 48-56.

Coughlin, E.K. Scholars see possible conflicts in academia's business ties. Chronicle Of Higher Education, 1981, 23, p.23.

Dershowitz, A.M. The Best Defense. N.Y.: Random House, 1982.

de Souich, B.P., et al. Clinical pharmacology, a 'me too' affair? Eur. J. Clin. Pharmacol., 1981, 2(3), 259-260.

Devereaux, P.M. Essential elements of nurse-physician collaboration. J. Nurs. Admin., 1981, 11, 19-23.

Epstein, C.F. Women In Law. N.Y.: Basic Books, 1982.

Evans, P. & Bartolome, F. Must Success Cost So Much? N.Y.: Basic Books, 1980.

Feinberg, A. Calls of academe, Washington POST, June 3, 1962, p. D-1.

Fitzhugh, M. Training doctors for the family of man, Washington POST, Book World, Nov. 15, 1981, p.17.

Freedman, A.M. Malpractice approaches the pulpit, N.Y.TIMES, 1982, June 6, p.F-8.

Friedman, P.L. The American Lawyer Guide to Law Firms. N.Y.: Am-Law Publ., 1982.

Galbraith, J.K. The New Industrial State. Boston: Houghton-Mifflin, 1967.

Gaylin, W. The Killing of Bonnie Garland: A Question Of Justice. N.Y.: Simon & Schuster, 1982.

Gero, R., et al. Advertising. <u>Dent. Clin. of North America</u>, 1981, 4, 721-724.

Giamatti, B. <u>The University and the Public Interest.</u> N.Y.: Athenem, 1982.

Gray-Toft, P., et al. Stress among hospital nursing staff--its causes and effects. <u>Soc. Sci. & Med.</u>, 1981, 5, 639-647.

Greiner, P.A. What has become of the traditional nurse? <u>Nurs. Outlook</u>, 1981, 29, 720-721.

Hardin, T.C., et al. Physicians' perceptions of a clinical pharmacy program. <u>Am. J. Hosp. Pharm.</u>, 1982, 39(1), 125-126.

Harris, J.C. <u>Stress, Power and Ministry.</u> Washington, D.C.: Alban Institute, 1980.

Harris, J.C. & Hahn, C.A. <u>Study Guide For Stress, Power and Ministry.</u> Washington, D.C.: Alban Institute, 1980.

Hofman, P.B. Accurate measurement of nursing turnover. J. Nurs. Admin., 1981, 11, 37-39.

Jasarnoff, S. & Nelkin, D. Science, technology and the limits of judicial competence. <u>Science</u>, 1981, 214, 1211-1215.

Kerr, C. <u>The Uses Of The University.</u> Cambridge, Mass: Harvard Univ. Press, 1963.

Kraus, W.A. <u>Collaboration in Organizations: Alternatives to Hierarchy.</u> N.Y.: Human Sciences Press, 1980.

Lataste, X., et al. Clinical pharmacology-training and career. <u>Eur. J. Clin. Pharmacol.</u>, 1981, 21(3), 261-262.

Lauder, L. <u>Defective Medicine: Risk, Anger, and the Malpractice Crisis.</u> N.Y.: Farrar, Straus, & Giroux, 1978.

Lavander, R. Nurse burnout: what can we learn? <u>J. Nurs. Admin.</u>, 1981, 11, 17-23.

459

Leas, S.B. A Lay Person's Guide to Conflict Management. Washington, D.C.: Alban Institute, 1980a.

Leas, S.B. Should The Pastor Be Fired? Washington, D.C.: Alban Institute, 1980b.

Legal Times of Washington, 1601 Connecticut Avenue, N.W., Washington, D.C. 20009.

Lipman, A.G. Analysis of information provided by clinical pharmacists. Am.J. Hosp. Pharm., 1982. 39(1), 71-73.

McDonald, K. Commercialization of university science is decried. Chronicle Of Higher Education, 1982, 23, 9.

McKay, A. Our judges, too, need continuing education. Legal Times, April 26, 1982, p.21.

McKinney, L.C. Lawyers have role in reducing soaring legal costs. Legal Times, April 26, 1982, p.23.

McNett, I. Community must be important part of therapy, APA Monitor, 1982, June, p.15.

Maccoby, M. The Leader: A New Face For American Management. N.Y.: Simon & Schuster, 1982.

Mazur, A. The Dynamics of Technical Controversy. Washington, D.C.: Communication Press, 1981.

Menges, R.J. & Dittes, J.E. Psychological Studies Of Clergymen. N.Y.: T. Nelson, 1965.

Meyer, P. The Yale Murder, N.Y.: Empire Book, 1982.

Miller, J.D., Prewitt, K., & Pearson, R. The Attitudes of U.S. Public Toward Science and Technology. Chicago: University of Chicago Press, 1980.

The National Law Journal. Am. Law Publ. Corp., 2 Park Ave., New York, N.Y. 10016.

Noble, K.B. The law. N.Y.TIMES, Educational Supplement, October 11, 1981, p.17.

Noble, K.B. The surge in business failures, N.Y.TIMES, Business Section, November 15, 1981, p.1.

Oswald, R.M. Your next job may kill you. Alban
    Institute Action Information, 1979, 6, 12-14.

Oswald, R.M., Rutierrez, C.T., & Dean, L.S. Married
    To The Minister. Washington, D.C.: Alban
    Institute, 1980.

O'Toole, J. Making America Work. N.Y.: Continuum,
    1982.

Ouchi, W. Theory Z. Reading, Mass.: Addison
    Wesley, 1981.

Pascale, R.T. & Athos, A.G. The Art of Japanese
    Management. N.Y.: Simon & Schuster, 1981.

Schein, E.H. Organizational Psychology (3rd Ed.).
    Englewood Cliffs, N.Y.: Prentice-Hall, 1980.

Schuller, D.G., Strommen, M.P., & Brekke, M.L. (Eds.)
    Ministry in America. San Francisco: Harper &
    Row, 1980.

Schuller, D.C., Strommen, M.P., & Brekke, M.L. (Eds.)
    A Study Of Contemporary Ministry. San Francisco:
    Harper & Row, 1980.

Scully, M. Moves to Control Abuses in Sports Eyed by
    Major Universities. Chronicle of Higher Education,
    1982, 24, p.1.

Smith, C.G. Doctors' Wives: The Truth About Medical
    Marriages. N.Y.: Seaview Books, 1980.

Smith, P. Questioning the conduct of lawyers,
    Washington POST, 1982, January 4, p.1.

Spedling, E.J., et al. Encountering reality: reactions
    of newly hired R.N.'s to the world of the medical
    center. Int. J. Nurs. Stnd., 1981, 4, 217-225.

Stahl, D.G., et al. Educational costs and the decrease
    in dentists. J. Am. Dental Assn., 1981, 6
    845-846.

Todd, L.A., et al. Women in dentistry. Dent. Clin. of
    No. America, 1981, 4, 745-755.

Veatch, R.M.   A Theory of Medical Ethics.   N.Y.:
     Basic Books, 1981.

Waldman, H.B.   Some consequences of the increasing
     number of female American dentists.   J. Amer.
     Dental Assn., 1981, 4, 563-567.

Washington POST article: Physicians' suicide rate
     high, October 21, 1981, p.2.

Watkins, B.T.   Doubt about wisdom of requirements
     slows continuing education movement, Chronicle
     of Higher Education, 1982, June 9, 24, p.16.

Wayne, L.   Management gospel gone wrong, N.Y. TIMES,
     May 30, 1982, Business Section, p.1.

Wolfe, A.   America's Impasse: The Rise and Fall of
     the Politics of Growth.   N.Y.:   Pantheon, 1982.